GOD, GUNS, GOLD AND GLORY

Studies in Critical Social Sciences Book Series

Haymarket Books is proud to be working with Brill Academic Publishers (www.brill.nl) to republish the *Studies in Critical Social Sciences* book series in paperback editions. This peer-reviewed book series offers insights into our current reality by exploring the content and consequences of power relationships under capitalism, and by considering the spaces of opposition and resistance to these changes that have been defining our new age. Our full catalog of *SCSS* volumes can be viewed at https://www.haymarketbooks.org/series_collections/4-studies-in-critical-social-sciences.

GOD, GUNS, GOLD AND GLORY

American Character and its Discontents

LAUREN LANGMAN
GEORGE LUNDSKOW

Haymarket
Books
Chicago, IL

First published in 2016 by Brill Academic Publishers, The Netherlands.
© 2016 Koninklijke Brill NV, Leiden, The Netherlands

Published in paperback in 2017 by
Haymarket Books
P.O. Box 180165
Chicago, IL 60618
773-583-7884
www.haymarketbooks.org

ISBN: 978-1-60846-836-2

Distributed to the trade in the US through Consortium Book Sales and Distribution (www.cbsd.com) and internationally through Ingram Publisher Services International (www.ingramcontent.com).

This book was published with the generous support of Lannan Foundation and Wallace Action Fund.

Special discounts are available for bulk purchases by organizations and institutions. Please call 773-583-7884 or email info@haymarketbooks.org for more information.

Cover design by Jamie Kerry of Belle Étoile Studios and Ragina Johnson.

Printed in the United States.

Entered into digital printing February 2019.

Library of Congress Cataloging-in-Publication Data is available.

Contents

Acknowledgments

Like most authors of a scholarly tract, we're much indebted to many other people who informed our approach, all the friends and colleagues who encouraged us to write this book and commented on many parts, and our families who supported us while we were much more engaged in writing.

First, let's acknowledge our indebtedness to the giants who provided subsequent generations with so much illumination. Marx talked about how political economy alienates, warps, thwarts and distorts human potential in its unbridled quest for profits, based of course on the exploitation of workers. The immense prosperity of the capitalist era also causes a great deal of human misery—poverty, wars, and environmental despoliation. Marx also witnessed the contradictions of capitalism that created diametrically opposed groups that would eventually overthrow the system. We agree with his diagnosis and vision but feel that his timing was off.

Max Weber provided us with an understanding of how the cultural and social psychological factors that resulted from the rise of capitalism led to the transformation of class relations and religious domination of Europe and culminated in the Reformation and the rise of Protestantism and its many denominations. Not least of which, for our purposes, Puritanism was both a consequence of the changing nature of market society and a way of life that expanded modern capitalism. Weber was also quite critical of modern rationality that entrapped people in rational systems, so while bureaucratic organizations were much more efficient, the price of that efficiency was dehumanization.

Finally, unlike many of our sociological colleagues, we openly celebrate Sigmund Freud. He was far from perfect of course. However dated his biological theories of motivation, however limited some of his sociological observations might have been, his work still helps us to understand how domination becomes internalized, how people quite often act contrary to their own self-interests and how strongly various defenses and denial mechanisms for individuals, as well as for societies, prevent people from knowing themselves or understanding the world clearly.

The most immediate influence on our work is Erich Fromm. Initally, he offered a synthesis of these perspectives to understand primarily how and why the Germans embraced Adolf Hitler and Nazism, which included a racist ideology that led to the systematic extermination of 12 million people, the slaughter of at least 20 million Russians, and many more millions of Europeans in war and its aftermath. Fromm makes us aware of the role of authoritarianism and its cousin, the nihilistic destructiveness he termed necrophilia—the love of death. Fromm was no bitter pessimist. On the contrary, he bequeathed a vision, the notion of a "sane society" in which the transcendence of capitalism, commodification, domination, and the pathology of normality in a capitalist society, is possible. A better future is possible.

As Critical Theorists ourselves, who work in the traditions of the early Frankfurt school and the entire career of Erich Fromm, so consequently, we don't really fit into the neat categories of academia. Although we are both housed in Sociology, the mainstream of social theory rejects our type of work as philosophical, and perhaps far worse, biased. We offer an emancipatory theory that critiques domination, and we completely disavow the so-called "value free" and allegedly unbiased ideals of the mainstream that believes one's personal values preclude the possibility of an objective, "scientific" analysis. At the same time our Marxist colleagues accuse us of abandoning social class and material factors and escape to the impressionistic and illusory areas of culture. Few see any value in associating the social world with the depths of the unconscious with all of its sexual and aggressive desires, defenses, ambivalences and anxieties from which there is no escape. As the reader will see, such critiques entirely miss the point of what we are doing.

Perhaps the most immediate appreciation should go to Professor Stephen Bronner who first encouraged us to integrate issues that we've worked on a long time and put them into a book. Given what we've said, matching our goals with a publisher was not easy and it was for this the reason we especially appreciate the work and support of Professor David Fasenfest, who is not only the editor of *Critical Sociology* but of the Brill series that has published a number of critical sociological analyses and in this case, some may feel that Critical Theory is not truly a Marxist perspective. Given that much of our discussion is based on the political economy that is the basis for alienation, immiseration and dehumanization should dispel that notion. Moreover, when we speak of "discontents," we begin with the economic consequences of growing economic inequality, hardships and a dysfunctional government owned and controlled by the capitalist elites. So perhaps more than anyone else we thank Professor Fasenfest for his support from the beginning to the end.

A number of friends and colleagues have influenced and encouraged us, and in many cases have read parts of the manuscript or at least heard us ramble. A few intrepid colleagues read the entire manuscript and offered valuable comments. These are Professors Neil McLaughlin, Roger Salerno, and Michael Thompson.

As our feminist colleagues have told us, the personal is political and in so far as our analysis of contemporary American society seeks political change we should note personal factors involved.

Lauren Langman first expresses appreciation to his wife Judy who has always been encouraging but has often questioned why her husband spends all his time writing and not enough time relating. But I would also note that having four grandchildren slants one's perspective on the future and hopes to mobilize social change so that they might have fulfilling lives in a more secure world, one free of war, conflict, exploitation and environmental devastation. Finally, I'm deeply appreciative of Loyola University-Chicago that provided me with the time to complete this work. While on the one hand, a Jesuit University has a very long tradition of supporting social justice, but on the other hand, as a bureaucracy, there are various forms and regulations, so I thank my past and present chairs, Professors Rhys Williams and now Anne Figert for all their support and encouragement.

George Lundskow would like to thank his wife Andrea, who provided the uninterrupted hours necessary to focus on this project. I hope this book contributes in some small way to a better world that our two young children, Vivian and Vincent, can enjoy and prosper in, free from the exploitation of people and the environmental degradation that enriches the billionaires at the expense of everyone else.

In addition to nearly everything that Erich Fromm wrote, I also found considerable inspiration from Huey Newton's autobiography, *Revolutionary Suicide*. More than his personal story, he presents both an analysis and a vision for a better future, and despite the bleak title, his vision is actually founded on wisdom and hope. In the *The Age of Reason* by Thomas Paine, published in 1794, he calls for a union of faith and science, and much like Stephen Jay Gould or Carl Sagan, that religion and science speak to different types of truth about the human experience. This spirit of progressivism in all its forms inspires my scholarship throughout.

Inspiration comes in many forms. While I hacked away at the keyboard, my faithful companions included the songs of The Black Keys; The Turnpike Troubadours for one of my favorite lyrics—"He was just a counterfeit James Dean\ And she had her feet up on the dashboard\Like a burned out Betty Page\But together they were something\ In a slightly stolen car." Like all the best Great Plains alt-country bands, Jason Boland and the Stragglers tell the stories of common people with no good choices, "His American Dream is like a county line sign that's been shot full of holes." Tanya Donnelly's songs capture my feelings so well they seem biographical. I should also mention my favorite metal bands: Iced Earth, the ageless lads of Iron Maiden, and the greatest work of popular music of all time, *Nightfall in Middle Earth* by Blind Guardian. Only a power metal band could turn *The Silmarillion* by J.R.R. Tolkien into a rock opera! Nobody does life, death, and faith like metal.

And finally, given that our perspective is a little unorthodox we would like to express appreciation to the readers of this book who simply by holding this book in their hands join us in our hopes and visions that a better world is possible.

Preface: What's the matter with the United States?

In the summer of 2015, the Supreme Court ruled in favor of recognizing gay marriage. In less than a year, close to 100,000 gay couples got married. For a number of Americans, those strongly wedded to notions of heteronormativity and patriarchy, typically religious conservatives, "real men" are straight, tough and assertive, while women are submissive, nurturing and primarily fulfilled in motherhood. For many such people, especially conservative, evangelical Protestants, homosexuality is a sin and the acceptance of gay marriage was an outrage. In 2015, Kim Davis, a conservative Christian, and a county clerk in Kentucky got her allotted 15 minutes of fame when she refused to recognize gay marriage and would not issue licenses. She became a heroine-martyr for the religious right. (The US District Court overruled her and her office did issue licenses but without her name.) How did this "perfidy" of perversion, the acceptance of gay marriage ever happen in the United States? In 2008, only about 9% of the population lived in a state in which same-sex marriage was legal. By the summer of 2015, given a decision by one of the most conservative supreme courts in America, that number rose to 100%.

What if the government called for a war and nobody showed up? That day hasn't arrived yet, but few believed that we would ever see same-sex marriage legal, the legalization of marijuana or a Black President in our life time. While these events may seem to have happened rather suddenly, nearly miraculously, we see them as the outcome of one set of progressive social forces in the United States that have long battled with a different, and more sinister side. This book focuses on the sinister side of American culture and its underlying character. A companion book, *A Sane Society in the 21st Century*, will follow this one and focus on the inclusive, compassionate, and progressive side. Ironically, but also factually, both the sinister and the progressive sides derive from the same history and experiences.

In looking at the 2004 election, Kansas, long a liberal state, indeed once a hotbed of the emancipation movement, populist radicalism, and relatively progressive Republicans such as Bob Dole who with George McGovern, co-sponsored legislation that created the food stamp program. In recent years, Kansas has moved in a more reactionary direction. Elections over the last ten years or so have brought in a far-right legislature that opposes higher education in any form, vehemently rejects science and has removed all income taxes on business, while defunding schools and infrastructure. Why did Kansas move so far to the right in such a short time? As Thomas Frank (2004) noted, the economic conservatives, the moneyed interests, often called "movement" conservatives, encouraged and mobilized the angry social conservatives, many of whom consist of religious "values voters" who saw their traditional values being challenged and even rejected. They voted against the liberal, secular, social and cultural value changes that challenged their traditional views on social and moral issues.[1] Their fundamentalist religious beliefs justified opposition to gay rights, birth control and abortion, while they strongly supported prayer in public schools. They attempted to ban the teaching of evolution and instead, impose requirements to teach creationism. Such authoritarian religious conservatives seek to entrench patriarchal family values and sustain social relations based on hierarchies of gender, race, ethnicity, church membership and sexual orientation. As a result, the bread and butter economic issues of the poorer voters were obscured by the politics of emotion that unwittingly generate support for economic policies that hurt the very people who vote for them. Although many conservative politicians may be sincere in their moral beliefs, for the most part, they well understand how the promises to defend patriarchy and traditional morality, especially sexual morality do enable them to win elections and implement a variety of strategies and policies that ultimately help the rich and screw the poor. And so the Kansas legislature cut social benefits, along with the taxes of the rich. In the decade that followed, especially since the ultraconservative Sam Brownback became governor, tax revenues plummeted which necessitated major cutbacks in infrastructure, education and social benefits. Kansas became a basket case, remarkably poorer and worse off than its neighbors. Kansas has now become the poster child of failed conservative economics that have led to stagnation, slashed budgets and wrought economic decline. As so many economists such as Krugman, Stieglitz or Baker have noted, conservative budgets just don't work in the real world. And this just in, by the fall of 2015, Brownback's approval sunk to 18% in a deep red state where Obama got 28%. How sweet the *schadenfreude* (the joy of seeing someone else's shame and misfortune), especially when Brownback and his supporters aggressively created their own failure, but unfortunately created misery for so many innocent victims as well. By the way, Brownback did come up with one idea to raise revenues: the state should sell sex toys and films from foreclosed adult businesses (Murphy, 2014). Brilliant!

---

1   For our purposes, "movement" conservatives are those generally tied to very conservative economic policies, reduced taxes for businesses, fewer regulations, opposition to unions, etc. Although such positions are typical of economic elites, the broader based "movement" began during the Goldwater campaign. "Values voters" are typically conservative Protestants who tend to support religious values-and extending them into state policy as patriarchy, anti-abortion and anti-gay values.

What happened to Kansas? Surprisingly perhaps, nothing new. Rather, long-standing authoritarian forces came to the surface and at least for the present, gained control of the state government. Forces of power, hierarchy, and aggression are just as American as cooperation, equality, and charity. From the 18th and early 19th Century for example, many Americans embraced Emancipation, Women's Suffrage, and The Progressive Era, while many other Americans promoted slavery, segregation and various forms of racism, discrimination, ethnocentrism and persecution. Xenophobic politics and the worship of money have always been part of American culture, yet in Kansas today and throughout the country, many poorer voters willingly forsake their own economic interests, or as we will argue, they interpret their economic problems as the outcome of alleged foreign contamination in the form of Mexican immigrants or middle-eastern Muslims. Social programs and government supported health care appear as subversive attempts to undermine the sanctity of impossible and fictional ideals, the Neverland of white male privilege, idyllic neighborhoods of picket fences and church picnics populated by clean, obedient kids that never use drugs, don't listen to rock "n" roll (or at least not rap/hip-hop) or ever have sex before they are married.[2]

We know that the serene community of the rural White Protestant imaginary, portrayed somewhere between Grant Wood's *American Gothic* and Norman Rockwell's Christmas dinners was never as pleasant and harmonious as it is "remembered." Or should we say retroactively constructed? The important point is that we would like to explore the question of why so many Americans fervently embrace cultural agendas and in turn make political choices that have led to economic stagnation and decline for most people while the very rich have profited massively. While the median American individual income is now just a bit above $30,000 a year and household income about 54,000 a year (2016 Dollars), the average for the top 10% is roughly $114,000 and the top 1% come in at about $380,000 a year. Meanwhile, the top hedge fund managers generally make over a billion or two dollars per year (Stevenson, 2016), almost all of which is taxed at the much lower capital gains rate rather than the much

---

2   Most research shows that almost half of Americans have become sexually active by the age of 18, by 21, it's about 80%. There are no longer major differences between male and females, rural or urban youth. It should be noted that even in more conservative parts of the country, where abstinence is the primary form of sex education, and many young girls attend "chastity balls" where they pledge their chastity to their fathers and future husbands (Valenti 2010), much like New Year's resolution to lose weight, the pledges are typically breached. Ironically, maybe not so ironically, even before losing their virginity, these young women pledged to chastity have high rates of STDs and when the threshold is crossed, they are more likely to get pregnant.

higher personal income tax rate. The managers of Goldman Sachs got an average bonus of $344,000, almost five times what the average family makes, and that was on top of their salaries. The changing economic profile of the USA has become more and more evident even to the mainstream media. Most Americans know that the rich make more that middle classes, but very few have any real idea of just how skewed are the income and wealth distributions, even as they struggle to make ends meet, let alone save for the future.[3] The ranks of the poor and near poor have swollen. There has been a massive contraction of the "middle classes," what political economists call a "hollowing out" as most job growth has been in lower skilled, lower income services such as retail sales, janitorial work, and fast food. As the middle class becomes an "endangered species" (Huffington, 2011), the incomes and wealth of very rich Americans, especially those working in the FIRE industries (finance, insurance, real estate), along with many of the Fortune 500 CEOs, have skyrocketed. Indeed, the top 10% own about 77% of the wealth of the USA. The 20 richest Americans that could fit in a Gulf Star jet own about 50% of the wealth of America. The six Walton heirs own as much as the bottom 45%. Yet the self-serving conservative agendas of the economic elites would not be possible without electoral support from the masses of angry, anxious and distraught older white people who fear and even hate the cultural and demographic changes taking place in the USA. Contrary to the platitudes of the pundit class, it's not the economy stupid, it's the preservation of traditional values and identities that are under assault that impels people to mobilize and vote for particular agendas of conservative elites, little understanding how elites that speak to their issues hijack their agendas in order to get their votes, and once elected, they serve the corporate elites who finance their campaign in order to enhance their profits by keeping wages and taxes low, minimizing regulations and in many places, polluting the land, water and air. As we will show, these traditional values and identities are deeply rooted in American history, and emotionally anchored in American social character. As such, these feel much more immediate and real than external economic and cultural changes. As we will explain, when these values coincide with authoritarian personality characteristics, people tend to be highly conformist, close minded, resistant to change and think in terms of mutually exclusive binary categories of good versus bad, right versus wrong, and us versus them. Moreover, such character types tend to be fearful and suspicious, easily angered and aggressive, and right wing politicians

---

3   There is an excellent video that shows just how much more the elites make than most people can imagine. https://www.youtube.com/watch?v=QPKKQnijnsM Accessed 03/24, 2015.

strategically know how to mobilize that fear, anger and suspicion. Right populism has a long history.

The Fault Lies within

A number of factors explain the growing inequality of the USA. Automation, robotics and CAD/CAM (computer assisted design/computer automated manufacturing) eliminated many jobs. Furthermore many other jobs of assembly, toy manufacturing, garments, appliances, and electronics. were outsourced to sweatshops in the Third World. These factors led to the demise of well-paid jobs with benefits. At the same time, the growth of globally based productive investment further contributed to growing income stagnation and decline for most Americans, but rapidly growing incomes for those at the top and thus inequality skyrocketed. In the 1950's, CEOs typically made about 20–30 times what workers made. Today, the average CEO of the top 100 corporations make 30 million dollars a year, about 300 times what the workers make; the top 10 best paid CEOs average about 73 million per year. These CEOs often have huge multimillion dollar pension funds and preside over companies that don't offer retirement benefits to their workers. The pensions of the top 100 CEOs is equal to the total pensions of 41% of the American work force.[4] Marx had argued that the State is primarily the executive committee of the bourgeoisie. C. Wright Mills (1956, 1970) subsequently demonstrated that a "power elite," consisting of the leadership positions at the top of the pyramids of the military, the political and the commercial sectors that in fact controls the bureaucratic organizations that run the society, quite independently of the "will of the people." In a major study, Gilens and Page (2014) argued that the American polity is now based on "Economic-Elite Domination," also known as rule by the rich.

In the sixty some years since, the mass media, a major aspect of the economy that advertises most goods and services and distributes government or corporate propaganda call news, which is really "infotainment." More recently, Wolin (2008) argues that we now have what can be considered a "managed democracy" best described as "inverted fascism," a system where the economic elites have total control of all three branches of government. In 2010, the Supreme Court of the United States (SCOTUS) through the Citizens United decision rendered corporations as people and political contributions as "free

---

4   http://www.alternet.org/economy/100-ceos-nest-eggs-retirement-savings-41-families
     Accessed Nov. 3, 2015.

speech." This codified the power of the wealthy to select and elect, indeed buy direct political power. While billionaires like Bill Gates or the Koch brothers are often mentioned in the daily news, they represent just the tip of about 358 mega-rich families and/or the corporations they control. About half of these mega rich donors each contribute over a million dollars, mostly to conservative Republicans. In the 2016 election campaign, the Koch brothers promised to contribute almost a billion dollars. And surely as we would expect, given the particular underlying social character of American financial elites that we will discuss later, these mega rich fully expect that if their candidate is elected to office, he, or perhaps she, will cut their taxes, cut "costly" health and/or environmental regulations that might protect workers and consumers and finally, they will cut, if not end various benefit and safety net programs and replace them with various forms of privatization that profit business. We should also note that elite economic power shapes tax codes and encourages offshore banking where the elites and their corporations park their money. Nevertheless, the cumulative consequences of the move from the semblance of democracy to plutocracy, coupled with the expanding costs of maintaining an Empire, are the major reasons why the United States is in a prolonged period of stagnation and decline. As we shall repeatedly note, while this new form of plutocracy has nearly ended democracy, it was not imposed upon the people and maintained by "secret police" or what Orwell would have called "thought police." There is no conspiracy. Many common people embrace it willingly.

But we would like to offer an alternative way of looking at what underlies and has enabled these economic changes and the politics they have brought. As Cassius might have said to Brutus, "the fault dear Americans, lies not in our stars but in ourselves." As we will argue, to understand the current social and political realities, we must understand the importance of American character. More specifically, below the surface of its collective identity and dominant values, we see a particular type of social character that joins fearful white males and many equally fearful females together with the economic elites into a political force based on a supposedly "normal" perception of social issues and events. This perception derives from commonly internalized values descended from a shared cultural history, now reinforced by the various media. This social character—religious, industrious, independent, and phallic aggressive—often racist, sexist, and xenophobic, undergirded by an authoritarian streak, has been facing economic stresses and cultural assaults on its traditional identity and the social status compensation of racial, gender, and sexual hierarchies. Thus a very common call of conservative and reactionary mobilizations, especially right populist movement has been something to the effect of "we want our country back," meaning a return to a time before their social and cultural power waned, when their status and esteem were unquestioned, when their values were unquestioned and identities valorized. This has long been part and parcel of reactionary claims that long antedate the current Tea Party and current Republican Party. At the same time, we see other, newer types of character types that unite other groups, from liberal-left coalitions to mainstream financial concerns to young progressives and even to apathetic nihilists. Each type derives from commonly internalized values descended from a shared cultural history. While often marginalized, ignored or repressed, as we hope to show elements of this more liberal, indeed progressive open-minded, tolerant social character, much like far-right conservatives, derive from the same cultural history.

To understand the plight of contemporary America, we will look at the nature of American character as it was first forged in the crucibles of the early Puritan theocratic colonies of New England, as well as in the mountain communities of Appalachia and on the slave plantations of the antebellum South. In New England, the earliest settlers were highly religious people whose primary concerns were the unfettered practice of their Puritan religion. An essential part of that Puritanism was the value of community and mutual support extolled in Winthrop's "City on the Hill" sermon (See p. xx). But a variety of factors, not the least of which was in fact their religious motivation, had a secular consequence. Puritan "this worldly" asceticism and its sacralization of work, that Max Weber called the "Protestant ethic" led to the worldly success and prosperity that it had abhorred. But this industriousness, seeing work as a "calling," one's life as a career and an anal retentive asceticism enabled saving not squandering one's profits. This orientation, actually a characterological pattern eventually led to the prosperity of the colonies, but in so doing, attenuated the social bonds that had held their communities together. This is what Bellah (1992) meant by *The Broken Covenant*. Appalachia further contributed the ethic of rugged individualism and distrust of government authority, while the South contributed beliefs of white superiority and narrowly defined moral communities that created strict in-group and otherness boundaries. Joined together, these elements formed a core of traditional American character that enabled the first "new nation" to ascend to the very top of the world's pinnacle of wealth and power, it simultaneously established certain contradictions of character and society that may have long endured, notwithstanding episodic eruptions, but as we will suggest, these underlying characterological changes and resulting characterological differences are not only irreconcilable, have indeed led to the current economic stagnation and portend future decline. (This may however diminish inequality and provide people with more gratifying lives.)

Subsequently, many of the policies, beliefs and agendas of the contemporary political system reflect a traditional American social character structure that no longer functions economically, politically or socially and now undermines the common good. Indeed, the founding fathers of the republic, loathing the tyranny of a monarchy, yet fearing the irrational rabble of the less wealthy and less educated masses, attempted to create a republic lead by a guardian class of affluent and educated men who were likely to be enlightened philosophers and statesmen, men of honor and integrity who would act in the best interests of all, even if that meant checking democratic tendencies of the masses that might challenge property rights.[5] Recall that as a result of the Revolution, George Washington who owned vast tracts of land became the richest man in America. And so a system of checks and balances of government was instituted to limit the power of the government and limit the power of the masses. Clear limitations of suffrage being limited to affluent white men were believed to insure the peace, prosperity and common good of all in the new nation. The new secular, non-hereditary American patricians would insure benevolent rule consistent with Enlightenment critiques of tyrannical monarchs and despots that characterized many parts of Europe. But this tenuous compromise between the patrician founders and plebes would not last, especially after the election of Andrew Jackson in which the legacies of Madison, Jefferson and Hamilton were challenged by the growing numbers of common people. The important point is the "benevolent democracy" of enlightened rule (perhaps an oxymoron) could not last, due ironically to the ways the nation emerged. On the one hand, the growing masses that had gained the vote were quite supportive of Jackson and with his election, there was a new era of popular Jacksonian democracy that created jobs, deeded land and increased social mobility often at the expense of the native population and the people of adjoining borders, especially Mexico. Secondly, between the abundant resources and the industriousness of its emerging social character, little more than 100 years after its Revolution, a growing class of talented, ambitious and completely unscrupulous industrial and financial elites arose. Their rapidly rising economic power also meant the power to elect lawmakers and leaders, and shape policies to secure their interests and profits. As will be noted, they encouraged the rise of urban police and private security firms, a form of personal militia, to suppress and control workers. By 1929, their greed and profligacy, coupled with indifference to the masses, crashed the economy in the Great Depression. And while lessons were learned, those lesson were later unlearned as a new glass of

---

5 See   Chomsky   http://www.truth-out.org/progressivepicks/item/34794-us-guardian-elite
   -rulers-date-back-to-nation-s-foundingAccessed 01/23/2016.

greedy elites appeared on the scene. In 2007, under Bush II, like Hoover in 1929, the economy again crashed into the Great Recession.

The haphazard response to the economic crisis of 2007–8 portends future economic catastrophes, while the quagmires in Iraq, Afghanistan, and now Syria, Yemen, and Libya, again rooted in American social character, portends continued political disasters in which the unexpected outcomes could include nuclear exchanges. Closing down the government to protest a president's fairly conservative, Heritage Foundation health care plan to aid insurance companies, big Pharma and medical equipment makers, also known as the Affordable Healthcare Act or Obamacare, goes beyond traditional bipartisan politics and introduces irrational elements that paralyzes government as a whole, undermines democracy and costs billions of dollars to accomplish nothing. Thank you Senator Cruz. When every policy, every decision becomes grounds for total governmental shutdown, something more than rational political interests motivates the people who hold public office. As we will argue, the traditional American character that historically played a major role in the ascent of the United States to broad prosperity immense power now serves to undermine that colossus. To paraphrase Pareto, history is the graveyard of empires, all of which, from Babylonia to Egypt to Persia, Greece to Rome and the Spanish, French and British, seemed so formidable and eternal in their time. Today, these former empires mostly endure as interesting tourist spots. We suggest, following Chalmers Johnson (2010) that the USA is now following the same trajectory as did Rome and the others. The fact that the notion of an American decline and fall has entered into mainstream discourse, such as with Chris Matthews (2014), more and more of the public realizes that collapse into third-world status is an increasing possibility. Not surprisingly, an increasing number of the world's poor now live in the USA.

Most critiques of American character have focused on the more or less overt aspects of that character, its collective beliefs and values, its identity and self-images, its myths and narratives that the founders allegedly held. Just what are these beliefs? Most observers ever since de Tocqueville have noted the enduring power of religious sentiments, industriousness and an avid quest for material pursuits, individualism, conformity and anti-intellectualism, mixed with a little racism, sexism and xenophobia. Today, these elements have become a reconstructed celebration of a mythical past. Patriarchy and racism continue to thwart the progress of women and ethnic groups. Collective narcissism that sees itself as "exceptional," as "indispensable," as the "best country in the world," wards off any serious self-appraisals or comparisons with other societies where most people have a far better quality of life. Meanwhile its underlying phallic-aggressive tendencies, easily manipulated by politicians and media, dispose general support for state-based violence and aggression against "undesirables" and allegedly inferior people, and legitimate America's interventionist geopolitics. This was already evident in the westward expansion of the colonies in the 18th Century, followed by the territorial expansion and moving frontier of the new nation in the 19th Century that stopped only when settlers got to the Pacific Ocean which marked the "closing of the frontier." This process involved the vast slaughter of Native-Americans, slavery, and the military takeover of northern Mexico to form what is now Texas, Arizona, and New Mexico. Such extensive and consistent violence greatly shaped American character.

To move forward then, we will go much farther into the historical origins and transformations of these elements over time. As we will endeavor to show in the following chapters, (1) the strong religious sentiments and values of the founders have persisted, but have also changed decisively. (2) We will show the necessity, if not propensity of the early colonials and post-revolutionary citizens to use violence against Native Americans as well as against African slaves has endured as a major quality of America's toughness (Wilkinson, 1984 p. 3) America has long embraced a fervent ambition for materialist ends, with far less concern for aesthetic values, humanistic goals, or sustainability. Finally, (4) the collective narcissistic sentiments tied to "American Exceptionalism" are such that the Americans considered themselves a "chosen people" who produced the greatest society in history of the world-or at least its wealthiest and most powerful. But today, we are falling behind many other countries and most Americans have some sense of that decline. However, those who travel to Europe or Asia discover that the US has the slowest and least reliable rail system, the worst roads, antiquated airports, as well as the slowest but also most expensive internet and connectivity services. The United States built the first skyscrapers, but today, the tallest buildings in the world today are found in the Middle East and Asia. Thus many who travel abroad begin to get a sense of what a truly modern country is like. As we shall argue, understanding what we see as the rise, decline and potential phoenix of American character depends on understanding its underlying social character, what Erich Fromm called the most typical psycho-social pattern in a society, one that has been shaped by social conditions to adapt to a particular political economy and cultural system, which thus enables people to function as members of a society.

Starting in the 1600s, the Puritan religion of the early colonial period valued a staunch work ethic. The colonizers were suspicious of government, and yes there was patriarchy, ethnic discrimination and slavery. Yet the frail colonies survived harsh conditions, frequent illness and death. But eventually the colonies prospered, became the first new nation which, over time, became the dominant global superpower. Today, these very same aspects of American character undermine the capacity to adapt to a new and changing world in which many other countries are now more ascendant. As the statistics on healthcare, poverty rates, and academic proficiency show, the United States is falling behind most other industrial societies. But American individualism tends to ignore social problems and/or blame them on particular individuals, the "bad apples" rather than structural factors or the ideological characteristics of the society, or the politically motivated social policies that may ill serve the society by primarily benefiting the wealthy. We now live in a world in which rampant materialist pursuits are fostering ecological crises that threaten the very viability of our species.

The current forms of American character that are dominant are extremely recalcitrant to change or transformation. That's the bad news. The good news is that given current social and economic realities, as we shall argue, that character structure is waning compared to an emerging, more progressive character type, or perhaps several types. These newer generations can hopefully adapt to the changing world and in the process create a more harmonious America that is more gratifying and fulfilling for far more of its people.

Enter the Frankfurt School

While the Enlightenment valorized Reason, extolled knowledge and promised an emancipatory vision of freedom, equality, democracy and brotherhood, scholars as diverse as Nietzsche, Weber and Freud noted the underlying irrationality of what seems to be the rationality of modernity. This prompted the critiques of Reason developed by the Frankfurt School of Critical Theory. The emancipatory visions of the Enlightenment that promised democracy, freedom, equality, brotherhood, and self-fulfillment, instead became a major source of domination and irrationality that culminated in the Holocaust and Hiroshima.[6] When the total obliteration of the enemy (or in the case of the Jews, real people turned into a fictional enemy) appears like a rational course

---

6 The critique of rationality, clearly evident in Weber's work, has been a central theme of the Frankfurt school of critical theory which has informed our perspective. The foundational document has long been Horkheimer and Adorno (1947) *The Dialectic of Enlightenment.* The most important subsequent critique was found in Stephen Bronner (2004) that would defend the principles of the Enlightenment's valorization of science and reason notwithstanding the many critiques from both right wing political leaders as well as the left wing postmodern fashionistas of cultural critiques who disdain the Enlightenment as just another "grand narrative" belonging in the dustbin of history.

of action, we must understand the contradictions and discontents of our age that make the mass annihilation of people seem legitimate and reasonable. We must understand social character, resting on Freud's understandings of character structure (the ego, superego and id), levels of consciousness that included unconscious desires, feelings and memories, repression, ambivalence and contradiction. Whatever else one might say about Freudian psychodynamics, people, individually and collectively are not always rational actors who seek to maximize their self-interests. People often act in self-destructive ways and engage in a variety of processes from repression to denial of aspects of themselves, and even when more self-aware, are quite often reluctant to make changes. In modern life, the obsessive ambition with individualistic achievement often fosters wealth as material success for the person, but often at the cost of loneliness and despair. As we will show, many of the social critiques of the USA note that it is a lonely society.

While we will cover this ground in more detail, our primary concern is understanding the underlying "social character" of Americans in order to reveal how many of its underlying motives, its emotionally anchored collective values, myths and fantasies, identities and many of its actions are not only self-defeating, but foster pain, suffering and quite often deaths of other Americans and people around the world. To understand American social character, its motivations, emotions and feelings and ways of seeing the world, we will largely follow Erich Fromm's (1992, [1973]) theory of social character as the most frequent constellation of social psychological traits in a given population. This does not mean that everyone, or even the majority share a similar character structure, rather, social character is modal, simply the most frequent, and typically found among people in positions of power as a leading type that people in general emulate. Furthermore, social character is historically contingent, adaptive to its historical context and is thus largely shaped by the necessity of an existing social system. As Fromm put it, people must *want* to do the things they *must* do in order for society to function.

One of the central arguments to follow is that the traditional "social character" of America is no longer adaptive to the contemporary, globalized world situation, that some aspects of American social character foster conflicts between traditional morality and more adaptive values. Ironically, patriotism and respect for wealth and authority now serve to sustain general stagnation and inequality in face of the growing wealth and domination of American capitalism by the very rich. In other words, for many people, the focus on changes in sexual values, gender relations, family structures and the growing populations of immigrants and minorities moves attention away from policies that allow the rich to get richer. There is little awareness of just how much the elites have gamed the system such that we have a growing economy, but growth that goes overwhelmingly to the top 1% and in turn denies prosperity to the great majority. Consequently, traditional American social character has largely become dysfunctional and unable to adapt to the current social and economic realities of the globalized markets of today. This maladaptation now undermines the nation.

Closely tied to the growing anachronism of traditional American social character is the question of "motivated reasoning," or in simple terms, accepting or rejecting evidence based on personal preferences. The real facts are the ones that support what I want to believe is true. Selective use of evidence tends to reduce the cognitive dissonance, that is, the discomfort between contradictions of one's beliefs and what evidence suggests. Why do so many people believe the claims peddled by right wing pundits and politicians, especially the ones that populate the Fox Noise Channel? Because such claims are congruent with emotionally-based value systems and identities that are not open to negotiation or revision. Since the Presidential election of 2008, a Pew poll in 2010 found that 34% of Republicans (compared to only 8% of Democrats) believed that Barack Obama was born in Kenya, and worst of all, he is both an ardent atheist and a devout Muslim who hates the United States. Some critics like that "astute" observer of contemporary America, batshit crazy former representative Michelle Bachman has even claimed that Obama was the Anti-Christ. When he finished his term, the Rapture would begin, he would lead the forces of Satan, the last days would start and Jesus would come back—or something like that. Two years later, a new Pew poll in 2012 found that the percentage of Republicans who believed Obama was a Kenyan Muslim had actually increased to 43%, and a 2015 poll from Public Policy Polling found that 66% of Donald Trump supporters believe this (Tesfaye, 2015). Alongside charges against Obama personally, we might also include creationists who believe the world was created 6,000 years ago exactly as it is now. And back then, Adam and Eve rode on dinosaurs with English saddles to get around in the Garden of Eden. We might also note the climate change deniers who reject any notion that carbon fuels have been responsible for global warming. Indeed, many people do not even believe that global warming is taking place, notwithstanding higher annual temperatures, droughts, rising sea levels, flooding, and hey, what's wrong with warmer winters anyway? The United States has the only major political party in the world that includes climate change, evolution, and all-around science deniers. Other anti-science beliefs include, for example, that homosexuality is choice and can be "cured" through prayer. Many religious Republicans see science as a liberal plot to undermine their beliefs such that they automatically reject anything scientists might say. As Mooney (2006) explains, mainstream Republicans not only reject established science but actually embrace a variety of bad science such as creationism, the notion that condoms cause AIDS, birth control pills cause cancer, and vaccines cause mental retardation. That people believe such things cannot be understood without a concept of "motivated reasoning" and that motivation is often unconscious. For many people, often highly educated people including doctors and lawyers, scientific evidence is undermining their religious-based worldviews and in turn their identities. As a result, they are incapable of accepting the evidence-based claims of scientists. Consider as a case in point, Dr. Ben Carson, eminent pediatric neurosurgeon who sought the Republican nomination for president. While on the one hand, his strong Seventh-Day Adventist religious beliefs may have helped his rise from poverty to medical school to chief of pediatric neurosurgery at Johns Hopkins, it surely distorted his views and understandings of history and society. He claimed Joseph built the pyramids to store grain. Yes, huge pyramids were built with very small rooms to store grain next to dead bodies! Moreover the story of Joseph took place 500 years before the pyramids were built.

Lastly, despite several decades of economic stagnation for most and decline for many, especially contemporary youth, many Americans still honor and respect the economic elites and their policies and, without any study of economics, believe that the tax cuts for the rich and the retrenchments of benefits, including their own will produce general wealth. As progressive economists such as Robert Reich or Paul Krugman have often noted, trickledown economics is a mythology that we would call tinkle-down, and the pissed-on masses can't afford umbrellas anymore. The vast multitudes of youth and underemployed college graduates no longer have such faith in the economic system or its elites—it was the Occupy movement that labeled them the 1%.

Given what we have said about American character, and its underlying social character that fosters a variety of economic, political, cultural and ecological dysfunctions and discontents, one might say we are heading down a primrose path that can only end as one of the dystopic or cataclysmic scenarios of *Mad Max, Blade Runner, Waterworld, The Terminator, Brave New World, 1984,* or *Elysium.* However, as the psychodynamic tradition maintains, character has a dialectical relationship to society and is not only capable of challenge and resistance to the established order, but as a basis of resistance more generally can impact society in everyday ways. Although social and underlying psychosocial change is gradual, we have been on a trajectory of change at least since the 1960s. So today there is a general acceptance of sexuality, the recent legalization of same-sex marriage and the increasing decriminalization if not legality of marijuana are themselves outcomes of progressive characterological change.

Changing American Social Character: The Prelude to Socialism

In progressive futuristic worlds as portrayed in *The Dispossessed, Star Trek,* and *Babylon 5,* science-fiction creators have explored alternative kinds of societies and imagine what an egalitarian society based on sharing, caring and mutual aid might be like without directly referring to socialism which many (older) Americans see as a dreaded anathema that undermines its "successful" capitalist system, thwarts individualism, denies personal "freedom" and gives undeserved rewards to the morally deficient, "undeserving" poor. Much like Catholicism in the 19th Century, some see socialism as an oppressive collectivism that gives priority to the community and not the individual and this feared loss of personal liberty in turn elicits irrational anger and rage. There is a long history of this irrationality, rooted in traditional American character; consider the Palmer Red Scare of the 20s, McCarthyism in the 50s, and more recently accusations that President Obama is a socialist, radical Muslim atheist who hates the United States.[7]

Sociologist Philip Slater (1970) suggested that the irrational hatred and disdain of the hippie counterculture of the 60's was based on their embrace of community, dependency, mutual-aid and collective engagement. These powerful, yet repressed unconscious needs were desperately desired by isolated and selfish individuals, but also resented and repressed because the desire for the collective, the yearning for community, exposes their inner isolation and fear of engulfment. Moreover, these qualities are considered "feminine," weak and passive qualities no tough, phallic-aggressive male should desire. Similarly, the counter-cultural celebrations of sexuality, often quite public in the 60's also offended the more typically sexually repressed segments of the population because again, it evoked free and open expression of passion and exposed the emptiness and inner torment of prudish conservatism that comes from a harsh, punitive superego that both represses and therefore heightens the desire for sexual gratification and thus loathes its expressions, especially the sexuality of women that seem "impure" and hence a danger to community standards that give men the power to define and control women's sexuality. Much as Nietzsche said about *resentment* as a form of repressed envy, there is disdain and hatred toward what is most wanted yet repressed and denied, but embraced by other less repressed and inhibited people. In retrospect, Slater's observations point to the cultural time where the dominant social character of America began its descent and a long suppressed, marginalized social character slowly became ascendant. As traditional repressive and individualistic

---

7   An excellent short documentary, "America's Unofficial Religion: The War on an Idea," https://
    www.youtube.com/watch?v=Hznlp-DwgSw Accessed Oct 16, 2015.

American character wanes, as newer generations express an openness to socialism, no longer associated with the horrors of the Soviet nuclear threat, and without any personal experience of the Cold War or memories of the days of the Cuban missile crisis. According to the Pew foundation, between a third and a half of the millennials now support socialism over capitalism.[8] Among registered Democrats, about as many support socialism as do capitalism.[9] This was first evident with the New Left of the 60's, more so in the Occupy movements, but clearly evident in the Sanders campaign of 2016 in which democratic socialism has become seen as a legitimate political position. We will try to show that this growing support reflects an underlying change in the American social character, and indeed, an alternative social character formation already exists that while not very typical, has been an essential part of American character ever since it's very beginning. Nevertheless, this historical legacy, like the underlying character structure that supports it, has been repressed, denied and submerged. As will be later shown in Ch. 7, there have been a much greater number of co-ops, collectives, etc. in American history than most people think.

Two major factors concurrently impact and erode the traditional American character, now thwart its continued reproduction in future generations and foster a new constellation. First, the stagnation of the economy and its adverse consequences impinge upon most people, but it is especially the young who are likely to find a depressed job market and many are likely to take jobs for which they are overqualified. The millennial generation, especially college graduates, has seen and experienced firsthand the economic downsides of the current system, few good jobs, but with monstrous debts, including 1.2 trillion dollars' worth of student loan debt that make it impossible to plan a life trajectory. Fewer and fewer have jobs that promise well paid, stable, upwardly mobile careers that provide both salary increases and various health and/or retirement benefits. Instead many have short term consultancies or freelance work, often with few if any benefits. Many indeed take unpaid "internships" for large corporations simply to have that experience on their records in hopes that it might someday lead to employment. As the Occupy Wall Street movements revealed, people throughout the class hierarchy, from students to wage workers to many professionals turned out in force to express their collective displeasure, indeed outrage that the rich were getting richer, often at government

8 Little Change in Public's Response to "Capitalism," "Socialism" http://www.people-press .org/2011/12/28/little-change-in-publics-response-to-capitalism-socialism/?src=prc-headline Accessed 09/12/2014.

9 One third of millennials support socialism, You Gov, see https://today.yougov.com/news/ 2015/05/11/one-third-millennials-like-socialism/Accessed Sept 12, 2015.

expense, while everyone else got the shaft. As they proclaimed, "the banks got bailed out, we got sold out." Much like other experiments in collective, democratic sharing such as the Paris Commune or the anarcho-syndicalist organizations of Republican Spain, the bourgeois state employed massive intimidation, pepper spray, water hoses, riot clubs, and tasers against the unarmed, peaceful Occupy community in Zucotti Park in New York City as well as many other of its encampments around the country. This use of state violence put an end to living examples of alternative types of communities that might be possible. At least for now. Given the authoritarian nature of police forces, between their hatred of nonconformists and preference for aggression they were quite happy to use violence to disperse the peaceful occupiers while the courts hammered many with severe fines and imprisonment.

Yet Occupy was mostly a moment, an expression of anger, discontent and indignation, and not a world historical event or sustained movement. While such emotions do not change the political system directly, they do impact social character and dispose progressive political action. True, Occupy was not the prelude to revolution, nor under the present conditions is any kind of revolution quite likely.[10] But that said, we should think of Occupy as an indication of major cultural change undergirded by and reflecting a changing underlying social character and an opening for counterhegemonic discourses and critiques.[11] The economic conditions and cultural forces that gave rise to Occupy are not going to go away. At the same time, these factors are fostering the kinds of characterological shift that we believe are underway and support a more rational, sane society that we consider in our concluding chapter. Finally, whatever else Bernie Sanders primary campaign of 2016 has accomplished, he has moved the concept of Democratic socialism from demonized threats of barbarians at the gates set to overthrow the government to a legitimate political position. Many Americans may be quite surprised to learn that many institutions of the US, its postal system, libraries, many utilities, public schools, fire departments, airports, seaports and roadways are really forms of socialism.[12] Bernie Sanders' critiques of oligopoly, inequality, access to healthcare,

---

10   In the last decade or so, we've seen the militarization of police forces such that most urban police forces more resemble combat ready, body armored soldiers often riding in armored personnel carriers armed with heavy machine guns. Moreover, since the NSA listens to every phone call and reads every email, most progressive groups include an infiltrator or two.

11   Many pundits have suggested that the spirit of Occupy is what motivated the Sanders campaign that positioned itself against the millionaires and billionaires of Wall Street.

12   While the very notion of socialism has been anathema in the USA, at least till the Sanders presidential campaign of 2016, for those who like Internet lists, here is one of the 75 socialist

education, and the extent to which big money controls society resonated with large numbers of young Americans who had felt the economic adversities, and were ready to "Feel the Bern." As Bronner rightly notes,

> Preserving a doctrinaire understanding of socialism...renders it politically irrelevant. Better to consider a notion of critical solidarity and highlight the 'socialist' elements of existing proposals that seek to regulate capital and redistribute wealth. Articulating criteria for judging this or that piece of legislation, while targeting and then pressuring conservative 'allies,' is part of the challenge facing contemporary socialists. Commitment to principles should not excuse refusing to engage what exists. After all, if it means anything at all, socialism is ultimately a political project rather than a model program or a prefabricated ideal.[13]

As of this writing, the sentiments of the Occupiers live on in the Bernie Sanders campaign for president in which an admittedly democratic socialist garnered a great deal of passionate support among the young who have flocked to convention centers around the country, even in staunchly conservative and rural states such as Mississippi and Louisiana. As we shall make clear, an emerging social character is likely to be the psychosocial foundation for very fundamental changes in the political economy, collective values, and everyday life practices that portend a kinder, gentler, more egalitarian, inclusive, democratic society. But as we previously noted, the centrality of individualism in American social character, along with its repressed fear of being engulfed by a collectivity, is such that socialists have been highly disdained. Since the growth of industrialization following the Civil War, with the rise of labor unions and worker co-ops, socialism has been the target of an irrational anger and aggression and of course, often the target of State violence. The growth of urban police departments as well as private militias such as the Pinkerton's emerged to control, if not thwart, labor unrest. These sentiments ultimately fueled fervent anti-communism from the time in 1918 that President Wilson sent 12,000 Marines to fight on the side of the Czar and the Mensheviks against the Bolsheviks. Then came the Palmer "Red Scare" raids in the 1920s. Since then, many very costly "anticommunist interventions," if not outright invasions, especially in third world countries have taken the lives of millions people, and usually

---

programs in America: https://www.dailykos.com/story/2012/03/29/1078852/-75-Ways-Socialism-Has-Improved-America?detail=emailclassic Accessed 11/26/2015.

13   Socialism in America http://readersupportednews.org/opinion/75-75/2483-socialism-in-america Accessed 07/08/2015.

install or uphold right-wing military dictatorships. The intense irrational anger toward socialism is deeply tied to traditional American social character and with it, deep-seated fears of the erosion of individualism and the attenuation of the tough, phallic-aggressive aspects of American social character and the belief that God gave American a special mission, along with its wealth and power to police the world for the sake of profits and Jesus.

One reason for the intensity of various right-wing mobilizations is that demographic changes are reducing the number of older white people while more and more youth abandon sexism, racism, homophobia, and perhaps above all, reject Puritanical sexual values. As Marcuse (1991 [1964]) demonstrated, "repressive desublimation" became one of the primary means in which people were incorporated into the administered and emotionally repressive society. Although "swinging" (swapping married partners) may appear progressive on the surface, most of the swingers in 1950s–1970s came from politically conservative backgrounds in which sex was the ultimate evil, but as the repression weakened, sexuality then appeared as the ultimate salvation from restrictive social expectations. To manage this contradiction, swinging allowed for a kind of deniability—they were still married after all. Over the last few decades, each cohort of young people experience the contradiction between conservative values and contemporary lifestyles at a critical period in the life cycle and with greater openness toward alternative values and meanings that often leaves conservative moral codes behind. Many young people leave conventional organized religion entirely such that the non-denominational, atheists, agnostics, Wiccans, mystics, and no affiliation are now the second largest denomination.[14] As we will argue, these two forces, the growing economic contradictions and hardships that many face in the current American economy, rendered especially blatant by the growing visible wealth of the very rich, together with more liberal social, political and even sexual values of youth in general, foster liberal social agendas. Many aspects of this emerging social character have been long present in American society. Insofar as the more extreme conservatives command the repressive power of law enforcement, authoritarian religions and vast monetary wealth from economic and cultural elites, these tendencies have for the most part marginalized and repressed progressive elements at both the normative and characterological levels. But as we argue, in an age of easy access to internet porn, Cosmo's 50 new sex secrets, hook up apps and female comediennes who routines focus on their sex lives and/or anatomies, lady parts, traditional sexual values have little influence—and aren't even worth a

---

14   http://www.alternet.org/belief/white-christian-america-decline-why-young-people-are
      -sick-conservative-religion.

joke anymore. While the values have indeed changed, actual behavior has been relatively constant for the last several decades. It has just become more visible and produces less personal guilt and shame.

In the economic world, various forms of communes, collectives, coops, and creative communities have existed alongside the dominant social and economic order that have challenged both the nature of private property and the hierarchies of class domination that has sustained that system (See Curl, 2007). The conditions of our times are fostering a "return of the repressed," not as the explosion anger, rancor, violence and chaos conservatives deplore, but as the caring, sharing, cooperation and empathy that have been repressed. For us, the return of the repressed promises a better, kinder more just world.

Chapter Outline

Chapter 1: In our introduction, we trace the origins of American character, rooted in the early Renaissance, then the Reformation that eventually led the Puritans to New England, where a unique social character was first shaped in the original colonies. With the Enlightenment, came a revolutionary war, soon followed by westward expansion and an ever moving frontier. We won't examine historical periods and particular incidents as such, but rather, we will look at the specific historical forces and events through the ages to arrive at an identifiable American character. This chapter also includes contemporary theoretical discussion with illustrative data and examples to establish the four essential expressions of the dominant social character and its values, namely, God, Guns, Gold, and Glory.

Chapter 2: Religion was the primary source and force of legitimation for leaving England, colonizing the new land, displacing native populations and shaping the early culture and social character. Nearly every American leader, whether the President or religious authority or populist activist invokes God as the origin and inspiration of their decisions and actions. The belief that America carries divine blessing and purpose pervades our politics, business (at least for much of US history) and especially, wars of aggression. It has also justified inequality, slavery, and oppression.

Chapter 3: Gendered violence, especially gun ownership is often sanctified as "moral redemption." Toughness and aggression at both the personal and political level, as well as the obsession with gun ownership and open display of firearms, as expressions of phallic-aggressive masculine toughness and virility has shaped America's social character as well as its politics.

Chapter 4: We will show how the worship of money often equates with the devotion to God. Money justifies itself and requires no further legitimation or concern for other people or the environment. While greed has always existed, wealth controls American politics and policies to crate immense inequality and dysfunctional social systems. The American plutocracy willingly sacrifices infrastructure, education, and even scientific advancements in order to hoard extreme wealth in private corporate and individual treasure troves while the rest of the country collapses.

Chapter 5: While not so named until the 20th Century, Americans have long and ardently regarded their nation as "exceptional," and in some ways it was, for example the persistence of religion defied the secular trend of European modernization. In the pursuit of wealth and power, we will see how the military consumes ever more of the national budget and resources, and the technology of weapons and combat systems is the only area in which the US remains preeminent. To sustain the military-industrial complex, we show how in the American context, a sense of honor and glory derived from killing, beginning with the annihilation of indigenous people, and the relentless slaughter of the foreign Other. We argue that victory is less important than the righteous death and destruction of the enemy which connects America to God's divine plan for the United States, and that each individual must be willing to fight, whether the enemy is an army, a terrorist organization, or "illegal" immigrants.

Chapter 6: We will then link the social psychological concepts we first introduced in Chapter 1 together with the subsequent chapters to create an understanding of the contradictions of American social character, to understand why the reactionary character type has become dysfunctional in relationship to the contemporary world that requires more inclusive and mutually respectful social relations both at home and abroad. The social character, attitudes, and social hierarchy that rich white men have used to dominate the country and shape the world no longer holds legitimacy, and the vast expansion of the US military demonstrates this lack of legitimacy abroad. Yet the more forcefully the US asserts itself, the less influence it wields, the faster it falls, the harder it will hit bottom, and the more devastating the final wreckage.

Chapter 7: For all the gloom and doom about the future of the USA, we remain optimistic and envision an alternate future which derives from the same cultural and historical roots as the now dominant, yet waning social character. Thus we will argue that today we are seeing the cultural version of what psychoanalysis calls "regression in the service of the ego" in which the person, or in our case the society, can recapture aspects of itself from an much earlier time that has been repressed, denied or marginalized. This in turn allows the "return of the repressed," and what we consider repressed is the spirit of the Commune premised on democratic values and egalitarian practices of caring, sharing and empathy that can be found in America's cultural history that has been either repressed, forgotten or denigrated and dismissed as "feminine." But as we will argue, the emerging social character, also rooted in a long cultural history, is more adaptive for the present and future by transcending capital, emphasizing being over having, universalizing what has been denigrated as feminine and bidding farewell to the phallic-aggressive kick-ass version of masculinity. We envision various possibilities of community, inclusion, tolerance, egalitarian relationships, self-fulfillment and better quality of life and honest faith.

Chapter 8: Sociology has generally looked at trends and processes, as do we who suggest that a new social character is emerging and likely to become the dominant type, enabling major transformation and restructuring of the society. But a short term, unique events such as a terrorist attack, another economic meltdown, or even however unlikely, a nuclear war can change all that. But we will still offer thoughts for the future that prefigure our next book, *A Sane Society in the 21st Century*.

Although we cite academic and other references to make our argument, we will not offer a comprehensive literature review or critique previous scholarship, though some of this literature will be cited.[15] Rather, we seek to:

1. Illuminate the nature of America's underlying social character that sustains its collective values and its identity. To this end, we have followed the traditions of the Frankfurt school of Critical Theory, especially the work of Erich Fromm on the historical nature of social character, dynamic character change, and what makes for a good, sane society.

---

15   Perhaps the most comprehensive analysis of American character remains that of Alex Inkeles (1997) with whom we have a great deal in common, especially his psychodynamic approach, a concern with the modal personality type in the context of multimodal distributions, his emphasis on the continuities of American character and as well as its major changes in the latter part of the 20th Century. With rather conventional inclinations, Inkeles noted a decline in the work ethic which has not occurred, but rather as we suggest people are seeking meaningful work rather than that which brings more individualistic forms of happiness. Writing at the end of the 20th Century, the sexual revolution was over and Americans had become much more tolerant of sexuality as seen in mass media, advice columns, and most of all in actual behavior. Despite the loud and vociferous counter-reaction of religious conservatives, especially fundamentalist Christians, the sexual behavior of Americans has only become more open and inclusive (the right to gay marriage, for example) since 1997.

2. American social character, dynamically understood can be thought of as a resolution of a number of psychosocial polarities, conflicts between desires, conflicts between desires and defenses and/or conflicts between social character and the nature of the world.

3. Moreover, we argue that the unique conditions that gave rise to American character, between its "inner determination" initially tied to Protestantism, the geography and topography of the land, rich in resources including arable land and for most of the early years of the Republic, Americans were relatively isolated from European conflicts. These factors led to increasing levels of prosperity and by the end of the 19th Century, the USA became an increasingly powerful nation state. Following World War II it ascended to the very pinnacle of power, a "superpower" and following the Bretton Woods conference began to assume the qualities of an Empire. At the same time, moments of its social character that enabled the rise of the new Colossus created conditions that would undermine that growth. Indeed, the primary attributes of it social character, its individualism, its religiosity, its disposition for aggression and indeed it's self-image as exceptional that enabled its ascent now serves to undermine its wealth and power.

4. Finally, and perhaps most importantly, we wish to articulate a political position that begins with a critique of domination based on the legacy of the Frankfurt School's syntheses of Marx, Weber and Freud. But that emancipatory tradition also suggests an alternative utopian vision of what might provide a better, more egalitarian, more fulfilling "good society." Thus we see in decline the conditions for the emergence of a more humanistic, egalitarian, nurturing society, what Fromm called a "sane society," in a post capitalist society in which people overcome alienation, reification and commodification and build supportive communities that provide nurturing relations. To live in peace and not war, to nurture creative potential and experience dignity and love, this is our vision for the future. Not only might people live in harmony with each other but in harmony with nature, lest our environmental despoliation bring an end to the human race. Although repressed, submerged and at times vilified, demonized and marginalized, the progressive aspects of American character have always been present, and as we will argue in this book, arose from the very same religious, cultural, and historical experiences as did the authoritarians, the social dominators, the narcissists that now dominate the USA. But some of them see the pitchforks coming and we see our work as clarion calls for nonviolent resistance because a different world is possible.

As will be demonstrated in the following pages, notwithstanding the endurance of the "culture wars" that began in the 6os, the rightward shift of the political center that we may perhaps date from the failed Goldwater campaign that led to the 1968 Nixon "Southern strategy," soon followed by the expansion of globalization, justified and celebrated by neoliberalism has seemingly left the country in a sorry state. As will be noted, neoliberalism has become the dominant ideology embraced by economic and corporate elites, both within the US among the transnational capitalist classes across the globe. It "explains" the nature of reality and the appropriate actions that privileges the marketplace and market based solutions and policies that promise general prosperity. Thus governments need to service debt not squander money on benefits and entitlements that should be privatized. Regulations need to be lifted so corporations can prosper. Neoliberalism promises that short term hardships will be overcome and the rising tide will raise all ships. Thus, like many religions, market fundamentalism promises that short term suffering now will bring rewards at a later time, but in this life not the next. While it has vastly increased wealth, as promised, most of that wealth has gone to the elites. We noted how 20 men own half the wealth of the USA, well 62 men own half the wealth of the world, and in that world, about 1/3 of the people live on about a dollar a day. This is why many critics of neoliberalism consider it simply a subterfuge to mask the organized theft of contemporary capitalism. Finance capital in particular functions more like a criminal syndicate that relies on rigged gambling and "too big to fail" extortion to cover the losses with public money. Yet wealth justifies itself, and for many who vote for the billionaires and their lackeys, rich people shine like a paragon of virtue to admire and emulate no matter how they made their fortune.

Our current political leadership, riven by intense conflicts and hatreds within the factions of the ruling classes has led to a dysfunctional government beholden to the economic elites that is unable to address the fundamental problems of our times, namely growing inequality and impoverishment, environmental despoliation and national decline. Unlike conventional academic tomes, we will look at current events, perspectives from outside the academy, and develop a decisively progressive agenda. We make no pretense of neutrality because such pretenses often make academic work irrelevant to the real world.

Introduction

The concern with national character may have begun with Herodotus, the father of history. He described the typical qualities of the various groups surrounding Ancient Greece and attempted to look at those distinct qualities of each group and to discern what today we call their "national character." Based on their shared cultural legacies, language, customs, values and habits, Herodotus wanted to know what makes each group different from the others. Today, 2,500 years later, it remains quite evident that the cultural legacies of generations past still bear down upon the present and shape it's social, political and cultural life. As Marx noted, people make history, but not always as they please. While surely every generation is shaped in part by its current realities, those realities nevertheless interact with historically specific versions of social character which emerged at an earlier time and may yet endure and/or perhaps change in response to new events. In the US, many aspects of social character have been consistent over time, and this consistency now produces the farcical and dysfunctional political system that has created a tragedy for most Americans. While costumed Tea Partiers may don tri-corner hats, play drums and fifes and wave the Gadsden flag with its coiled serpent, most of the Tea Partiers who "want their [white patriarchal, homophobic] country back," the colonials and the colonial way of life they imitate in dress have been dead for over 200 years. Indeed, many if not most of the anti-government, anti-socialist populist right would not be alive had not the government financed medical research, subsidized health care and paid the medical bills of those over 65.

While there is no simple answer to the issues of continuity and change of social character, in any culture, variations in the distributions of the kinds or types of people might be found. Given the nature of the economy and the values of a particular group, some people will better adapt than others, and what may have been random variations at one moment becomeconsistent patterns in thought and behavior. Surely there are differences of race, class, gender, and today, ethnicity, but at the same time, the ranges of variation are not unlimited. Certain patterns or constellations are more compatible with existing economic, political and cultural systems than others. The patterns of values, meanings, practices and collective identities that become dominant constitute social character. The specific dominant social character may not be the most numerous, but most of the population shares many of its personality traits and values.

America began its legacy when the early Puritan settlements faced struggles against both harsh elements from which many died from conflicts with the native populations who didn't like being forced from their ancestral and now colonized lands. But the early colonial era was followed by growing prosperity and claims for political independence led to its Declaration of Independence from England. Following its armed revolution, the thirteen colonies became the first "new nation" (Lipset, 1979). With its modest beginnings as a colonial backwater, with its democracy and prosperity, and subsequent ascendancy as a world power, America and American character has been a topic of interest and analysis since the late 18th and early 19th Century when French observers such as to De Crevecoeur and de Tocqueville first charted the young democracy in America, noting especially America's individualism, dynamism, the industriousness of its people and their materialism. Some 60 years or so later, in 1893, Jackson Turner claimed that these distinctive qualities of American character, unlike Europe, were due to an expanding frontier and the necessities of adaptation to the conditions of frontier life. As Rojek (2016) says, the wide-open frontier "denotes an imaginative expanse where social being may be tested, reinvented, reframed and, crucially, for our purposes, admired and relished." Louis Hartz (1991 [1955]) argued that the distinct quality of America was based on its not having a feudal tradition and a hated aristocratic class. As De Tocqueville noted, Americans did not hate the rich, they wanted to be them. In America, its individualism and ethic of self-reliance forged a barrier against class consciousness that mitigated against the possibility of socialism. We will later argue that the barrier is far less formidable today and larger segments of the population see the rich increasingly like the despotic nobility of aristocratic Europe.

In many ways, we follow works such as David Riesman's *The Lonely Crowd* (2001 [1961]), a study of individualism and conformity written at a time of alienation compounded by the fear of communism. Philip Slater's *Pursuit of Loneliness* (1970) charted the underlying psychodynamics of that loneliness, written in the during the war in Vietnam and rise of the counterculture, the times revealed some of the very deep fissures in America's underlying social character that differentiated the older, traditional American character that was more authoritarian, patriotic and sexually repressive, from the newer, emerging social character of the countercultural youth that tended to be more critical of authority, disdainful of patriarchy and more likely to reject traditional norms, especially norms of sexual repression. His work exerts major influence on our own scholarship. More recently, Robert Putnam's *Bowling Alone* (2000) speaks to the decline in civic participation and social connections such as social clubs and bowling leagues at a time when globalization has undermined the middle-class dreams of financial security and attenuated social connections. While many people maintain relationships via social media ... but when someone has 800 friends, the notions of intimacy, sharing and connection become a bit tenuous. There have been many other important contributions by other people as well.

As almost any and all observers note, part and parcel of American character has been its individualism, but individualism itself explains only part of the equation. As the following chapters will unfold, we will also discuss the importance of religious based (Puritan) morality which engendered the individualism that flourished along with the growth of capitalist commerce, urbanization and the expanding frontier. Moreover, and at the same time, up until recently, religiosity has remained an important aspect of American social character and in turn, a determinant of American political policies, especially attempts to regulate gender roles and sexual "morality." This has been especially true in the states of the Old Confederacy that includes the Bible Belt where conservative evangelical religion is firmly entrenched. However, a growing cultural and social psychological gap between older and younger cohorts means that even children of conservative families are ever less likely to maintain these traditional values. Moreover, the USA is become more and more multicultural as new immigrants bring new ways of life from different parts of the world. For these reasons, the more conservative, authoritarian segments of American society, who are the most dogmatic and least open to change, are especially angry that the right-wing, often reactionary politicians they support and who actually control the House of Representatives can do nothing whatsoever to reverse the realities of a massive cultural shift despite control of Congress.

Similarly given the history and nature of colonizing settlers occupying the lands of other people, there is also a phallic-aggressive quality of American character, a value of male toughness, for many, this can be seen in gun ownership (Wilkinson, 1984). Perhaps one of the most important recent critics of American character, Seymour Martin Lipset, has offered extensive accounts of how America became a "new nation," and how *American Exceptionalism* (1998) that stressed individualism and dismissed traditions of deference to authority, led the United States to become a much more dynamic society, but at the same time one more disdainful of authority and prone to have greater levels of violence among its own people and abroad, compared to other countries such as Canada which retained stronger notions of national law and collective benefit.

Most scholarship seeks to understanding national character as a pattern of historically based collective values, as its self-referential narratives, its identities, and/or it's more or less distinct cultural expressions in art, literature, poetry, film, and music. Indeed, American character can be seen in everyday life where Americans tend to be more dynamic and assertive. Notice how much louder Americans are in restaurants. The emphasis on free expression has created the most innovative and diverse forms of music that find audiences all over the world. Unfortunately, much the same can be said about US foreign policies and the enthusiastic invasion of other countries and reckless overthrow of foreign governments. So, we attempt to understand national character at the level of values by illuminating the underlying social character that is more often than not ignored by rationalist scholarship that avoids both the psychological aspects of character and the system that heaps lavish rewards on those who own it—capitalisists. Capitalism rests on alienation, exploitation and reification; people only exploit other people if they see them as objects, as something less than human or even more typical in the history of the US, as deserving slavery or poverty so that others may prosper. A comprehensive account of thoughts, values, and behavior in the United States must include its underlying social character.

Erich Fromm and Social Character

The political and cultural conflicts and struggles in America today are not simply battles of liberal versus conservative ideologies or Democrats versus Republicans. Nor are these simply battles between the religious conservatives and the more secular liberals, nor white versus non-white, patriarchy versus feminism, discrimination versus inclusiveness, or even the 1% versus the 99%. While all of these ideological battles are part of social conflicts often called "culture wars" in the US today, diverting attention from actual class wars and less obvious psychological differences, we argue that a much more essential and profound conflict is unfolding which informs the economic, ideological and political stances that people take over the particular battles that result from class, race, ethnicity, gender, and sexuality inequality. This is the conflict over the changing nature of American social character. What is social character? Following Erich Fromm (1992 [1973]), social character consists of the most typical social psychological characteristics found within a group that make people in that group psychologically similar to each other, different from others, and thus, social character constitutes a link between the individual and society. The individual feels connected to others precisely because they share internal sentiments that are also manifest socially.

As Erich Fromm explains, "the concept of social character is based on the consideration that each form of society or social class needs to use human energy in the specific manner necessary for the functioning of that particular society" ((1992 [1973 p. 283). For the sake of simplicity, we see social character as a the most frequently found pattern of socialized desires, internalized values, understandings of the world and conscious self-awareness, including one's self-conceptions, such as narratives of identity and self-images through which one defines him or herself. The dominant social character may not include the majority of people, but everyone shares at least some of the key characteristics. However, it is strongly typical among the elites.

For our purposes, the most basic dimension of social character is along a humanistic versus authoritarian axis, but most people lie in the middle, not the extremes. The humanistic orientation emphasizes empathy, caring, sharing, and nurturance as well as encouraging creative self-realization and bringing benefits to other people. While not everyone in such a group is equally empathetic, caring, and so on, and a few not at all, everyone expresses or conforms to these traits to some extent, and the leaders of the community most of all. In contrast, authoritarians value strength, power, toughness, conformity, and maximizing benefits primarily for one's local group or community. Like the community of humanists, not everyone is equally authoritarian, but everyone has some elements of it, and the leaders most of all. Authoritarians see and understand the world quite differently than more humanistic types. People see what they want to see, and depending on their social position, their social character and what they are forced to see. But they may selectively discard and reject what may be discrepant, counterfactual or disconfirming to their values and identities. Cognitive dissonance, the differences or contradictions between various beliefs, or between beliefs and reality fosters various degrees of stress, anxiety and discomfort. People seek consistency and so employ a number of strategies such as motivated reasoning, which may include denial, splitting and so on to ward off discrepant information that might challenge one's self, identity, one's community and/or one's value orientations. Thus underlying motives and feelings that are part of one's character structure act to "accept" information compatible with one's beliefs and character, in other words, confirmation bias. Meanwhile, they actively reject and deny evidence and information that is inconsistent with one's identity, values and peer groups. Motivated reasoning provides people with a degree of comfort, it enables individuals and groups, or in our case a nation, to function on a day to day basis. But at the same time, the rejection of certain beliefs or aspects of reality can have adverse consequences. Consider for example how many people selectively disregard(ed) the relation of smoking to lung cancer.

Consciousness, is always contingent on social relations and experiences, especially the experiences that take place in the various institutions that inscribe socialize ideologies and hegemonic social norms such as the family where folks learn obedience or creativity, schools that celebrate a national history and culture, peer groups and media that disseminates propaganda called "infotainment." Today some might add social media. Moreover, sometimes personal experiences may change one's ways of looking at the world. As we earlier noted, losing a job and/or house can change one's views on capitalism. One reason why the US had to leave Vietnam was when the troops saw the futility of fighting, they began to "frag" officers. Later many joined antiwar groups.

For Kant and the legacy of the social constructionists, the mind is an active agent that constructs the world on the basis of the sense data that enters consciousness. Thus for example one's position in the social hierarchy is a major influence on how one sees, if not constructs social hierarchy, if one sees it at all. Some evaluate it as perhaps natural while others see it as created and imposed. Indeed, one's position in social hierarchy and the kind of character that emerges determines how one sees the world and other people in general. Subordinates are more likely to see hierarchy than elites. And in a likewise manner, gender, itself a hierarchical status, leads to different forms of consciousness, and so for many generations feminists have emphasized the unique nature of "women's ways of knowing." These and a multitude of other forces shape our desires, identities and cognitive frames all of which in turn influence the way we see the world, evaluate it, and act upon it. Otherwise said, one's underlying social character, of which we are typically unaware, acts as a prism that refracts reality in particular ways that are consistent with the person's character that has been socially shaped. Note the world views of conservative politicians, talk show hosts, and Donald Trump compared to leftists like Bernie Sanders. Conservatives see the world as more fearful and precarious, enemies are everywhere and we must be tough and strong whether the enemies are criminals or murderers here, ISIS over there, or immigrants allegedly coming to steal, plunder and rape. Their world views often border on the paranoid and sometimes cross into delusion when embracing various conspiracy theories. Negotiation is for wussies—not real men with balls. What gay men do is disgusting, makes you want to vomit. For a strong authoritarian, social hierarchies are normal and natural and those on top are usually "better" people. But humanists like Bernie Sanders sees the dangers of crime and terrorism as the products of injustice, especially when due to hierarchies of wealth, race, and gender that rob people of their dignity and livelihoods. People should negotiate to everyone's benefit rather than fight. As for what gays do, a liberal mayor like Bill De Blasio of New York City is married to a bisexual Black woman.

For our purposes, we might see how attitudes and perceptions impact the relation of capital punishment to crime. Many people, typically highly religious and/or political conservatives, given an underlying sadomasochistic, punitive orientation, feel that "offenders" must be harshly punished to prevent future crime as well as affirm collective values. However, 50+ years of solid criminological, research, and a vast litany of philosophy have shown, as Dostoevsky concludes in *Crime and Punishment* or as Tolstoy in *War and Peace* has concluded, harsh punishments do not deter crime, but this undermines the beliefs which many still hold. Many believe that the death penalty reinforces the power of the government and the sanctity of the law; but the death penalty does not reduce crime or violence. It may actually increase violence as the State becomes a model for violence. For many States, recent fiscal pressure has moved legislators to accept the reality that with an average cost of $25 million or so for an execution, the money might be better spent on education, infrastructure or aid to the disadvantaged. For those lawmakers with less devotion to the public good, reducing the costs of executions enables more tax breaks for rich people and corporations. For us however, one of the consequences of such "motivated" reasoning is for most people to ignore how American national character has become dysfunctional in the contemporary world-supporting policies and politicians that ill-serve the public good.

As the Frankfurt school first demonstrated, and more recently a number of social scientists have pointed out, emotions and feelings have greater impact on people's beliefs, thoughts and action than rational considerations. Consequently, morals and values serve and reflect the particular interests and agendas of one's social character, in contrast to scientific perspectives or objective reasoning which seeks the most complete knowledge possible to ascertain a sense of truth without distortion or concealment. Instead, people act more like lawyers than like scientists and typically engage in highly selective ways to gather "evidence" to support their identities or position. People employ what is called a "confirmation bias," to support their opinions and buttress their claims, especially their political or moral positions. At the same time, they disregard, deny and/or debunk that which contradicts their own beliefs or agendas desired. This discrepancy often leads to cognitive dissonance and in many, perhaps most cases, people embrace their beliefs and reject evidence all the more vehemently because few people are willing to admit they were wrong in a society that values power and toughness. Our concern however is not so much the individual, but what is most typical kind of social character in a group and not the individual character. Thus for example, hiking through the forest some groups of people might see the glories of nature, stand in awe of natural beauty and envision a society living in harmony with Nature and the environment. But other groups, trekking through the same forest might see a source of timber, wood pulp or even Christmas trees all of which might yield profits. And the next travelers might view the same land and envision possibility of subterranean mineral resources that can be strip-mined or fracked to bring oil to the surface.

In a similar vein, Paul Krugman has termed the claims of many conservative politicians as "zombie ideas," such as austerity eventually creates wealth and/or trickle-down economics would promote economic growth, tax cuts for the rich create jobs, while the "advantages" of privatizing social security and ending the Affordable Healthcare Act (Obamacare) have all been empirically disproven. Yet such mantras, devoutly believed by conservatives, rejecting all disconfirming evidence, leads to policies that adversely impact a national economy and quite often devastate the very poor. Despite all counter factual evidence, these ideological mantras remain part of the stump speeches of conservative politicians which emotionally resonate with the character structures of their followers. We would hope that when Krugman reads this book he can understand how and why such ideas appeal to aspects of traditional American character and serve emotional needs, even if privatizing prisons, social security and Medicare appeal to rich conservatives, they are only a small number of people. Child labor, eliminating OSHA and the EPA also appeal to billionaires and their corporate managers, but once again, they need the conservative values voters to gain office and pass this kind of legislation—which adversely impacts most of these very same voters that support them.[1]

Finally, social character includes various interpersonal "mechanisms of escape," Erich Fromm's term for the defense mechanisms that people use to repress certain thoughts, feelings, and desires and keep them unconscious where they nevertheless remain active and exert influence, though unknowingly. As every intro psychology text notes, defenses such as intellectualization, rationalization, projection, regression, reaction formation, denial, or acting out, and even sublimation are ways of avoiding certain desires and feelings. Without getting into the intricacies and more technical details of psychoanalytic theory, defenses often suppress unpleasant desires and feelings, stigmatized thoughts, traumatic early memories and other unpleasant feelings and keep them out of conscious awareness. Classical psychoanalysis considered these kinds of defenses that distort, deny and/or manipulate reality as aspects of

---

1   In his failed quest for the presidency, Governor/Reverend Michael Huckabee suggested revisiting slavery as a form of punishment for criminal offenders. But ironically enough we already have such a system namely prisoners who work for sometimes between 10 and 25 cents an hour working in state or local infrastructure. We have seen similar ideas that poor, meaning minority, school children work as janitors in their schools. We need another Charles Dickens to expose the ugly underside of American Empire, just as he did with the British Empire.

the "horizontal split" in which certain, often "prohibited" desires, feelings and thoughts were kept below, kept down in the unconscious and out of awareness to avoid guilt, anxiety, or shame. The goal of therapy was to bring the unconscious into conscious awareness and thereby give the ego power over the id, or as Freud said, "where id was ego shall be." But what is especially crucial for our analysis of American social character is the mechanism of "splitting," which tends to be an ego function in which people deny one part of reality in order to sustain another part of reality based largely on their own needs and values. In early infancy, a child splits experiences into simplistic good and bad categories.[2] Later, as the child develops greater cognitive ability and emotional development, s/he can, or should be able to integrate the contradictions that are entirely normal. In some cases, however, when a person continues this kind of splitting into adulthood, a pathological connection develops to other people as well as with the entire society. While our concern is not the psychopathology of individuals, we nevertheless will argue that the use of splitting is an important ego process, that as a defense that has long been typical of the American social character which enables the blanket denial, if not vehement rejection of that which may question, if not contradict one's beliefs and understandings. Often found along with splitting, projection allows a person to project his or her feelings or desires outward, especially what they least like about themselves onto others. People typically project their greatest fears and/ or repressed desires. So for example the racialized Other cannot be a complex human being with wide variations within his or her group, nor may the Other have any contradictions. Rather, s/he is often the embodiment of projected aggression and rendered evil, or perhaps s/he is the object of projected sexual desire and thus rendered an immoral, sinful monster. A primary tenet of white supremacy in the American context has meant that Black and Brown people simply cannot be real people, their humanity was not recognized. They are either subservient, if not grossly deficient, or else they are vile, filthy, lazy, corrupt trespassers, typically oversexed and likely criminals. Hence, Donald Trump, as an embodiment of traditional American characters (successful businessman, carnival barker, snake oil salesman), became the Republican presidential nominee in 2016 by saying that Mexican immigrants were drug dealers, rapists and murderers. First, he splits off all the most negative qualities, and then projects them onto all Mexican immigrants (and later, all immigrants). Similarly, many

---

2   For those more familiar with psychoanalytic theory, this is Klein's distinct of the good and bad breast, paranoid and depressive positions that eventually find integration. But for many, especially conservatives whose thought cannot deal with contradiction, everything is either-or, good, as in in-group, or bad, as in outgroup.

other conservatives view Obama as a Kenyan Muslim who hates America, an atheist, a communist, spineless dictator-king. Don't worry about the apparent contradictions in this alternative reality, it is clear to the believers.

Given the Puritanism of the early American settlers that divided humanity into the chosen and the damned, splitting and projection became essential mechanisms of defense for the emergent American social character and subsequently, the damned were denied all humanity which thus justified the most heinous torture and public executions. Puritan leaders, men in particular as we will see later, cast moral transgressors from their own community, including women. The Native-Americans were seen as servants of Satan or subhuman savages. This of course "justified" the genocide of the native populations. In World War I, the Germans were considered Huns and spikeheads that impaled babies on their bayonets. In World War II, Nazis were krauts, little more than pickled cabbages. The Japanese were rendered Japs, Nips, and monkey-men and needed to be eliminated. When America came to Vietnam, the enemy consisted of gooks and slopes. Similarly, in Iraq the people became camel jockeys, rag heads, and Hajis. In all such cases of racism, misogyny, and other forms of bigotry, "those people" aren't really people with any humanity, but simply bad objects to use, abuse, discard, torture or kill. The very same dehumanization was clearly seen in the pathological ravings of the "good" Christian Chris Kyle, the *American Sniper* who viewed all Iraqis as "savages" which justified taking out women and children. We also see this same splitting and projection taking place among the religiously inspired creationists or climate change deniers that simply refuse to accept hard "evidence" of evolution based on scientific inquiry and empirical methods, moments of an evil liberal conspiracy. After all, the Bible doesn't say anything about radiocarbon dating.

The George W. Bush administration officials like Dick Cheney and Chief Legal Counsel John Yoo claimed that "enhanced interrogation techniques" like waterboarding were not torture. Religious conservatives have a great deal of trouble accepting the fact that the majority of Americans do not share their values over issues of sexuality, patriarchy or homosexuality, the reality that most Americans become sexual by 18, and that patriarchy is on the decline and most support gay marriage.

Finally, as we will discuss in more detail, the celebration of American character is such that America is seen as the best, richest and happiest country in the world, a democratic, moral country that is the primary force for good in the world. It is a place where people from all over the world supposedly come for jobs, superior medical care and the finest education. Americans can do no harm even when invading, destroying and occupying other lands which is often necessary to promote peace, freedom, democracy and human justice. Any individual who actually holds such beliefs might be considered a bit daffy, but when the benevolence of America becomes a distinct quality of American social character, not only do such beliefs become normalized, but serve to justify despicable practices and policies.

The Social Character of Elites: Dominators and Destroyers

There are many different expressions of social character, even within its own parameters. Whatever the commonalities, some people tend to be authoritarian and some more democratic, some are life-affirming, or life-thwarting, exploitative or cooperative, hierarchical or egalitarian, and engaged or perhaps indifferent. Most importantly, social character determines the manner in which people interact, both in terms of their overt behavior and the experienced emotions that resonate as meaningful. As Erich Fromm (1992 [1973]) pointed out, the members of any society (or any group or class) "must *want* to do what they *must* do if the society is to function properly" in accordance with their assumptions and beliefs about life. Consequently, a cooperative and compassionate person wants to be cooperative and compassionate, and feels right and fulfilled whenever they have such opportunities whether in work, politics, leisure and recreation and personal relationship. Similarly, the more sinister expressions of social character may include exploitative and aggressive people, typically authoritarians with a sadomasochistic streak, who feel joy and fulfillment whenever they can dominate, exploit, and oppress others and find gratification in their suffering. And many of these are narcissistic as well, superficially charming manipulators, indifferent to the feelings of others, who need constant admiration and recognition.

Today, an exploitative, life-thwarting version of American social character, a product and legacy of centuries long past, ascendant to the elite pinnacles, dominates much of the politics, economics, and culture in the United States. This kind of person tends to be highly individualistic, hard-working, and can readily use or at least justify violence for the sake of moral redemption. Such people are typically authoritarians that are strongly anti-intellectual and uncritical over the use of power and the impact that power might have on people. In general social dominators have an extremely callous disregard for people other than themselves. Other character types exist alongside the more dominant types, and some even resist the dominant type and his or her world views, policies or practices. Nevertheless, most of the top 1% didn't become rich and powerful because they gave away (or even invested) their money for the common good. The well-known richest man in America, Bill Gates does give away millions every year, but he also makes billions every year. In 2013, he received 11.5 billion in total income (La Roche, 2013). Whatever Gates' individual traits, his social character is that of a member whose income is at the top .01% of the world's population. Beyond the software business, Gates believes that his expert genius can solve problems that he sees in our educational system. Core curriculum, "objective" assessment, the standardization of learning to serve corporate interests are all part of the Gates Foundation's efforts to transform the entire education system in the United States into Gates' personal vision—if you can't answer a question with an equation, the question is of no concern. As Henry Giroux (2014) argues, such kinds of educational pedagogy that valorizes "objective" and "data-driven" assessment are just one part of a larger effort to transform the university's mission. Rather than broaden the individual into a knowledgeable, imaginative and compassionate citizen capable of creative and quite often critical analyses of the society, the neoliberal view seeks instead to reduce people to servants of corporate interests over and against any sense of a common good:

> The mantra of neoliberalism is well-known: Society is a fiction; Sovereignty is market-driven; Deregulation and commodification are vehicles for freedom; Higher Education should serve corporate interests rather than the public good. In addition, the yardstick of profit has become the only viable measure of the good life, while civic engagement and public spheres devoted to the common good are viewed by many politicians and their publics as either a hindrance to the goals of a market-driven society or alibis for government inefficiency and waste.
>
> GIROUX, 2014, p. 24

Since the calculation of profit and loss is considered the only viable measure of success or failure, the only viable orientation to education is a coldly calculating instrumental rationality. In this view, counting money and counting "learning outcomes" are no different. At the same time, institutions and systems cannot hold worldviews, advance agendas, and make decisions. Only people can. The cold calculations of instrumental rationality are not just the outcome of business interests, but the expression of an underlying social character typical of social leaders like Bill Gates that interprets the world as a collection of objects to control, manipulate, and exploit for personal satisfaction and gain.

Is it OK to intimidate and embarrass students in the classroom, or undermine a friend or spouse in public, or even shoot up a school or place of work? The lives of other people have no relevance to the pursuit of personal gratification. Is it OK to destroy a business and eliminate jobs to gain a profit, or move a factory to a poor country with cheap labor costs where sweatshops employ young women and even children in hazardous conditions? Many factories knowingly pollute the environment and endanger public health, but public health is just an "externality," so dumping waste into a river that becomes highly cancerous to a downstream community is just another calculation. Should countries go to war for the sake of oil or other resources? Sanctions on Iraq meant that about 500,000 children died, while former Secretary of State Madeleine Albright said it was worth it. The best estimates suggest that over 1 million Iraqis died as a result of the American invasion that devastated a relatively stable, although not democratic nation, noting of course that it was the CIA that helped put the Baath socialist party into power that enabled Saddam Hussain to become its dictator. Then the USA encouraged his invasion of Iran. In the world in which we now live, the lives of other people have no relevance to the quests for profit and power. Of course, not everyone would make such decisions, but those who do, will do so enthusiastically, and they find glory and reward in any social setting that promotes greed, ambition, and all manner of personal gain. In Michigan, the conservative Governor Rick Snyder appointed an emergency manager for Flint, Michigan who knowingly sourced water from the Flint River to save money, even though the water was highly toxic with high levels of lead and other contaminants. The Governor then tried to blame his staff for his own lying and attempted cover-up (Detroit Free Press, 2016).

Our critique does not arise solely from the left. As the extremely rich transnational capitalists and their corporations detach themselves from their own communities and nations, they become self-serving and often hostile to anything that might protect the health and welfare of a community and nation, such as wage and environmental regulations when such regulations infringe on profit in any way.[3] As longtime Republican Mike Lofgren argues, the extreme rich and the corporations they own have seceded from their home countries. Billionaires such as Bill Gates, Sheldon Adelson, the Koch Brothers, the Walton family, and others openly finance, that is, buy candidates for public office, "Our plutocracy now lives like the British in colonial India: in the place and ruling it, but not of it" (Lofgren, 2012). For Lofgren, following an argument by the late historian Christopher Lasch, the threat to the United States does not come from the poor and the masses. It comes from the rich, "and not just the

---

3   In the summer of 2015, the State of California discovered that Volkswagen intentionally rigged the software in its diesel cars to comply with environmental standards when tested but in fact the level of pollution was 40 times the legal limit under normal operation. European regulators then discovered the same cheating in EU markets. This was not the work of a few rogue programmers but corporate policy.

super-wealthy but also their managerial coat holders and professional apolo-
gists who are undermining the country's promise as a constitutional republic with their reprehensible greed, their asocial cultural values, and their absence of civic responsibility" (Lofgren, 2012). Although they have little regard
for their followers, the rich and powerful depend on their managers and some
degree of public support, because without commitment and support from
some segments of the population, people like Bill Gates would be just another
nerdy wanker who thinks he knows everything, or the Koch Brothers would
just be two greedy old geezers grumbling about Mexicans, Blacks, and hippie
environmentalists.

In the contemporary social environment that worships money and power
above all, personal traits such as arrogance and aggression, also rooted in
American character, become celebrated as the personal manifestations of having wealth and power. Money lets people say and do whatever they want, and
not just because people can use wealth to buy the privilege of self-expression.
The Koch Brothers have pledged 889 million dollars to support radical-right
candidates in the 2016 election season (CBS News, 2015). We allow big money
to control politics because we worship money in the United States, we extol
the rich and believe that wealth sanctifies anyone who has a lot of it. Wealth
buys more than airtime. It buys hearts and minds in a society that worships
money as a god. This is changing, especially among the younger cohorts, and
we will return to this change. In order to understand contemporary America,
it's contradictions and indeed growing discontents we need to examine how
we got to the present point, and the important role of social character that is
shaped by historical context, is a major factor impacting social and political
life and yet the is generally both invisible to the individual and ignored by most
academic scholarship.

Character and Contradictions

Insofar as social character changes in response to the social environment, the
contemporary conflicts within American character developed over time. Different eras reward and reinforce particular character traits over and against
others. For ten years, Erich Fromm witnessed how the transition from a pre-
modern village to a modern town in Mexico also changed the predominant
character types (Fromm, 1996 [1972]). Using a multi-method approach of interviews, questionnaires, and participant observation, Fromm concluded that
in its pre-modern form, the village emphasized the "receptive character." Based
on long traditions, a receptive character expects to receive whatever would

normally accrue to a person, based on their class and status of birth. For example, a farmer's son expects to inherit the farm. A farmer's daughter expects that her family will marry her to a farmer's son. A blacksmith's son expects to inherit the forge, and so on. For the receptive character in a traditional society, inheritance and one's trade, the passage of property, skills, and status in the community are not choices and not earned either; they are dictated by tradition. The receptive person sees anything that follows in accordance with tradition as fair and just. Social ties to family and community are strong, as tradition dictates. Each person is born into a particular set of obligations and privileges, and each person expects that everyone else will uphold the obligations of their social position. The highest virtue of all is fulfilling the expectations of birth and keeping your place in society.

As the traditional village transitioned to a modern industrial town, the predominant social character type changed from the "receptive" to the "hoarding type." The "hoarding type" relies much less on established social ties and instead lives as an individual who is free to accept or reject the social relations of their birth. This makes social ties much freer, but also less secure. As an individual, they feel free to make of life what they can, and so they apply whatever abilities they have to earn as much as they can. Fromm calls this type a "hoarding type" because they expect to keep whatever they earn, with no particular obligations to anyone else. They expect nothing from others, and others should not expect anything from them, except by mutual contractual agreements for a fixed duration. Unlike traditional society, social relations in modern society are fluid and determined by individual effort, not by tradition. Fairness for the hoarding type means that everyone has a fair chance at life (though not an equal outcome) and justice means that everyone gets what they themselves earn. Neither the receptive nor the hoarding character is inherently better or worse than the other, but rather it depends on how well one type or the other functions in a given society. We may not like a strongly restrictive traditional society, such as medieval Europe, but traditional forms of social organization were viable for thousands of years. The modern industrial type is less stable and viable. What of the present post-industrial United States? What if a society is so dysfunctional that it produces pathological character types? In this book, we argue that the contemporary United States rewards and valorizes at least two highly sinister pathological character types, the authoritarian-destructive, and the social dominance orientation both mentioned earlier. We will return to these concepts later in this chapter. First, let's consider in more detail the rise of the hoarding type, the most common type in the modern capitalist era and how this has given way to the pathological types (but also progressive types).

The Origins and Rise of the Modern Social Character

With the rise of trade that began in Renaissance Italy, the *nouveau riche* merchant classes sought a distinct cultural identity of their own since they were neither born into the aristocratic dynasties, nor were they peasants. The quest for what we might now call "distinction," on the basis of valorized identities based on their "cultural capital" led to the "rebirth" or Renaissance of Greco-Roman art, sculpture, literature, philosophy and architecture that would provide the foundations for the emerging identity. Further, much of the trade was with the Byzantine Empire (the eastern half of the Roman Empire) and with the Islamic world, for example, Venice and Genoa had extensive trade with Sidon, Palmyra, and Baghdad. Ironically, much of the classical texts of the Greek and Roman playwrights, poets and philosophers had been translated into Arabic by the Muslim scholars and thus endured during Europe's Dark Ages that began after the fall of the Roman Empire in the West in 476 CE. This repository of wisdom later introduced Europeans to Arabic medicine, science and mathematics, including Arabic numbers and the favorite of high school students, algebra. Exposure to the far more advanced Islamic sciences opened the West to a range of thought that suddenly made the world far bigger and more complex. During the Renaissance, roughly from the 14th to the 17th centuries, the Roman Catholic Church as the ultimate institutionalized representation and moral enforcer of collectivism and hierarchy, began to lose its hegemony over religion, the economy and the culture. Protestant reformers, early scientists such as Galileo and Copernicus, and humanist philosophers such as Erasmus and Pico della Mirandola opened up a world that could no longer be contained within the monistic theology of the Church that dominated the entirety of feudal social life. The Church in Rome became not so much ignorant (since many clergy were highly educated) but were rather grossly incomplete and outdated as the nature of commerce and culture changed. An institution of faith could no longer manage and contain the rapidly expanding areas of science and commerce. The rising bourgeoisie were the bearers on an individualistic, "this worldly" egalitarianism that challenged the traditional views of the Church.

As the market economy emerged, flourished and spread across Western Europe, cultural changes followed and swept across the region. An "elective affinity" fused the rational, individualistic economic and cultural forces of capitalist modernity against the collectivist forces of medieval feudalism. As the bourgeois class of merchants grew in numbers and in wealth, the contradictions between their economic interests and that of the Old Order became more evident. Similarly, moral conflicts and theological disputes with the Church, grew more and more evident. Even as early as the Avignon papacy (1309–1377), we see the emergence of theological challenges to the Church. Perhaps more importantly, we saw the beginnings of serious critics of the Church's corruption, such as Jan Huss and John Wycliffe. Huss, with a few followers and little power was asked to repent his heresy, he refused, and he was burned at the stake. Years later a Dominican monk named Martin Luther, echoed the words of Jan Huss, criticized the letters of indulgence and the commercialization of grace by the Church. He posted his 95 theses on the door of the Wittenberg Church. But following the invention of the printing press and the growth of a literate population, Luther's influence spread far and wide. In 1517, the Reformation quickly spread across Europe, especially central and northern Europe.

The media explosion brought on by the printing press meant that Luther's message was much more widely diffused than if it had been limited to face to face discussions within a small locality. This put him at the center of all sorts of religious, spiritual, political, and economic discontent. The right to read and interpret scripture on one's own lead to the throwing off of the chains of papal and ecclesiastical authority. This also fostered more political and economic freedom as well and the German peasantry broke into widespread revolts against feudal domination. John Calvin's critiques soon followed in France and Switzerland. His *The Institutes of the Christian Religion* was published in 1536. The Reformation radically changed Christendom in many ways, including the premise that science could challenge religion on important areas of knowledge. The broader notion that nearly any person or groups could challenge established authority based on Reason not only promoted reformers to break away from the Church of Rome, but also to pursue alternative means of understanding, seen especially in the rise of critical philosophy and science. Enter the Enlightenment.

As Kant (1784) put it, "the Enlightenment would free humanity from its self-imposed immaturity ... the inability to use one's understanding without guidance from another. This immaturity is self-imposed when its cause lies not in lack of understanding, but in lack of resolve and courage to use it without guidance from another. *Sapere Aude!* [Dare to know]."[4] The Enlightenment promised not only freedom of thought but political freedom that was heretofore thwarted by dynastic rule legitimated by God's will, or at least what the elites of the Church proclaimed as God's will. Radical thinkers like Locke, Voltaire and Rousseau attacked the systems of domination, inequality and oppression inherent to theologically justified dynastic rule, especially the *ancien régime* that was legitimated and sustained by the Church. Human reason, the unity of logic

---

4 Immanuel Kant (1784) what is Enlightenment? http://www.columbia.edu/acis/ets/CCREAD/etscc/kant.html.

and passion, inspired revolutions of thought, word, and deed. It was in this context of a great deal of religious ferment that various religious schisms and movements emerged. For our purposes, there were two major consequences. Firstly, Protestantism encouraged literacy and in turn the individual could read scripture on his/her own, without the mediation of the Church. Thus Protestants founded public schools and even universities and this took place in the New World as well. We will get to that story later. Second, Protestant individualism and asceticism provided ideological support for the emergent market society, as well as fostered the "hoarding character" type who was better able to adapt to the rise of market society and its demands for self-reliant autonomy and ascetic self-denial. However unintentionally, Protestantism provided a moral justification for work that became seen as a moral "calling" in which endless work was as a means to alleviate "salvation anxiety." At the same time, work provided a basis for self-esteem and meaningful collective norms. But as Weber also noted, Protestant asceticism, often meant the saving and/or investments of profits that led to an unintended prosperity, yet Protestant asceticism condemned ostentatious displays of success and self-indulgence. Ironically, the moral path of endless productive work, savings, and reinvestment created even greater wealth which eventually undermined the ascetic morality that made the accumulation of wealth possible. We might note that an important theme derived from this theodicy of the distribution of fortune, that the hard working people were blessed, their success a wink from God that they had it made, while the less industrious, typically lazy, and hedonistic, meaning sexual rather than ascetic, were immoral. This has been a typical trope of right wing populism, what Berlet and Lyons (2000) called "producerism" a doctrine that divides the world into the "makers" and "takers," the makers are the good, hardworking, industrious folks, blessed by God, versus the lazy parasites the takers, parasites who would live off the efforts of others. These takers, the parasites, are typically racial and/or ethnic minorities, perhaps gays, that are seen as enemies, dangers. This trope was evident in the Know Nothing party in the 19th Century. and the core of the working class support for Donald Trump and his condemnation of Mexicans and Muslims.

Writing at the beginning of the 20th Century, Max Weber predicted that mass consumerism would become all pervasive by the end of that Century and he was right. As he said, "the pursuit of gain, where it has become most completely unchained and stripped of its religious-ethical meaning, the United States, tends to be associated with purely competitive passions ... these passions directly imprint the pursuit with the character of a sporting contest" (Weber, 2002 [1920], p. 124). This purely competitive passion in the business realm often fosters the nihilistic social dominator devoid of any moral compass or human capacity for empathy. We will explore this later.

Those likely to embrace Protestantism were typically the petty bourgeois peasant landowners or artisans and learned professionals living in the towns rather than in the countryside. This included workers in new areas like printing, bookselling and new manufacturing technologies like silk making. Thus, given the occupational based "elective affinities" of those engaged in commerce with Protestantism that in turn legitimated, sacralized and motivated work, we would see the growth of new, commercial classes. And given the asceticism of early Protestantism, the economic fruits of labor were not seen as the goals or rewards, but perhaps, and only perhaps, a subtle hint at salvation. Work itself served as a defense mechanism to suppress "salvation anxiety," while economic success that provided people with a degree of pride and respect, further lessened anxiety.

The Mayflower Arrived and Its Legacy Endured

Among the many Protestant denominations that would emerge as part of the Reformation, the "Puritans," the name given in the 16th Century to the more extreme Protestants within the Church of England who thought the English Reformation had not gone far enough in reforming the doctrines, liturgies and structure of the church. The Puritans wanted to purify their national church by eliminating every shred of Catholic influence. Many of its rituals were viewed as superstitions. More specifically, a group of separatists completely rejected the Church of England and chose total separation and formation of their own, autonomous congregations. In the 17th Century many Puritans immigrated to the New World, where they sought to found a holy Commonwealth in New England. They came to be known as Pilgrims. In 1608 they went to Holland, in 1620 they arrived in Massachusetts and as they say, the rest is history; Christianity in one form or another has remained the dominant cultural force in New England and the later United States even into the 21st Century. Dominant, yes, and consistent in some ways but mutable in others, as we will also explore.

For the moment, however, beginning close to 400 years ago, a small group of 102 staunchly religious, persecuted "outcasts," the early Puritans, wandering through Holland and England, left England to sail aboard the good ship Mayflower to arrive in the New World where they founded a number of small agricultural communities and established New England. Here they would freely practice their version of Protestantism. They saw the New World as a redemptive vision unlike Europe whose corrupted religions needed purification and reform. In 1630, while still aboard the Arbella, in his now famous sermon on Christian charity, Sir John Winthrop proclaimed that with God's help the new Christian community would be like a "city on the hill" with charity, affection, and community that would shine like a beacon to all mankind. Thus were planted the seeds of what would eventually become America's "civil religion," a set of religious/moral beliefs that are broad cultural values rather than tied to specific denominations (Bellah 1992 [1976]). An intrinsic aspect of this "civil religion" was the glorification of America whose fortunes represented "God's will" that would become essential qualities of American exceptionalism, a topic we will discuss later.

During the earliest years of the colonies, given the topography and climate, life in the colonies was a constant struggle just to survive, and many did not survive for long. All would likely have perished without help from some of the Native Americans, especially the Wamponoeg, who better understood how to hunt game and cultivate crops. For their help, the next generation of European-Americans exterminated them. Instead of gratitude for the help of the native populations who taught them hunting and planting, the settlers attributed their survival to divine Providence, which also justified the extermination of the Native Americans. For whatever aid given to the colonists, they were repaid with diseases for which they did not have immunities, they were relocated, often forcibly. Then following the Pequot War of 1637, then King Phillips War of 1676, for the most part, the Native American populations were displaced as more and more settlers arrived and grabbed their land. Since God was on the side of the good Christian settlers, whom He had also blessed with guns, we would see this pattern repeated over and over. American social character developed a unique blend of religion, violence and the quest for wealth as a "chosen people," chosen by God to direct the world. This remained a powerful cultural meme that has played an important role in what would become known as "American exceptionalism." Between natural growth and subsequent immigration, the colonies survived, and then prospered (Potter, 1954). With abundant land for farming, vast forests of timber that enabled ship building, shipping, whaling and distilling rum, and later textile production, prosperity came to the Northern colonies to shape American character as a "people of plenty." Given an individualist religion that valorized and sacralized work, expectations of literacy, rich land with abundant resources, including rivers to transport goods, without any existing and competing social systems or institutions of government, together with a powerful work ethic, the Puritans eventually prospered in commerce. While the early years of the community were characterized by strong community ties and covenants of mutual aid and obligation extolled in Winthrop's sermon, as they prospered and their settlements grew and colonialization expanded to the West, the covenants of communal obligation waned, and indeed broke apart (Bellah, 1992). As De Crevecoeur noted in 1782, the conditions of the colonies were quite favorable for the more industrious white people. In a little over 150 years after landing at Plymouth

Rock, their population had swollen to a few million people, mostly farmers, seafarers, skilled tradesmen, and various business people from small dry goods stores, bakers, printers, and silversmiths, to larger merchants and shipping companies, rum distilleries and even some plantations. Not only did the native born populations prosper and swell, but immigrants from many other European countries came to the colonies, and later the nation, to seek and most often find their fortunes. Meanwhile African slaves toiled on plantations that were similar to feudal manors to produce tobacco and cotton bringing vast wealth for the landowning/banking and commercial classes of the South. In 1776, a number of well-educated business and local government elites, inspired by the ideas of the Enlightenment, declared the independence of the thirteen English colonies, and achieved a military victory over the British Empire in 1783.[5]

Within 200 years of landing at Plymouth Rock, a highly motivated, highly individualistic, "American character" had been forged, that would little change for the next 200 years except in one crucial way. The Puritan lifestyle did not necessitate devotion to God, but only to a systematic, individualized, intensely focused lifestyle. Puritanism dictated a way of life; it did not promise an outcome (since salvation was reserved for a select few). Consequently, nearly any object could take the place of God as an object of worship. Over the next 250 years, people would find God and divine blessing in wealth, power, and status. And those who had not attained such advantages, then still could identify with those who had and imagine they, or surely their children would gain the pots of gold. As De Toqueville (1945 [1840]) observed, competition, hierarchy, judgment, suspicion, and intolerance guided their lives and their personality.

One of the factors leading to "American Exceptionalism" was the fact that Puritans, inspired by God, founded what would later become the first "new nation." Puritanism, rested on four basic convictions: (1) personal salvation was entirely dependent on God's will, (2) the Bible provided the indispensable guide to life, (3) the church should reflect the express teaching of Scripture, and (4) society was one unified whole. Puritan leaders such as Increase and Cotton Mather, Thomas Hooker, Roger Williams, and John Cotton, although of different political orientations, articulated highly similar conceptions of humanity. In particular, they taught the absolute sovereignty of God, the total depravity of man, the complete dependence of human beings on divine grace for salvation, and the importance of personal religious experience. God speaks through individual divine experience, not through religious institutions. People

---

5   The fact that the French armed, financed and gave the colonialists military guidance and support is little noted in the history texts. But when the US forces came to France in WWI, one of the leaders said, *Lafayette, nous voila,* a note of appreciation for the French aid, especially that of Lafayette.

were seen as wicked, evil, and corrupt. Divine grace alone could change them. This however, did not absolve anyone of responsibility for their actions. On the contrary, God holds everyone duty bound to do His will as revealed in scripture and divine experience. Temperance and self-control must begin in childhood. Thus Puritan childrearing practices were harsh and intolerant, following the "spare the rod, spoil the child" policy of the Bible (Greven, 1991; Straus and Donnelly 2001). Since a child possessed a "will" that needed to be broken, physical punishment, justified by the Bible, was seen as the means to "beat the devil out the child," Proverbs 13:24. This "strict father" morality as Lakoff (2009) has called it, has important consequences, not the least of which is fostering, more typically reproducing an authoritarian, aggressive form of independence and self-reliance, devoid of empathy for others, especially those who suffer the same unforgiving physical discipline that reproduces those patterns. In other words, the "strict father" encourages submission to authority, admiration of the strong and hatred of the weak, and aggression towards anyone perceived as an outsider, as "different" in some way and weak. Accordingly, there is no capacity for empathy for those who suffer pain and suffering, beginning with pain they inflict upon their own children which is rationalized as loving desire to make sure they grow up the one and only "right" way. Moreover, as we now know so well, it is not simply the physical pain that is so hurtful, but the shame and humiliation that quite often lead to the reproduction of that abusive treatment.

As hinted by Freud in the Schreiber case, physical punishment may dispose paranoia, and we might note that using or receiving physical punishment may have been one reason why conservatives are typically fearful, suspicious and bearers of "the paranoid style" in America (Hofstadter, 1964). Indeed, as we listen to the rantings of many right wing conservatives, especially the Glenn Beck side of the religious right and current Republican Presidential nominee Donald Trump play on the paranoia of the enemy that is everywhere and threatens us from within and from without. Whether Mexicans allegedly streaming across the border to rape and murder, or Islamic terrorists plotting acts of mass destruction, Trump calls for widespread use of torture and construction of a thirty-foot wall between the US and Mexico (as John Oliver remarked on his show *Last Week Tonight*, this would create a big market for thirty-one-foot ladders). Far-right rival Ted Cruz calls for a massive bombing campaign throughout the Middle-East, apparently including nuclear weapons to "... carpet bomb them into oblivion," Cruz said at a multi-candidate event in Cedar Rapids sponsored by the Tea Party-aligned FreedomWorks group. "I don't know if sand can glow in the dark, but we're going to find out" (McCormick, 2015). When confronted by military experts who warned this was contrary to US policy and might kill or wound several hundreds of thousands of non-combatants, he refused to back down. Recall when the abuses of Abu Ghraib became public,

40% of Americans were fine with it. And let us recall that Abu Baghdadi, the self-proclaimed Caliph of ISIS spent 5 years in an American run torture facility. Yes, this was campaign posturing, but it also reveals how such sinister and sadistic promises appeal to one side of American social character. It also demonstrates the intersection of religion, violence and an irrational paranoia that enables consent to all kinds of interventions and wars.

The Waning of Puritanical Sexuality

Given their staunch commitment to a divine order, Puritanism exerted considerable influence during the colonial period, and subsequently became an established and enduring feature of religious thought and cultural patterns in America that has endured to the present day. It provided a particular Christian vision for America. Their isolation, the harshness of survival when most folks died relatively young, and their sense of being a "chosen people," made their religious convictions especially severe and intolerant of either sin or criticism. There is no doubt that the moralism of the Puritans, together with their worldviews, and zeal to realize those views, greatly shaped the subsequent course of the nation, long after the more austere practices waned, and left only the ethic of endless work and gain as a "sporting contest." Yet those austere practices endured for at least 200 years and waned only gradually, at least in public. *The Scarlet Letter* remains one of the classical American novels. The repression of sexual desire makes its gratification ever more desirable and for the moral gatekeepers, their sermons, entreaties, condemnations of the sexuality of others is an attempt to control their own sexual lusts and passions, but those various attempts to control what is forbidden make the desire all the more powerful. That sometypically male conservative clergy and political leaders preach purity and abstinence but also rape young women and boys has long endured as a hidden consequence.[6]

Ascetic moralism often became violent. In 1692–93, 26 women and two men stood trial for witchcraft in and around Salem Village, Massachusetts. Convicted of allegedly unnatural acts allegedly provoked by insatiable lust that came from cavorting with Satan, 20 souls were executed and some of their children died in prison. The Salem witch trials often included "inspections" of the genitals of the accused by a "witch pricker" (Cotton Mather was one) who poked the genitalia and other body parts with a needle or knife. Such "inspections" would reveal devil's teats where demons could suckle (Barstow, 1994). Early asceticism was so

---

6 This is not unique to either the United States or any denomination, Christian, Jewish or Muslim.

intolerant that ascetics couldn't even agree with each other. For example, Roger Williams and Anne Hutchinson went to Rhode Island as heretics expelled from Massachusetts because they advocated for co-existence with Native-Americans. The Quakers, devoted to peace and nonviolence settled in Pennsylvania. But as a part of American social character, asceticism endured for centuries beyond the demise of the original Puritan communities. About 300 years after Salem, in the 1990s, Bill Clinton's sexcapades with intern Monica Lewinsky, Zippergate and ci-gar-gate, inspired the conservative right and its "moral" political leaders to vote for his impeachment. Just like the Puritans of Salem, the far-right political and religious conservatives assumed that all Americans condemned the President's extramarital affairs and allegedly insatiable lust which they perceived as a great moral travesty and atrocity. Some did in fact see it as a great offense, but the far-right misjudged the reaction. Most Americans were relatively unconcerned, and indeed, there were significant numbers of men and women that would have gladly traded places with Bill or Monica. And by the way, the accusations against Clinton were led by Newt Gingrich, Henry Hyde and Bob Livingston, themselves compulsive, serial philanderers. Their compatriot and Speaker of the House, Dennis Hastert, now sits in prison due to his payoffs for abusing young boys. Does hypocrisy have no limits! We shall return to this story later.

Consider former governor Mike Huckabee, ordained minister who entered the 2016 presidential primary campaign—which led nowhere. He wrote a book with a similar title to ours, *God, Guns, Grits and Gravy* (2014) and contends that America has two cultures, bubbas and bubbles. The bubbas who typically live in the "flyover" states are the moral, decent folks who respect women who practice the womanly virtues of sexual abstinence and loyalty (subservience) to fathers and husbands. They keep the house clean and take care of the kids. But in the bubbles, places like New York, Los Angeles and San Francisco, many people, especially women, extol the crudest and most morally offensive, vulgar forms of culture, they have become "trashy" in his words, they use profanity, drop F—bombs in public and even have sex before they marry. Imagine the horror! During an appearance on Fox News to plug his book and advance his presidential quest, he was interviewed by Megyn Kelly, herself a rather con-servative reporter. She responded to Huckabee by saying "I've got news for you gov'. We're not only swearing. We're drinking, we're smoking, we're having premarital sex with birth control before we go to work, and sometimes, we boss around a bunch of men." Dejected, the former governor replied, "aw, I just don't want to hear it."[7] The fact that people like Mike Huckabee or equally

---

7   The interview is very much worth seeing, go to https://www.youtube.com/watch?v=881UYXaHamE or http://www.nydailynews.com/news/politics/megyn-kelly-hits-back-mike-huckabee-trashy-comments-article-1.2096296 (Accessed 01/26/2016) to see her rebuttal.

conservative Rick Santorum cannot accept the possibility that many, and actually most people see the world quite differently reminds us that the Puritans of Salem Village couldn't accept that the governor of their day, William Phips, didn't believe in witches. A very pragmatic man, Phips not only ordered the witch court disbanded when he returned from England, he ordered the judges to offer relief from the suffering they had imposed. As Phips states (spelling included):

> I caused some of them to be lettout upon bayle and put the Judges upon consideration of a way to reliefe others and to prevent them from perishing in prision, upon which some of them were convinced and acknowledged that their former proceedings were too violent and not grounded upon a right foundation ... The stop put to the first method of proceedings hath dissipated the blak cloud that threatened this Province with destruccion
>
> PHIPS 1692.[8]

Even as they repressed sexual desire, or at least attempted to do so, however, the Puritans nevertheless valued individualism, literacy, education and hard work (as a moral virtue), all of which enabled the colonies of New England to survive and prosper. As this happened, the religious fervor waned and the covenant eventually broke apart. And yet as individualism flourished, one of the main ways that its underlying loneliness was assuaged was through membership in faith based communities, maintained through churches and parochial schools.

Commerce and the Colonies

By the mid-18th Century, with growing prosperity a new kind of elite arose. Men of business and commerce, often quite educated, sometimes in England or elsewhere abroad, became the dominant social players. Such men were equally devoted to a tireless, systematic life of work, but not in service of God

---

It might also be noted that when she introduced him to the show, she flubbed and introduced him as Governor Fuckabee. Further, we might note that today the more conservative, religious "Red States" have greater rates of family violence, sexual abuse, unwed motherhood and divorce than the liberal "Blue States." While Red State Conservatives blame the government, liberals, and the "lame stream media," they cannot see how their repressive values foster what they most abhor, yet most desire.

8   http://law2.umkc.edu/faculty/projects/ftrials/salem/ASA_LETT.HTM Accessed July 24, 2015.

or even seeking his blessings. Instead, they were on quests for evermore capital. As Puritanical moralism waned in some places, especially seaboard cities like Boston, New York and Philadelphia that were more likely to be centers of cosmopolitanism, puritanical moralism migrated to rural areas and in the process, assumed different forms, different denominations and different moral codes such as Baptism, Methodism, Pentecostalism, and others. To the extent that social change creates crises, schisms, religious awakenings and/or the proliferation of religious entrepreneurs, they, despite doctrinal differences, by the early 20th Century they typically agreed on one thing—the need for renewed moral purity. Seventh-day Adventists, Jehovah's Witnesses, Christian Science, and Mormonism all call for the purity of mind and body, and quite often the avoidance of all pleasure, not just sexual pleasure. No alcohol, caffeine, or for some, abstaining from meat, which much like sex is quite pleasurable and indulgent and hard to give up. William Keith Kellogg and John Harvey Kellogg invented toasted corn flakes as a pure, healthy and mostly tasteless food for Adventists seeking the cherished purity of body and mind. Corn flakes were supposed to curb that deadly sin, "onanism," which is masturbation. Didn't work. However, one of their lead developers, William Post, had more interest in making money than in promoting sexual purity. He left Kellogg's to found his own cereal company where he would achieve much greater wealth as the owner than as an employee. He ingeniously added a few dried grapes to those dried grain flakes and created his first product, Raisin Bran, which became a longtime favorite of children as well as the constipated. As we argue, a conservative Christian moralism remains an undercurrent in contemporary culture, as well as in domestic and foreign policy. As the country expanded, other cultural groups, namely the people of the Appalachians and of the Deep South, also contributed elements to American character. We will return to that discussion by region in the chapter on religion. For now, we will highlight the central characterological elements that developed from the intersection of Yankee Puritanism, Appalachian individualism, and Southern white supremacy.

The Polarities of Social Character

It should now be evident how the conditions of a religiously inspired settler society prospered and grew. In the process, the people became ever more culturally and psychologically different from their English and/or European roots and we saw the emergence of both its distinct national character and the underlying social character of America. But how do we understand the characterological questions as we've stated? A person cannot be reduced to less than an embodied consciousness, inherently constituted partly within the mind, and partly as engaged in social relations. However dated some aspects of Freudian theory may now be, Freud always regarded the person as having been shaped by the nature of his or her society. People think and behave differently if they live amongst a primal horde of hunters, for example, compared to Renaissance Italy. The level of technology is not primary, but rather, it shapes the type of social roles and relationships that are possible. A Renaissance artist like Michelangelo, who sought truth in beauty like all artists of his era, could not exist among hunter-gatherers, nor could abstract modern artists like Man Ray or Max Ernst, who sought to reveal the contradictions of modern society by chopping notions of beauty into pieces, exist during the Renaissance. Time and place is crucial. Whatever we call it, psychoanalysis, as depth psychology, provides us with a dialectical theory of character structure shaped by the need to adapt to social conditions, in our case modern civilization, which requires systematic work, individual accountability, and promises a harmonious community and cultural attainments of civilization such as beauty, cleanliness and orderliness that stand in marked opposition to the "natural" tendency of the person to seek his/her self-interested forms of pleasurable gratifications.[9] Thus one of the fundamental qualities of people is ambivalence, the desire for the stability of civilization and harmonious social relations, but at the same time bearing costs of the repression of desires. One major contradiction of modern times is the emphasis on individualism, yet also commitment to community (church, club, team, neighborhood, or nation for example) which can only happen to the extent the individual subordinates their individualism to the collective. The pursuit of individualism has meant the repression of deeper longings for community, and the contradiction intensifies because a person feels their individuality as internal, and the community as externally imposed. Even if a person can choose community commitments, they can only choose from the products offered rather than actively shape their community. This is changing, however, and active community formation will prove decisive in our next book.

Erich Fromm rejected Freud's biological basis of desire, and developed a more sociological theory of human relatedness rooted in Hegel, especially the struggle for recognition or what today we call validation. People need to feel important in some way to someone. Marx saw alienation as thwarting creative

---

9   A glance of the history of medieval hygienic practices indicates that such things as washing, bathing or changing one's clothing were indeed quite rare events. The wigs of the aristocracy were often infected with lice. And thus far as bathroom practices were concerned—just look it up on the Internet.

self-realization and validation, and Nietzsche envisioned a "will to power," that people need to feel like they can accomplish things that people find meaningful. We are not however ignoring relationships of sexuality, sensuality and aesthetic sensibilities. Can someone watch Game of Thrones, Outlander, or peruse the Sports Illustrated Swimsuit Issue and not feel sexual desire? The fulfillment of various desires depends on socially available outlets, and thus social relations become a kind of contract—I will behave properly if society allows some means of fulfillment—but unlike theorists like Hobbes or Locke, Freud and psychoanalysis illuminate the unconscious, and how and why certain desires, memories and images are repressed and how that repression has personal costs of frustration or guilt. For some individuals that cost was neurosis, but even for people in general, the guilt-based repression demanded by civilization meant that all suffered its discontents.

As mentioned earlier, social character manages individual drives and desires by fashioning them into socially useful forms of motivation. If the potential relationship between the person and his/her society is variable, then social character, as a compromise formation, stands as a tentative resolution between conflicting desires and social demands or conditions. Since social conditions and demands often foster social change, and when this happens, then social character must adapt as well, otherwise there will be a disconnect between people and their social world. In other words, legitimation crises arise in which social institutions appear detached, unjust, and oppressive. In a psychoanalytic sense, the history of the United States has been a history of legitimacy crises that arise from conflicting polarities in American social life. The polarities we will focus on are individualism versus collectivism, moralism versus pragmatism, and toughness versus compassion. Within those conflicts, anti-intellectualism has often been an important part of American character but is more of a derivative than an actual mode of social character, that is to say, much like what we earlier called motivated reasoning, anti-intellectualism serves defensive functions that assuage the potential anxiety between one's identity and values that might be undermined by alternative interpretations and/or evidence. Similarly, authoritarianism is a separate dimension that cuts across the others, that is we can have authoritarian individualism as well as authoritarian collectism.

Given what we will note as the polarities of character, we can see that when for example we talk about individualism versus community, we find that each may vary along authoritarian-democratic lines. Consider one major difference between American right wing conservatism and German Fascism. Americans, given both their tradition and underlying character embrace individualism and demand "liberty" whose meaning is quite nebulous though seemingly has something to do with disdain for government regulations that might restrict or redistribute profits. Meanwhile, the Germans valorized the *Volk*, the community of its people which Nazi propaganda attempted to forge as a de-individualized mass based on *Blut und Boden* (blood and soil). At the same time, while authoritarianism is often associated with aggression, at least to out-groups, authoritarians can be quite compassionate, highly loyal and supportive of each other within the in-group (Haidt, 2012). Conservatives value loyalty to the in-group quite highly, thus they are typically quite supportive of some of their "exceptional" nation's often aggressive military interventions against non-Americans, whose deaths in the millions are irrelevant. Similarly, the widespread use of torture and even mass surveillance and incarceration at home is OK so long as it is directed against brown people or religious outsiders. Social character is thus more subtle and multidimensional than any one particular attitude or set of beliefs or modes of behavior.

It is important to note that given the nature of ambivalence, individuals or groups can easily shift from one side to the other side of a polarity. People quite commonly find themselves caught betwixt and between and consistently high ambivalence creates anxiety, insecurity, and fear. We would like to briefly lay out the dimensions of social character as binary oppositions that create significant ambivalence, that is, feelings of being pulled in competing directions at the same time, which most people are.

A   Individualism versus Collectivism

One of the most fundamental moments of American culture, character and its social character has been its individualism, a legacy of the rise of market society, the Renaissance but most of all the Reformation and rise of Protestantism with its stress upon salvation as between the person and God that was not mediated or dispensed by a Church. This individualism would become one of the most salient aspects of American culture, American character and its underlying social character. A foundational truth in both sociology and psychology is the dual nature of human existence. The famous sociologist Robert K. Merton (1967 [1949]) observes that each person hopes to assert and develop one's self, to differentiate one's self from the group, but at the same time, people want connections to others, membership in groups of people that provide warmth, comfort and connection. Reference groups become the way in which any society mediates individual and collective identities into a coherent unity; the social and the psychological models "are not sharply separable; in part they overlap, and in part, they complement one another" (Merton 1967 [1949], p. 281). Given that any discussion of diversity is really a discussion of varying reference groups, as a sociologist, Merton calls the one(s) we identify with as "normative," and the ones we see as different as "comparative" types (Merton 1967 [1949], p. 283). This corresponds to psychological terms of in-group and out-group, but the terms explain the same things. Today, we may use the term "identity" as a fusion of the social and psychological perspectives. In actual practice at any given historical moment, a society may favor either individual or collective identities. For the most of human history, collective identity has been dominant insofar as individualism has generally been rare and indeed, in some societies, a violation of collective norms and values. Nevertheless with the rise of capitalism, Protestantism, modernity and urbanization emphasized individualism.

Nevertheless, for sociological purposes, our concern centers on collective identity rather than individual identity, because widespread individualism is itself a type of loose collective identity. Thus even in individualistic societies, people may share collective identities such as nation-based citizens, an occupational group, a political movement, a fandom of a celebrity, members of a Church, or a delinquent gang. But such identities have different degrees of salience and centrality to one's individual identity.

In many traditional European societies, as well as other traditional societies, honor and status accrued through one's family, clan or tribal affiliations, so the glory or dishonor of one became the glory or dishonor of all. Kinship was seen as a juridical unit; if the entire family enjoyed the fame of its most successful members, so did the entire family suffer the infamy and guilt of any crime perpetrated by one of its members.[10] The cultural origins of individualism in the West can be first seen in the 11th Century when the Church institutionalized confession, rendering the person responsible for his/her own sins and salvation. With the rise of ever greater trade, individualism flourished. During the Renaissance period, perspectivism in art, think how Giotto, Da Vinci or Rafael, individualized the viewer much as Renaissance portraiture moved from the hagiography of religious figures to the distinct features of the subject who was typically a member of the affluent merchant classes who could afford to hire an artist. Perhaps we should also note what Aries (1962) called the "invention of childhood" and emergence of privacy within households that were increasingly separated from the workplace. Houses now included diverse rooms, some for cooking, entertaining, sleeping and often for reading. Between having their

---

10   Think of honor killings in which a women rejects traditional norms in favor of more modern norms. Her sexual activity shames the entire family and a male member of her family, father, uncle, or brother must punish or kill her. Such societies have no independent courts or civil police force.

own clothes, toys, and even bedrooms, childhood became explicitly a time of preparation for later life, especially schooling and career.

As collective identity waned, so too did collective success and justice. Cooperation, egalitarianism, forgiveness, and curiosity had guided people's lives and personality. These values were derived from community membership, which formed alongside ethnocentrism and competition. Nevertheless, the notion of community has always been problematic in American culture. As Salerno (2003) argues, the community would give us social support and connections, yet always threaten to engulf, limit freedom, stifle individuality, and swallow up the person:

> A history of the American community is the story of escape and hope. It is a tale of leaving home and starting anew. It is a story of fear and bloodshed, slavery and war. But it is also a quest for regaining something that had been lost—the pastoral ideal. ... They want to be engaged with their physical and social environment but also want considerable independence from it. Working against the building of viable communities was their fear of losing themselves in sameness—becoming nothing. While the desire for community is expressed in the arts, theater, cinema and novels, individuals pursue loneliness and privacy in their personal lives: private homes, gardens, separate rooms, and separate schools. There is a desire to be free from commitment to others, a quest for isolation, yet a simultaneous unconscious yearning to be a part of something bigger than oneself. Again, it is the self-other borderline that is most relevant in the struggle for both community and identity
>
> SALERNO, 2003 p. 254.

Similarly, decades ago Erich Fromm (2013 [1976]) argued that people yearned for community, engagement, and mutual reliance. Slater (1970) reiterated Fromm's point, yet in the American context, given the important of hegemonic masculinity as the cultural expression of underlying phallic aggression along with radical individualism, social ties and connections of any type suggested dependency, weakness, passivity and indeed, a questionable, denigrated masculinity that is more like a form of femininity. When a male is less than a kickass, big-balls "tough guy," such males are labeled wussies or indeed, pussies (Kimmel, 2008). While stable social ties and strong connections provide comfort, support and assurance, collectivities such as communists, socialists and hippies allegedly promote conformity, dependency, and a lack of productivity, while even more sinister collectives such as Al Qaeda and the Islamic State reduce all individuals to nothingness as both their supporters and their victims die for the cause. And so the dialectic of individualism and collectivism is a major polarity that impacts the dynamics of American character. The compact signed on the Mayflower promised democracy and a strong community, but as we saw, with growing affluence that covenant was broken. We no longer have either. America was the first "new nation" that promised to embody and exemplify the Enlightenment values of science and Reason and in turn liberty, equality, and democracy. The US envisioned itself as a model for the world. How ironic that the French monarchy, giving financial support to the revolutionaries, in blockading Cornwallis at Yorktown and forcing a British surrender, also contributed to their own demise when provocateurs like Thomas Paine carried the spirit of the American revolution to France, *Liberté, Egalité, Fraternité*. The secular values of the Enlightenment tended to be quite critical of superstitions, religious dogmas, eternal "truths" and theological explanations. While science and reason flourished in some places, especially seaboard cities, religion was, has always been, and remains one of the major cultural forces in the United States. Needless to say, the conflict between science and conservative religion, seen for example in the now famous Scopes trial has remained an important part of American society and the debate has not changed very much since then.[11] But the conservative rejection of science keeps many very bright young people from pursuing science which, whether we like it or not, is absolutely essential for the 21st Century. Indeed, the decline of native born American science students is especially telling. Notice how the science laboratories of the leading graduate programs in perhaps biology, chemistry or physics are largely populated by Asians, especially from China and India. Then look at the relative standings of American students compared to other countries. Thus the Republican war on science has adverse consequences for preparing students for careers in the sciences. We've heard of cutting off one's nose to spite one's face, but the attack on science is more like blowing one's brains out. (And thanks to the NRA, that "victory" is done quite easily.)

B   *Moralism versus Pragmatism*

Two outcomes of Puritan moralism are crucial for us. Pragmatism and its frequent ally anti-intellectualism arose as rivals to the religious moralism that created them. The Puritans, many of whom were highly educated in England, soon created schools and even religious colleges. Harvard University was first established to train ministers and eventually to provide higher education in general. This is where the first printing press in America was used and the

---

11   This has been evident in so many policy debates over such things as gay marriage, abortion, and now transgender rights.

people preferred to publish their own books rather than import them from England. Although Americans were literate, American thought quickly became anti-intellectual. In 1642, the Puritan writer John Cotton wrote "The more learned and witty you bee, the more fit to act for Satan will you bee." Similarly, the dominance of theological literalism limited scholarship to biblical commentary rather than criticism and debate. Book education apart from Scripture was frowned upon. While that would change over time as intellectual and literary groups flourished in cities and university towns, anti-intellectualism would not so much disappear as migrate away from commercial cities and centers of learning and cosmopolitanism to more rural, less educated locales. De Tocqueville noted how America was a land where people were reluctant to deal with abstract and/or controversial ideas, because to do so would make one a bit "unusual" and might fray already tenuous social bonds. Thus people avidly discuss the popular culture of cars, sports, vacations and celebrity gossip (who was doing whom), or discussions of the last episode of whatever TV show is popular. But people generally avoid complex subjects that might reveal their limited knowledge, as well as controversial issues that might strain relationships. Outside of encapsulated realms of academies and cultural centers, most Americans are reluctant to articulate political criticism or debate complex ideas. Thomas Sowell notes that:

> From its colonial beginnings, American society was a "decapitated" society—largely lacking the topmost social layers of European society. The highest elites and the titled aristocracies had little reason to risk their lives crossing the Atlantic and then face the perils of pioneering. Most of the white population of colonial America arrived as indentured servants and the black population as slaves. Later waves of immigrants were disproportionately peasants and proletarians, even when they came from Western Europe ... The rise of American society to pre-eminence as an economic, political and military power was thus the triumph of the common man and a slap across the face to the presumptions of the arrogant, whether an elite of blood or books
>
> SOWELL, 2001, p. 187.

For Hofstadter (1963), anti-intellectualism has a long history that had preceded the emergence of our national identity and has remained a powerful trope in American culture. While Hofstadter was influenced by the research on authoritarianism, more recently, Pierce (2009) argued that "American idiocy" was based on its democracy, if enough people believed it, if it was said often enough, it was "true" and as we have pointed out, for a number of folks, especially the more authoritarian, evidence does not impact beliefs. To be an egghead, a scholar is a term of derision. If you're so smart, why ain't you rich?[12] In more recent times, especially since the Cold War and the rise of religious conservatism, fundamentalism became politically supported by economic elites to secure political power, and in turn we have seen a number of religious based expressions of anti-intellectualism, especially the growing power of literalism, home-schooling, and so-called reconstruction or restoration of some allegedly glorious past.

Consider only creationism (see below), climate change denial, Obama as a socialist Muslim and his ACA setting up death panels. Or again, in 2015, a multistate military exercise, Jade Helm, set off the wildest conspiracy theories that went to the limits of political paranoia, one-third of registered Republicans believed that the US army was planning to take over Texas, confiscate people's weapons and prepare the way for a takeover by Chinese soldiers. We can see the consequence of this religiously rooted anti-intellectualism by just noting how a large number of fundamentalist Christians embrace creationism and who reject all scientific evidence of evolution. Millions of people visit the Creationist Museum in Petersburg, Kentucky, where strategically clothed Adam and Eve frolic about in a simulated version of the Garden of Eden riding upon simulated, animatronic dinosaurs, ironically using English saddles. In case you wonder why Adam and Eve did not become dinosaur dinners, you should note that the dinosaurs were vegetarian until Original Sin took place. Forget all that stuff you learned about razor like claws, teeth like steak knives, and powerful jaws that evolved for breaking bones and shredding flesh. Furthermore, the Bible describes a land dinosaur (Behemoth) and a sea dinosaur (Leviathan). Scripture also says that lightning bolts shoot from Leviathan's eyes and flames pour from its mouth (Job 41:18–21). Were the lightning and fire a unique quality of Biblical animals and now a lost biological ability, or was it a magical ability that has been lost? Creation science continues to investigate. And again, how did Noah manage to get so many such huge and perhaps dangerous beasts aboard the Ark? The Bible makes it clear that God willed the animals to be docile, and "Two of every kind of bird, of every kind of animal and of every

---

12   When Adlai Stevenson was running for president, one of his supporters told him that every thinking American will vote for him. To which he replied, I'm glad ma'am but that surely won't be enough to get elected. We might however note that the average American family makes about $53,000/year in 2016, the average salary for associate professors is $80,000 and full $100,000. Might this express another aspect of *ressentiment* toward folks who babble in classrooms, often advocating communism or speaking in tongues, or writing books like this one, and wind up better paid?

kind of creature that moves along the ground will come to you to be kept alive" (Genesis 6:20). And by the way, the developer of the Creationist Museum has just built a replica of the Ark.

Contemporary anti-intellectualism might be said to have begun with the Goldwater campaign of 1964 (Cf. Mooney, 2005). As his campaign said, "In your heart you know he's right," to which Democrats replied, "In your head, you know he's nuts."[13] Representative Louis Gohmert of Texas, notwithstanding his law degree, has been considered the dumbest member of Congress. One example was his claim that Muslim terrorists with Ebola were coming across the Mexican border to infect Americans.[14] Anthony Fauci, the head of the NI-AID dismissed this as preposterous nonsense, because Ebola infected carriers would not live long enough to cross the Atlantic, cross the treacherous border, get to a major city and infect Americans. But what does one of the world's foremost disease doctors know? As one commentator put it, Republicans seem to pull "facts" out of their ass. We suggest those asses are products of American character. Remember that it was Ronald Reagan who said that facts are stupid things. As Karl Rove was reported to have said, we create our own realities. And yet let's give credit to Richard Nixon for realizing that "there are a lot more horses' asses in the world than there are horses."

Between the legacy of scriptural literalism, the isolated ecology and idiocy of rural life in America did not disappear with capitalism in the US as Marx predicted, but rather with the valorization of the "tough male" who fears articulating "lofty" ideas, and the no-nonsense practicality of the gun, America became the land where might makes right and nothing speaks louder than material success. Long before Pierce, James, Dewey or Mead described the foundational texts of pragmatism, "Yankee ingenuity" had become a part of American culture. The inventors or tinkerers or manufacturers who came up with brilliant inventions and practical solutions to problems became popular heroes. Ben Franklin, Thomas Jefferson, Eli Whitney, Oliver Winchester (repeating rifle), Samuel Colt (revolver), Dr. Richard Jordan Gatling (machine gun), Cyrus McCormick, Alexander Bell and Louis Armour all became rich and popular. In the 20th Century Orville and Wilbur Wright, Henry Ford, Ray Kroc, Steve Jobs, and Bill Gates are as much a part of American mythology as its Puritan founders. The massive arms industry and the rise of banksters continues this tradition of innovation, power, and the daredevil risk of financial wheeling and dealing.

---

13   Ironically, today, his moderate positions on many social issues would make him too moderate to be a Republican.

14   http://aattorg/americas-dumbest-congressman-claims-undocumented-future-democrats
-bringing-ebola-to-u-s-video/ We couldn't make this up.

Today however, these values and practices in the globalized political economy now undermine that wealth, power, and success for the majority of the population. The United States is in the twilight of empire.

The major American contribution to the realm of ideas has been pragmatism, which has generally been a secular philosophy. Pragmatism rejects abstract and absolute truths whether religious, scientific or humanistic. It sees usefulness or practical consequences as the basis of any meaningful truth claim. It clearly opposes any kind of supernatural, authoritarian set of absolute and enduring truths, values and ideas, and affirms instead various kinds of individualism, empiricism or temporalism (constant change so that the "truth" of one time is likely to be replaced by another). Common to this substantial core of pragmatism is that whatever explanation works better and gets us where we want to go is the true one, whether it is more abstract or more concrete, whether it serves particular or general interests. William James defined pragmatism as:

> The whole function of philosophy ought to be to find out what definite difference it will make to you and me, at definite instants of our lives, if this world-formula or that world-formula be the true one" (1898: 50). Thus, when one is confronted with the evidence in favor of the formula "the human soul is immortal," and then turns to the considerations put forward by the skeptic in favor of the formula "the human soul is not immortal," what is he to do? If he is a Pragmatist, he will not be content to weigh the evidence, to compare the case for with the case against immortality; he will not attempt to fit the affirmative or the negative into a "closed system" of thought; he will work out the consequences, the definite differences, that follow from each alternative, and decide in that way which of the two "works" better. The alternative, which works better, is true. The attitude of the Pragmatist is the attitude of looking away from first things, principles, categories, and supposed necessities; and of looking towards last things, fruits, consequences, facts.
>
> JAMES 2000 [1907], p. 55.

At the personal level, this polarity of character reflects a fundamental conflict between a repressive, fearful, punitive super-ego guarding against any transgression of thought or deed, vesus a more relaxed, flexible ego ideal based on hope. In the former case, there are moral absolutes that are fixed and unchangeable, in the latter case, there are no permanent absolutes.

The legacies of populism, popular democracy and "civic activism" resulted in a common belief that ordinary folks didn't need the aid of fancy "experts" who "knew it all." The self-made man (and later, woman) never needed no fancy book learnin' to make a fortune. Quite the opposite, as Dean Manders (2006) shows, Americans overwhelmingly believe that good old-fashioned "common sense" is all anybody ever needs. This fits into a larger and well-known theme in American culture, there is a much more widespread condemnation of intellectuals as lazy, useless and often treacherous (Jacoby, 2009; Hofstadter, 1963). In 1843, Bayard R. Hall wrote of frontier Indiana, that "(w)e always preferred an ignorant bad man to a talented one, and hence attempts were usually made to ruin the moral character of a smart candidate; since unhappily smartness and wickedness were supposed to be generally coupled, and incompetence and goodness." Intellectuals are often disdained as not only arrogant, but prone to trick and hoodwink ordinary, decent folks with their big fancy words and high falutin ideas. All a decent person needs to know about Islam is that it is wrong and evil. Case closed! Researching the origins, causes, and support for militant Islam just shows that intellectuals basically side with the terrorists rather than their fellow Americans. Many of the loudest voices and exemplars of anti-intellectualism include people with post graduate degrees from elite universities. Ted Cruz and Louis Gohmert have law degrees, while Mitt Romney and George W. Bush have MBA's, yet none of them ever mentioned their formal education as a qualification for public office. No, on the contrary, the goal of American policy should be to kick ass, destroy our enemies, and not to understand them or why they became enemies. Violence is the best way to solve any problem. In the 2016 Republican primaries, the "policies" to deal with ISIS included carpet bombing, making sand glow, taking out families of terrorists with drone strikes, and of course full-scale invasion of several more countries. No one mentioned that ISIS originated in American prison camps in Iraq, it was built from angry people who lost their families to the US invasion and also from former Iraqi officers the US dismissed from service. While much of the anti-intellectualism might be sadly humorous, such as the displays of Adam and Eve riding dinosaurs, beliefs that prayer can "cure" homosexuality, God sent hurricane Katrina to punish New Orleans for tolerating homosexuality and "The Big Easy" lifestyle, He also punished the East Coast with hurricane Sandy because New York is, well, you know New York (left wing, tolerant, unmarried have casual sex and the place where the money hungry Jews control the world economy), and God is still punishing California with a drought because of the decadent Hollywood and various other alternative lifestyles, and maybe because most American pornography comes from Southern California.[15]

---

15   Actually much of the industry moved to Nevada when California passed condom requirements in all porn. Much porn also comes from "amateurs" uploading their antics to get

This recently flourishing wave of anti-intellectualism, typically inter-twined with fundamentalist religion and Republican politics, coincides with America's fall from world leadership in science and technology to the medi-ocrity of mid-pack (except in military technology). As Susan Jacoby (2009) argues, "exceptionalism" allows Americans to exempt themselves from the rigors of logic, reason, factual evidence, and especially, from critical thought. Of course, all those economists, historians, political scientists, engineers, and sociologists who marshal evidence to point out the challenges that America faces are just a bunch of liberal eggheads, perhaps socialists, gay friendly if not actually, foreign-born, and none of them are worth a grain of salt nor worth listening to. If you want to understand what's going on in the world, watch the Fox Noise Channel (aka Faux News), listen to Rush Limbaugh or Pat Robertson and read Glenn Beck and take note of his explanatory charts.

C   *Toughness versus Compassion*

One consequence of the Puritan emphasis on sexual repression, indeed the general repression of erotic desire, is to dispose a great deal of aggression, and this aggressive quality of America, what Wilkinson (1986) called "American Tough," a combination of masculine strength, bravery, and resolute willingness to kill is a defining American quality. This toughness is not simply an aggressive predisposition, but a resolute form of strength as much based on self-assurance and conviction of righteousness as on physical power. It suggests that the per-son cannot only express aggression, but endure pain at the hand of a brutal enemy or authority figure. He can take it like a "real man," but the enemy's ag-gression will be avenged. This toughness is associated with individualism, the tough guy can handle himself and he doesn't need anyone to tell him what to do unless that authority is strong enough to enforce compliance.

Toughness was an essential quality for survival in the early years of colonial life and westward expansion. It was as important for the Puritan village as the frontier town. As we earlier noted, this aggression was present from the begin-ning when the Native Americans needed to be eliminated. It was essential to white domination in the South. And of course it was essential for the Revolu-tionary War, the War of 1812, the Civil War, and nearly 400 years of genocidal wars against Native-Americans and the subjugation of women.[16] Whenever

---

15 minutes (or less) of fame. So it may be coming from a next door neighbor's house, or perhaps a dorm room down the hall.

16   As has been pointed out, the tough kick ass Americans fought a war of independence against Britain. About 75 years later, the Canadians had a peacefully negotiated indepen-dence. Of course the American myth included the acumen of rural sharpshooters, even

power was threatened or challenged, the response was likely to tough it out and stand tall in the face of adversity. It is thus no accident that even to this day, the most ardent defenders of the rights to gun ownership are found in the South and West, former slave states and regions of genocidal wars against Native-Americans settled mostly by Appalachians (discussed later). Moreover, for most of its history, the USA was a collection of small towns scattered across a vast rural landscape where hunting was an essential and quite desirable part of social life and family traditions, at least for the men who owned and cared for their guns and bequeath them to their male children. Joe Bageant (2008), who came from a small rural town in Virginia and subsequently went to college, became a socialist and eventually moved back to his home town has offered a very sympathetic view of rural gun culture as part of family traditions that he calls *Deer Hunting with Jesus*. Such regions are among the strongest opponents to any kind of gun control. But that said, most of the guns that rural hunters have are not the semi-automatic military weapons like AR-15s and Uzis or Glock pistols typically used by urban Street gangs or mass murderers. Thus the gun was not only the symbol of power in the form of phallic aggressive masculinity, but gun ownership individually as well as collectively became an essential part of American character and identity. Despite so many murders every year, logical gun control eventually confronts the emotionally anchored values and identities of social character.

Just as Americans may be prone toward a phallic aggressive stance to the world and even toward various "outgroups" from within, there is also a long standing tradition of compassion, charity and philanthropy. Again recall that Winthrop's classical sermon had hoped that the city on the hill would be "a model of Christian charity." One of the first acts of the new American government was to establish hospitals in the seaports of the "new nation" to care for sick sailors coming from other parts of the world and unlikely to have friends or family to care for them while in port. In face of many major natural disasters, including floods, earthquakes, hurricanes, tornadoes and droughts, more so than many other cultures, Americans are likely to reach deeply into their pockets to support the victims of man-made catastrophes such as the many wounded and maimed in many of the ongoing wars. Many Americans volunteer their time and money at local food pantries and homeless shelters. The massive rebuilding of Europe and Japan enabled their democracies to flourish and created two strong allies in the process.

Though as we noted, it was French money, French arms and French military assistance that turned the tide. *Lafayette, nous merci.*

American Mythology

Endless wars and relentless westward expansion promised ever new adventures in wondrous lands. Westward across the Appalachian Mountains they went, along the Pennsylvania trail to the confluence of the Allegheny and Mongohelia Rivers where they form the Ohio River, which flows to the Mississippi and points South. Across Old Man River lay the magnificent expanse of the Great Plains until the Rocky Mountains rise high and cold. The Rockies are impassible except for a few places more treacherous than Thermopylae. Moving further Westward across timeless deserts, one comes to the Sierra-Nevada Mountains, the windy chaparral, and finally the Pacific Coast. How does a national character persist over changing terrain and centuries of time? How could the legacies of small Puritan New England colonies, and as we will see, mountain folk and patrimonialism in the Deep South, founded almost 400 years ago, both wane and endure?

One of the ways in which ideologies and identity endure over time is through the psychosocial mediation of culture. Values that emerged under one set of material conditions can be transmitted to many subsequent generations long after material conditions might change (Horkheimer, 1972). Cultural values are also transmitted through shared memes embedded in myths and narratives that are passed from one generation to the next. While certain more overt aspects of a narrative will change over time, its underlying themes are often remarkably persistent. These narratives are the stories we tell ourselves, the stories of success and failure or good and evil that provide vivid illustrations of "vital truths" that define reality and often decide the difference between life and death, between salvation and damnation. These narratives tell us who we are as a "people." One of the most persistent of these narratives is the notion of the "*American Monomyth*" as the basis of an aggressive nationalism (Jewett and Lawrence, 2003). In this myth, the hero, skilled in the use of violence, is on a quest to realize a vision of a free society extricated from corruption or oppression, often with a sidekick to restore the virtue that has been lost. Joseph Campbell found this theme so often, he refers to it as the "monomyth" or the one myth that stands above all others. As was seen in the Bible, liberators such as Moses and Jesus best qualify as examples of loss, the recovery of identity, and eventually, of redemption. In Greek mythology, Perseus, Jason, Achilles, and Odysseus are its exemplars. Campbell's description is an enlargement on the basic formulae represented in the rites of passage: separation-initiation-discovery-return. The quest of the hero is an extended search for something that has been lost or taken away, something that ought to have been one's birthright. The hero encounters formidable forces, suffers trials and tribulations, and yet wins a decisive victory. The successful completion of this search reveals to the hero the secret of his true identity and enables him to return from his mysterious adventure and take his rightful position in society (although this may be in spirit form). Stories from ancient Greece and the Bible are not about individuals, but individuals as the leader of a collective mission. Jason and the Argonauts, Odysseus and his twelve ships, Achilles and the Myrmidons, Moses and the Israelites, Jesus and the disciples.

In its American versions, the lone hero ventures forth strictly as an individual, though at time he may have a sidekick, much as the Lone Ranger had Tonto or Batman has Robin. As he, and more recently she, ventures into the wilderness, the frontier, upon the seas, or into the far reaches of outer space, the American hero faces a struggle of good and evil for redemption, but in decisive contrast to earlier versions, the hero seeks to redeem himself, not a people. His success restores some lost principle from the past, and thus American redemption centers on the past, not the future. In James Fenimore Cooper's *Deerslayer*, or in Hawthorne and Melville, the hero faces a darker universe, for example as Ahab seeks his personal revenge against the "great white one." That same theme echoes through Thoreau, Emerson and Whitman. Hemingway, Faulkner, Steinbeck, Wright, and Updike bring the hero into the 20th Century. The rugged individual of the Old West and the frontier now faces the stifling refinements of civilization that cloud his masculine identity with notions of politeness, gentleness, and the ever-feared complexities of intellectual thought. As Richard Slotkin (1998 [1985]) documents through primary evidence, American culture views the natural world with hostility; it is *The Fatal Environment* that offers innumerable forms of death, and only the toughest will subdue it adequately to make a living or a fortune. Similarly, modern civilization offers only useless softness and a servile gentility; real Americans believe in the salvation of violence, that *Gunfighter Nation* (Slotkin, 1998 [1992]) means more than just the right to own guns, but that guns connect us to a glorious past and instill power in the present despite the relative ease and security of modern life compared to the frontier. Hemingway strongly represents Slotkin's argument, that modern man must turn to hunting as a kind of gladiatorial combat against the primordial power of nature represented by a massive swordfish in *The Old Man and the Sea*. No other experience, however, compares to the sanctifying purity of war. In *For Whom the Bell Tolls*, the desperate struggle for survival takes the modern man to his authentic primordial roots where he can once again drink in the raw life forces of nature without apology. Kill or be killed; the simplest and best truth available to the American man.[17] As Rojek (2016) has argued, the

---

17   We will later note how these cultural mythical themes play out in American geopolitics, consider only how in face of pure evil, Al Qaeda, the tough sheriff from Crawford Ranch, got rid of all them Iraqi desperadoes and their leader in the black hat and moustache,

Turner "frontier thesis," glorifying and justifying the Westward expansion, also known as God-willed Manifest Destiny, became the basis of the mass mediated commercialized myths of glorious and tough guy heroes beginning with Wild Bill Hickok's Wild West show, traveling rodeos, dime novels and most of all, 20th Century Hollywood in which the strong, tough and "virtuous" heroes like John Wayne, Clint Eastwood and even one of the onetime host of Death Valley Days, Ronald Reagan, who seems to have never left the set. But most of the settlers and "heroes" of the West were veterans from the Confederate army, well trained in weapons and tactics, imbued with racism and valorizing "toughness." They were not the weak, helpless, yet God fearing settlers, ranchers, or townsfolk who needed a hero. Frank and Jessie James, for example, were former Confederate soldiers who became outlaws still fighting the system (that is, union law and order) who supported their independence as armed robbers and mass murderers for hire.

While the mythical hero is a staple in many cultures, the particular elements of each ideal represent, in the minds of the believers, exemplars of the real. In the American version of the monomyth, the hero, as the avatar of cultural values, embodies and realizes a pure individualism. In *Captain America and the Crusade against Evil: The Dilemma of Zealous Nationalism* (Jewett and Lawrence, 2003), the tale begins with a community in a harmonious paradise now threatened by evil; normal institutions fail to contend with this threat typically an invasion or corruption by an evil person, a nameless entity or faceless mob, or a horrible mutation. The people are impotent, they are either women or emasculated men and consequently, helpless in the face of this adversity. From out of nowhere comes forth a special hero, a selfless superhero unusually talented in the use of violence to restore harmony, the bliss of Eden having been ripped asunder. He has to renounce temptations to carry out the redemptive task; aided by skills and his fate, his decisive victory restores the community to its paradisiacal condition; the superhero then recedes into obscurity. Sometimes he dies just as he achieves success. Sometimes he moves on down the road, breaking the heart of the woman who loved him.

This is the archetypical theme of heroic redemption as a religious allegory rooted in the Bible. The hero is typically innocent (often sexually virginal) or at least indifferent to love and sexuality. He is independent, self-reliant.

Baddy Hussein. And look what happened when mythic reality, visions of vindication, confronted actual geo politics. But what must be noted, is no matter what happened in Iraq/Afghanistan, the 2016 Republican primary candidates each replay the movie we have seen before, this time its ISIS.

The present zombie craze of *The Walking Dead* TV series or the movie *World War Z* gives us armies of dead and decaying people—polluted and fetid miscreants who feed on the living. Zombie killers Rick Grimes in *The Walking Dead* and Brad Pitt as Gerry Lane in *World War Z* are the reluctant saviors who don't fit in with the world nor with the people who they endeavor to save.

In the past, John Wayne, Clint Eastwood or Chuck Norris as gunslingers in numerous westerns, or Mel Gibson and now Tom Hardy as Mad Max (the former colony Australia shares many aspects of American mythology), or fictional characters like the Lone Ranger, Superman, Shane, Travis Bickel or Captain James Kirk, Bruce Willis in the *Die Hard* movies, Charles Bronson as the avenging vigilante in Death Wish or the defiant Wolverine in the X-Men, the hero uses his own prodigious skills in violence and killing to annihilate or otherwise rid the community of its malevolent evil doers and restore the pristine harmony of Eden. Despite exhortations to remain, and often promises of erotic love, social esteem, and/or political power, he dashes off into the wilderness at sunset, perhaps with his trusty and platonic companion Tonto, Robin or Mr. Spock.

Wolverine is the ultimate self-reliant loner, who kills or tries to kill his women (namely, Jean Gray and Mystique) when they become more powerful than he is—and therefore inherently a threat, no matter what their intentions. As Jean Gray takes on the phoenix power, which among other things enables her to transform reality with a thought, this power consumes her (although many male characters in the Marvel universe can handle this level of power, such as the Silver Surfer, Thanos, The In-Betweener, and Galactus). If men are the heroic saviors, women are the victims, both when they are too weak and too strong. Although TV and film have recently presented powerful female characters, Katy Gilpatric (2010) found that 58.7% were submissive to a male character, 42% were romantically linked to him, but the most problematic fact was that women who become more powerful than male characters (such as Xena Warrior Princess and Jean Gray) had to die in the end because they couldn't handle their power. Xena dies in a hail of arrows, betrayed by her romantic male counterpart, Julius Caesar, a reluctant decision but necessary to save Rome from Xena's independent female power. Wolverine impales Jean Gray with his adamantium claws, tears in his eyes as he kills his lover. He is both tough and compassionate. In the American monomyth, powerful women are inherently a threat, both to themselves and to others. Male heroes stop women who can't stop themselves. Only Buffy the Vampire Slayer triumphs over evil, men, and evil men. In the process, she not only wields her power successfully but does something unusual in American culture—she *shares* her power with other women. Although male, the strongly feminist Joss Whedon (creator, writer, and producer) and his staff of mostly female writers intentionally moved Buffy beyond the outlaw heroes of Thelma and Louise who remain defiant, but find they cannot escape the world of men and commit suicide rather than submit to the laws of men. Instead, Buffy changes the laws of men. If American culture is ready to accept true female heroes like Buffy (still one of a kind, whose story ended back in 2003), the pace of change so far has been glacial.[18]

In the 19th Century women needed to stay in their place, just like in the 20th Century, although sometimes they didn't, just as in the 20th Century. Phoebe Ann Mosey and Martha Jane Canary, better known as Annie Oakley and Calamity Jane, respectively, learned tracking and gun slinging, and often passed as men. Women broke from conventional gender roles in other ways. "Mother" Mary Harris Jones was a socialist and active labor organizer. Perhaps her most famous moment came when, at age 75, she stood with miners in Ludlow, Colorado against hired thugs, also known as the Colorado National Guard who opened fire on the miners and their families, and killed about 30 men, women, and children (Martelle, 2007). Shortly thereafter, she had a face-to-face meeting in New York City with the mine's owner, John D. Rockefeller, who finally enacted some labor reforms.

For the most part though, America was moving Westward, and women had their subordinate place in the grand scheme of Manifest Destiny. Conflict between men inevitably arose at the point where the advancing frontier and the wilderness collided. It is from the opposition of city and country, of civilization and the wilderness, of the restraint of custom and the freedom of the Western expanses that the American hero quester emerges. However unfortunate, ever since settling New England the hero must either leave or die. The American hero is neither us nor them and instead constitutes a unique Other, really a charismatic hero whose power and skill in the use of violence transcends the mundane and with this uncanny blessing, he purifies the community yet not for the sake of the community but for his own redemption and divine mission. Still, his quest for personal rather than collective redemption also restores the status of the elites, the ranks of social hierarchy, and destroys the evil Other and thus restores social order. The American monomyth depends on violence

---

18   Much of the intense animosity toward Hillary Clinton by conservative Republicans, is not simply her politics, but the fact that she has very long been a tough, assertive woman. Unlike leading conservative women such as Sarah Palin, Ann Coulter or Phyllis Schafly, Hillary has refused to support traditional gender ideologies. Consider only her work/support for the Children's Defense Fund, her support for women's issues, as well has her highly aggressive, testosterone driving foreign policy from support for the dictator Mubarak during Arab Spring, cheerleading the invasion of Libya, support for a military coup in Honduras, and so on. She never saw a war or intervention she didn't like.

for moral redemption, because violence is the surest means to destroy the Other, not just an enemy who would attack you, but the Other, the ones who are not God fearing American, whether other people, other beliefs, or even nature. As D.H. Lawrence put it:

> The American Man gets his deepest thrill of gratification, perhaps, when he puts a bullet through the heart of a beautiful buck, as it stoops to drink at the lake. Or when he brings the invisible bird fluttering down in death, out of the high blue. "Hurt nothing unless you're forced to." And yet he lives by death, by killing the wild things of the air and earth. But you have there the myth of the essential white America. All the other stuff, the love, the democracy ... is a sort of by-play. The essential American soul is hard, isolate, stoic, and a killer. It has never yet melted. White America only kills when it is forced to, yet killing is the whole point of life (2003, [1910] p. 65, p. 111).

Lawrence argues that the popularity of the Western story, the obsession with and emulation of frontier values even after the frontier was long gone persists because the mythology remains not just as a story, but as the core of American identity and penultimate embodiment of American values of God, Guns, Gold and Glory. Deeply anchored in American social character, they seem normal and desirable, and whether they make any logical sense in the present or not, they resonate as emotional gratification.

Social Character Today

Today, the antagonisms of the past have intensified as the American Colossus wanes from within, its infrastructure crumbles, its government is dysfunctional and it heads toward collapse. Unable to fulfill its promises of an ever better standard of living and expanding the ranges of social justice, the ambivalence of the polarities of social character become more pronounced as legitimacy unravels. The super-rich and their toadies, racists, misogynists, homophobes, religious extremists and other miscreants claim exclusive possession of truth, of power, of privilege, and seek to crush all opposition. And yet they are just as much a product of American culture and history as the emancipationists of the 19th Century, as the suffragettes and feminists, as interfaith movements, labor organizers, civil rights activists, peaceniks and others who seek a more cooperative, sustainable, and mutually beneficial society. To sort out the types and trends, we adapt a Pew Center model of political affiliation into a model of social character. First, the Pew center research reveals a more nuanced depiction of American political affiliation today (Table 1).

We further modify the conceptualizations of the respective categories (Table 2). In our case, we adjust the concepts to better illustrate the direct

TABLE 1   *The 2014 political typology: Polarized wings, a diverse middle.*

	Percent of ...		
	General Public	Registered Voters	Politically Engaged
	%	%	%
The Partisan Anchors	36	43	57
· **Steadfast Conservatives**	12	15	19
Socially Conservative Populists			
· **Business Conservatives**	10	12	17
Pro-Wall Street, pro-immigrant			
· **Solid Liberals**	15	17	21
Liberal across-the-board			
Less Partisan, Less Predictable	54	57	43
· **Young Outsiders**	14	15	11
Conservative views on government, not on social issues			
· **Hard-Pressed Skeptics**	13	13	9
Financially stressed and pessimistic			
· **Nest Generation Left**	12	13	11
Young, liberal on social issues, less so on social safety net			
· **Faith and Family Left**	15	16	12
Racially diverse and religious			
· **Bystanders**	10	0	0
Young, diverse, on the sidelines of politics			
	100	100	100
N	10,013	7,999	4,767

2014 Political Typology: Figures may not add to 100% because of rounding. The politically engaged are registered to vote, closely follow public affairs and say they always or nearly always vote
SOURCE: PEW RESEARCH CENTER 2014

TABLE 2   *Some character types in critical social psychological work.*

Pew typology	Lundskow-Langman
Partisan Anchors	**Consistent Characters**
Steadfast Conservatives—socially conservative populists	Far-right Conservatives—authoritarian populists and destructive nihilists
Business Conservatives—pro-Wall Street, pro-immigrant	Corporate Conservatives—social dominators interested only in personal gain
Solid Liberals—Liberal across the board	Solid Liberals—open-minded and pro-social
Less Partisan, Less Predictable	**Ambivalent Characters**
Young Outsiders—Conservative on government, not social Issues	Young Outsiders—suspicious of formal authority, support helping others
Hard-Pressed Skeptics—Financially stressed and pessimistic	Consumerists—defined by satisfaction of purchasing appetites
Next Generation Left—Young, liberal on social issues, less so on safety net	Anti-Establishment Youth—Reject conventional institutions and culture, but also seek a more egalitarian world
Faith and Family Left—Racially diverse and religious	Faith and Family Left—faith as a specific guide to an egalitarian world
Bystanders	**Apathetic Character**
Young, Diverse, on the Sidelines of Politics	Indifferent to the world and their role in it

SOURCE: PEW RESEARCH CENTER 2014

correlation of political views and social character, as long-demonstrated in decades of research (for example, Adorno, Frenkel-Brunswik, Levinson, and Sanford 1950; Altemeyer 2006, 1996, 1988; Diamond 2008; Ekehammar, Akrami, Gylje, and Zakrisson, 2004; Stenner 2005; Zizek, 1994).

Although our model emphasizes underlying character types, we do not exclude the role of cognition. People make active choices, absolutely. However, these choices follow from their character. As Jonathan Haidt (2012) shows, people of sincere moral conviction make different choices as a result of different character orientations. Thus for example, people with strong conservative leanings place higher value on in-group loyalty and purity than do more liberal people. Similarly, as Erich Fromm (1992 [1973]) demonstrated in an analysis of authoritarian and necrophilic leaders, people who commit mass murder have no remorse or regret at all. Quite the opposite, in fact. They feel very proud of their work. Recent research on the Boston bombers (Reitman, 2013), shooters and serial killers (Babiak and Hare, 2006) shows similar insight. These killers feel fully justified and proud of their work. They knew exactly what they were doing.

At the other end of the spectrum, consistent liberals feel fully committed to policies of genuine democracy, tolerance, inclusion and even appreciate diversity. Similarly, they also support more equitable distributions of wealth and services to be paid for by more progressive taxation. Their activism, whether in mass movements such as Occupy Wall Street, or more individual commitments such as supporting Doctors Without Borders, derives from capacities for empathy, caring about others and the need to improve the condition of others which overrides factors that divide people by race, creed, gender, national boundary, and other prejudices. Nevertheless, far-right, corporate, and liberal personalities all draw a kind of fortitude from the confidence that arises form a consistent personality. All will take varying degrees of personal risk to achieve outcomes they perceive as meaningful. People seek to support polities consistent with their character type.

Likewise, people with ambivalent personalities feel less committed to particular policy or action, yet still feel a longing to actively define their lives and the world. To the extent they feel outside of, or exploited by conventional society, yet still connected to parts of it, they will feel torn between the demands of society to conform, against their personal sense of faith and individual autonomy. To the extent this conflict remains unresolved, their character remains ambivalent—torn in competing directions with no resolution in sight. In contrast, the apathetic person feels no particular commitment to themselves, society, or their place in it. This differs considerably from the ambivalent person, who lives in a highly charged emotional state. The apathetic person is indifferent and without passion.

Toward a New Character Typology

Consequently, our adaptation of the Pew typology follows in brief.

· Far-right Conservatives tend to be populists, supporting the "common people" but given their ethnocentrism, the "people" are members of their own in-group, which has generally been Caucasian. Moreover, they typically share fundamentalist religious beliefs. Those conservatives who see the power and privileges of white male America challenged, if not undermined by a younger, browner, more liberal America, and facing demise, like caged animals, are becoming increasingly angry, aggressive and nihilistic.[19] When they "want their country back" they refer to a pristine white community long past. Recently, white Americans have formed militia groups to deny sanctuary to 59,000 Latin American children fleeing poverty and violence in Guatemala, Honduras, and El Salvador. Right-wing populists have blocked buses, and even detained a group of children on a YMCA camp outing, believing them to be illegal immigrant children (Inskeep, 2014). The signs, raised fists, and the middle-finger with loud shouts of "fuck you!" and "go home wetback!" at protests and at public forums throughout southern Arizona and California express the same ethnocentric attitudes of hate and violence usually directed at adult immigrants. Apparently, the protesters feel no less hateful towards helpless children (Serna, Linthicum and Hansen, 2014). Perhaps this racist ethnocentrism has been most evident when most Republican governors and primary candidates would bar Muslim refugees, mostly women and children, all totally vetted, and all attempting to escape the havoc and devastation the US caused. At the level of character, right-wing populists fear impurity and contamination, especially racial mixing. And of course, one of the dominant themes of right-wing conservatives has been fear, resentment and anger of the growing number of non-whites in positions of power, especially President Obama who is seen as a Kenyan born Muslim, socialist, definitely "not one of us." These conservatives see life in terms of strict hierarchy, and one's individual place depends on one's group affiliation. In the US, this depends first and foremost on racial affiliation, although gender has also been significant. Members of higher racial and social status groups should thus have inherent privileges compared to members of lower groups. In short, the far-right populist is a right-wing authoritarian, or RWA.

· Corporate Conservatives, perhaps a better term than "business conservatives" which would include businesses of any size. Although mid-size business owners, especially car dealers and construction companies tend to be staunchly conservative (Hetherington and Weiler, 2009), they typically belong in the far-right populist category. In contrast, the very structure of the corporation conceals its managers from attention, and most importantly,

---

19   This reactionary anger was clearly evident in the 2016 Republican primary win which
      Trump and Cruz thrived on the anger and frustration of frightened, angry Americans.
      Trump showed no constraints in calling Mexicans rapists, baring Muslim immigrants,
      denigrating women, claiming Hillary got schlonged and reiterating a supporter's claim
      that Cruz was a pussy.

from accountability. In this environment, the corporate conservative is free to indulge their passions for self-gain, usually in the form of money, but which could also include power as one rises through the ranks and even gains notoriety. First and foremost, the corporate conservatives justify their actions by a sense of inherent personal superiority, this is the social dominator orientation, or SDO who typically feels that his or her "superiority" justifies greater wealth, power and rights to rule over others.

- Solid Liberals embrace values and attitudes of inclusion, appreciation of diversity and equality. Like their conservative counterparts, these values and attitudes coincide with emotional sentiment. Rather than hate and exclusion, liberals value love and forgiveness. As the Pew study finds, they are liberals "across the board." Just as conservatives remain consistently judgmental and suspicious, liberals remain consistently inclusive and curious. In short, liberalism in the US expresses an underlying character type that is open-minded, imaginative, and in general, embraces a much larger and more diverse sense of community than do conservatives.

Rather than a catalogue of the various types indicated above, we collapse them into two competing trends in social character in the United States today, authoritarian-dominance-destructive tendencies and progressive-caring tendencies.

The Authoritarian-Dominance-Destructive Orientation

Instead of summarizing the vast history of authoritarian studies, suffice to say that decades of research can be captured as three elements of character. In simplest terms, three key elements define the authoritarian: conventionalism, submission, and aggression (Altemeyer, 2006).[20]

- Conventionalism—The authoritarian submits to conventional thoughts, attitudes, beliefs, behaviors, group affiliation, and anything perceived to be familiar and normal. They fear anything new or different from themselves and their familiar way of life.
- Submission—The established and familiar norms require submission, they shouldn't be questioned, only obeyed. Nonconformity in practice is

---

20   We note that other variables associated with authoritarianism include conformity, anti-intellectualism, anti-intraception (self-reflection), superstition, stereotypy, cognitive rigidity, and preoccupation with sexuality, especially that of others.

disdained. This applies to all aspects of life, including politics, culture, and religion. More than anything else, an authoritarian worships power. Might makes right in all areas of life—better to be strong and wrong than weak and right.

- Aggression—Authoritarianism is rooted in sado-masochism which is the basic template for their social relationships, world views and/or political agendas. Authoritarians idealize authority and readily submit to "higher powers" even as they demand submission from those below. Those who will not submit to what is believed to be right and just, must be punished, and if necessary—eliminated. Perhaps the most extreme example in the US was the tradition of lynching "uppity" Blacks for either disobedience (such as looking up when spoken to) or imputed sexual desires toward "pure" white women. Prior to the frequent hanging or burning, the victims were often beaten, castrated and their bodies mutilated which gratified the phallic aggression of the dominant white males who delighted at the destruction of Black masculinity.[21] Thus, destructiveness often becomes part of the authoritarian identity, because violence, as previously mentioned, is the surest means of destroying the Other, especially since some transgressors are inherently evil and can never be anything else. They can only be destroyed. At the time of this writing, President Obama has successfully negotiated a nuclear reduction treaty with Iran. It was encouraging to see that the American public supported the deal, 56% were in favor, 37% opposed but authoritarians have decried it as a bad deal (ABCNews/Washington Post poll July 16–19, 2015). Mike Huckabee said that Obama should just "march the Israelis to the door of the oven" (Markon, 2015) while Charles Krauthammer (2015) on Fox News labeled the deal as "quite insane" and as "capitulation." Senator Lindsey Graham believes that the President has now become the biggest supporter of global terrorism (CBS This Morning, July 21, 2015). In their view, Obama is not just weak, but a member of the evil Others (African-Americans, Muslims and effeminate males who would rather negotiate than kill). In classic authoritarian fashion, Obama is perceived as weak, and must be opposed. A Black man in a position of power is inherently unconventional, and in combination with alleged weakness, the authoritarians express aggression in the form of rebellion against his false authority. Consider for example the "occupations" of the federal Malheur

---

21   Authoritarian sado-masochism continued in Vietnam, Iraq, Afghanistan and many lesser interventions, where the US practiced and taught various techniques of torture to South and Central American dictators. Just as African Americans might have been castrated, a favorite technique of Americans has been electric shocks to the genitals.

Wildlife Refuge in Oregon from January 2–26, 2016 by Ammon and Ryan Bundy, two sons of Cliven Bundy, a rancher who has refused to pay federal grazing fees for his cattle on public lands for the last 22 years. Along with seven other men and one woman (all white), they occupied the facility in order to spark a general uprising against the US government which they believe has no right to own or regulate land, or require that ranchers pay fees or taxes (Choksi, 2016). In the absence of an authority that seems legitimate, an authoritarian will rebel against the authority figure they perceive to be illegitimate. Who would authoritarians perceive as legitimate? Matthew MacWilliams (2016) found that 49% of Republican voters score in the top 25% of authoritarian tendencies, and Donald Trump in particular has captured at least 43% of strong authoritarian voters and 37% of authoritarians overall. In fact, MacWilliams found that authoritarianism is the one and only variable that predicts Trump support—not race, class, gender, income, education, or religion.

The Dynamics of Fear and Power

Despite the obsession with power and toughness, authoritarianism arises from fears of freedom, loneliness and abandonment. The three characteristics of authoritarianism, conventionalism, submission, and aggression produce a fear-power dynamic. The authoritarian feels fearful, bordering on paranoiac; they are always on-guard against enemies and transgressors who will violate the purity and certainty of their lives and communities as they imagine them. In response, they idolize power in all its forms, and hope to gain a sense of security through submission and subservience. Even the suggestion of deviance, a mere thought or word could invoke a fear response and in turn, an aggressive reaction. Submission to a superior class, a leader or God's Will alleviates one's responsibilities, so that whatever happens in life was due to external factors. When the Nazi war criminals pleaded *nicht schuldig* (not guilty), they were "just obeying orders." Thus whether a person wins the lottery, survives an airplane crash or the nation prospers or declines, it is because of a superior external power, usually God, who has intervened. It always strikes us as interesting when for example airplane crash survivors say it was God's will that they walked out unharmed, but where was that same God's will when the other passengers died, or when the Nazi regime murdered 12 million people and at least as many died in America's genocidal slaughter of Native-Americans? Clearly, God bestowed no favor on such people.

The authoritarian experiences high levels of anxiety and fear, which Crouse and Stalker (2007) show arises from perceived threats to self-preservation, feelings of powerlessness, insecure sexuality, and perceived aggression or the invasion of undesirable elements, whether people, religions, or anything unconventional. Consequently, "the same unpleasurable affects aroused by these impulses (affects connected with death, uncertainty, sexuality, and aggression)" produce particular reactions that closely resemble "[M]any forms of psychopathology that are characterized in terms such as self-deception, self-estrangement, and a narrowed or false consciousness" (Crouse and Stalker, 2007, p. 40).

We would like to emphasize this conceptualization sees authoritarianism as a type of psychopathology. It is not a choice, nor the result of any sort of logical decision-making, no matter how detailed a belief system may appear nor how carefully articulated one's views on an issue may be. Recent longitudinal research shows that, as the authoritarian personality develops, his or her cognitive skills develop more slowly in direct correlation to the strength of authoritarian characteristics (Heaven, Ciarocchi, and Leeson 2011; Leeson, Heaven, and Ciarocchi 2012; Perry and Sibley 2012). The more authoritarian a person becomes, the weaker their cognitive ability, and the less they value creativity and critical reasoning.[22] This remains consistent across generations, such that if parents raise their children to be authoritarians, they also transmit their dislike of critical thinking as well as their prejudices (Duriez and Soenens, 2009).

Following Crouse and Stalker (2007), the authoritarian constructs an argument in order to conceal their real emotional defensive reactions to their own internal anxiety and fear. In the US context, we will discuss the issue of white authoritarianism, because white ethnicity is the dominant standard even as non-whites become a larger proportion of the population, this has not reduced feelings of white hegemony. In fact, quite the opposite, authoritarian whites view the relative growth of the non-white population as an invasion and corruption of the nation (Crawford and Pilanski 2014). When they say: "we want our country back," what they mean is they want an imaginary, idealized nostalgic past when no one openly questioned white, Protestant heteronormative male domination, nor the subservience and inferiority of women, African-Americans and other minorities. They want a time when gays, lesbians, and other kinds of "degenerate perverts" stay hidden or remain in their sewers and

---

22   The earlier noted research on physical punishment, one of the main ways authoritarianism is instilled, shows that in and of itself, spanking or whipping children impairs cognitive development.

not clutter the clean, pure landscape of America with their despicable, sinful behavior.

In general, authoritarians live within a fear-power dynamic. They fear anything they perceive to be uncertain; anything new, unfamiliar, creative, or anyone different from themselves which becomes a threat to their worldview and quite often, there very identities. They are intolerant of ambiguity. They much value obedience and conformity. To assuage their fears, they seek overwhelming power and thus they surrender to "rigid, closed boundaries, internal homogeneity and consensus, they strongly embrace orthodox and belief systems and associated world views along with ritualized practices, profound ethnocentrism, hierarchical structure, and emphatic leadership" (Hogg and Adelman 2013: 441). Through strict rules, rigid boundaries, unreflective attitudes, and aggression towards perceived transgressors, authoritarians hope to gain a sense of security (Altemeyer, 2006) which does not generally differ by gender (Rajan and Krishnan, 2002), although it does by ethnicity (Duckitt and Bizumic, 2013). Dominant ethnic groups (in our case, white Americans) are much more prone to authoritarian tendencies. In short, the authoritarian is a type of social character with a specific fear-power orientation to the world.

In everyday life, authoritarians hold strong in group-outgroup prejudices (Altemeyer, 2004), especially against gays (Crawford, Jussim, Cain, and Cohen 2013; Gormley and Lopez 2010), and particularly in the US, against black people and other ethnic minorities (Cribbs and Austin 2011; Norris and Reeves 2013). They support whatever restrictions on human rights and freedoms they feel might be necessary in order to safeguard against imagined acts of terror or other perceived uncanny threats to US security (Crowson and Debacker 2008) such as an Ebola invasion.

The Social Dominator

As Professor Quirrell remarks in *Harry Potter and the Sorcerer's Stone*, "A foolish young man I was then, full of ridiculous ideas about good and evil. Lord Voldemort showed me how wrong I was. There is only power, and those too weak to seek it" (Rowling, 1997: 291). Perhaps the real-life gangster Salvatore Lucania, better known as Charles "Lucky" Luciano offers a more nuanced perspective. Reflecting on his own life, Peter Lupsha (1992) observes that Luciano never realized how truly mainstream American he was. Luciano says that

> I had Masseria and Maranzano knocked off. What I did was illegal; I broke the law. Roosevelt had us and other guys like Hines and Walker sent to

the can or squashed. What he did was legal. But the pattern was exactly the same; we was both shitass double-crossers, no matter how you look at it. Now, I don't say we elected Roosevelt, but we gave him a pretty good push. I never knew that a guy who was gonna be President would stick a knife in your back when you wasn't looking. I never knew his word was no better than lots of racket guys

in HAMMER and GOSCH, [1975] 2013, p. 276.

Luciano expected legitimate men of power to behave better, but he also grasps the truth, that "the pattern was exactly the same." We do not contend that Franklin Roosevelt was simply ruthless and self-serving, but rather, that he was following particular American values that tough guys use whatever means necessary to get what they want, and the more immediate and direct, the better. Only weak losers and suckers wait for the rule of law, follow moral principles, or trust in the goodwill and compassion of others. Voldemort, gangsters, Presidents, capitalists, and anyone willing to assert their interests over and against others by any means necessary constitute a particular expression of American culture and character when individualism and aggression are conjoined and a person lacks any conscience or capacity for empathy, they freely employ the most direct means available. The Social Dominance Orientation (SDO) is motivated by personal gain and satisfaction. These characters illustrate the social dominance orientation. They do not submit to anyone, nor do they seek followers. They relentlessly pursue their own self-interest with no regard for anyone or anything. As a sociopathic character, the social dominator will readily use people, but only as instruments towards selfish ends and never for any collective benefit. In a general sense, a social dominator is "one's degree of preference for inequality among social groups" (Pratto et al., 1994). However, in actual practice, a social dominator has no particular group allegiance, except to the extent the group serves their personal agenda (Densley, Cai, and Hilal 2014; Sidanius, Pratto, and Rabinowitz 1994). This is especially true if a group already has high social status which the dominator can use to their own benefit (Levin et al., 2002), or the SDO feels some sort of external threat (Cohrs and Asbrock, 2009; Morrison and Ybarra, 2008) and they can use a group as a shield to deflect any possible attacks directed at them personally. John Dean, longtime Republican and member of the Nixon staff, having carefully read Altemeyer's work on authoritarianism, discussed the character of various "conservatives without conscience," as he called the key figures in the Nixon administration. In his assessment, Dick Cheney is a consummate SDO. One of the most powerful men in Washington, Cheney's ego "did not need the spotlight, and his dark view of the world and life was in any case, better suited to working behind closed doors" (Dean, 2006 p. 157). Cheney wants obedient minions, not followers or admirers. Cheney is aggressively pro-war, pro-torture, and always prepared to send other people to do the fighting he was never willing to do himself, all classic SDO behavior. He strategically avoided the draft during Vietnam. He said that he had "more important things to do." As involvement in Vietnam intensified in 1963, Seelye (2004) documented the following chronology. Cheney quit his job with a power company in Wyoming and enrolled in Casper Community College and sought his first student deferment on March 20, according to records from the Selective Service System. After transferring to the University of Wyoming at Laramie, he sought his second student deferment on July 23, 1963. On Aug. 7, 1964, Congress approved the Gulf of Tonkin resolution, and the war escalated. Just 22 days later, Cheney married Lynne Vincent. He sought his third student deferment on Oct. 14, 1964. In May 1965, Cheney graduated from college and his draft status changed to 1-A (available for service). In July, President Johnson announced that he was doubling the number of men drafted. In response, Cheney obtained his fourth deferment when he started graduate school at the University of Wyoming on Nov. 1, 1965. Unfortunately, on Oct. 6, 1965, the Selective Service lifted its ban against drafting married men who had no children. By a remarkable coincidence, nine months and two days later, Cheney's first daughter, Elizabeth, was born. On Jan. 19, 1966, Cheney applied for 3-A status, the "hardship" exemption, which excluded men with children or dependent parents. It was granted. In January 1967, Cheney turned 26 and was no longer eligible for the draft.

After that, Cheney served as a Congressional aide, then failed as Gerald Ford's campaign manager against an unknown Democrat, Jimmy Carter. He served in the House and the Senate, rarely voted, and sponsored no legislation of consequence. When the Cold War ended, President George H.W. Bush decided that his administration would deliver a "peace dividend" to the American people as a major part of his legacy (Sparrow 2014). His Secretary of Defense, Dick Cheney, disagreed with this policy and insisted on increasing rather than decreasing military spending in order to support a much more aggressive deployment of military power abroad. Bush overruled him. On the surface, Cheney remained silent in public and compliant in meetings. At the same time, he used sympathetic reporters and others to spread the notion that the US was becoming weak, and that the base closings were politically motivated when in fact a bipartisan committee had spread the closings more or less equitably around the country (Engel 2014). Undermining his boss from within the administration, Cheney made Bush look weak, contradictory, and biased against his own conservative principles. They don't call him "Dick" for nothing. In the next election, Bill Clinton limited George H.W. Bush to one term.

Later, as Vice President under George W. Bush, Cheney's lurid fascination with torture, and his policies to detain enemy combatants without trial or charge and torture them indefinitely, and also terrorize the occupied Iraqi population with random raids and arrests, destroyed any remaining favorable Iraqi opinion of the US. Officially, the only authority the Vice-President has is to break tie votes in the Senate. Unofficially, Cheney utterly dominated George W. Bush. By the middle of his second term, it had become "abundantly clear that [Bush] is a mental lightweight with a strong right-wing authoritarian personality. ... Cheney, it appears, knows how to manipulate the President like a puppet and handles his oversized ego by making him believe ideas or decisions are his own when, in fact, they are Cheney's" (Dean 2006, pp. 168–169). The power behind the throne is the perfect position for an SDO like Cheney, where he can make all the decisions and bear none of the responsibility, such that "Cheney is the mind of the Presidency, with Bush its salesman" (Dean 2006, p.169).

Why would Cheney be assertive in some roles, and uninvolved in others? In the absence of a perceived threat, particular personal interest, or instrumental needs, an SDO has no concern or use for other people. If he can advance his career through the House and Senate with only minimal participation, there is no need to waste time and energy. Once he had arrived in the Vice-Presidency, Cheney knew he held the true seat of power compared to clueless George, the President. He could use all his connections to run the executive branch and indulge his vicious personal fascination with torture (Holtzman and Cooper, 2012; Mayer 2009). In any case, Cheney advanced his own career, with the least effort when possible, and by sacrificing others when necessary. Further consideration suggests that, given his willingness to undermine and destroy his own President, which he did twice (Ford and Bush I), as well as his voracious fervor for war and torture, Cheney seems to manifest elements of necrophilic destructiveness, although no investigation has been done in this regard. If accurate, that would explain his policies towards the Middle East and some chilling possibilities. Maybe the real motivation was to destabilize the region and guarantee new enemies? Maybe even control of Iraqi oil and guaranteed contracts for Halliburton (of which Cheney was the former CEO and still a major stock holder) was not the primary goal.[23] The widespread destruction of Iraq, the indiscriminate bombing, killing, and torture would provide ample, ghastly

---

23   The initial acronym for the invasion of Iraq was Operation Iraqi Liberation, but when it
      was noted that that spelled OIL, the name was soon changed. And one of the ironies of
      history is that much of Iraq's oil has gone to either China or Isis.

and compelling carnage for a necrophilic personality.[24] On December 3, 2014, the Senate Committee on Intelligence released a 6000-page report on the CIA's use of torture after 9/11. The report provides vivid descriptions of gruesome techniques, and although torture revealed no new intelligence, the CIA continued to use it. In response, Dick Cheney condemned the report as a "load of crap" (Dwyer 2014). When asked if he would promote those techniques again, Cheney said "absolutely."

Based on the findings of Durieza and Van Hiel (2002), we define the SDO more specifically by three traits. (1) An obsession with power. Even money or popularity is merely a means to domination and control, not an end in itself. (2) They are convinced of their own inherent superiority; they aren't pretending or compensating for some internal insecurity. In contrast to the typical authoritarian who seeks security through affiliations with powerful groups, leaders or ideologies, the social dominator sees him/herself as the embodiment of power and superiority. (3) Rules and morality are for the inferior and the weak. A dominator does whatever they want and even defines reality as they go. It is important to note that the SDO is a cause of hierarchy, exploitation, and inequality, and not an outcome of group dynamics (Kteily, Sidanius, and Levin 2011). In other words, the SDO actively shapes social relations to suit his or her interests, and does not simply respond or adapt to prevailing circumstances.

For the most part, domination depends on willing submission, and for those authoritarians so inclined, the occasional boast about America's strength and exceptionalism will suffice. The vast middle of the population who waiver between authoritarianism and emancipation, require more subtle and also more persistent manipulation. The standardization of education, uncertainty of employment, corporate ownership and control of the mass media beginning with the propaganda called "news" or escapist entertainment and multiple kinds of diversion such as celebrity gossip, all minimize creativity, critical awareness and the potential for critique, let along challenge to the system. For Marcuse (1964) this was the essence of "one dimensional thought" that led to a cheerful, uncritical acceptance of the status quo, notwithstanding its adverse consequences. As Ray Bradbury (2013 [1951]) describes it in *Fahrenheit 451*, with our schools "turning out more runners, jumpers, racers, tinkerers, grabbers, snatchers, fliers, and swimmers instead of examiners, critics, knowers, and imaginative creators, the word 'intellectual,' of course, became the swear word it deserved to be" (2013 [1951], p. 48). Bradbury is not entirely correct.

---

24   For Fromm (1992 [1973]), necrophilia refers to the love of death and destruction, it is the reaction to those who tend to be thwarted in their capacity for creative self-fulfillment. Thus they find empowerment in the love of death.

The United States has never revered, nor even much respected intellectuals. At the same time, not everyone can rise to greatness, yet society must still function. In this regard, we "give the people contests they win by remembering the words to more popular songs or the names of state capitals or how much corn Iowa grew last year. Cram them full of non-combustible data, chock them so damned full of 'facts' they feel stuffed, but absolutely 'brilliant' with information" (2013 [1951], p. 56). The internet intensifies the feelings of brilliance, in that anyone can find the answer to any question, whether the answer is accurate or makes sense is irrelevant compared to the pleasure of taking possession, taking ownership of information and "the answer." Consequently, everyone feels like "they're thinking, they'll get a sense of motion without moving. And they'll be happy, because facts of that sort don't change. Don't give them any slippery stuff like philosophy or sociology to tie things up with" (p. 56). In other words, anything that helps a person interpret facts, discern accuracy from inaccuracy, sense from nonsense, should be avoided. As our ever more standardized tests today require, memorization and conventional ideas dominate education because they are most easily measured on standardized tests. We end up with attractive numbers to demonstrate achievement, and also a compliant populace whose very complacency conflicts with the reality of declining earnings, decaying infrastructure, and perpetual uncertainty.

The Contradictions of Social Character

In this book, we trace the rise of American social character focusing on its central themes of religiosity, violence, materialism and exceptionalism. Moreover, its underlying social character, psychodynamically understood, has been seen as various compromises over ambivalences of individualism versus collectivism, toughness versus compassion, and repressive moralism versus pragmatism. Cross cutting these polarities of character are tendencies toward authoritarianism that have given rise to the sinister social dominator as well as general anti-democratic social characters. But to a lesser extent, there has also been a progressive social character that while not a frequent, not widely supported, and while more often ignored, ridiculed or marginalized, has been at the forefront of progressive change. As we shall conclude, through the processes of dynamic character change, a major shift is taking place that is fostering a more tolerant, humanistic, caring, sharing, inclusive, democratic social character. These character types are not new, they also derive from political-economic and cultural legacies and trends rooted in US. The competing trends are possibilities, not certainties. As we argue, character determines allegiances. People make choices and choose their actions based on an internal emotional orientation, what feels right when making choices of war or peace, charity or condemnation, empathy or hostility. Insofar as many of these desires, emotions and feelings are unconscious, people do not consciously identify themselves as an "authoritarian" or "dominator" and only rarely as "progressive." On one hand, people see themselves as law-abiding, morally upstanding, and patriotic. Many, perhaps most Americans identify as Christian. And these positions are regarded as normal, natural and should apply to everyone. On the other, many people see themselves as dedicated to social justice, human rights, and equality. Many also identify as Christians and indeed many are involved in antiwar efforts, aid to the sick and the poor and abroad range of progressive causes. Indeed, we will argue that religion plays a central role for both types of character.

Dualities pervade American cultural history and identity. American culture teaches self-reliance and toughness, but also patriotic unity. We worship a god of money and power, but the same god also teaches love and forgiveness. We are supposed to be ambitious individuals, who also submit to the law. Honest and virtuous, cunning and unrelenting, always strong enough to make the hard decisions in life. As Rupert Wilkinson (1986) argues, toughness has been a constant in American life, beginning with rugged life on the frontier, but also in factories, both for the hard-driving owner and the bosses, as well as for the workers.

If Lord Voldemort and Dick Cheney constitute one familiar archetype, then so do people like Jane Addams, Mother Jones or Martin Luther King and all the other people who risked jail, their livelihoods and lives to change the culture and politics of the United States for the benefit of others. It also includes the many regular people who volunteer their time in public schools, at food pantries, crisis centers and homeless shelters and carry on their lives with decency and kindness toward others, with innumerable small acts of courtesy, friendship, and love. They raise socially responsible children and build community life in an age of social fragmentation, frequent moves, short-term temporary employment and fractured social networks. Compliant, conflicted, stagnated, and angry. Welcome to the United States in the 21st Century!

Summary

For many social observers, especially historians, economists, political scientists, and perhaps especially sociologists like the authors of this book, the events of the past few decades may seem confused, contradictory and without rhyme or reason. On the one hand, thanks to globalization and the emergence of a deterritorialized world market, legitimated by neo-liberalism, has enabled the rapid growth of finance capital and in turn, we've seen an enormous explosion of wealth. However, the vast majority of economic growth goes to the top 1%. But this concentration of wealth has also concentrated political power in the hands of the 1%. Moreover, this plutocracy has failed the majority of the people worldwide. Partisan politics has become especially bitter as our political parties see the with acrimony and rage toward each other, especially over social issues and laws that would regulate morality. Political compromise and bipartisan agendas that might benefit most of the voters whose taxes foot the country's bills are no longer aspects of legislative process. While benefits and even various aspects of research are cut back, there is plenty of money for "defense" that really means expensive weapons that either don't work or aren't needed. With the most powerful military in the world, the US has not won a war since 1945. But trillions of dollars have been squandered while millions of people have died as a result of imperialist interventions. Still the most powerful economic and military power in the world, the US economic Colossus is rapidly deteriorating. Roads, rail lines, bridges, water and gas lines, airports and seaports, are all crumbling, rotting or rusting away. 85% of the most heavily travelled bridges in the country were built before 1970 and almost all of them are in need of major repair, if not replacement, which is not likely since no legislation has been proposed to address infrastructure. Save for its elite universities and graduate schools, its educational system is failing as its average academic scores fall ever further behind. Except for military technology, the US has ceded innovation to the rest of the world. We may not need the tallest skyscrapers or more landings on the moon, but we have no new achievements to stand in their place.

How are we to understand the many paradoxes and contradictions of today? We would like to suggest that to understand the events of our day requires an examination of what is generally considered "American Character," the more or less distinct values, mores, and reflexive narratives of a particular people. While the notion of American Character is generally understood by most scholars and ordinary people as well, we would like to suggest that while on the one hand, the concern with national character is essential for understanding how and why most citizens of the United States may be subtly different from Canadians and extremely different from Nigerians or the Japanese. But and how did those differences emerge, how are they reflected in everyday life, governance and culture? As we will argue, that while the notion of national character as generally used and understood is extremely important, underlying that character, is a "social character," which according to Erich Fromm is the most common, most typical underlying, if not unconscious psychological constellation of often ambivalent motives, desires, memories, defenses, ways of seeing, understanding and experiencing the world Social character shapes one's self-image and the typical ways that people relate to each other.

In the following pages, we will note certain aspects of America's national character that that are generally evident to most people, its religiosity, its propensity for violence intertwined with widespread possession of firearms, its materialism and ambition to attain wealth, and finally its "exceptionalism," its identity as not only being a special and unique country, but a "chosen" people, blessed by God and a general force for good in the world. But these aspects of its national character are emotionally anchored within its underlying social character which generally tends to be individualistic, moralistic, and prone toward toughness and violence. Moreover, that character is often quite authoritarian. American social character is one of the main reasons that the United States is facing decline and as it does, we see various expressions of discontent and the emergence of various social movements—some reactionary, some are progressive, and some completely escapist.

As we will conclude, given the nature of dynamic character change, we're seeing the emergence of a "new" constellation of social character. But as we will also show, most elements of that character are already within ourselves and given what psychoanalysts have called "regression in the service of the ego" that allows the "return of the repressed," the same cultural history that has given us the more individualistic, religious, and often aggressive social character has also given us a legacy, often ignored, repressed and/or marginalized, of a more communal, more secular, more compassionate social character. As we shall argue, this characterological change is not simply one deemed desirable by the standards of our progressive values, but this emergent character, itself an adaptation to the conditions of our times, is in fact adaptive to the kind of world we now live it. Indeed, unless humanity evolves and moves away from its tendencies toward the unbridled accumulation of wealth, which all too often has required violence, then between the possibilities of nuclear war and/or pollution bringing ever more violent climate change and environmental despoliation, our society may not last. But we are hopeful, as we witness various social changes that are taking place before our eyes, we see the erosion of what Fromm called "the pathology of normality" and the growing possibilities of a "sane society."

God and His Chosen People: Act II

Exodus tells the story of how after nine plagues, boils, frogs from the sky, and water turned to blood, followed by the slaughter of all firstborn Egyptian children, the Pharaoh said enough, now you can go. He probably used some expletives to make his point, but we have no records. The Jews left Egypt, headed to the Sinai Desert and crossed the Red Sea which the manly Judeo-Christian God conveniently parted for them. God then beckoned Moses to climb Mount Sinai to receive the Torah, or at least the Ten Commandments. After 40 years of wandering through the desert, Joshua led the Israelites to the Promised Land and thereupon attacked the city of Jericho. And when it was conquered, the Israelites began the slaughter of every man, woman, child and goat. The goats too? That's harsh. From what we have already noted, since the Israelites were "chosen" by God to leave Egypt, receive the word of God, then invade and settle on someone else's land and claim this "promised land" as their own, they felt empowered to slaughter the previous inhabitants. With this holy model in mind, the Puritans and others came to the New World, invaded it, and slaughtered the people.

Like the children of Israel, the Puritans came to claim the land God had promised them. Many of the early colonialists did indeed think of themselves as a "chosen" people, a lost tribe coming to the Promised Land to build a New Jerusalem. There is something about being chosen by God that makes a people "special," or as Americans proclaim today, we are "exceptional." God typically rains blessings on His chosen people and then encourages and legitimates a variety of beliefs and practices, not the least of which is dispossessing the heathens and infidels, relieving them of their land and then killing them if they complain or resist. The Native-Americans did not have goats to slaughter, but later, as the frontier moved west, there were buffalo.

The outlines of American character, and its underlying social character were thus initially shaped by the combination of Puritanism and settler colonization of abundant, verdant land, rich in natural resources, and while there had been natives living there for thousands of years, the land and its resources were part of their Commons.[1] But the Puritans had a few guns to enforce

---

1 Settler colonies whether English, French, Spanish, do share certain characteristics that include weapons to enforce claims, and denigration of the indigenous cultures and peoples as inferior, if not subhuman.

their claims. And yes, they were fruitful and they did multiply. Many more people crossed the ocean to join them, especially when economic opportunities became more of a draw than Puritanism. Those subsequent generations of colonists, whether native-English speakers or not, shifted the cultural and characterological trajectory away from the Puritan roots yet nevertheless, as we will discuss, America retained some aspects of this legacy. Indeed, one quality that is often denoted as part of American exceptionalism has been the persistence of religion in general and it's extremely conservative forms, rooted in particular. Scholars of religion has long asked why America has been resistant to the forces of secularism.

The colonies did not have a landed aristocracy that had been blessed by God that held titles to the land and wielded power. Few traditions kept people in a particular place or locked them into a fixed social status. In order to freely practice their Puritanism, and the fact that the settlers chose to sever all ties to their home countries, individualism flourished unfettered and most (white) people seemed to have an equal shot at prosperity. Class differences were less blatant than throughout Europe. Thus a new social character emerged, the American who was first described by De Crevecoeur as a "new race of men." We would like to first look more closely at the origins of the American Character.

Puritanism today is often simply equated with repressive sexuality, premarital chastity, and sometimes prohibitions against alcohol.[2] Repression of the erotic was not unique to early Puritans since that was also typical of Catholicism teachings and values as well, though Catholics knew the "flesh was weak" and if confessed, sins could be forgiven when sinners repented, especially when repentance meant the sinner donated to the Church. Catholicism also allowed various festivals through the year to allow sinful pleasures. As Bakhtin (1968) clearly noted, the medieval Carnival was a brief moment of toleration for all kinds of indulgence in drink (mead was the preferred and most available form of alcohol), food, profanity and debauchery. They made Spring Break in Cancun look like a Sunday Afternoon Baptist church picnic. Few revelers today know that Mardi Gras was (and is still for some) a religious event to celebrate life before the austerity of Lent. To be sure however, for the early Puritans of America, adultery was harshly punished and so too was premarital sex, at least in theory. Puritanism was an inter-denominational movement of dissidents from within the Church of England and the Catholic Churches of the European continent, especially in Flanders (Belgium and the Netherlands) and various places in the Austro-Hungarian Empire. Congregationalists, Calvinists,

---

2 The import of Caribbean sugar cane and production of rum was a major industry in early America.

Presbyterians, Baptists, Methodists, and others broke from their established churches (and some broke away from those who had broken away) and became entirely new and separate churches. Still, why would certain people cross an ocean and embark toward an unknown, uncharted and far off land where their future was quite uncertain? We might hazard a guess that for some reason or other they were more individualistic, more motivated to pursue their faith, or more likely to be risk-takers. Or, perhaps they heard stories of Spanish sailors who told their English counterparts during the battle with the Armada that the climate was sunnier, milder and more pleasant than Northern Europe. Whatever the case, for our purposes, the most important factor encouraging their journey was their dream, their vision of building a divine kingdom on Earth which inspired their intrepid voyages across the ocean. Puritanism in particular and asceticism more generally, fostered industrious shaped the earliest culture of the North Eastern American colonies which soon became the economically most successful and influential region in the nation. Although this vision of divine purpose would go through permutations over the next several hundred years, American culture, its national identity and of course, it's social character have been inextricably intertwined with religion since day one. This has been as true of progressive expressions of religious inspiration as well as its more reactionary forms that garner far more attention. And indeed the persistence of religion as a major factor, has been a major element of "American exceptionalism" as a central moment of America's "civil religion" about which we shall have more to say.

At the same time, given ethnic and regional differences, there were variations in the ways of life such that while most Americans were deeply devoted to Christianity in ways that in some cases were quite compatible with and in some ways in conflict with Puritan asceticism. In the mountains of Appalachia, life both differed from and resembled life in the rocky woodlands of New England. Both were frontier areas where white settlers forcibly removed and/or slaughtered Native Americans. Both initially consisted of fragmented communities that were widely dispersed across an unfamiliar countryside. Culturally, the different European settlers were similar and different from each other. English, Scots and the Dutch (if we include New York as part of Yankeedom, a sociological boundary) settled New England and the Northern Eastern seaboard, while the Scots-Irish and Irish settled Appalachia (Germans followed slightly later but in large numbers). The Puritans were largely drawn from the emerging middle-classes of England, while the Scots-Irish came from oppressed groups suffering under English domination, first in their native Scotland, and then as invaders of the Northern counties of Ireland. Encouraged to migrate to the New World, the Scots-Irish and Irish neighbors served under circumstances similar to Northern Ireland, as shock troops to subdue a Native population in order to establish and maintain English hegemony.

Thirdly, wealthy planters from England, France, and Spain established large plantations in the Deep South. The first North American colony was in fact Spanish; St. Augustine, Florida, was established in 1565, while Jamestown, Virginia, the first English colony, did not appear until 1607. The French Colony of New Orleans was established in 1718, and functioned primarily on the basis of a plantation system. Slaves from Africa toiled in the fields providing the labor needed for the agricultural foundation of the Southern economy. Each plantation, like a medieval manor, was a more or less self-sufficient fiefdom where the owners dominated all aspects of social, economic, political and cultural life. His domination extended into the sexual realm where male slave owners and/or their sons had unlimited access to female slaves. Similarly, patron-client relationships, quiet similar to feudal notions of fealty, loyalty, obligation and honor, permeated social relationships between the plantation owners and their landless and often impoverished white vassals.[3] The image of the Southern Gentleman and Southern Belle derive from the Antebellum social conventions of the wealthy slave-owning elites who viewed themselves as even more sophisticated and superior than their European progenitors; they were Roman patricians reborn in the New World. Given family lineage and notions of racial hierarchy, wealthy white Southerners enforced a strict social and racial hierarchy and principles of violent domination, both through slavery and patrimonialism under which most ordinary white people lived as tenant farmers dependent on the patronage of wealthy whites. Patrimonial class-culture relations governed Southern institutions so thoroughly that most of the Confederate Army consisted of poor whites risking life and limb for their patrons. Like medieval knights and vassals, they were bound by codes of fealty and honor that might cost life or limb. Nevertheless, Southern elites, much like feudal lords, took their responsibilities seriously, and they typically served in their Confederate military and often died in combat, unlike American elites today (such as we saw with Dick Cheney) who eagerly send the children of the lower classes to do the killing and dying they are not willing to risk themselves. Besides, the elites are often too busy making money and consolidating power. After all many serve their country by acquiring emerging companies, managing portfolios or hedge funds, trading currencies or managing mergers and acquisitions.

---

3   Many of these feudal like qualities of the antebellum South still endure today. Similarly, the feudal elites were typically warriors, and to this very day, the US military disproportionately consists of those from Southern and Western backgrounds. And of course feudal societies were highly religious. It is in the military that cultural legacies of honor, toughness, and conservative religion join with economic opportunity.

We could divide the early colonies into more specific regions, but our goal is not to catalogue all the cultural and religious variations. Rather, we wish to focus on the three aforementioned regions that we group by their culture, character, and economic form. On that basis, we argue that each region contributed early and long-standing aspects of American life and character— New England, Appalachia, and the Deep South. This roughly follows the boundaries that Colin Woodard (2011) uses in *American Nations*, although his boundaries and the interests that established them are almost entirely political. In contrast, we also include class, cultural, and characterological factors. Despite the vast hardships of the earliest times, the small bands of colonists in all three regions established viable communities, although with very different outcomes.

New England

In New England, where the Puritans first settled, they bequeathed to the colonies and subsequently the new nation, its distinctive social and cultural qualities that joined Christian piety, work as a calling and a bit of salvation anxiety with economic opportunity. We also include New York, New Jersey, and Maryland in the Yankeedom region, which generally became far more prosperous than Appalachia and the wealth was certainly more broadly distributed than in the Deep South. Our notions of "middle-class" arose from this more equitably distributed Yankee prosperity that Americans embrace today, however nebulously. As we have said, one of the most important expression of the values and visions of the early period was the proclamation of John Winthrop, Governor of the Massachusetts Bay Colony:

> The Lord will be our God, and delight to dwell among us, as his own people, and will command a blessing upon us in all our ways, so that we shall see much more of his wisdom, power, goodness and truth, than formerly we have been acquainted with. We shall find that the God of Israel is among us, when ten of us shall be able to resist a thousand of our enemies; when he shall make us a praise and glory that men shall say of succeeding plantations, "the Lord make it like that of New England." For we must consider that we shall be as a city upon a hill. The eyes of all people are upon us. So that if we shall deal falsely with our God in this work we have undertaken, and so cause him to withdraw his present help from us, we shall be made a story and a by-word through the world.
>
> WINTHROP, 1838 [1630]

For Winthrop, the American beacon would bring people to the shining "Mount Zion, to the city of the living God, the heavenly Jerusalem" (Hebrews 12: 22). Since the colonies were founded by divine grace for divine purpose, the US would be inherently exempt from worldly laws and historical forces that affect other countries. Like the heavenly Jerusalem, the American version contained contradictions. Like their biblical counterparts, Americans should "Keep on loving one another as brothers and sisters. Do not forget to show hospitality to strangers, for by so doing some people have shown hospitality to angels without knowing it. Continue to remember those in prison as if you were together with them in prison, and those who are mistreated as if you yourselves were suffering" (Hebrews 13: 1–3). Alongside the love fest and comradery, people must remember that "Marriage should be honored by all, and the marriage bed kept pure, for God will judge the adulterer and all the sexually immoral" (Hebrews 13: 4) and also "Have confidence in your leaders and submit to their authority" (Hebrews 13: 17). Compassionate and yet judgmental, free yet committed to authority, loving and yet uptight and chaste; we will trace the impact of these contradictions through American history and its effect on social character today. And then the Bible has a lot of justifications for slavery as well as stoning and smiting.

Given the importance of religion in legitimating and motivating the settlers to first embark across the seas to the new lands, then justifying their colonization, later, their subsequent independence from England and then the westward expansionism, the settlers had the absolute certainty that their survival, eventual prosperity and military successes were due to God's blessing. We might well say "and so it came to pass" that the small ragtag group of devoutly religious Puritans established colonies in New England and wider Yankeedom that eventually prospered greatly, following the conviction that God willed their dominion over this new land, and further willed that its morals, values and ways of life would be a model for all men to follow. How did this happen?

For Max Weber (2002 [1920]) and R.H. Tawney (1926), ascetic (Puritanical) Protestantism encouraged the spread of capitalism as well as the disenchantment of the world that in turn fostered the growth of science which became conjoined to became the essence of modernity. Asceticism emphasized a systematic and pure way of life, every moment of every day was part of a "career" not just episodic moments or on Sundays. Each person was expected to calculate the moral significance of all thought and action in order to fulfill God's will. Besides God's will, nothing else mattered. This attitude and way of life, that all people must at all times concentrate on work that serves God's will and exclude everything else also excluded personal sentiments and desires. In other words, the ascetics routinized moral living. Given its divine importance, they routinized everything, including the economy. With the systematic and endless investment and re-investment of money in order to make more money, capitalism in turn turned life into a systematic career of endless work and the accumulation of wealth and reputation. Science became the systematic accumulation and interpretation of observable facts revealing the glory of God, void of personal sentiments. Robert Merton (1938), in his classical essay on Puritanism, pietism and science suggested that Protestant asceticism contributed directly to the rise of 17th Century English science in which the scientists saw as their work as investigations into God's creations.[4] Moreover, their no-nonsense attitudes, high levels of self-control and commitment to work fit well with the goals of careful and patient research. This legacy would cross the pond, inspire many early American scientists, and pave the way for entire universities dedicated to technology and engineering, first and foremost was the Puritan-founded Massachusetts Institute of Technology, MIT.[5]

As the New England colonies grew and capitalism flourished, small villages became towns and towns became cities. As general prosperity increased, a number of processes were set into motion that would eventually undermine both the Church and dynastic rule in the South. The distinctive feature of Protestantism at least back then was not simply the encouragement of hard work combined with asceticism, but a compulsivity toward accumulation without bounds. To understand endless devotion to work as more than just a means of support or as a means of chasing wealth, but rather as a form of obsessive-compulsive behavior, if not a neurosis, we need to consider the unconscious dynamics of character structure that subsequently shaped historical development.

In the early colonial period, much like Europe at that time, the dominant character type was the "hoarding character" mentioned earlier, that is, the collective version of the restrictive obsessive-compulsive asceticism that worried continually about controlling his or her impulses, especially sex desires and the pursuits of other physical pleasures. Cleanliness and order are essential. Control becomes a preoccupation, such that the wallet as the fruit of labor becomes a source of both satisfaction and temptation, both a source of confidence and a source of guilt. Ascetic qualities of orderliness, tireless work, and self-control were highly adaptive in the emerging capitalist society, but

---

4   We are of course reminded that the Republican disdain of science is relatively recent and that indeed, up until the 1960s Republicans tended to be more supportive of science and scientific research than were the Democrats.

5   Parenthetically, many of the Big 10 universities were founded by the Morrill Land Act grants to create agricultural research centers.

contained an inherent contradiction: it exalted individual virtue, but simultaneously condemned individual gratification. As we argue, Puritanism encouraged individualism, freedom, equality and transformed a religious "calling" into social compulsions of duty and self-sufficiency that instilled feelings of accomplishment but also feelings of insecurity. One must do one's duty, the conscious expressions of pride in early sphincter control, often learned in coercive ways. Alongside the certainty of productive work was the uncertainty of personal adequacy and lures of temptation. In order to avoid feelings of uncertainty and inadequacy, the Yankees worked tirelessly. Consequently, American individualism acquired a unique aspect as it became intertwined with work.

At first, American individualism was rooted in Protestant doctrines that stressed a direct, unmediated relationship between the individual and God which did not require a hierarchical Church or any superior clerical authority. We are reminded that De Tocqueville was the first scholar to systematically use the newly coined term of individualism to describe America character. He noted that the very destiny of America was evident within the first Puritan who landed on its shores. The salience of Protestant based individualism was more fully developed by Bellah who saw how its contemporary expressions, as "habits of the heart" might have inspired economic success in America, but as he had earlier noted, it attenuated the bonds of community.

This religiously based individualism would morph, migrate to, and flourish in other realms. Indeed, it facilitated the spread of science and modernity as a cultural framework and capitalism as its economic base. However, the same science and Reason, as well as prosperity and resulting inequality would introduce a serious set of contradictions and intensify personal insecurity through the very same lifestyle that that served God's will. Puritan doctrines, especially Calvinist notions of pre-destination, promised the possibility of salvation, but simultaneously made it highly uncertain. Protestants were likely to suffer from "salvation anxiety" about their fate in the afterlife. Catholics could find comfort in a deathbed confession and/or buying a letter of indulgence in which earthly cash enabled a passage to heaven, or the continuation of their family and community. Unfortunately, Protestants needed some other means to assuage their anxieties and they found it by turning work into a "calling," a moral obligation above and beyond any practical concern. For Christianity, work had heretofore been one of the curses that befell Adam, Eve and all humanity for eating of the forbidden fruit, for women pain in childbirth was the other legacy. Ironically enough, the Puritans embraced the monastic traditions of the Catholic Church that had already made work a "calling," a spiritual vocation, a moral obligation to work for the glory of God, whilst living a simple, Spartan life in the monasteries and convents. Thus for Protestants, work in general not only became a moral obligation, but served a defensive function to counter salvation anxiety.

Worldly success was not so much for the pursuit of wealth, but an indication of God's choice as to the person's salvation. Even more unfortunately, tireless work as a calling and the wealth that resulted also indicated God's grace, yet only in earning and saving wealth, not in spending and enjoying it. Puritan asceticism was such that profits were saved and reinvested, not spent on luxuries. This in turn legitimated endless economic expansion as a moral achievement. As Weber noted, this resulted in creating the very conditions of material wealth and temptation that the early Puritans disdained.

Altogether, their world created tensions and anxieties, especially over salvation that prompted a compulsive work ethic and worldly asceticism in which work acquired a specifically moral purpose in this world, while also fulfilling a transcendent and divine purpose. Puritan theology promoted both individualism and a moral life, but this also created individual anxiety because liberty and self-autonomy also meant individual accountability. No one could help those who would not or could not help themselves, and even Jesus died only for the elect, those who were predestined for salvation, and not to redeem everyone. The individual stood utterly alone in this life, while facing an unforgiving and judgmental God on the way to the next life. Yet, the individual needed to fulfill certain social obligations to family, church, and community.

As a result, life always involved tension and fear because God had predestined the fate of everyone even before He created the Heavens and the earth, so one's works could not guarantee salvation no matter how relentlessly one pursued his or her calling and simultaneously avoided sin. As far as any mere human knows, all of our efforts to serve God's will may in fact be the very works that lead us away from God. For the Puritans and other ascetic Protestants, God was remote and unknowable, while temptation was close and familiar. American Protestantism involved an inherent contradiction, God allowed individual free will and autonomy, but also demanded very specific service in the form of a "calling" but provided few if any indications of success or failure- until the final judgment. Consequently, one could only persevere in the presumed "calling" as a righteous individual, all the while suspicious of everyone and everything that might distract or mislead from divine purpose. In the end, one could only hope for the best, because ultimately, God may have decided that we don't measure up.

Appalachia

The Puritans were not the only religiously based cultural group. Throughout the mountains, especially along the Appalachian chain which runs from northern Alabama all the way through the Green mountains of Vermont, another expression of Christian culture emerged. Initially steeped in a harshly judgmental and brooding form of Calvinism, new forms of Christianity swept the region in the Great Awakenings of the 19th Century. Methodism, Baptism, and later, Pentecostalism transformed mountain religion into highly emotional, often ecstatic expressions. In some of these congregations, people spoke in tongues, while others handled rattlesnakes as proof of their faith in God's Will. Compared to Calvinism and other ascetic forms, these new forms of Christianity provided a haven from the harsh reality of mountain life, and legitimated personal gratification and independence. This suited mountain culture far better, given its history of rugged independence and rejection of government beyond the local level, whether the British crown, the Continental Congress, the State or the US federal government.

As de Tocqueville travelled along the Ohio River, he noted the stark contrast in lifestyles on the Ohio side compared to the Kentucky side of the river. In southern Ohio (settled mainly by New England Puritans), strict chore schedules and moral codes determined the daily farming routine. On the Kentucky side (where Appalachian culture predominated) people worked hard, but as little as possible they devoted much time to music, dancing, drinking, and fighting. A favorite pastime for men was "purring," whereby rivals would hold each other by the shoulders and kick each other in the shins until one relented. This was not to settle disputes; purring was for fun (Nisbett 1993). For disputes, men preferred fist-fighting in which the first one unconscious or unable to continue loses. Dueling with swords and firearms was for men of privilege, but all classes embraced rugged individualism. Born to wealth, Andrew Jackson killed several men in duels (Brands 2005) as part of political negotiations in his home state of Tennessee. He killed more men during service in the Revolutionary War (at age 13). In the War of 1812 and numerous wars against Native-Americans, he often issued blood-curdling oaths and called upon God to help him annihilate his enemies with righteous vengeance (Brands 2005). Violence was his main claim to fame for the presidency, proudly proclaiming that he killed a lot of Brits, as well as Creek, Seminoles, Shawnee, Cherokee, and Choctaw (Remini, 2001). Once elected President, his Indian Removal Policy of 1830 displaced several tribes and included the Trail of Tears in which thousands more died from exposure, starvation, and disease. Jackson was an Appalachian man by birth, belief, character and lifestyle.

Mountain culture thus shared certain things in common with their ascetic neighbors to the North. They shared a strong sense of individualism and personal honor, tied to religious devotion that in turn sanctified the righteousness of the individual. They also valued work as a virtue, but only to the extent that it was necessary to produce a livelihood of some kind. For mountain people,

work did not integrate the individual into a moral community as in Protestantism. Rather, work reinforced the virtue of individual self-reliance and toughness. Work of any kind that supported a person was legitimate, whether it
was intrinsically moral or even legal was irrelevant. For example, the Whiskey
Rebellion of 1791–1794 was not simply a rebellion against a formal tax on
whiskey. Sociologically, it represented a direct conflict between a local barter
economy (whiskey was often used as a form of currency) and goods for services
connected to a culture of rugged self-reliance. Appalachians relied on personal
reputations and a firm handshake, not on lawyers and contracts. The rising
power of a central national government, official authority, and dispassion-
ate formal legality clashed with the folk customs of mutual respect in which
people settle their own affairs. If you have a problem, you take it up face to
face. The tax was not just an economic imposition, but an imposition of a very
different worldview on a long-established local culture.

Perhaps more than any other quality, passion separated mountain culture
from asceticism. Soon after their arrival, mountain culture embraced a much
more free-spirited orientation to life. Religion, lifestyle, and music of greater
Appalachia reflected this free-spirited version of individualism. This created
space for a much looser gender division. Women as well as men faced daily toil
to eke out a living in a harsh environment. Logging, and later mining, required
large investments of capital, and so even when these industries developed,
local people served only as cheap labor and benefitted relatively little form the
wealth extracted from natural resources. Neither men nor women benefitted
much from endless hard work amidst falling timber, the treacherous bleak-
ness of the mine, or domestic labor under poverty. Similarly, women stood
alongside men in the two main sanctuaries of life: in church, and in festival
celebrations.

Originally called mountain music or hillbilly, country music arose from the
harsh struggle to live in the mountains. Women struggled under the same conditions as men, and as such, earned the right to tell the stories of mountain
life no less than men. Women featured prominently in mountain and country
music from the very beginning. Born into poverty as a coal-miner's daughter,
married at 13 and with five children by the age of 21, Loretta Lynn sang boldly
from a woman's perspective:

> Well nobody knows where you're goin'
> but they sure know where you've been
> All their thinkin' of is your experience of love
> their minds eat up with sin
> The women all look at you like you're bad

and the men all hope you are
But if you go too far you're gonna wear the scar
of a woman rated X.

Speaking to the patriarchal standards of male sexual freedom and the virgin-whore dichotomy forced upon women, Loretta also follows the usual country culture standard—don't complain. Be tough and move on. No matter how unfair life is, stand up for yourself and move on.

Similarly, songs abounded about the grim reality of mining, poverty, but also faith in Gods' grace in the everyday struggle for survival. Passions ran high, and songs often portrayed the sudden and frequently senseless violence of desperation. For example, the anonymous 19th Century mountain song "Banks of the Ohio" (covered by Johnny Cash and many others) tells the story of a young man who asks a girl for marriage. She doesn't respond one way or another. Impatient to hear a decisive yes or no,

I plunged a knife into her breast
And told her she was going to rest
She cried "Oh Willy, don't murder me
I'm not prepared for eternity"
I took her by her golden curls
And drug her down to the river side
And there I threw her in to drown
And I watched her as she floated down

In this and innumerable other songs, from the first troubadour songs to travel from the British Isles to the Appalachian mountains to present-day country music, we see a powerful sense of individual autonomy. Not even murder conjures up an apology or sense of regret for one's actions. In this song, the boy simply goes home. The famous "Folsom Prison Blues" by Johnny Cash also tells the story of a man who commits murder. As he says, "I killed a man in Reno, just to watch him die." Not for money, or revenge, or even thrills; he killed a man for no reason at all. Still, the song only speaks of regret, not remorse. The blues of prison life arise from getting caught and the consequent loss of personal freedom—not any kind of apologetic remorse for murder. No matter what happens in life, whether stories of travel, love, war, violence, poverty, or death, mountain and country music never apologizes for past actions or calls for collective change. A person can only roll with the vicissitudes of life as a tough and self-reliant individual.

Appalachian religion thus became more of a highly personal choice rather than social obligation as well as a respite from the harshness of daily life. Far from the dour and judgmental severity of asceticism that affirmed moral status, mountain religion affirmed an enthusiastic, even ecstatic embrace of joy whenever possible. Alongside, however, stood the sense of personal honor. One's name must carry weight. Although the first references to bare-knuckle boxing come from the Boston area around 1733, the New England version was prize-fighting—a purely entertainment spectacle for money. In Appalachia, fist-fighting became an unregulated and ingrained way for men to settle disagreements (Gorn, 1986 pp. 36–39) and build a personal reputation in the process. Appalachians carried their sport and sense of justice westward to the Great Plains, where boxing became even more brutal as personal reputation blended with prizefighting, with fights sometimes lasting 100 rounds over several hours (Mee, 2001). A winner must be decided, and although the other must therefore lose at some point, surrender was far worse than defeat. Promoters often included boxing as part of larger spectacles of roping, shooting, carnival games, and dances, such that boxing became part of family entertainment (Agnew, 2011). Tied to the land with a fixed sense of place and purpose, farmers, ranchers, and shopkeepers typically did not participate in boxing. Loggers, railroad men, miners, teamsters, and others with no fixed sense of place were the willing participants in bare-knuckle bloodsport from which they earned no money, and often lost their ability to work as a result of broken jaws, fractured skulls, torn ligaments and tendons, and damaged internal organs (Agnew, 2011).

Even itinerant preachers would enter the ring to earn the respect of the men whose souls they were trying to save. Beyond the boxing ring, they would brave any river, open expanse, dust bowl or storm as well as hostile Native-Americans to reach any audience that would join them in open-air revivals (Brown, 1995; Phares, 1971). Methodist Preachers such as William Cravens (Wakeley, 2014) and Peter Cartwright (Bray, 2005), both from the mountains of western Virginia (now West Virginia), often sermonized about the virtuous hard work and bravery of the men who were claiming the land for God. Like the men in their audience, they were hard-fighting preachers who would fight any man who challenged their toughness. By the time fighting and religion migrated to the prairie lands of the North American interior, frontier culture now integrated religious revivals, carnival games, farmer's markets, and fighting into a unified spectacle of faith, community and violence.

It is here that we see American anxiety at work, a constant struggle of men to prove their masculinity and their worth in a world where they stood as lone individuals, always on the move from one job to the next, or no job at all. Women were few and would only tie down a man whose livelihood depended on mobility, and so prostitution flourished on the plains where men viewed women and nature as objects of conquest (Merchant, 1989) to use and then move on down the railroad line. Hard-working, hard-drinking, and hard-fighting; the uprooted man of the frontier lived a high-risk lifestyle with potentially great rewards but with death always nearby from accidents at work, disease, or the gun. To go down swinging was preferable to fading away. Today, festivals of masculine prowess and identity retain many of the features of frontier culture. In spectacles such as NASCAR and the Sturgis Motorcycle Rally, men from mostly working-class backgrounds drink, fight, and celebrate the unity of God and country (Krier and Swart 2014) to aging but still hard-charging riffs of Ted Nugent and Lynyrd Skynyrd that promise truth and transcendence for the man who always goes his own way and never surrenders.

In a region with a fierce sense of independence and self-reliance, with a concurrent distrust of anything official, personal reputation becomes the standard of conduct and dispute resolution. As Nietzsche argued, "the will to a system betrays a lack of integrity" (1990 [1889], p. 63). Although unlikely that many, if any mountain folk ever read Nietzsche, they certainly embraced his ideals of the independent individual who meets life head-on, with intense enthusiasm every step of the way and without regret until fate or God lay claim in death. Laws, official rules and formality of any kind violates the primacy of personal integrity. Mountain culture developed both from its historical origins and from the particular conditions of mountain life.

Firstly, the Scots and Irish brought with them a herding culture. With large areas to protect and only family members available, one's personal reputation by itself must be enough to scare away poachers. Strength and self-reliance were inherent aspects of the herding life and central to survival (Fischer, 1989). In addition to basic economic survival, family alliances through marriage and mutual support generally required displays of strength and integrity (McWhiney, 1988). Scattered across harsh and infertile terrain, projections of personal power occupied the same social space that, for village and urban populations of Puritans, the community occupied. In Scotland and Ireland both, where feudalism developed only vaguely compared to England, lords offered little protection or accommodations of justice. In all matters, individual men as heads of extended families could rely only on themselves. Transplanted to Appalachia, mountain life similarly separated households into relatively isolated, autonomous and typically impoverished livelihoods. With influxes of German settlers and Black people from the Deep South, Appalachia became increasingly diverse, yet it fragmented along racial and ethnic lines rather than become a synergistically unified cultural groups. As a consequence, mountain

culture emphasized a contradiction between individualism and ethnic solidarity, and a contradiction of self-reliance with loyalty to the extended family.
The moral community thus included only those of familial relation, and much
more loosely, those of similar livelihood and ethnicity. As we will next see in
the Old South, Appalachia was not the only place to develop a strong sense
of in-group versus outgroup sense of rivalry, but also in contrast to the South,
social commitments tended to be attenuated. There was nothing comparable
to the egalitarian communities of Yankeedom nor the genteel sense of manners, customs, and devotion to social authority as in the South.

The Deep South

Often conflated with Appalachian culture, the Antebellum culture of the
Deep South differed in certain key ways. Religion specifically served as a social adhesive, binding the wealthy plantation owners and their impoverished
clients in mutual dependence. Far from a divine call for equality, Southern religion sanctified social inequality and blessed racial and class domination as
an expression of divine order. Socially, the living conditions of most whites
differed from their enslaved counterparts mostly in terms of justice and a
vague concept of freedom. Poor whites were allowed a greater range of voli-
tion compared to a slave, but "agency" always remained within the bounds of
servitude that resembled the feudal relations of agrarian Europe. Much like
feudal Europe, religion enforced patrimonial servitude as a moral obligation.
Wealthy plantation owners rented land to poor whites, either as tenant farmers or sharecroppers, and also provided some semblance of justice, much as
a feudal lord held dominion over all matters within their territory. Like their
peasant counterparts in Europe, poor white Southerners practiced a kind of
fealty to their plantation masters, pledging their loyalty and support in times
of war. This gave them a certain level of status, one notch above the slaves,
but also ensured their continued impoverishment. Tenant farming never produced enough surplus to move up in the world.

Taken together, the economic and moral sanctity of patrimonial class-
cultural relations also reinforced a strongly authoritarian social character that
involved certain inherent contradictions that were however different than in
Appalachia. Although a man was expected to show the same strength and
toughness as his counterparts in the mountains, he was also expected to maintain his subservient social position. In other words, he was supposed to stoutly
uphold his name and self-reliance, but at the same time, defer to his social
superiors. He should be both autonomous, and subservient. For authoritarians,

the more dominant and overbearing the authority figure, the better, assuming the authoritarian perceives that authority figure as a legitimate authority. In the South, a legitimate authority figure could only be wealthy and white. Given its history of slavery and racism, white Southerners are still reluctant to recognize the legitimacy of a Black President, and the overlapping "birther," creationism, and Tea Party movements that emerged or strengthened in response to Obama's election tended to be strongest in the old Confederacy. In turn, people with racist attitudes throughout the country celebrated the battle flag of the Army of Northern Virginia (the command of Robert E. Lee), which became known as the Confederate flag and primary symbol of white supremacy when Strom Thurmond and the Southern Dixiecrats split from the Democratic party in 1948. Prior to that moment, the actual national flag of the Southern Confederacy during the Civil War looked entirely different—three horizontal bars and a circle of seven to eleven stars, one for each of the states that joined the Confederacy.

Southern theologian Charles Hodge argued for a doctrine of "particular" salvation, as distinct from "general" salvation. While this was already found in older versions of Calvinism as predestination, particular salvation added another factor-race. When the Southern Baptist Convention (SBC) was born in 1845, it officially adopted a modified version of "particular" Baptism, in that only those who were born again would be saved, and only from among those to whom God offers the possibility of salvation. Furthermore, Southern Baptists reflected popular notions of the day and codified them into a belief of white spiritual superiority that not only accorded whites the opportunity for salvation (and denied it to others), but also promoted a "manifest destiny." The godly way of life, embodied by white people, especially those of high social status, should determine the destiny of America. Hodge proved uniquely qualified to articulate a doctrine of wealthy white salvation. He held a doctorate from an elite school (Princeton), yet often expressed his views in the local vernacular which gained a widespread populist following. His leadership, which influenced many ministers at a local level, provided a theological and scholarly cover for race, status, and class domination (Hewitt 1991). Beyond race by itself, Hodge emphasized that anyone could sin, but the select few possessed an inherent grace that corresponded to the high manners and customs of the plantation elite, which shielded them from "the enduring power of sin" which otherwise manifested as social failure. In short, Hodge's theology and that of the early Southern Baptist Convention "personified social conservatives in the South" (Hewitt 1991 p. 88). Hodge's preoccupation with sin and temptation led him to condemn most forms of social unrest, as well as any form of social change that challenged established and conventional routines. Overall, Hodge represented an antimodernist thinker who supported everything old in the

Old South. He rejected universal suffrage and advocated slavery as a natural and divine order.

Most significantly perhaps, Hodge argued that "the person and the soul are completely passive," whereas God is the only active force. For this reason, "sinners are by themselves unable to perform any holy act," (Hewitt 1991 p. 56). The "real" people of God therefore accept their fate rather than try to make their fate. For Hodge, people can only submit to God, and if God wanted to change the social order, He would do so. According to Hodge (1866), "God approves certain individuals and predestines them for eternal life. The ground of this choice is His own sovereign pleasure; the end to which the elect are predestined is company to Jesus Christ" (Hodge, 1866, p. 459). Hodge exemplifies the attempt to reinstate predestination as an element of modern Baptist belief and justification for the social domination of one group over others. For Hodge, predestination not only determines the fate of one's soul, but also establishes the social order of this world.

Consequently, Southern Baptist culture would appeal to and reinforce an authoritarian relationship based on submission to God and an authoritarian social character in general. This is appreciably different from Yankeedom and Appalachia, in that self-sufficiency and work are not particular virtues in life. Rather, the one virtue that supersedes all others is keeping your place and fulfilling the obligations of your station. Authority flows from God, to white men, to white women and children. Black men, whether slaves or not, occupied a rung below "whippersnapper" white boys. As the Poet Sterling A. Brown (1996) tells it:

Old Lem

I talked to old Lem
and old Lem said:
"They weigh the cotton
They store the corn
   We only good enough
   To work the rows;
They run the commissary
They keep the books
   We gotta be grateful
   For being cheated;
Whippersnapper clerks
Call us out of our name
   We got to say mister
   To spindling boys

They make our figgers
Turn somersets
We buck in the middle
   Say, "Thankyuh, sah."
      "They got the judges
They got the lawyers
They got the jury-rolls
They got the law
   They don't come by ones
They got the sheriffs
They got the deputies
   They don't come by twos
They got the shotguns
They got the rope
   We git the justice
   In the end
   And they come by tens.
... I had a buddy
   Six foot of man
He spoke out of turn
At the commissary
They gave him a day
To git out the county
He didn't take it.
He said 'Come and get me.'
They came and got him
   And they came by tens.
He stayed in the county—
He lays there dead.
... They don't come by ones
They don't come by twos
But they come by tens."

The Civil rights movement revealed innumerable such stories. How strange that allegedly tough men would come by tens to get one man, for nothing more than speaking out of turn or some other offense such as walking on the wrong side of the street or eating at the wrong lunch counter. Recall that keeping your place was the primary virtue in life. We no longer argue that such so-called crimes of African Americans represented white racism and domination, and punishments often carried long prison terms or the death penalty at the hands of a lynch mob. We condemn them as hate crimes today. We do still argue about why they happen(ed). The argument we present here is that for the highly authoritarian character, even the smallest offenses as resistance to authority evoke powerfully emotional and often violent reactions of hate that arise from the fear that the social order will unravel and one's superior status with it. In the Old South, from the slightest to the greatest transgressions, all sense of social order and meaning, as well as divinely ordained order and meaning might collapse if one unpunished domino after another falls.

Of course, Black emancipation threatened both the economic power and social status of the plantation owners who owned the vast majority of slaves. At the same time, emancipation also threatened the patrimonial bond between rich and poor that slightly elevated the impoverished white tenant farmer above the Black slave. Without a strong sense of racial superiority, the impoverished white Southerner would truly have nothing. This attitude also flourished in Florida and Southern Louisiana where Spanish and French culture predominated and where slave plantations dominated the economy. In the history of the United States, white culture and economy dominated Black people so ruthlessly and completely that Black Americans have been one of the most oppressed and exploited people on earth, although the genocide of Native-Americans certainly rivals antebellum slavery in brutality. Slavery and genocide have been the basis of white supremacist identity in the United States.

Religion, Contradictions and Character

On the surface, asceticism, mountain religion, and patrimonialism appear similar. All were Christian, typically Protestant, and committed to a strong sense of individualism, social status and a moral obligation to work. At times, these similarities have produced social, cultural, and political alliances in American history. Yet beneath the overt similarities, we see particular differences that create contradictions in American religion and social character. These contradictions contribute to the anxiety in American life. American religious life contributes to the anxiety of contradiction in that each person should adhere to God's will, yet also live as they feel is right. Higher powers will address all wrongs and both the righteous and the wicked will receive justice in the end, but before that happens, each person needs to take charge of their own life and also punish the wrongdoers among us. Religion reinforced both individualism and social responsibility at the same time, and often in contradiction.

As a consequence, American individualism has always had a problematic, ambivalent relation to community, strong social attachments, mutual support and loyalty to one's community were strongly desired. Fears of abandonment are among the most archaic and powerful experiences that shape character since without connections and support, one is rendered helpless and the fear of annihilation and death may be the most basic and powerful emotions (Cf. Becker, 1974). Yet at the same time, given all we have said about individualism in American, community is also feared, there is a dread of being swallowed up by someone or something more powerful, and even God can be fearsome, and yet compassionate. Thus we would argue that as many observers of American social character have noted, the compromise between individualism and community has been loneliness and ambivalent attachments. Moreover, for American social character, individualism becomes tied to strength and power, and any dependency on others, especially the community or worst of all, the government, even dependence on God, is a sign of weakness if not failure. One resolution to this paradox has been to create homogenous communities that distrusted any outsiders who might embody even the most minimal variations in lifestyle and or appearance. It was not by chance that the main victims accused of witchcraft in New England were outsiders like Tituba, a woman of color, as well as unmarried men and women. Since then, bohemians, celebrities, gays, liberals and the worst of the worst, socialists, communists and dark-skinned Muslims have become the hated outsiders.

The Puritan settlements articulated the quintessential narrative of American community. It was a place wherein rugged individuals confronted the ravages of untamed nature, where the mass slaughter of indigenous peoples gave testimony to Puritan religiosity. It was a place of fence building and church going, but also a place of repressed sexuality and intolerance of difference. It was a place of sacred covenants between settler to settler and settlers to God in a continuous hierarchy that required protection from internal threats of weakness and temptation, as well as from outsiders with different beliefs and ways of life. The Puritan community placed the church at the center of the town, of social life and the patriarchal family as the first locus of control. Without the church and without the family, there was no community. The early New England settlement was an outpost: a bastion of God in a godforsaken land (Salerno, 2003).

However, the Puritan communities were not rigid or stagnant. On the contrary in fact, as a result of their economic dynamism, Puritan communities grew and traveled westward following the frontier. Although still committed to homogeneous communities, in the Midwest and the West Coast, the Puritans assimilated Native-Americans, although often in very forceful ways.

One favorite way was to separate children from their parents and place them in special boarding schools (Stout, 2012) specifically designed to strip native children of their religion, culture, and language and then instill the English language and Yankee values, which included a strict daily routine and regulation concerning classes, clothing, meals, and all manners and behavior (Coleman, 1993). They also expected that any settlers enclosed in their territories would conform to a Yankee-Puritan way of life. In other words, the Puritans carried their essential work ethic to the frontier life they sought to tame. In the Yankee mind, the chaos, freedom and liberated sexuality of the frontier town demanded the realization of the order, control and repression of the Puritan community. Freedom from old restraints, both moral and economic, also meant greater insecurity, and amidst a hostile land inhabited by indigenous peoples.

Frontier communities were structurally diverse; many were short-lived and disappeared from memory altogether or lived on as ghost towns of legend. Others continued and prospered. Compared to the early Puritans, many of whom had been college educated abroad, these new western settlers were unrefined, mostly uneducated and illiterate farmers from Germany and Scandinavia or poor whites from the Deep South. As Yankeedom lost its religious fervor in favor of economic expansion, Yankee culture no longer offered a moral covenant to create community, but instead gave in to the emerging culture of individual economic success unfettered by religious or other moral obligation. Life in the Midwest and the Great Plains unified the economic expansion of Yankeedom with the individualism of Appalachia and the white supremacy of the South. There were no covenants holding people together. Westward expansion was in part a history of daily violence to clear the land of buffalo and all other indigenous species and people until the exploitation of resources no longer provided a basis for livelihood. First bleed the land of oil and ore and then move on in a kind of slash and burn rampage. Christopher Lasch has noted, "Whereas the pioneer gave vent to his violence and murderous cruelty, he saw the result as a goal of community—a safe place for his wife and children" (1979 p. 39). Violence became the key to both economic and social security. The loner-bandit was romanticized in the tabloids as the true heroic man. The James Brothers and Billy the Kid, murderous and heartless as they were, became romantic icons. The range cowboy, typically a poor, crude uneducated former Confederate soldier, doing work that was poorly paid, dirty and dangerous, was transformed by Southern newspapers into the rugged individualist, the non-contemplative, quick shooting, hard fighting, and untamed individual. Separated from the laws of the land, proudly alienated from his own humanity, he was reckless and wild in taking whatever he wanted (Salerno, 2003).

Religion and Culture

Nevertheless, the conservative moral sensibilities did not disappear, but morphed into a more authoritarian form, live within the law, unless the law proves weak and ineffectual. Then, a real man makes his own laws. Ascetic toughness is crucial, because a real man must be self-reliant and ready to exact justice at any moment. For at least 400 years, American religion has retained certain essential ascetic characteristics. While often associated with conservative, literalist or fundamentalist versions of Protestantism, ascetic individualism has also shaped American Catholicism, as well as business customs, bland suits, and humorless focus on task, of time-clock regimentation and conventional homogeneity in popular culture that promises personal gratification through mass produced commodities (Marcuse 1991 [1964]). Individualism, asceticism, work as salvation, and the dualism of the sanctified versus the damned, have remained enduring characteristics of American character. Such values and social character do not correlate directly with church attendance, but in fact manifest as central aspects of American culture across a wide variety of social contexts, including religion and regardless of denomination.

As mentioned, early asceticism typically barred women from direct participation in church. While clearly patriarchal, such decisive gender division not only located women as subordinate, but as inherently inferior in the eyes of God. As the sociologist Elizabeth Reis (Reis 1999; 2014) concludes, early colonial men committed sins, but women had sinful natures. Made in the image of God, men not only held a divine authority over women, but further carried the responsibility to wield that authority to contain the evil they believed is inherent in the nature of women. Consequently, early Protestantism contributed to the phallic aggressive side of American culture, often tied to a sense of individual manhood and honor.

However, Christian scripture and culture includes a different and opposite message. In contrast to judgment and intolerance, the other message teaches love and compassion. Whether one or the other predominates in the Christian tradition and scripture is a matter for religious scholars. Nevertheless, many Christians have embraced the message of love and compassion. For example, Abraham Lincoln's parents believed, based on lessons from scripture, that any form of physical punishment would harm a child both mentally and spiritually (Donald 1996). As a young man, Lincoln read voraciously, including the Bible, and consequently refused to hunt animals, even for food, because he believed that killing was wrong (Sandburg 1939). Apparently, the Lincolns did not especially embrace the work ethic, however, as the young Abraham devoted all of his time to reading, which the work-centric community regarded as loafing

(Sandburg, 1939). The main point, of course, is that scripture inspired the Lincoln family to approach life with a general sense of respect and even compassion, rather than judgment and condemnation. Just like the more belligerent interpretations of scripture, so the compassionate view continues today.

The Midwest

The Midwest serves as useful illustration of change as a fourth area that draws partially from New England and Appalachia, yet in direct conflict with the South and hence generated its own culture from the diverse waves of immigration in the 19th Century. Returning to the Lincolns, they lived in Kentucky, Indiana, and finally in Illinois, all of which at the time were frontier areas. Abraham grew up amidst a newly developing religious morality, one that combined the sentiment of social justice from Yankeedom with an emerging practicality derived from the diversity of migrants and immigrants, including mountain folk, settling in the region we now call the Midwest. Descended from English lineage, the Lincolns lived in communities that also included Scandinavian, German, and Dutch immigrants. Although racism appeared as well, Southerners tended to migrate westward rather than to the North. Thus, Midwestern towns developed a unique sense of practicality and egalitarianism. Most of the people lived and worked on family farms; each family owned more or less the same acreage, earned similar incomes and lived similar lifestyles. Practicality arose from this general equality, simply as a means to conduct daily affairs with as little friction as possible. Although not driven to promote religion in social life in the manner of the Yankee Puritans, the Midwesterners practiced a kind of practical frugality—if something serves no useful purpose, it's not so much a matter of sin as a matter of irrelevance. Similarly, work beyond what is necessary to maintain the farm and earn a decent living is excessive. Don't be greedy, and why not enjoy life a little?

In contrast to the Southern plantations, the family farmers of the Midwest owned far more modest plots and thus could not support the lavish excess and conspicuous opulence of wealthy Southern aristocrats with their grand mansions and estates. Nor, as partial descendants of Yankee Puritan culture did they desire to possess or display opulence. Family farmers owned and worked their own land, and thus differed substantially from Southern tenant farmers. And further, they earned a much better livelihood than did the subsistence farms of Appalachia. Economically, the family farmers had direct reasons to oppose the expansion of slavery; moreover as business owners (along with tradesmen and shopkeepers), they required a level of education far higher than tenant farmers of the South. Lacking the wealth of the plantations or the commercial masters of New England, they had very obvious reasons to support public rather than private education. Similarly, they were likely to support governmental regulations of land use, ownership, and commodities markets that ensured a continued livelihood for everyone. The Civil War thus revealed considerable socioeconomic differences in the United States, despite the apparent superficial similarities of Christianity and European descent. The demarcation of North versus South was more of a political demarcation of Union and Confederate forces. Much of Appalachia, like the entire state of Kentucky sought neutrality, while eastern Tennessee attempted to become an independent state loyal to the union when the state joined the Confederate side. Meanwhile, 22 counties in Virginia seceded and joined the union in 1863 as the new state of West Virginia. Missouri officially joined the Confederacy but a popular uprising ousted the governor and turned the state neutral. In short, North and South were the two largest players among several other sides that marked substantial economic, cultural, and characterological differences.

In the years leading up to the Civil War, many devout Christians condemned and battled against slavery just as Hodge promoted it. Notably, Charles Finney advocated "the freedom of the human must supersede and happen at the expense of divine sovereignty" (Hewitt, 1988 p. 88) a bold statement in any day. Finney sought to understand freedom of choice as something ordained by God and thus, as an aspect of divine will, emancipation takes many forms. Theodore Dwight Weld and Arthur and Lewis Tappan joined the abolitionist movement and called upon all good pastors to fight slavery as part of their regular gospel sermon and all good people to fight against slavery in their daily lives. William Lloyd Garrison, a Northern Presbyterian, harshly attacked any church or congregation that would not denounce slavery. His abolitionism rested squarely on deeply felt religious beliefs (Swift, 2008 [1911] p. 132). His aggressive and at times vitriolic attacks on parishes that remained silent on the slavery issue earned him widespread public notoriety and many political enemies.

As fervently as people like Garrison saw the battle against slavery as an expression of divine will, pro-slavery forces saw divine will as an absolute law that stipulated slavery (and later justified segregation as divinely ordered). Divine will required unquestioning submission, which differed decisively from the abolitionists who saw divine will as unfolding through active, thoughtful, conscious engagement with all aspects of life. They also continued the tradition that sought to unify all people under God. In contrast, pro-slavery leaders held that Christianity and salvation are only for the chosen, and race was the primary factor. The major denominations split over the political issue of slavery, and the spiritual issues of free-will and salvation. Presbyterianism split in 1857, into the New School sect (in the North) and the Old School sect (in the South). Baptism split in 1840, and the Southern Baptist Convention officially formed in 1845 (Swift 2008 [1911] p. 33). Although the SBC officially held no position on slavery and maintained that it was a civil matter outside the affairs of religion, their first president, William B. Johnson, declared "the South is now free to promote slavery" (quoted in Swift 2008 [1911] p. 133).

Religion and Culture Today

Today, the US remains about 78% Christian, but being "Christian" means very different things depending on whom you ask. Although the US has a long history of racism, being African American is still seen as a particularly inferior status for many whites, closely followed by people of Latin American descent. Racism in the South during the Civil Rights era is well-known, but even today, racism is not limited to the South. However, and this is crucial, social movements and individual sentiments to transcend racial and ethnic prejudice overwhelmingly appear outside the South. In other words, racism exists everywhere, but anti-racism arises predominantly in New England, the Midwest, and the West Coast—an area settled by Yankees, Midwesterners, and Hispanics. Although the Civil Rights movement started in the South and many of the first acts of civil disobedience took place there, the South also had much further to go towards some semblance of equal justice. Perhaps the starkest division in American religion was in the South during the civil-rights era where the Southern Christian Leadership Conference (SCLC) stood in opposition to the Southern Baptist Convention (SBC), the SCLC efforts moved towards equality for people of all races while white churches and the SBC in particular tenaciously maintained a commitment to racial segregation. Consequently, the various iterations of Christianity follow the contours of the underlying social character as shaped by race, regional culture and economics.

New England still retains many expressions of its ascetic origins. Up until 2012, Massachusetts, Maine, and Rhode Island enforced the so-called "blue laws" which completely prohibited many forms of business on Sunday and Christmas and placed limitations on just what business is permitted on Sunday. For example, up until the 1980s, Massachusetts prohibited the use of any word specifically associated with alcohol, liquor, spirits, beer, or wine in any public advertising. Liquor stores were typically called "package" stores, and these package stores could sell nothing else. Similarly, convenience stores, supermarkets, and other vendors could not sell alcohol. Bars simply had a name with no particular indication of their business. When one of the authors (George Lundskow) was living in Boston in the 1980s, he frequented music clubs known as The Rathskeller (aka the Rat, where many jazz and later rock legends were discovered), Bunratty's, and TT the Bear's Place. Curiously, all of these establishments were primarily bars that introduced live entertainment to cash in on the vast college student crowd in the greater Boston area. Nothing in their name distinguished them from restaurants or any other business. Names that included bar, tavern, or pub were banned. Massachusetts prohibited all commercial business on Sunday until the 1980s, and some still may not open before 12 noon. The State began to allow alcohol sales on Sunday after 12 noon in 1990. On July 25, 2014, the State passed a new law allowing alcohol sales starting at 10am on Sundays. Shock and horror! And this even before all church services have concluded! While every state regulates alcohol and business in some way, those localities, states, and regions with strong religious asceticism and not just strong religious values in general have enacted laws based directly on ascetic religious morality. Most ironically perhaps, the world famous Jack Daniel's distillery in Lynchburg, Tennessee is in a dry county where mountain people are both hard-living and pious. While not surprising perhaps, such laws shape and in turn illustrate the social character of the people who live under them.

Closely connected with religious asceticism, as argued earlier, is the strong sense of social justice. Those areas most known for progressive social activism, the Northeast and the West Coast, as well as parts of the Midwest, all developed from either Yankee asceticism or frontier-farming practicality. Whether in the name of God or functional social relations in business and daily life, social justice serves everyone, who are in all cases equal in certain unalienable ways either before God or their community. Consequently, the opposition to slavery was strongest in New England and the Midwest, just as was the opposition to the US entering World War I. Although the Civil Rights movement started in the South where conditions were most grievous for Black people, it caught on strongly wherever social character demanded social justice. The Black Panthers started in Oakland, California. Malcolm X was shaped by his experiences in Detroit and Chicago where he joined the nation of Islam. Midwestern state universities became some of the most militant in opposition to the war in Vietnam, and the famous SDS (Students for a Democratic Society) socialist and non-violence activist organization started in Michigan. Although Berkeley was a hotbed of radical leftist student and community activism, so too was the University of Wisconsin-Madison, Ohio State, and the University of Michigan. The National Guard shot and killed four protesters at Kent State University in Ohio. Needless to say, Southern universities did not join in the civil rights or the anti-war movements. Whatever their personal beliefs may have been, social commitment and activism are just not in their history or character. It is only quite recently that some Southern universities and statehouses have removed the Confederate flag (originally only the battle flag of the Army of Northern Virginia, as mentioned earlier) and now the predominant symbol of white supremacy, that is generally vehemently denied by many white racist Southerners. Imagine contemporary Germans telling Jews that the swastika is simply a symbol of German pride.[6] Since the swastika is banned in Germany and other countries, neo-Nazis and other right-wingers in Europe and South America often use the Confederate flag in its place (Taylor 2015). Everyone around the world knows that it really stands for white supremacy.

Although the numbers are slowly rising, only 14% of the overall US population claims no religious affiliation, and only 6% of the population identify themselves as atheists (Pew Research, 2012). Aside from the atheists, nearly all of the unaffiliated hold some type of spiritual beliefs and 68% of them do believe in God (Pew Research, 2012). Moreover, the number of Americans who currently say religion is very important in their lives (58%) is little changed since 2007 (61%) and is far higher than in European countries such as Britain (17%), France (13%), Germany (21%) or Spain (22%). Over a longer period, the percentage of Americans who say that prayer is an important part of their daily life was 76% in 2012, the same as it was in 1987 (Pew Research, 2012). Rather than completely reject religion, the trend in the US is moving toward deinstitutionalized religion. Americans still pray even if not in church. Not only does religion still play a strong role in US society, but the particular versions that a person follows are those that resonate with his/her social character. As we pointed out in the previous chapter, Christianity in the United States today includes both a traditional segment of steadfast, indeed authoritarian conservatives, but at the same time, while having historical roots, today there is a rising faith and family left.

To be sure, the totalitarian and authoritarian side of American faith includes some of the New Atheists as much as fundamentalists or other religious-right perspectives. Like their fundamentalist religious counterparts, the New Atheists claim a monopoly of the truth, see the world through a Manichean prism of pure good versus pure evil dichotomy, and hold to the far-right of the political spectrum. Christopher Hitchens, Richard Dawkins, and Sam Harris all call for

---

6   It is of course one of the ironies of history that today, various gay, artistic and leftist Israelis seeking to leave the reactionary government in Israel have made Berlin the most desirable destination for expat Israelis. The fact that one of the most rabidly intolerant societies in history could so radically change in a few generations, is precisely what gives us hope.

an end of faith and religion in any form. While none of them consider their brand of atheism a type of religion, their categorical and automatic rejection of the divine, religion, and faith in any form is a position of faith itself; their rejection of religion is universal and absolute. They won't tolerate anything that in any way resembles faith or religion (Amarasingam, 2010). Indeed, Stahl (2010) sees a clear consistency between the New Atheism and fundamentalist religion, the only difference is that the great enemy is people of faith, rather than the faithless or the infidel. In his book, *The End of Faith*, Sam Harris goes so far as to call on the United States to use its nuclear arsenal to annihilate the Middle East as a means to cleanse the world of the Islamic threat:

> ... the only thing likely to ensure our survival may be a nuclear first strike of our own. Needless to say, this would be an unthinkable crime—as it would kill tens of millions of innocent civilians in a single day—but it may be the only course of action available to us, given what Islamists believe.
>
> HARRIS 2004 p. 129

"An unthinkable crime," he laments, but perfectly acceptable if it achieves the desired outcome of annihilating a religion. Presumably, he would leave Indonesia alone, perhaps because they are not in the Middle East or he is unaware of their existence as the largest Muslim country. He doesn't say whether he would annihilate the more secular countries of Morocco, Tunisia, Algeria, and Turkey, where the populations are nevertheless predominantly Muslim and do include some enclaves of Islamism. Iran strongly opposes the Islamist movement and has done much of the fighting against ISIS, but Harris seems oblivious to factual details, how ironic it is that his thinking mirrors the Abbot of Citeaux Arnaud Amalric in 1209 who, when asked how to differenti-ate faithful Catholics from the Cathar heretics, he infamously told his troops to "*Caedite eos. Novit enim Dominus qui sunt eius.*" That is, "kill them all, and God will know those that are His." In his subsequent *The Moral Landscape* (2010), Harris asserts that the only correct source of morality comes from science, which for Harris boils down to a dispassionately calculated cost-benefit analysis. In any case, one of the great atheist leaders and systematiz-ers of all time, Adolf Hitler, would certainly approve of Harris, as does an admiring segment of the American public that put both *The End of Faith* and *The Moral Landscape* in the top ten on the New York Times bestseller list. As real Americans know, whether Christian or atheist fanatics, righteous violence solves all problems.

The Religious Right and Left

Not all conservative evangelicals are part of the religious right, which also includes the atheist-right, which really constitutes a position of faith premised on devotion to instrumental rationality, not science in a larger sense of curiosity and inquiry. For us, the religious right is not only politically conservative, but what is especially important for us, these political and religious, as well as social and cultural values, reflect an underlying authoritarian character structure. A religious authoritarian believes that the inerrancy of religious scripture or doctrine supersedes science (Apple 2001). In the case of religion specifically, God judges and punishes. He rewards servile devotion to power and simultaneously rewards aggression towards transgressors. Hatred and aggression towards the unbeliever (which includes both false beliefs and non-belief) is not particular to Evangelical Christianity, but is quite typical of any religion that supports or indeed may be part of an authoritarian social order. Here, the Ayatollah Khomeini's version of Shia Islam, the Wahhabist Islam of Saudi Arabia, the fundamentalism of Ultra-Orthodox Jewish settlers in the occupied parts of Palestine and the evangelical Christians of the United States are remarkably similar.[7] A central communality of authoritarian religion is the construction of evil enemies as the negation of the ideal group. For authoritarians, there can be no pure good without pure evil, and this eternal battle rages across all time and places, in every aspect of life (Juergensmeyer, 2003; Wessinger, 2000).

For these reasons, the religious right, including some members of the Tea Party groups, insist that President Obama is not a fellow Christian, but a despicable, socialist Muslim who hates America. To the far-right, he appears to be the archetypal unity of outsider traits, he is Black, liberal, foreign-born and Muslim. And a socialist to boot. And with his fancy college degrees such as Harvard Law School, then teaching at the University of Chicago, he is an intellectual which as we saw means weak and impractical to many conservative Americans. While he is certainly Black (African-American), he is not so liberal as supporters hoped, nor as liberal as opponents have accused him. Of course, he is neither foreign-born nor Muslim. For the authoritarian however, given what has been said about "motivated reasoning," facts and evidence such as a state of Hawaii birth certificate matters less than the emotional unity of

---

7 Many of the settlers on the occupied lands are from secular Russian backgrounds. For them, their fervent nationalism acts much like religion to support the egregious treatment of Palestinians.

perceived and believed outsider characteristics. His birth certificate must be a forgery and part of a Hawaiian (as in, non-white) conspiracy in which left-wing CIA agents planted a birth certificate in the hospital records and put announcements of his birth in Hawaiian newspapers back in 1961 as part of the plot to install the "Kenyan Candidate." We personally prefer the alien, reptilian shape shifter theory in which the Nephilim aliens assumed human forms; Obama and other world leaders including Vladimir Putin, Xi Jinping, Francois Hollande, and Angela Merkel are really the advanced scouts from a protein deficient planet seeking to gather humans for food.[8] Star Trek meets Soylent Green!

Consistent with historical patterns, the Faith and Family Left is interdenominational—much as expressions of the religious right have been. While often lumped together with Evangelicals generally, the Faith and Family Left (FFL) understand scripture and the life of Christ very differently. They also include Jews and Muslims as well. Who are they? As Eboo Patel argues, the important distinction across all the world's religions is the difference between "religious totalitarians" on one side, and those who respect diversity and interfaith cooperation (Patel 2012 p. 94). Furthermore, progressivism in general depends on all people of good faith, regardless of their particular religion or whether they practice any religion at all. Patel identifies a "faith line," which distinguishes the forces of hope and love from the forces of fear and hate. With this basic distinction, we see the contrast of social character that plays out across progressive authors and activists from various faiths, all of which embrace hope and love in opposition to fear and hate. Given the same scriptures, the same social facts, people will interpret and apply religious thought and faith in different ways consistent with their character. For this reason, people interpret and create meaning from faith, in combination with facts and reason.

Although only vaguely considered in academia, numerous expressions of progressive faith abound. For example, Joerg Rieder (2009) draws explicit connections between economic exploitation and a call for Christian activism. Drawing upon Critical Theory and psychoanalysis, Rieder sees a nexus of wealth and power that shapes culture and morality in ways that legitimate

---

8   We could not make this up if we tried. Rather, like the birthers who see Obama as a Kenyan Muslim, other conservatives, especially religious ones, embrace the alien theory and claim that one of Obama's body guards is also an alien shape shifter that was seen at an AIPAC meeting. As we earlier said, they pull these "facts" out of their ever constricted butts. See: http://beforeitsnews.com/alternative/2014/03/reptilian-shapeshifters-from-hell-obama-our -government-and-in-our-society-ultimate-plan-of-destruction-and-the-time-is-now-mind -blowing-videos-and-photos-2918252.html.

the exploitation of labor and endless consumer desire. In the end, he makes a strikingly straightforward conclusion that "like the crucifixion of Christ, the fate of the people on the underside of society has to do with repression. As Christ experienced repression by the religious and political leadership of the time, working people often experience repression by the leadership of their own times, whose goal is to profit as much as possible from the so-called free-market economy" (Rieder, 2009 p. 115). Like Marx before him, Rieder is not content simply to understand the world; he wants to change it.

If we accept the notion that private property is the basis of "freedom" in a capitalist society, then the more private income-producing property a person owns, the more freedoms they enjoy. Moreover, the premise of private property involves force. Owners want to maintain their exclusive domination and control. Rieder (2009) thus argues that capitalism and private property violate the Christian ideals of peace and justice. Citing a long line of Christian theologians, including Augustine, Anselm of Canterbury, and John Wesley, as well as numerous Biblical passages, he argues that God and Jesus emphasize grass-roots rather than top-down authority, mutuality and service rather than control, fulfilled labor that parallels God's redemptive work, cooperative rather than competitive accomplishment, and labor that addresses need rather than profit (Rieder, 2009 p. 152). If a Christian accepts that Jesus called for a radical reorganization of human relations, then the common good, rather than private gain, should be our central principle. Yet, the common good is "not a commitment to some statistical middle-ground" (Rieder, 2009 p. 156). Rather, the Common Good is only as good as the condition of the weakest and least capable. In place of private accumulation then, we should devote ourselves to the "oppressed and despised" as Jesus did. In short, resources should be distributed based on need, not greed. This is what liberation theology called the preferential option for the poor.

Over and over again, FFL writers condemn consumerism as an immoral system that appeals to greed, selfishness, and all manner of unlimited desire. An entire society based on unlimited desire requires unlimited production, which requires an endless and ever-intensifying flow of energy, resources, and the exploitation of labor. This destroys families, society, and nature. Walter Brueggemann (2014) calls for a constant resistance to consumerism and private accumulation, in all ways large and small. He sees the gods of Egypt and other false idols as the gods of commodities. These deities represent the worship of power and wealth. In contrast, the Judeo-Christian God condemns wealth and power. He frees the oppressed by opening the door to radical alternatives, and at least one case, parted the Red Sea so that the oppressed might escape the armies of Pharaoh.

Like the ancient Hebrews, the modern Christians should employ all means available not to simply avoid excess, but to challenge the system that depends on it. Since the commodity system has permeated nearly all aspects of life, resistance can always happen on an everyday, familiar level. For example, multitasking. Although it may appear innocuous on the surface, Brueggemann sees multitasking as an embodiment of the commodity system in which "multitasking is the drive to be more than we are, to control more than we do, to extend our power and our domination" (Brueggemann, 2014 p. 67). Brueggemann also attacks more conventionally significant problems, namely anxiety, which he sees as the inherent outcome of a society based the accumulation of more, and the attendant, coercion, exclusivism, and endless unfulfilling work.

Through interviews Tom Krattenmaker (2013) sees an emerging progressive Christian movement already at work in the streets, a reclamation of sorts to embrace the redemption that Christianity offers, the restoration of community, and in general, to transform social relations from a relation of commodities to commodities and people as objects to relations between real people in common purpose. He argues that this work, so far, has gone largely unnoticed because it works within established legal, business, and congregational frameworks. Christian businesses such as the Noonday Company, a fair-trade company that deals in third-world jewelry, and Food of Life that produces organic breads and other baked goods (with recipes from the Bible) both see social justice and detoxification of the environment as part of God's covenant. Greyston Bakery in Yonkers, NY, founded by a monk, employs the unemployable, such as drug addicts, convicts, and gang-bangers as a means of bringing sustainable prosperity to an impoverished community. When a job opens, Greyston hires the next person on the list; they have no interview of any kind, no background checks, and no drug testing. The company provides all workers with healthcare, daycare and a retirement pension. They still make a profit, and they have been doing it for thirty years. The management team argues that their model of social responsibility as a required aspect of profitability should be rolled out everywhere and codified as law.

Religion and Social Character

As history shows, Christianity in the United States offers two competing visions. One, the more evident and widely known, legitimates the dominance of capital and wealth. Indeed, some televangelists preach the prosperity gospel, that Jesus helps you get rich, at least if you send some money to the preacher who will personally bless the money, at least before buying a mansion or private plane. The other version of Christianity, born when Jesus chased the money changers (early financial speculators) out of the Temple, challenges the legitimacy of capital and wealth and emphasizes social justice. While not a critique of class domination as such, with calls for humans rights and for much higher minimum standards of living, they are now inherently challenging class hierarchy because respect for human rights cannot be achieved within class or race, or gender, or other hierarchies of domination. Given that inequality is inherent in capitalism, and especially, since this inequality is increasing and impacting more and more Americans, the moral values of Christianity clash more directly with the values of accumulation and exploitation.[9]

Nevertheless, American Christianity, like all religion, perhaps like all creeds, philosophies, and belief systems, depends on interpretation, and interpretation depends on underlying social character. Any scripture, and perhaps any complex tome lends itself to multiple readings and interpretations. The words on the page do not speak themselves, but only convey meaning when a mind interprets the words. The Bible supports at least two main lessons, which Erich Fromm (2013 [1976]) sees as a message of patriarchal domination, but at the same time, a competing lesson about peace and love that is achieved when people develop their own full potential. In this effort, people recognize the beauty and frailty of life, such that humanity gains the potential to unite around the one thing that all people truly have in common—death. Only in this realization can we ever live a truly meaningful life.

To have or to be? To devote one's life to accumulating objects and possession, or to enlightenment and creative self-realization? We will return to these questions in our concluding chapters. At the moment, let us just mention that for Erich Fromm, these are the two essentials messages in the Judeo-Christian tradition, and thus in Western Civilization. These doctrines have moved through our history ever since the time of the Roman Empire that valued

---

9   Given our concern is with social character as that which is most typical, our discussion has largely been focused on various Protestant denominations. But we should know that even within Catholic or Jewish American thought the same polarity exists. Thus one author, Lauren Langman, teaches at a Jesuit University and is sometimes asked how a Jesuit University tolerates a sociology department with a number of left-wing radicals. Simple! The Jesuits have long embraced social justice as recently articulated by Pope Francis, himself a product of "liberation theology" that stressed its preferential commitment to the poor and the obligation to resist oppression. Similarly, a number of very progressive Jews, for example, Rabbi Michael Lerner, editor of Tikkun, have long advanced arguments for social justice, both in the United States and the larger world, being especially critical of the ways Israeli governments have treated the Palestinian populations.

domination, conquest, and power. Although many dominated people rebelled against the Empire, there was only one real challenge to its core values and that challenge was based on the radical teachings of an itinerant Jewish carpenter. Mark 6: 3 identifies Jesus as a "tekton," usually translated as "carpenter," but this is mostly by tradition established in early Christianity. A better translation would be more general, perhaps "tradesman." In any case, resistance to the values of Empire came from common people, not from rival elites who only seek to seize the reigns of Empire or replace it with their own form of domination. Western civilization has never resolved this internal conflict between empire and mutual aid, even as the contemporary expression of Empire, neoliberalism, now dominates the world. Just as the struggle between empire and mutual aid rages at the level of political-economy, so does a corresponding battle rage at the level of character. American religion legitimates both, each against the other.

Property rights require enforcement through the force of law and arms to defend boundaries and maintain boundaries between the haves and have-nots. At the level of character, the necessity of exclusion and its possible violation creates suspicion, arrogance, and fear. These emotions become the basis of hate and aggression. The Bible speaks to this character type, with numerous examples of possession, domination, and aggression (Fromm, [1972] 1992). At the same time, the Bible speaks to peace and love, and the joy of true freedom, freedom from property and all manner of desire. Only through forgiveness and mutual aid can we make life better for more people (Fromm, [1972] 1992). This message appeals to people motivated by love. This path leads to true freedom, the freedom to live without suspicion and fear, especially the fear of loss, whether property, money, status, or even one's life. We are free to live with each other, to trust in the goodwill of others and devote ourselves to others, with the real faith that love will inspire others to reciprocate the same mutual aid, respect, and devotion to a common good. As Jesus says (Matthew 5: 38):

> "You have heard that it was said, 'Eye for eye, and tooth for tooth.'"[10] But I tell you, do not resist an evil person. If anyone slaps you on the right

---

10   The initial acronym for the invasion of Iraq was Operation Iraqi Liberation, but when it was noted that that spelled OIL, the name was soon changed. And one of the ironies of history is that much of Iraq's oil has gone to either China or Isis.

cheek, turn to them the other cheek also. "You have heard that it was said, 'Love your neighbor and hate your enemy.'" But I tell you, love your enemies and pray for those who persecute you, that you may be children of your Father in heaven. If you love those who love you, what reward will you get? Are not even the tax collectors doing that? And if you greet only your own people, what are you doing more than others? Do not even pagans do that?"

Jesus overturns the old eye for an eye morality, and then instructs his audience to be good to everyone.

To further reinforce this point of universal benevolence, Jesus tells the story of the good Samaritan (Luke 10: 25–37). The parable begins when an "expert" on the law asks Jesus how to be good. Jesus tells him to be good to your neighbor. The expert then asks, in essence, who the real and deserving neighbors are. Jesus then tells the story of a man who was robbed, beaten, and left for dead. Two people step over his body and keep going. Finally, a Samaritan comes along, whose people are hostile towards the Jews. Nevertheless, he feels sympathy for the man, takes him to an inn and cares for him, and then tells the innkeeper he will return to check on the man and pay any additional bills. The Samaritan asked for no recompense, recognition, or reward. He simply and plainly did all the good he could. Everyone listening to Jesus agrees that the Samaritan did the right thing. Jesus then concludes: "go and do likewise." Taken in context of all the other stories of Jesus in the Gospels, our neighbors whom we should care of are anybody and everybody in need. The real message that Jesus delivers is not to treat others as you want to be treated, but rather: Be Good To Others No Matter How They Treat You.

If this vision seems idealistic, it is. That's the point of religion, to envision an aspirational ideal. The Faith and Family Left takes it seriously, but so too does the authoritarian right who see Jesus as judge, jury, and executioner. To the extent that religion offers multiple and conflicting visions, this reflects corresponding conflicts within the society that creates different religious orientation. In the United States, the competing visions teach unrelenting hard work, aggressiveness, exclusion and punishment of the undeserving, especially those who cannot or will not earn their own way. In today's America, monetary success is the only measure of success that counts. Even laws are for suckers too weak or inept to create their own success. Most of all, there are no guarantees. Hard work and making all the right choices can still lead to mediocrity or failure, just as the devotion to the calling and avoiding sin did not in any way earn salvation for the early Puritans. We all need to accept that life is unfair and unequal. Suck it up, grin and bear it, or takes some risks to change your situation. Legal or illegal, each person stands alone and should expect no help, and give none to others. In this vision, no amount or type of laws or regulations can change the natural and divine order of the strong dominating the weak. This worldview also reformulates the Golden Rule: Do Unto Others Before Others Do Unto You.

In a world of alienated social relations, people experience the world as a collection of commodities, including most public space which is itself increasingly privatized retail or residential space, populated not by people, but by commodities for sale or use. The high importance of prayer in daily American life speaks to this alienation. God is the only one available to hear our hopes and assuage our fears. To the extent that God appears as an authority figure more than as a friend or mentor, then religion reinforces the authoritarian personality, especially in the absence of real, compassionate, human interaction. Nevertheless, people need emotional fulfillment as decisively as they need food and water, and like food and water, emotions can be mass-produced and consumed in commodity form. But just as fast food is high in calories and low in nutrition which necessitates ever more consumption, so commodified emotions provide immediate gratification in the most visceral forms, whether righteous revenge or dick and fart gags, idealized romantic love (e.g. chick flicks) or mindless sex and violence and lots of people and things getting blown up (dick flicks). Such simplistic emotions do not correspond to the complex vicissitudes of real life or the human search for meaning. Unfortunately, a constant diet of simple, "one dimensional" thoughts and emotions creates simple personalities that become easily polarized in a polarized culture reinforcing the dogmatic, black and white thinking that reflects an underlying authoritarianism. Submit to strength. Dominate the weak. Buy a branded identity that promises happiness at a nearby mall or perhaps shop online. This orientation allows very little room for humane tenderness and connection, yet which people crave the more desperately it is denied.

Perhaps Rupert Wilkinson captures modern American identity best, in that the authoritarian personality "has a conscience which is divided against itself with warfare between values of control, namely orderliness and uncompromising strength versus a humane tenderness ... and impulses of affiliation" (1972 p. 34). Americans are "broken rebels" in Wilkinson's view, whose freedom is always plagued by guilt and anxiety, and whose social relations are empty experiences of self-gratification. For this reason, rebellion is against someone or something external and alien, sometimes projected onto actual people perceived as the Other, but in a social psychological sense, the enemy is really one's own insecurity and dissatisfaction with empty consumer abundance and meaningless choices.

Narcissism, which often correlates with authoritarianism, manifests similar feelings of emptiness as one confronts the contradiction between self-conceptions with exaggerated levels of self-worth and the actuality of limited self-accomplishment. This is especially the case when self-worth derives from membership or identification within a "privileged" hegemonic racial or other reference group. For example, it becomes apparent that some white males live far better and accrue far more status and fortunes than other white males. The narcissist feels even more insecure and fearful when non-whites achieve more and the result is narcissistic rage. Default membership as a white person no longer guarantees as much as it did in earlier times. Just as it is for the authoritarian, the god of the narcissist takes on the characteristics of the narcissist, but without the insecurity. God takes on the idealized attributes of the dominant group, especially when the attributes cannot be achieved or forfeited such as race and gender (Prothero 2003). When a valorized identity provides compensation for a lack of social interaction and validation, God serves as the ultimate validation of self-worth that finds no confirmation in recognition in the real world. The authoritarian God reinforces in-group solidarity and exclusion of the Other. Faith in heroes, obsession with uncanny events, doom and gloom attitudes pervade societies rife with alienation and god-figures that replace human interaction (Crouse and Stalker, 2007; Mirisola et al., 2013). Specifically, Teymoori et al. (2014) found that it is only religion that correlates with both authoritarianism and moral authority (and not such things as family or government). The authors carefully note that while all forms of religion correlate with moral authority, only some also correlate with authoritarianism. In such cases, intolerance and aggression increase significantly as the authoritarian believer feels that God sanctifies their own sense of righteousness and simultaneously sanctifies hostility towards transgressors (Blogowska, Lambert, and Saroglou, 2013; Liberman 2014; Lerner, Goldberg, and Tetlock, 1998; Pachterbecke et al., 2011; Shaffer and Hastings, 2007). Americans embrace religion far more than any of their first-world counterparts, and as research shows, authoritarian notions of the divine create sharp in-group and Other divisions and in turn, justify hostility towards anyone perceived as transgressive. On the other hand, religion also provides a countervailing vision that motivates people towards very different notions of empathy and kindness, charity and compassion, mercy and forgiveness, cooperation and equality. Such religious ideals are visions of community, ideals of what Robert Bellah and his co-authors (1992) called the "good society." In their view, impersonal institutions have replaced collective social ties, such that our required commitments are to institutions, not each other. Personal and social ties between people are optional and easily dissolved at any time. This reinforces alienation, social fragmentation and the perception that the world consists of objects which are exchangeable and exploitable as commodities independently of time, place, and self. In other words, the having orientation sees the world as acquiring possessions that can be chopped up and reshaped as desired. People become bodies, or body parts for sexual gratification, or fair-weather friendships based on a mutual contract of ease and convenience. Similarly, as we have noted, contract work, "gig jobs," short term projects and temporary employment precludes commitments to organizations or fellow worker, perseverance, and dedication. Even white collar professionals have become increasing disposable. The good society requires a nexus of personal and social commitment to the collective good based on common conceptions and mutual aid. Towards, this end, a "good society," or what Fromm would call a "sane society" absolutely requires the very human qualities that our modern institutions, by their inherently impersonal, rational structures, functions and logic cannot provide namely love, empathy and compassion.[11] The emotions of religion speak to character, and thus religious devotion is felt as much if not more than thought. Religious beliefs are not really the issue. Community is the issue. Who gets to socialize with whom? Who benefits and who suffers from our way of life?

Whatever our neighborhoods may offer today, genuine and enduring human connections are difficult and uncommon at best because the average American moves every six years. As Roger Salerno argues, community today consists mostly of nearby amenities, such as schools, employment, shopping, and entertainment (Salerno 2003 pp. 179–180). If not forced to move to maintain or improve employment, people typically move to improve access to more and better amenities. However dominant this corporate consumerism may be, Putnam, Feldstein, and Cohen (2004) also see resistance, which they document throughout the country. Religious groups, civic groups, neighborhood improvement groups, social justice groups, and many others continue to organize against the having orientation and attempt to replace it with collective responsibility and shared prosperity, the foundation necessary to support the being orientation and genuine fulfillment through living, through meaningful relationships, rather than consuming and having more and more things.

---

11   This was quite clear to Weber who warned that modern, rational capitalism, entrapped
      us within "iron cages" and gave us "Specialists without spirit, sensualists without heart;
      [and yet] this nullity imagines that it has attained a level of civilization never before
      achieved."

Should we construct our lives on our appetites, or on our hopes and dreams for involvement and understanding, especially of the greatest mystery of all—death? It seems very human that death should be the greatest inspiration to make the world more conducive to life. How should we live, and what happens when we die? Profoundly religious questions, seemingly.

With some ideas about how we should live, a local coalition of progressive activist groups rallied in downtown Raleigh, North Carolina in February 2013 to protest economic injustice and racism (WRAL News, 2013). In February 2014, the largest progressive rally in the South since the Selma to Montgomery march in 1965 occurred (Berman 2014). The 2014 rally and march brought more than 140 coalition groups together to challenge racial, gender, and economic oppression as interconnected systems of injustice from both a moral and political basis. The rally specifically sought to show that people of all races, creeds, orientations, and ages will no longer tolerate racism, sexism, homophobia, the grotesque wealth inequality of our times and a lack of access to quality public education and healthcare. In a similar way, church groups all over the country feed the poor and homeless, operate organic farms, and start up fair trade businesses as part of a new nexus of religious faith, environmental concerns, and social justice. One of the most popular evangelical pastors of the faith and family left, Rob Bell, has always argued simply but fervently, with full faith in God, that no matter what, Love Wins. A loving God would never condemn anyone to hell forever. If God forgives all, then so should we (Bell, 2011). He's not the only evangelical to call for benevolence and solidarity. As Brian McLaren (2012) asks, "Why Did Jesus, Moses, the Buddha, and Mohammed Cross the Road" to which he adds, "not to mention Lao Tzu, Nanak, and Wovoka" (McLaren, 2012 p. 5). Whatever the punchline, McLaren concludes that "is it a joke to think that they would respect one another and be drawn towards one another as friends, allies, and collaborators?" (McLaren, 2012 p. 6). After all, they all teach the solidarity of all people, that everyone has a purpose, and value, and a soul, it's not a sin to be glad you're alive, and death is not the end.

Given the history of the United States, and the extent to which religiosity is deeply anchored within its social character, in the near future, secularism is unlikely to sway the masses towards progressive social relations, but maybe religion, especially the more progressive version of Protestantism, the liberation theology of Pope Francis, and/or the largely Jewish network of progressive spirituality. Let us share the sentiments of William Phips in 1693, who ordered a halt to the witch persecutions, because the "former proceedings were too violent and not grounded upon a right foundation ..." We must likewise abandon the belief that the United States has a special divine mission that our heroes will lead us through blood and fire, annihilate our enemies both here and abroad, so we may rule the world as god intends. Instead, let us recognize a global humanity and common purpose, with the faith and hope that Phips brought to Salem so that we may dissipate "the blak cloud that threatened this Province with destruccion" before endless war and gruesome concentrations of wealth and power dooms us to a cataclysm of each against all.

Summary

The history of a nation and the shaping of its national character, as well as its underlying social character, much like an individual, owes much to the past—yet change still occurs. The persistence of religion has been one of the outstanding features in the United States in contrast to the secularism that accompanied modernity in Europe. Although the Puritanism of the early colonials waned over time and was also transformed in relationship to other versions of Christianity from Appalachia as well as the South, a number of awakenings and schisms increased the diversity and the passionate commitment of people to Christian faith-based groups. Even as its founding fathers declared their independence from England and established the country with a very clear-cut constitution guaranteeing the separation of church and state, most Americans maintained strong religious beliefs and high rates of church membership that has endured till this very day, notwithstanding increasing levels of prosperity and education.[12] Indeed, as we suggest, the persistence of religion may be one of the major qualities of American exceptionalism. But why is this the case?

This question had intrigued de Tocqueville who asked the question as to why, in the absence of a state religion and mandatory church attendance people "voluntarily" attended church and maintained religious beliefs. Anticipating Durkheim, he suggested that religion provided solidarity in a widely dispersed, mobile society. There have basically been three main strands of Christianity in the USA, the ascetic Puritanism of the Yankee North, the more emotional expressions in the central, Appalachian Mid-states, and finally the more patrimonial religions of the antebellum South that basically upheld racial and gender hierarchies. At times the beliefs and practices might well

---

12   There are certain extreme versions of Christian fundamentalism, the Dominionists that
        reject the notion that the US was a legacy of the Enlightenment in which church and state
        were separated, but the US, founded by and for Christians, is a Christian dominion that
        should be led by the truly righteous who will insure Biblical law is the law of the land.
        Among these Dominionists are Ted Cruz, Jerry Falwell, Jr., Sarah Palin and Glen Beck.

overlap, especially when justifying westward expansion and claims to the land whether displacing indigenous peoples or wars against Mexico and Spain.

In the last several decades or so, a major sector of the ruling economic classes have encouraged many religious conservatives to vote for Republicans on the basis of religious issues ranging from women's choice, ready availability of contraception, gay marriage and prayer in the schools, but the result of such voting has been to make the rich richer and many of the religious conservatives, especially small business owners and/or working class people all the poorer by having supported economic policies that have undermined their wealth and status. As we point out, religious beliefs are not homogeneous, and that the majority of Americans are members of more moderate, and in some cases even progressive church-based organizations. Lest we forget, many churches, especially Northern churches, reflecting the more egalitarian social structures of the Midwest, strongly supported emancipation. While the civil rights movement was in large part a movement of progressive African-American churches, opposed of course by the more conservative Southern congregations, especially Southern Baptists, a great deal of material and personal support for the civil rights movement came from northern congregations. Today, for example while most Republicans from dog catchers to would-be presidents proclaim their devout authoritarian versions of Christianity, more progressive faith-based organizations, typically interdenominational, work for various aspects of social justice. As a cultural pattern, anchored within social character as an enduring aspect of subjectivity, religion has had a major impact on American life and will surely do so in the future. Having said that, the fervor of authoritarian religion is more typical of the older, whiter, and more typically, Southerners. Contemporary youth are rapidly eschewing institutional religion in general and conservative denominations in particular. In the 2016 presidential campaign for example, the conservative Christian messages of Rick Santorum and Michael Huckabee fell upon very deaf ears and they dropped out quite early. Although Ted Cruz garnered the evangelical vote, that bloc by itself was not nearly enough to gain the Republican nomination. Unlike many other progressives, and surely quite unlike the "new atheists," we believe that shorn of its authoritarian beliefs and practices, a progressive religious orientation, one that valorizes a general inclusive community, that emphasizes awe and humility, that encourages a quest to understand the meaning of shared experience and the one true reality of death as an inspiration to provide the means to live life to the fullest, must be an essential part of a more humanistic America.

America: Chasing the Pot of Gold

Character and Political-Economy

Let us briefly summarize some of the crucial points we previously made, beginning with the historical nature of social character and the basis of its dynamic change in response to economic and cultural changes. Following what Fromm argued, the rise of the market society shattered the often violent, but highly ordered, highly stable feudal societies of European Christendom. If we start with the installation of Charlemagne in 800, and end in the mid-1600s after the Thirty Years War which devastated Europe and undermined the social relations of feudal patrimonialism and hereditary status, feudalism endured about 850 years; or perhaps over a 1,000 if we see WW I as the end of dynastic rule. In feudal society, each person had a more or less fixed rank, place and identity in the social hierarchy largely determined by birth, gender, territory and sometimes one's occupation or guild membership (many people were thus named, for example Smith, Carpenter, Baker and so on).

The dominant character type of the feudal system, the "receptive character" was not well adapted for dealing with the new and changing conditions and demands of the emerging market society. Economic rewards and "success" were now more likely based on individual effort, people needed to be more independent, assertive, self-controlled and at this point in time ascetic. People were freed from the shackles of the feudal class system, but with that demise, the emergent market society, with its rising bourgeois class undermined, indeed replaced the stable class relations of feudalism. But the changing economic realities and breakdown of the old class system meant there was a great deal of fear, anxiety and uncertainty as economic survival was problematic, social ties were attenuated and people felt more freedom. This prompted what Fromm called the fear of freedom. Slowly but surely, in order to overcome that fear and anxiety, we saw the ascent of an anal retentive-compulsive character structure that Fromm called the "hoarding character" previously mentioned that become the most frequent social character. Given the qualities of thrift, parsimony, orderliness and self-discipline associated with the hoarding character type, not only did such character types readily adapt to the new social conditions of emerging capitalism, but they eventually became the bearers of major economic and cultural transformations. They would spearhead new and different, and more rational religious, political and economic ethics that would require a fundamentally different character structure. Whereas the receptive character expected to "receive" their rank, status, and overall place in the world through tradition, the hoarding type expected to earn their place in the world on his own and "retain" whatever surplus their work produced. This might also include a certain degree of social mobility and self-autonomy and while upward mobility might be economically rewarding, this might lead to "status anxiety" as people moved into newer social locations.

While the hoarding character readily adapted to collapse of feudal traditions and the new and social conditions of capitalist class relations, at the same time the uncertainty of capitalist markets, and the waning of stable communities and networks of support brought a great deal of anxiety, especially for people who sought a more regularized, routinized life. Anxiety of course is a form of fear but unlike fear, the basis is often unclear. Psychoanalytically, the ultimate basis of fear and anxiety is the fear of annihilation, itself rooted in the fear of death. People attempt a variety of ways to deny their own mortality (Becker 1997 [1973]). Thus to overcome this anxiety, in Fromm's words, to "escape from the freedom" that came along with the individual's isolation and more fragile social bonds typical of a market society that left one more vulnerable, some people embraced various "mechanisms of escape" such as submission to a perceived "superior" powers whose "love" and authority would allay one's anxiety. Thus many people readily embraced the authoritarian versions of Protestantism in which a more aggressive male God and his son entirely displaced Mary and the feminist virtues of the caring, sharing, nurturing, and empathic mother who was thrown out of the Holy Family, as Lloyd Warner et al. (1963) so argued in the Yankee City study, a monumental exploration (in five volumes) of Christian family life in America.

While clerics like Hus and Wycliffe gained a small following by criticizing Church practices from nepotism to the sale of indulgences, as the new petit bourgeois classes grew in size and wealth, ever greater numbers began to reject the Catholic Church and embrace the highly authoritarian teachings of Luther, Calvin and Zwingli that stressed submission and in some cases, predestination that evoked "salvation anxiety" that was assuaged by both submission to higher powers, and hard work. Moreover, as we already noted, Protestantism, especially its Calvinist forms, emphasized that salvation was a process between a person and God, not mediated by or dispensed by the Church. Protestantism created a "priesthood of the believers" that required they be literate enough to read the Bible, and just coincidentally the Gutenbergs had developed the printing press to make mass distribution of books possible. When Luther posted his 95 theses criticizing many of Church's teachings and practices, especially the sale of indulgences, he directly challenged the established Church authority and the Reformation had begun. On the one hand, Protestantism "disenchanted the world," and dispelled any sense of spirits, animism, magic, mystery, and even godly miracles. One reason many young people today flock to various Harry Potter, horror, sci-fi, vampire and other supernatural movies and TV shows, is that for a few brief moments, they can be transported back to a time before Protestantism dispatched dragons from the world and erased magic and imagination and replaced it with instrumental rationality. All of existence was now seen as derived only and directly from God's master plan in which each individual had a particular instrumental role. Protestant asceticism also dismissed the saints and reduced the role of the Virgin Mary to a supporting figure. This rationality, Instrumental Reason, also played a major role in fostering the rise of modern science, and eventually, rational modernity. The "new" modern, more masculine world no longer had a place for "feminine" qualities such as compassion, cooperation, and forgiveness which were relegated to the household as a new and emerging "private sphere" which would become the site of "true womanhood" and eventually become a bourgeois "haven in a heartless capitalist world." Despite the ascetic notions of (Protestant) Christian virtue, as Marx noted, the bourgeois not only had the wives and daughters of their proletarians at their disposal, but common prostitutes as well. Nevertheless, seducing each other's wives became its own sport.[1]

Moreover, the rise of mass literacy further enabled the direct, individual relationship to God and fit better with the kinds of economic individualism now required in the new market society. But while the embrace of Protestantism solved one set of psychological problems of fostering a new iteration of social character better adapted to the new market society, its theology created another set of problems, namely uncertainty and anxiety over one's salvation in the next life. Having transformed work from an odious curse or a plain necessity into a "moral calling," it legitimated and sanctified a compulsive commitment to work as a long term, routinized career, which along with asceticism, became a typical quality for the new social character. For some adherents of the new Protestant faiths, the mainstream versions had not gone far enough in either liturgy (practices of services) or doctrines and

---

1   We have few details the about the actual sexual practices of the American bourgeoisie much before the late 20th Century Century. They did not parade their sexuality in public like the Kardashians and many others do today. We do know that the Puritans were not quite as Puritanical they claimed. Southern slave-owners and their sons often raped slave girls and women. Indeed this was quite acceptable and in fact legitimated as "whitening up" the slaves and increasing their labor supplies since the offspring were considered slaves. Yes, the one drop of blood rule.

they demanded a greater level of purity and reform. In response, they established their own Puritan churches. The "narcissism of petty differences" can often lead to the most violent of internecine conflicts over issues that would seem invisible or irrelevant to outsiders. And thus, a small number of devout Puritans left England and the Church of England that needed purification, and came to settle in a new and then unknown land. While to be sure the early years of the settlements were quite trying and difficult, and many perished, ultimately they not only survived but within a generation or so, the colonies began to prosper. There are many reasons why this was the case but among the important ones that we've noticed were the "freely" available and abundant resources of the verdant land, isolation from European wars and conflicts, the absence of landed estates and the absence of a State mandated religion that required membership and tithes. These conditions would prove quite conducive to creating an unfettered opportunity structure both economically and spiritually to create a sense that anything is possible with enough work and determination. As long as success, especially wealth, accrued from one's own work, the accumulation of wealth was considered morally acceptable, but this very economic success led to at least two adverse consequences.

First, the early colonial leaders regarded their settlements as moral communities that were held together by strong bonds of commitment and devotion as exemplified in the covenant and embodied in Winthrop's "city on the hill" sermon. Spoiled by their own success, the rapid the growing prosperity broke social commitments of the covenant of believers and eroded the values of asceticism (Bellah, 1992). While the first generations or two of settlers barely eked out a subsistence, the opportunities of the new land were such that in time some people prospered more than others. This was especially true for the various skilled tradesmen and artisans, ship builders, whalers and sailors, living in the growing small towns or cities. Meanwhile, the plantation owners of the South prospered as their tobacco and cotton were much in demand, especially in England.

In 1636 Harvard University was established by the Massachusetts Bay Colony largely to train ministers, but nevertheless it was home to the first printing press in the early colonies. In 1700 Yale was created. By the middle of the 18th Century, the Crown still appointed the governors, but most of the members of the colonial parliaments, as well as local magistrates and many clergy came from the educated classes of native born businessmen whose economic positions and educational attainments had somewhat tempered and moderated the harshness of early Puritanism. Thus for example, Max Weber considered Benjamin Franklin as an exemplar of the "Protestant ethic" given his emphasis on work, frugality, honesty, and practicality. The extent to which Franklin practiced his own preaching is inconsistent at best. He may have been "early to bed," but that was probably because of his "rock star" popularity among the damsels he encountered as the American ambassador to France. Was the bed to which he so early went his own? Perhaps there was some truth to Mark Twain's assertion that Franklin had proclaimed that "masturbation was the best policy" although prior to modern plumbing, there was no shortage of cold baths as well.

Secondly, Franklin and many of the others that constituted the leadership classes of the revolution and new nation were typically Deists who believed in some kind of God or Supreme Being, but the founding fathers were surely not fervent hellfire and damnation believers like John Winthrop, Increase or Cotton Mather. As previously discussed, religion played different roles in different regions of the early nation. Moreover, religion was further transformed as it moved further west. Southern religiosity was especially authoritarian and supported racial and social hierarchies, slavery, as well as patriarchy. It was particularly punitive toward transgression. That legacy is yet evident today insofar as most of the executions that still take place in the United States are in the states of the old Confederacy or Western states to which Southerners, especially Civil War veterans migrated. Texas is of course the number one executioner and their governors and states attorneys pride themselves on rarely giving clemency.

The rising business classes that were just a few generations removed from the early settlers became well-schooled, often in English universities where they learned arts, sciences and indeed philosophies of their time. These philosophies included the various scholars, critics, and *philosophes* of the Enlightenment which would have included Hobbes and Locke, especially the notion of legitimacy resting upon the consent of the governed. However radically different their thought, they argued for social contract theories that undermined the religious legitimations for dynastic rule in favor of human choices of trading "freedom" for security. The American Thomas Paine went even farther to declare the union of church and state to be the most heinous and oppressive form of government possible. However, they all seemed to miss reading Rousseau on the scourge of private property. Even while the radical Paine critiqued authority and government, he was willing to leave class relations intact assuming that a civilized society could guarantee a decent minimum quality of life for everyone by sharing the wealth. "I care not how affluent some may be," Paine writes in *Agrarian Justice* (2010 [1796]) "provided that none be miserable in consequence of it." So, their class based educational background that we now call "cultural capital," would become evident insofar as these people became the vanguards of revolutionary class that deplored monarchy as tyranny, valorized liberty and equality and in turn declared independence from Britain. They were themselves willing to fight in that conflict and eventually they won to establish a democratic republic, even if only rich, white men could actually vote. Paine later went to France and actively joined their revolution.

Back in the newly formed United States, the founders crafted a constitution that established a very strict separation of church and State. As Article VI, clause 3 of the US Constitution states, "No religious Test shall ever be required as a Qualification to any Office or public Trust under the United States." The First Amendment also adds that "Congress shall make no law respecting an establishment of religion, or prohibiting the free exercise thereof." As for the personal thoughts of the Founders, consider:

> I contemplate with sovereign reverence that act of the whole American people build a wall of separation between Church & State.
>
> THOMAS JEFFERSON, letter to the DANBURY BAPTISTS (1802).

> Christian establishments tend to great ignorance and corruption, all of which facilitate the execution of mischievous projects.
>
> JAMES MADISON, letter to WILLIAM BRADFORD, Jr. (1774).

> The purpose of separation of church and state is to keep forever from these shores the ceaseless strife that has soaked the soil of Europe in blood for centuries.
>
> JAMES MADISON, Letter objecting to the use of government land for churches (1803).

Although the Founders strongly supported the separation of the church from state power, they still supported the leadership claims of white, male, economic elites. Let us recall that in the late 18th Century, the majority of people were still rural farmers. The "big cities" like Boston, Philadelphia and New York, and even New Orleans (still part of France), were relatively small towns by today's standards. New York did not become a relevant economic actor until the late 1840s when the Erie Canal enabled the movement of goods from the Midwest and frontiers to the Atlantic Ocean. Then of course it mushroomed and eventually became the largest city in the United States. But what does become important for our argument is a growing class of business elites and how that class largely controlled the government. To a great extent, the political history of the United States is the history of the business class and its battles and victories over various rival elites and other possible challenges, especially over the Southern plantation owners, family farmers, and organized labor.

We previously pointed out how the landowning plantation owners of the Deep South embraced an aristocratic style of gracious living more similar to European nobles than the more frugal business classes of the Yankee Northeast. But as the northern states began to industrialize and diversified trade, Northerners would become wealthier. Economically, we see the basis of the Civil War as the outcome of fundamental conflicts between the industrial systems of the North based on "free" wage labor paid to workers and the independent family farms of the Midwest, versus the neo-feudal, agricultural society of the South based on slavery. Despite their conflicts, the Northern textile industries relied on Southern plantations to provide the needed cotton. At that time, slavery was highly productive. the brutality of whips, guns, and splitting of families are powerful motivators. Once the Civil War began, the South of course cut off cotton to the North as well as from Britain as an attempt to force Britain to join the Confederate side. Suffice to say, Britain refused this attempt for many reasons, and among other things, quickly developed cotton production in its other colonies, particularly in Egypt, the Sudan and India. Napoleon III committed France to support whatever Britain decided. This isolated the South politically and marginalized it economically. From our critical social psychological perspective, wealthy Southerners went to war to not only maintain their profitable slave based system, but to maintain their patrician values, identities and lifestyles, that depended on a sense of racial superiority that was legitimated through religion that morally elevated rich whites above poor ones, and poor whites above the Black slaves. While racist attitudes appear throughout the United States, racism was the single most powerful and meaningful element in Southern white identity across all classes. A similar dynamic has informed many other conservative, reactionary populists mobilizations in American history such as the Know Nothing Party, the KKK, and more recently the Tea Party (Langman and Lundskow 2012; Lundskow 2012) and the Trump campaign.

After the Civil War, industrialization, already more developed in the North, proceeded quite rapidly, and four things become important to us at this point in our story. With the rise of industrialization that included railroads, now spanning the new nation, mining and steel production, we also saw the rapid growth of cities, the rise of large hotels and department stores and growing stock markets and banks to finance the ever-expanding production. When the expanding railroad networks connected the Great Plains to the Eastern seaboard, Chicago became a meatpacking center and an important innovation emerged, the assembly line or perhaps we should be more accurate and say the "disassembly" line. Cattle and hogs came in one door and were then continuously proceeded along a number of steps where the animal was first slain, its skin removed and its carcass was broken down into various cuts of meats, bones, organs, connective and vascular tissue. As the meatpackers said, all that was left was the oink and the moo. In the early 20th Century Henry Ford reversed that disassembly line and began to use an assembly line to mass-produce cars and as they say, "the rest is history."

By the end of the 19th Century, we began to see the rise of a new aristocracy of industrial-financial wealth led by the "robber barons" or "captains of industry" depending on one's own values. Think of Carnegie, Vanderbilt, Pullman, Field, Duke, Rockefeller, Morgan, Gould, Harriman, Frick or Orfield. These business leaders, the .01% of their age, garnered vast amounts of wealth and lived in opulent estates that rivaled Versailles or the Czar's Summer Palace. On the one hand many of these men had come from modest backgrounds, but on the other, the qualities of the typical social character of that era, the hoarding character that we have described, individualistic, ascetic, aggressive, and perhaps an authoritarian or a social dominator, were such that these men were especially ambitious, some would say extremely ambitious, as well as ruthlessly determined to acquire wealth and power by any means necessary. They seemed to have little empathy for other human beings and often acted in ways that might cause people harm, ranging from job loss to outright deaths when safety standards were ignored. Indeed, strike breakers were explicitly hired to use violence against strikers. Thus, private paramilitary forces such as the Pinkerton's were often employed to suppress labor unrest and at times they acted like contemporary "death squads" to eliminate progressive leaders. As we previously saw with Mother Jones and the Colorado strikers, John D. Rockefeller was only moved to enact safety reforms after months of strikes that ended in a barrage of gunfire that killed 31 people. Although authoritarianism and the Social Dominance Orientation are different characteristics, they are not mutually exclusive. As Robert Altemeyer (2006) found, the double-high is both rare and extremely dangerous. Such people believe that they are both inherently superior to everyone else, and they perceive themselves on a divine or other transcendent mission to change the world and will tolerate no hindrance.

As the barons of industry ascended the economic ladder, they moved further and further away from typical strivers who still held to firm moral commitments. In contrast, the new industrial rich were motivated by an achievement orientation that discarded the moral regulation of the Puritan work ethic and morphed from asceticism into insatiable greed and a lifestyle of opulent ostentation. As that happened, they became more and more isolated from both their own origins and the plight of ordinary people. When they get married and have children, they employ various servants to raise and pamper their children who learn class domination quite early in that nannies, maids, drivers and servants are there to serve them. From the earliest years their children learn to dominate, control and subordinate the less fortunate. They attended elite private schools and employ tutors to help them get into the elite schools, although legacy status and monetary "contributions" facilitate the process. Between family connections, exclusive social networks of private clubs for golfers or yachtsmen, philanthropies for elite cultural pursuits, e.g. museums, symphonies or opera halls, elite social networks facilitate entry for well-paid careers. The subsequent generations of elites moved even further from ordinary people and completely lose touch with them.

Chris Hedges recalls that as a student on scholarship at an elite prep school, he got to know these people firsthand. He learned just how vile, venal and morally bankrupt was the oligarchic class and soon realized how they were in fact his class enemies and as such, he learned to hate them more and more (Hedges, 2015). As a foreign reporter, he could see firsthand the death and destruction this class saw as legitimate expressions of the national interests in the form of their wealth and profits. As we will see, this upper class, whether drawn from the older types of "hoarding characters," or the more recent and seemingly personable types, more typical of the more narcissistic, manipulative "marketing character," have themselves morphed into permutations of traditional American social character that are highly driven, talented, yet morally bankrupt. Sennett (1998) argues that the demands of neoliberal globalization require flexibility, and not simply as the capacity to readily change jobs in order to earn a living, but a highly flexible sense of moral values that justifies insatiable greed. Yet these elites with an unlimited sense of entitlement and complete indifference to the workers they dehumanize, they regard other people, workers and even their own families as disposable. As they gain more and more power, citizens in general become disposable and elite concerns with the general welfare of the nation wane. Economically, these extremely wealthy individuals collectively constitute a plutocratic class that has grown ever more isolated from and indifferent to the concerns of ordinary people. They live in various mega million dollar condos, gated and guarded estates with a variety of servants to clean, cook and tend the grounds. And quite often then have a number of residences that might include ski chalets, tropical villas, and mega yachts.[2] They have chauffeurs to drive everyone around, they often use private

---

2   Many of the yachts for the uber-rich today, sometimes exceed 600 feet long with billion-dollar price tags. Indeed, one yacht, a mere 100 footer belonging to an anonymous Malaysian, was plated in platinum with a gold bottom and cost close to 5 billion dollars. No, not a typo; that's five billion dollars. Meanwhile, Paul Allen, a founder of Microsoft just ran his mega yacht through a coral reef in the Cayman Islands destroying three basketball courts worth of coral.

helicopters to avoid traffic and when they travel far, they fly on comfortable private jets. No TSA lines or checks for them—nor cramped coach seats and dreadful airplane food.

Psychologically, these elites constitute a class of social dominators, as we discussed in Chapter one. On the surface, their finely honed marketing personalities may appear easy-going, jovial, and friendly, but they didn't get or stay rich and powerful by being nice or generous. Their well-honed social graces are purely ingratiating and self-serving. The film *Born Rich* (2004) by Jamie Johnson, heir to the Johnson and Johnson fortune, reveals how self-centered, selfish, and arrogant his class compatriots are. Men and women both typically display various expressions of grace and charm. Some pose as intellectuals, some as shy, and some as modest, and some even pose as hard-working professionals. In all cases though (except maybe Jamie himself) that act fades quickly in each interview to expose the complete lack of interest in anyone or anything beyond their own privileged lives. Some play at a career, such as Cody Franchetti who designs some truly hideous men's sport coats, but it's a hobby only; he doesn't slog it out with designers in the hypercompetitive fashion scene that is New York City. None have any sort of skills to actually earn a living or any interests beyond money and the indulgent lifestyle it buys.

While most of the newly rising industrial elites of the 19th Century or the finance elites of the present may not have studied economics or sociology, they have supported and embraced Sumner's "social Darwinism," which intentionally or not, fused classical, liberal economics with ideological interpretations of Darwin's theory of natural selection to contend that the successful capitalists were the "fittest," as in the most superior of people, and that superiority enabled them to survive and prosper. Such views were already foreshadowed by the Protestant distinction of the chosen, the elected that had been blessed by God and the unchosen, the damned who were morally deficient. For Darwin, the "fittest" refers to the best adapted, or as he concluded, it is not the smartest or the strongest or the fastest that survives; it is the best adapted. Most of the higher animal species, and indeed for most of human history, it has been sharing, caring and mutual support that enabled a group to survive. In contrast, the notion of "survival of the fittest" in the social Darwinist sense is not a scientific theory at all, but rather an ideology that justifies class domination and legitimates the economically successful dominators as being inherently "better" than other people. It is definitely not a theory of collective (species) adaptation, but in contrast, one that celebrates shrewd, ambitious individuals who, more often than not, are quite unscrupulous. While not formally stated, the late 19th Century of industrial capitalism and the current 21st Century era of finance capital represent the classical expressions of free-market economic theory (that is, unregulated market capitalism) rooted in Smith and Ricardo. Such people are personifications of the ideals of the bourgeois classes. The basic point of this self-serving ideology is that the economy should be unfettered by government regulations and controls. Thus when the market is free, given the nature of comparative advantage, then the "invisible hand" will insure the prosperity of the best and brightest. The function of government was to maintain domestic harmony, or more aptly, more accurately, expressed, the function of government is to monopolize the means of violence to control and suppress workers, limit their pay, and keep supply lines open, which means to use armies to invade and plunder resources of other people and navies to protect that plunder from other plunderers.

In the late 19th and early 20th centuries, the financial and industrial factory empires of America, including mines, railroads, packing houses and the great department stores and hotels required large armies of poor workers and thus at that time, the United States welcomed the "huddled masses" of immigrants, primarily poor Irish, Germans, Italians, and central Europeans, especially oppressed Jews from Russia and Poland. Millions flocked to the new "land of milk and honey" where the streets were "paved with gold," the same gold that filled the pots at the ends of the rainbows where the leprechauns frolicked. Nevertheless, with the growth of factory production, the newly dominant industrial capitalists created their own contradiction, an organized proletariat class might become a counterforce. Danger lurked among these masses of immigrants and workers since many of these Europeans had been members of labor unions and/or left wing parties, sometimes even socialist parties. Membership in such parties was quite typical for European workers. There had of course been indigenous socialist movements like the Knights of Labor. And so the late 19th through the mid-20th Century, became a time of labor organization, agitation and strikes along with strikebreakers and goon squads to suppress workers' demands for better pay and safer working conditions.

Like all the other demarcations in US history, capital versus labor was not clearly demarcated. Many American labor unions, including many American socialists held nativist views toward immigrants which of course served to divide and separate workers from each other, much of the history of labor struggle in America has been the use of private security firms, ethnic goon squads and strikebreakers to displace workers and then replace them with another ethnic group, only to find that one day the newer workers were protesting the same oppressive conditions. The capitalists then hired a different ethnic group or population to break the new round of strikes and replace the workers once again. Ronald Reagan, for example, used military flight controllers to break the PATCO air traffic controllers strike and then decertify the union.[3] Now of course, this processes has generally come to an end insofar as most industrial jobs have been automated or exported, while many companies have moved to right to work (for less pay) states. Today unionized labor includes only about 6.6% of the private sector (Bureau of Labor Statistics, 2015). This is too small a number to exert much pressure.

Capitalists and government long attempted to violently suppress the labor movement, as for example with the Colorado miners and strikes at Pullman and demonstrations at Haymarket Square. This was the time that saw the growth of the Pinkerton's and urban police departments that were primarily concerned with defending the properties and interests of the wealthy from the onslaughts of the "barbarians." While there are many struggles and many victories for workers, the economic collapse of 1929 and the Great Depression hit hard. Following the utter ineptitude and inaction of the Hoover administration, foreshadowing the George W. Bush tragedy, FDR won the election of 1932 and began to initiate a number of progressive social programs and aid that were very unpopular with the capitalist elites. These would include the NRA (National Recovery Act), the CCC (Civilian Conservation Corps), the WPA (Works Project Association) and the TVA (Tennessee Valley Authority) for starters.[4] Of course the economic elites accused him of being a socialist and/or a communist (though most capitalists might not know the difference), and some even suspected he was a Jew (at that time anti-Semitism was still a powerful force, Henry Ford even published the *Protocols of the Elders of Zion*). In fact, a cabal of the very rich capitalists allegedly tried to organize a military coup that would replace the "communist" FDR with a more fascist-friendly leader, someone more likely to join with Nazi Germany than with Great Britain and France, perhaps a popular figure like Charles Lindbergh, who would "save" the United States or at least preserve the profits and properties its elites.[5] But when they picked the most popular military officer, General Smedley Butler to organize

---

3   Reagan's appeal included authoritarian appeals to working class Democrats, the "Reagan Democrats" who supported Reagan for cracking down on the unwashed, oversexed hippies as well as promising to end the alleged welfare queens in pink Cadillac's, collecting welfare under 5 names for 6 children, each by a separate father. Thus people are more likely to vote their identities and prejudices than their class interest. And by the way, Reagan had once been the president of the Screen Actors Guild. Moreover, the general wage stagnation began with Reagan.

4   Such investments in public infrastructure were indeed socialistic, but Roosevelt was not a socialist. Public investment was a means to facilitate commerce and therefore in the long run, promote capitalism.

5   http://www.dailykos.com/story/2005/02/27/95580/-The-Real-Plot-to-Overthrow-FDR-s -America Accessed 03/23/2015.

the military, they found out that for some soldiers, American patriotism meant love of one's country and not love for its scheming elites.[6]

Although the Depression intensified class conflict and brought the US closer to a broad socialist movement, this proved fleeting. FDR's New Deal saved American capitalism from itself. The federal government employed vast armies of men to build roads and infrastructure from coast to coast, while regional efforts such as the TVA brought electricity and the modern world to remote and impoverished rural areas, particularly throughout Appalachia. Artists were hired to decorate post offices and other public places. While not quite a socialist revolution, programs of redistribution, government assistance, and "pump priming" entered the mainstream. After World War II, Republican Dwight Eisenhower promoted the Federal Interstate System, which once again brought federal organization and money to many regions, states, and localities. And thus groups like the John Birch society, a prominent right-wing group of the 1950s, called Eisenhower a conscious agent of the Communist Party, and as we have pointed out before, one legacy of the Protestant work ethic and early American forms of "civic activism" sharply disdained any government involvement in the economy, except of course for morally permissible activities that would police morality (especially in bedrooms), punish the undeserving or spread American greatness abroad through subversion and overthrow of "unfriendly" governments with military force if needed. Thus there is considerable support for government spending such as for prison construction, domestic spying, military deployments to resource-rich areas, and purchases of extremely expensive military hardware with very little use in most contemporary conflicts. Nevertheless, the post war government programs have created jobs, kept money in circulation, and in conjunction with federal assistance programs, raised vast numbers of people out of poverty, put many people through college, and created a huge middle class that could look forward to a comfortable retirement. It's nearly impossible to imagine today how once upon a time a leading Republican and leading Democrat in the US Senate, Bob Dole and George McGovern, collaborated to invent the food stamp program in 1970 (Armstrong, 2014).

Although the 1930s were largely a period of economic touch and go, ups and downs, and despite the many programs of FDR, the economy did not show consistent growth. Then, on December 7, 1941, the Imperial Japanese Navy

---

6   Butler is best known for his memoir and analysis of his military service in which he claimed "war was a racket" that basically served the economic interests of the rich who got richer, while the poor were slaughtered or wounded. See: https://www.youtube.com/watch?v=EI3lckqaSko Accessed 09/14/2016.

attacked Pearl Harbor. A few days later Germany declared war on the United States. Thereafter, the federal government embarked on one of the most massive and concentrated periods of government supported mass production of guns, tanks, ships, planes and various other war material in history. The era culminated in the Manhattan project that developed the first deployable atomic bomb.

What concerns us however is that after the war, when German and Japanese factories had been leveled to piles of rubble, the United States, with half of the world's production capacities left intact, had become the most powerful economic, political and military power in the world. Meanwhile, millions of returning veterans from World War II would not return to the small towns and farms they came from. They wanted job training or college educations to pursue different and better lives. The GI Bill enabled millions of soldiers to attend college who would otherwise be unable to afford it, and the bill became the model for financial aid that opened college to millions more people. Between the allocation of almost all production toward the war effort and the lack of any but the most basic consumer goods, there was a huge pent up demand. At the same time, households accumulated large amounts of cash during the war years when consumer goods were scarce, the huge market in war bonds to fund the war and to control inflation could now be redeemed for cash. Bingo! An explosion of mass consumption led to ever growing consumer markets with an ever growing cornucopia of goods as factories again produced cars, appliances and radios. The textile mills and apparel industries moved from making military uniforms to civilian fashions. These developments meant that the large corporations began to employ vast numbers of relatively well-paid union workers to produce the goods, and at the same time, the corporations enabled growing numbers of the newly minted veterans, now college graduates, opportunities to join the managerial classes. VA loans enabled many of the returning veterans to buy homes in the rapidly expanding suburbs that were dependent upon a massive roadbuilding project and the Interstate Highway System that enabled people to get back and forth to their homes. This vastly increased the need and market for automobile production. In order to get this massive spending bill through the Congress, Eisenhower "sold" it as an essential part of America's defense that would enable the rapid transportation of men and material in case of an atomic war. By the time the system was completed, Russia had enough hydrogen bombs to incinerate the US a dozen times. But we could have destroyed them at least 50 times.

American individualism and the concurrent ethic of self-interest rapidly grew from approximately 1945 to about 1980 as a consequence of two things. First, we saw and as Thomas Piketty (2013) argues, the postwar bubble of rapid economic growth was an exception to historical trends because World War II destroyed much of the world's industrial capacity and especially of US free-market rivals—Germany, France, Britain, and Japan. The only other surviving industrial capacity and infrastructure was in the Soviet Union which had other priorities and technologies that were not oriented to consumerism. They made and still make some of the best weapons in the world, and produce some good software and can still grill some tasty big-ass steaks, but they struggle to make a decent car, cellphone, or refrigerator.[7] To this day, nobody does theme parks as well as the Americans. Second, we note that the power of individualism in America has been such that people attribute their economic success to their own virtues and talents and ignore the massive federal government investments that have provided the necessary infrastructure (highways, dams, railroads and air traffic control system), food, medicine, support for their education, and product safety.[8] Farmers and ranchers, now corporations, not Grannie and Gramps on the small farm, as well as oil, gas and coal companies receive huge subsidies to make them profitable, while those who profit the most are often the most vocal supporters of "free trade" who decry government involvement in the economy. The availability of capital, and widespread prosperity after the War gave large segments of the population ever growing disposable income while government subsidies for food and education, and tax deductible mortgages kept costs low. Vast numbers of Americans moved to suburbia, bought cars, often two, and could even afford a family trip to enjoy the manufactured magic of Disney.

After a dramatic and decisive victory against Fascism, the unchallenged power of the United States, and the rapidly growing affluence, signs of divine Providence guiding American destiny seemed eerily and profoundly real. At the same time, a new evil enemy appeared, godless communism. Although United States Marines had invaded Russia to fight alongside the czar's armies, they soon learned that the great masses of people were opposed to their incursion and the hostility toward the czar and Boyars was quite widespread, they

---

7   Moreover, governments out side the US often provide direct financial support for research-intensive industries, especially the automobile industry.

8   It is only when large numbers of people are struck by salmonella or e-coli in their burgers, pizzas, salads or tacos, that people see some of the functions of government and the FDA and CDC. Of course the high fat, high salt and high sugar contents of such foods, indeed most fast foods, soft drinks and most processed food is a clear risk for obesity (and here the USA is only #2 behind Mexico), diabetes, heart disease and cancer. But in this case, the power of agribusiness joined with food producers to minimize, if not hide the health risks of this "normal" diet. And much of that "normal diet," perhaps fast food burgers as the best example, is a major cause of environmental despoliation.

wisely left. That lesson was lost to history. After World War II and the expansion of the Soviet Union through military conquests in Eastern Europe, a bipolar world emerged based on different geopolitical interests and there ensued a Cold War. Within a short time, the Soviets had developed an atomic bomb and for many years the world was again a very dangerous place. The communists not only threatened America's economic and political interests, but threatened to undermine our very way of life that had so pleased God and shined like a beacon of salvation for everyone yearning to breathe free, worship God and go shopping in the newly sprouting shopping centers and malls. Communism threatened to close both the department stores and the churches that had become interchangeable sites for meaning, community and identity. Intense fear and hatred of communism, rooted of course in the deeply rooted individualism of traditional American social character that disdained government, valorized an amorphous freedom and love of God became the dominant theme in American culture and politics until the Soviet Union fell. Rabid anti-communism not only enabled popular support for interventions into Korea, Vietnam, and dozens of lesser incursions, but authorized a revival of the Un-American Activities Committee, this time with Senator Joseph McCarthy leading a charge to purge alleged communists from the government and eradicate communist influence from and every book, mind and utterance. Communist plots were "seen" everywhere, and Senator McCarty, with a list of names in his hand, accused the State Department of being riddled with spies and collaborators. The most sinister threats to the American way of life allegedly came from the "culture industries" in Hollywood in which a number of eminent screenwriters and actors were seen as communists and put on blacklists such that they could not work. Finally, when ethnic music, the jazz and blues of African Americans had morphed into rock "n" roll in the late 50s, conservative religious leaders deplored its decadence, immorality, and not so hidden sexuality in the vibrant oscillations of hips and lower body regions that supposedly disposed youth to atheism, premarital sex, and of course communism. Who knew?

Despite the many fears of communist infiltrators everywhere, and the threat of all-out nuclear war (yet somehow the back yard bomb shelters of suburbia offered unassailable protection, at least in the minds of suburbanites), the country generally prospered. A rapidly expanding middle-class of well-paid factory workers, corporate managers and other professionals enjoyed increasing standards of living as evidenced in the proliferation of shopping malls, television programs, the vast numbers of new cars with style, power, and luxury replete with huge tail fins, and endless advertising on billboards, radio and television. Middle-class economics and politics promoted a kind of give-and-take centrism. The rich will still be rich, and some people will still be poor, but far more people would live somewhere in the middle income brackets, such that broad-based growth and prosperity created a social stability that rewarded people who prefer cooperation, consistency, and commitment.

Society has changed dramatically since the halcyon days of William H. Whyte's *The Organization Man* (1956), in many ways a testament to, more than an analysis of middle-class ethics, manners and worldviews. The organization man subordinated his personal feelings and ambitions to the organization, and in exchange for his conformity, loyalty and devotion to the organization, whether corporate, government, educational, management, or research, he received job security, regular pay raises, healthcare, and ample vacation time. As Whyte (1956) observed, "Only a few are top managers or ever will be ... but it is their values that set the American temper" (p. 4). The values and dreams of the vast middle of Americans provided their lives with work and leisure consisting of almost Norman Rockwell like images of warm, loving nuclear families congregating around a backyard grill on a patio overlooking a neatly groomed bright green suburban lawn around a house accessed by a tree lined road. Sitting in the driveway was the American made automobile of ever advancing style and power. Subordination of the self to collective goals, from which the individual also benefits, seems decisively un-American by today's standards. Even at that time, however, a growing bohemian culture of resistance and discontent drawing upon French existentialism and a beat generation emerged that critiqued and rejected the emptiness, sterility and even the dominant sexual norms of the time that Alfred Kinsey found most Americans had privately rejected in actual practice. While surely the beatniks were a rather small segment of the population, they provided the seeds that would blossom as the counter culture of the 60s that, as we have mentioned extolled sex, drugs and rock "n" roll and began the culture wars that have lasted till this day. And as most know, the fornicators won, the bible thumpers lost, but they have not yet formally surrendered.

How distant seems the postwar social contract and growing affluence. Between the forces of automation and globalization, especially its neoliberal forms, stable, long term, organizational careers have disappeared. The work of Sennett (2006; 1998) has shown how the changing nature of work in today's flexible economy has led to fundamental conflict of self and the nature of work compared to the earlier generation of the organization man. The demands and nature of work today in the "winner take all economy" requires lean, mean, flexible organizations with limited hierarchy that can rapidly change, grow or contract in relationship to market forces. These flexible institutions expect flexible kinds of people who can easily change skills, cope with episodic work who may only work on a specific project then move to another company. Today, people are likely to have eleven employers in their lives and often change locations throughout life. Consequently, identities must be flexible as well. Instead of the hierarchy of managers and long term relationships with co-workers who often become close friends, the flattened hierarchies have been replaced by short term teams that are often put together in order to accomplish a specific goal or project and upon completion, members go off in different directions, to different companies, to different cities and given air travel, to different countries. While perhaps more democratic, such organizations require workers to assume a false persona, a pseudo cooperation and the ability to say and do the things that make one seem to be a good team player, all the while aware that only a few of many will ever win the permanent hire that brings benefits and security. The rest will work piece rate forever. Such work demands and geographical mobility ill-serve individual needs for a sense of attachments to a supportive community and undermine capacities for loyalty to an organization, co-workers, family, or people in general. Contemporary flexibility denies a cohesive sense of self with clear purposes and goals. Finally, as organizations and their goals rapidly change, and certain people are no longer "needed," not only are they dismissed, but given the individualistic nature of American social character, they often blame themselves for the structural changes they experience. As Sennett (1998) pointed out, when the PCs replaced the refrigerator sized main frame computers, the older IBM engineers who lost their jobs eventually blamed themselves for not having upgraded their skills. Such is the American way, but in most of the northern European countries that have different economic models, not only does the government retrain workers, but provides them with economic support while they're unemployed. Meanwhile many sales and service workers today may not know if they're working until they get a text message from the company computer that analyzes the customer or service needs of the day. Thus we see that the world of short term contracts, "internships" (unpaid work to provide a line on a resume), consultant jobs, limited team projects and temporary relationships erode any sense of loyalty, community and continuity in one's life, which then undermines any consistent value system, integrity, and character traits such as loyalty and commitment that are valuable to society. This is what Sennett (1998) has called the "corrosion of character."

Temporary jobs and expendable workforces are transforming the most essential institutions. As most readers of this book are well aware, higher education is moving increasingly towards temporary faculty in the form of visiting professors, adjuncts, and non-tenure-track affiliates. Many K-12 teachers suffer endless bashing from Republicans who want to privatize schools and from Democrats who want standardized assessment of learning outcomes to determine salary such that pay decreases, no matter which party controls the statehouse and many teachers need food stamps to survive. No wonder schools of education struggle to fill their programs (Saccaro, 2014). To be sure, we now live in an age of digital millionaires and billionaires, while the vast majority of Americans today, especially youth, no longer find consistent economic success. By the way, the computer and the Internet were largely developed by government-supported research, a fact seldom mentioned by the techno-billionaire gurus and their aspiring minions. How do you like them Apples? Microsoft? Google? Amazon? EBay? Facebook? Twitter? Oh well, grab your smart phone, go to your Tinder App and find the nearest person with whom you can share neoliberal fantasies, free-market dreams, and perhaps a few other things that are not the topic of this book.

Back to the Past

As the defeat of the Axis appeared increasingly eminent, in 1944, the Allies held a conference of their financial leaders in Bretton Woods to restructure and rebuild the post war economy. Not only did the dollar replace the pound sterling as the basic currency for international commerce, but the conference established exchange rates between the dollar and other major currencies. Further, the foundations were laid for what would become the World Bank, the International Monetary Fund and the World Trade Organization that would encourage investment, global trade in general and the economic development of poor nations. One of the major consequences of Bretton Woods was to secure trade and currency advantages that would provide profits for American exporters, while for many developing nations, American dollars were expensive. Shortly thereafter, following WWII, with its massive factory system intact and half of the world's production facilities, spearheaded by American domination of the world economy, the world's economy was restructured around US hegemony. Many of the countries of Europe, and surely Japan, were devastated during the war, but nevertheless had skilled labor forces, first rate engineers and educational systems. Consequently, as the factories and transportation networks were rebuilt, foreign-made goods became relatively cheap compared to their American counterparts and their quality showed a great deal of improvement. By the late 1960s we began to see what sociologists and political economists called the "deindustrialization of America" and the beginning of rust belts spreading across the industrial heartlands of the United States as steel production, tire production and other manufacturing began their decline as it became cheaper to ship steel from Japan to Pittsburgh than to manufacture the steel in Pittsburgh. As more and more companies moved their facilities overseas or expanded already existing networks, more and more corporations assumed a multinational form. Increasingly, large corporations, whether banks, automobile companies, or appliance makers, became more and more autonomous from the countries of their origin and assumed a transnational character. These global companies were ever more likely to operate in a deterritorialized, global system of production and consumption. Globalization brought two important developments.

First came the rise of a transnational capitalist class (Sklair, 1998; Robinson, 2004). Like capitalists before them, the first and foremost goal of this class is capital accumulation, providing profits to shareholders and increasingly inflated salaries to the managers, especially the upper echelon elites. But what fundamentally differed about the emerging form of capitalism, was that its global nature meant that corporations became less committed to the local workers and the communities and even to the nations of their origin as they shifted priorities to benefit their global owners, often financial organizations, whomever and wherever they may be. The advanced technologies of production, namely computerized robotic design and production, together with "just in time" delivery of raw materials, vastly increased the productivity of workers such that fewer and fewer workers were needed to actually produce more and more goods. Secondly there were increasing numbers of imports of both finished goods and subcomponents. For example, "American" carmakers could calculate much more precisely which components could be produced abroad and imported to the US, and even entire finished cars. Global shipping lanes and global fuel markets allowed for consistent and relatively low transportation costs that could be figured into the overall calculations of costs. The major consequence was pressure on wages and from about 1980 on, the wages of most American workers stagnated or declined with a positive bump from 1995 to 1999 and then severe decline after 2007 (OECD, 2013). Ironically, wages have sufficiently stagnated so much that car production is returning to the US because cars are heavy, easily dinged in transport, and US labor costs, given new technologies and wage structures, are relatively less than they were in the 1960s. Of course, few of those workers can afford to buy the cars they make, which raises another issue, efficiency gains and lower wages have made many consumer goods, especially expensive durable goods, out of reach for increasing segments of the population. The workers in Mercedes plants in the South, starting at $12/hour, will never afford to buy the cars they make.

As the economic system changed from local to national to multinational and finally global/transnational, the legitimating ideologies of capitalism also changed. In the 1960s, a radical free market economist, Milton Friedman of the University of Chicago who was then considered somewhat of an oddball, advocated primarily monetarist policies in face of the generally accepted Keynesian consensus of most economists at that time. The received wisdom of economics was of course the Keynesian text of Samuelson. But somehow the theories of Friedman and his colleague Hayek endured and indeed found a small following. Then Salvador Allende, a democratic socialist, was elected President of Chile. Among other reforms, he dared to nationalize the copper industry to provide funds for health and education. After having failed to dislodge Castro from Cuba, there was no way the United States would tolerate another socialist country in Latin America. As we have noted, the American animosity toward communism was not simply based on economic rivalries, but deep-seated aspects of social character, and individualism, long a part of that social character prompted a deep-seated resentment of collective values, especially when "those" kinds of people, socialists, when in control of central governments, undermined the freedom of the marketplace and allegedly squelched individual initiatives. Then they might promise sex and atheism, but perhaps not in that order. Using methods similar to those employed to dislodge the democratically elected Mohammad Mossadeq government in Iran in 1953, as in Guatemala, they "successfully" undermined the Allende government and promoted a military coup led by General Augusto Pinochet. Now came the "shock doctrine" (Chomsky and McChesney, 2011; Klein, 2007). Enter the right-wing, a group of young Chilean economists trained at the University of Chicago under Milton Friedman, also known as the "Chicago boys" who began a radical transformation of the Chilean economy. They retrenched social aid programs, freed companies from regulations, privatized a number of resources and services including higher education, and loaded the government with development loan debts from the IMF and the World Bank, which they can't pay back because the terms of the loans forced the government to lower taxes and sell off any assets that produce revenue. The Chilean stock market grew, foreign corporations converted Chile's arable land to cash crops, the wealthiest Chileans made huge piles of money while and the rest of the country fell into poverty.

Given the globalization of the economy that we have discussed, following some of the economic problems of the 70s ranging from inflation to unemployment, a new economic doctrine, neoliberalism, gradually emerged, or perhaps it was not so new in that in many ways it represented a return to the market economies advocated by Adam Smith in 1776. Conservative Republican elites embraced Hayek and Friedman and the 1980 presidential campaign introduced the country to the Laffer curve, scribed upon a napkin, which suggested that lowering taxes actually created more government revenues because lower taxes would cause the economy to grow and generate more overall revenue from lower taxes because the entire economy would be larger. Cutting corporate taxes was not a new idea, because corporations always want lower taxes. In 1924, for example, Andrew Mellon called for lowering taxes from 73% to 24% and it did create more income for the government—until the crash of 1929. The other concept that Ronald Reagan and his economic hitman David Stockman frequently advocated was "supply side" economics that would trickle-down to general prosperity. If the rich got richer, they would invest more money, buy more goods and create more jobs so that the success of the rich would "trickle down" to everyone else. It quickly became apparent, both in the 1980s and especially since 2007, when the rich get richer, no one else benefits save the small coteries of those who serve them or produce 50K watches, 500 K cars, multi-million dollar yachts and homes like the 90,000 square foot Versailles of Florida of David Segal, the "time-share" king.[9] As we said in our introduction, trickle down = tinkle down, as in the people get pissed on.

In 1979, after nearly 20 years of 60s activism and 70s liberalism, the world turned sharply to the right. A diverse popular revolution overthrew the Shah of Iran whom we had imposed through a CIA/MI-6 coup. Many Iranians hoped that the country would reestablish the socialist democracy of the Mossadeq years. Unfortunately, the Islamic religious right proved the best organized, the most militant and skilled in the then new technology of delivering messages on tapes. Ayatollah Khomeini became theocratic dictator. In the same year, Margaret Thatcher became Prime Minister of Great Britain. In 1980, the former B-grade actor Ronald Reagan became President with a folksy charm that belied his aggressive character and rigid law-and-order management as governor of California. In 1982, the conservative Helmut Kohl replaced the liberal Helmut Schmidt as Chancellor of Germany. This period marked the ascent of neoliberalism in the West and some parts of Asia, as well as the rise of Islamic theocracy in the Middle East.

Although both theocratic, Sunni Saudi Arabia and Shiite Iran have become rivals, while many stateless groups such as Al Qaeda and ISIS consist of militia armies and terrorist operations across national borders. After the dissolution of the Soviet Union in 1991, many hoped for a "peace dividend" as mentioned

---

9 Mr. Siegel warned his workers that if they voted for Obama in 2008 and he became president, then he would retire and they would lose their jobs. Well, his time-share rip off business prospered and he has had to hire more workers to keep up with the improved economy that was not supposed to happen. Appreciation? Forget it. See https://www.yahoo.com/realestate/blogs/spaces/florida--versailles---nation-s-largest-home--is-back-from-the-brink-185715511.html?ref=gs Accessed September 24, 2015.

in Chapter 1, which would herald major reinvestments in infrastructure, education, social services, and aid programs. Many hoped that the military-industrial complex would finally recede into history, and for a while, George Bush I and Bill Clinton did decrease military spending. After September 11, 2001, when Islamic terrorists flew planes into the World Trade Centers and the Pentagon, George Bush II more than doubled military spending of the Clinton era. Barack Obama continued the increases, though at a slower pace (Jaffe, 2015). In a fashion similar to the Islamic militants and terrorists, the United States would draw upon its own history and its long-standing penchant for phallic aggressive violence. The US invaded Afghanistan and Iraq, although fifteen of the nineteen hijackers on 9/11 came from Saudi Arabia and none from Iraq. Then we attacked Libya, the government fell, and the country was left in chaos. Then we attacked Syria, and there we remain, bombing and slowly escalating involvement in a war that has at least nine different sides.[10] Why are we there? Does it matter, as long as military action asserts US power and defense contractors make money? Money and the gun have since been well-acquainted, and we look at the gun in American identity in the next chapter.

While most Americans may be little informed of the details of globalization, in many ways, it's promises of individual freedom, prosperity for both the individual and the nation, along with the rejection of the feminist "nanny state," getting governments off one's back had a great deal of emotional appeal that resonated with traditional American social character. But as the old cliché points out, be careful what you wish for, sometimes your wishes come true. Unions were outflanked, wages stagnated, well-paying "middle-class" jobs disappeared, and household debt soared to the present one trillion dollars of credit card debt, 8.1 trillion in mortgage debt, another 1.2 trillion of student load debt, and an overall household total of 11.85 trillion (Chen, 2015). And so the dreams of ever greater prosperity, and ever more consumer goodies turned into a nightmare of economic stagnation and decline, artificially sustained by massive deficit spending. Bought out by the economic elites, the US government shows no inclination at all to address household debt, the rising cost of education, or any other social problem so long as the profits continue to flow at the top in the current "inverted totalitarianism" (Wolin, 2008).

The major corporations and rich individuals, unshackled by *Citizens United,* not only control all three branches of government, but they strongly sway consciousness as well through media outlets that "explain reality" to the public. We should note that most of the mass media is owned by a few major

---

10   The Assad government, The Islamic State, Turkmen, Kurds, Turkey, Saudi Arabia, Iran, Russia, and the USA, all of whom fight with and against each other in different configurations.

corporations, while other big corporations spend vast amounts of money sponsoring various programs from escapist entertainment to the "infotainment" of news and/or current event/political talk shows, etc. NBC owned by GE, the #8 defense contractor never airs critiques of the military or its weapons systems. America's best known public intellectual, Noam Chomsky never appears on mainstream television. The control of consciousness through the mass media serves hegemonic purposes that shield and even celebrate the system, and marginalize its dissenters, critics and whistle blowers.

Consider how Americans "just knew" things, like Saddam Hussein had Weapons of Mass Destruction (WMDs).[11] Some elites might have read Judith's Miller "germ of the week" column in the "official voice" of the New York Times. No less than the otherwise intelligent, respectable Colin Powell presented a litany of embarrassing, cockamamie "evidence" of WMDs in the form of a few fuzzy aerial photos of warehouses and 18-wheeler rigs. Warned by his deputy, Lawrence Wilkerson that the "evidence" was sheer nonsense, Powell persisted and spent his credibility promoting war. Maybe Powell regrets that moment of calumny. By the time of Bush II's invasion, three teams of independent investigators had come up with nothing. Meanwhile, outside of the academic/activist communities, how many Americans knew that the CIA had previously engineered the takeover of Iraq by supporting the neo-fascist Baath Socialist Party as a bulwark against the spread of socialism and fundamentalism, deposing Qassim and eventually, installing Saddam Hussein as a CIA asset? Subsequently, the USA supplied Iraq with weapons, including Sarin nerve gas, to be used against both internal enemies and, with encouragement from the USA, Iraq invaded Iran and fought an eight-year. How many Americans "knew" for sure that Saddam, was a whiskey guzzling, compulsive womanizer who jailed if not murdered fundamentalists? Did they ever consider that it made no sense to believe that a secular dictator would ever work with a fundamentalist like Bin Laden? Quite simply, dictators like Hussein do not share power with anyone. American political debates and battles occur within extremely narrow boundaries as highly ritualized, feigned combat, and the winners are always the same economic elites who buy the candidates, fund the elections, then provide staff and advisors to legislators, the executive branch, and government

---

11   Three separate investigations of Iraqi weapon storage sites by Scott Ritter, Mohamed El Baradi and Han Blix did not find WMD or delivery systems for them. See: http://www.npr.org/templates/story/story.php?storyId=4996218 Accessed July 12, 2015. http://www.nationofchange.org/2015/03/01/china-accelerates-into-the-future-racing-past-america/ accessed February 28, 2015.

agencies.[12] Quite often, generous donors become ambassadors—at least to the choice destinations like London, Paris or Rome. And yes, the elites all give speeches praising democracy.

They're Back!

A common trope of Hollywood horror movies that end with the death of the monster, alien, an undead fiend, or other baddie, is a bit of ambiguity over the enemy's demise that prepares the audience for the next sequel. Perhaps a mangled hand shoots up from a grave, or an eerie beak cracks an eggshell, or the "scientist" sighs, "they are gone ... at least for now." In the real world however, with globalization, financialization and the new technologies that produce vast wealth by moving numbers around in global security markets, climate-changing pollution and displaced workers, we have seen the return of a new Gilded Age in which a small cadre of the very rich, the top 1% of the 1%, again completely control the State. The influence of big business on government policy is nothing new. Extremely rich individuals and organizations have been major players in the past, and so are they again. Of the 34 nations in the OECD, only Turkey, Mexico, and Chile have higher income inequality than the United States (OECD Report 2013). This inequality is the systemic result of regressive tax policies, and disinvestments in public works and services (OECD 2011). The wealth gap in the US is now the biggest on record and is increasing (Fry and Kochhar, 2014). This massive differential allows millionaires and billionaires to make unlimited campaign donations to "friendly" candidates, especially since a right wing Supreme Court decision, Citizens United, rendered corporations "people" and campaign contributions became forms of "free speech." The rich can buy votes in legislative bodies and dictate policy through perks, luxurious gifts, third-party political advertisements, lobbying, promises of investments, and threats of disinvestment. The control is so overt that most elected officials spend much of their time raising money and as such, are nothing more than mouthpieces for their big-money masters. Although some very rich individuals occupy positions in government such as former NY mayor Michael Bloomberg or former California governor Arnold "Terminator" Schwarzenegger or Representative Nancy Pelosi, most of the rich are not themselves likely to seek offices or win elections, therefore they buy control from the outside, such as do Bill Gates, Warren Buffett, George Soros, Sheldon Adelson, and David and Charles

---

12   The popularity of Bernie Sanders and Donald Trump in 2016 was in large part a rejection of plutocracy as usual.

Koch. A major consequence of this plutocratic power has been that income for the middle 40% of America has fallen to the lowest level since 1983, and most folks now carry far more debt (Pew Research Center, 2012). Middle-class income levels defined as 67–200% of the median income, have declined in every state since 2000, while the median income has declined an average of $13,946 in the same period (PEW Charitable Trusts, 2015). Extremely rich individuals, and even richer corporations, are the big money players that runs the US government.

What about manufacturing? Manufacturers have already received almost everything they wanted since 1980. Various international trade deals such as NAFTA or the possibility of TPP force American workers to compete with desperate and impoverished workers in other countries who often live under oppressive governments. Most of the manufacturing jobs that remain in the US, after union busting and wage cuts, are those that actually cost less to keep here, namely, anything too heavy to affordably transport long distances. Nevertheless, even the auto industry has moved considerable facilities to Mexico, and many vehicles in the premium segment that command higher prices can easily absorb the transportation costs from Europe and Asia. Companies like Apple epitomize out-sourcing; Apple designs products in California, and then uses mostly women and children who build them for poverty wages working for FoxConn, its Taiwanese subcontractor whose facilities in China make it the largest manufacturer in the world. Despite the ongoing outflow of jobs, manufacturing still remains a player that runs the US government. The only manufacturing jobs that remain are those few highly skilled jobs in aerospace and defense industries that not only have vast lobbies, but provide high paying jobs for ex-military officers and former congressmen and women. Boeing remains one of only two large-frame airplane manufacturers in the world. Billions and billions of public dollars have gone to develop highly advanced stealth planes (the B-2 bomber, its successor the LRS-B long range bomber, F-22 fighter and the F-35 fighters) and ever newer and evermore expensive naval vessels such as Ford class aircraft carriers, Virginia class subs and Zumwalt class stealth destroyers. The F-35 joint strike force stealth fighter, the most expensive weapon system in history is a case in point. As of 2016, it is still not ready for combat, and if it were, its mission is not clear. Why would a supersonic stealth fighter be useful when most combat today is against terrorist or militia groups that do not have planes and no fixed location to attack? An all-out war with China, which only neo-cons can envision, would likely go nuclear and destroy most human life, and besides, China depends on US markets and capital investment and the US depends on Chinese labor, so neither side would benefit from a war with the other. Russia is barely better than a third-world country and poses little military threat. Most defense expenditures have nothing to do with military need, but rather the fact that the non-functional F-35 has already produced huge profits for Lockheed-Martin. Despite the trillions of dollars spent, the thousands of lives lost, and many thousands more maimed and wounded, countries destroyed around the world, the technologically advanced American war machine has utterly failed to bring peace, freedom, democracy and equality to Afghanistan, Iraq, Libya, Syria, or Somalia. Indeed they have not won a war since 1945. Still, defense contractors gloat at the long term, low intensity conflicts that use millions of dollars of munitions every day.

In the past, industrial capital enjoyed nearly exclusive control of government, but the Great Depression and World War II forced elites to concede power, submit to regulations, and pay much higher taxes. Even during the Cold War years, many Presidents and politicians remained independent enough to exert some degree of civilian control over corporate power. For example, President Eisenhower faced a call for massive military buildup after the Soviet Union launched the Sputnik satellite in 1957 (the first human-made satellite). Instead, Eisenhower called for massive spending on education and infrastructure, a simultaneous build-up of scientists and civil engineers—all of which he regarded a vital to the long-term success of the United States. At the same time, his Vice President Richard Nixon emphasized the need for the humanities and social sciences as necessary to create well-rounded and dynamic innovators and not just technocrats (Lofgren 2013 pp. 145–147). Former military leaders familiar with the horrors of war such as Ulysses Grant, Dwight Eisenhower, and John F. Kennedy brought a somewhat independent perspective to politics that proved somewhat resistant to corporate domination. Although definitely friendly to business interests, they all worked for a balanced approach to public policy and thought that a healthy public required substantial public investment and protection. As a result, the manufacturing era produced regulations and oversight that now cover all aspects of design, engineering, and production in order to achieve various safety and energy outcomes. Cars and working conditions now far surpass the reliability, longevity, and performance of previous decades, and in general they run on far less fuel. And if we ignore VW, cars today emit far less pollution. Safety, efficiency, and durability are certainly positive social outcomes. Oblivious to the reasons for American success in the 1950s and 60s, right-wing politicians generally avoided military service and firsthand experience in war, nor have most experienced destitute poverty. Deregulators, public disinvestors, and war hawks such as George W. Bush, Dick Cheney, Bill Kristol, and Paul Wolfowitz were born wealthy, and have not served in the military, or the case of Bush, spent most of the time AWOL drinking, toking weed and snorting blow. Without any experience of economic deprivation or the lifelong nightmares of mangled bodies or comrades maimed and killed in combat, they have not heard the screams of the wounded or inhaled the fumes of burning flesh. Thus the social dominators have no qualms about sending young men and women, mostly poor, mostly minorities, to die in, or return broken from, far-off places. And when they return, perhaps maimed or suffering from PTSD, a woefully inadequate and underfunded Veterans Administration provides less than optimal care. Many of today's homeless were yesterday's veterans—used, abused and then discarded. Yes, some got medals, but medals don't pay the bills or resurrect dead comrades.

Unlike the manufacturing industries however, few comparable consumer protections now govern finance, fossil fuels and agribusiness. When the subprime loan crisis hit, the taxpayers of the United States provided billions of dollars to bail out the banks, financial companies, and carmakers. Following that, quantitative easing gave banks money at no interest which they used to buy government bonds that paid 4%. Many executives from companies like Chase, Citibank or Goldman Sachs got multimillion dollar bonuses for jobs "well done". Iceland's bankers got jail sentences. The millions of Americans who were conned into buying the subprime mortgages with artificially low down payments and teaser interest rates suddenly faced much higher payments while their homes went underwater (worth less than they paid). As a result of the implosion, millions lost jobs as companies went bankrupt and millions of others, often the same people, lost their homes. No bailout for them, but instead they received a rude awakening from a lesson in capitalist economics that neither they nor their children will hopefully ever forget.

Billionaires pay minimal taxes, even Warren Buffett, a Democrat has noted that he pays a lower proportion of his income to the IRS than does his secretary.[13] Consequently, the ruling powers today need not conform to governmental regulation and oversight; indeed, given the musical chairs between big government and big business, the corporate interests provide "experts" to write the very rules they more often than not ignore anyhow. And even when found guilty, their fines generally amount to chump change for large corporations. At one time, big businesses paid a considerable portion of the tax burden and were often involved in many projects of civic improvement and cultural life of supporting concert and opera halls, museums, public parks, and other investments. But insofar as so most commerce today is global, the transnational

---

13   Most Americans are little aware that their taxes are among the lowest in the industrial world while part and parcel of its cultural history, as well as its underlying social character, is a deep resentment toward taxation, much of which is often seen by conservatives as providing handouts, "free stuff" for the poor that keeps them poor.

capitalist classes are less likely to participate in the local society where they might live for a few years. They dominate it.

Moreover, they dominate from afar. The elites live in secluded mansions or atop tall skyscrapers protected by the latest in electronic surveillance as well as highly armed security guards. As we earlier noted, they do not travel in the same lanes or planes as the rest of us. Given their isolation from most people, and limited interaction with various service providers, they are often quite clueless about the general consequences of their economic policies and agendas that have made them so very wealthy. At one time we might have said they were clueless about how the other half lives, but now we might better say how the other 90% live. At the recent 2015 Davos meeting of the WEF (World Economic Forum), Wall Street mogul, Steve Schwartzman, CEO of Blackstone Equity said:

> I find the whole thing astonishing and what's remarkable is the amount of anger whether it's on the Republican side or the Democratic side ... Bernie Sanders, to me, is almost more stunning than some of what's going on in the Republican side. How is that happening, why is that happening? What is the vein that is being tapped into across parties, that has made people so unhappy? ... That is something you should spend some time on ...

Schwarzman's private equity firm, Blackstone, manages and makes fees from billions of dollars of pensioners' assets, was recently fined by federal regulators for not properly disclosing fee terms to its investors. The investors harmed by Blackstone's conduct included public retirement systems in California, Florida and New Jersey.[14] Among the top .1%, Schwartzman is well known for his lavish multimillion dollar parties like his 60th birthday party where Rod Stewart performed. Donald Trump was a guest. The Bar Mitzvah party for his son was equally elaborate. Meanwhile, Leon Black paid Elton John one million dollars to sing at his 60th birthday party. And David Brooks of DHB spent 10 million dollars on his daughter's Bat Mitzvah with entertainment that included Kenny G, Aerosmith and 50-Cent.[15] Much of his money was made selling defective body armor to the military. He was charged with fraud, insider trading, tax evasion and raiding his company's coffers for personal gain including

---

14   http://www.ibtimes.com/inequality-rising-billionaire-steve-schwarzman-expresses
        -surprise-american-voters-are-2273633 Accessed 02/12/2016.

15   http://www.history.com/this-day-in-history/aerosmith-and-50-cent-headline-a-10
        -million-bar-mitzvah Accessed 04/19/2015.

for the $10 million he used to pay for his daughter's lavish party. Screw the taxpayers, get a raise and a bonus, but if you endanger troops fighting imperialist wars, then, maybe, you are in trouble.

The Pitchforks are Coming!

While Schwartzman, Black and Brooks and much of the rest of the billionaire social dominators have recreated the Gilded Age, it is ever more obvious that growing discontent over both inequality and an indifferent government is more and more widespread and more vociferous. This is clearly evident in the rise of the Tea Party as a form of right populism intertwined with racism, as well as the progressive Occupy movement and support for Bernie Sanders. Thus we see a great deal of support for both Trump and Sanders, outsiders to the mainstreams of the political class; while they are each supported by different groups and different character types, both reflect growing discontent with the economic system and its political servants. Some of the elites do see the writing on the wall or perhaps pitchforks and torches coming down the pike. Multi-billionaire Nick Hanauer, a co-founder of Amazon and 30 other companies, recently noted:

> Seeing where things are headed is the essence of entrepreneurship. And what do I see in our future now? I see pitchforks ... the rest of the country, the 99.99 percent is lagging far behind. The divide between the haves and have-nots is getting worse really, really fast ... Some inequality is intrinsic to any high-functioning capitalist economy. The problem is that inequality is at historically high levels and getting worse every day. Our country is rapidly becoming less a capitalist society and more a feudal society. Unless our policies change dramatically, the middle class will disappear, and we will be back to late 18th-Century France. Before the revolution[16]

Some billionaires, are vaguely aware of the growing discontent and indignation and now fear the peasants may revolt are devising plans to permanently distance themselves from the masses they exploit. Many are building isolated villas in places like New Zealand. Peter Thiel (to whom we will return later) and Patrick Friedman, the grandson of unregulated markets zealot Milton Friedman, have teamed up to finance the development of the Seasteading

---

16 http://www.politico.com/magazine/story/2014/06/the-pitchforks-are-coming-for-us -plutocrats-108014_full.html#.VrfWy_krKUk Accessed 05/15/2015.

Institute, an island where the richest people in the world will be able to live with each other, free of any laws, regulations, or common people. Equipped with the latest technology, Seasteaders will be able to monitor global financial markets, conduct trades, and carry on whatever enterprising research strikes their fancy, all without oversight or taxes (Lynch, 2015). Accessible only by sea or air, Seasteading would be a utopia for billionaires. Given that Thiel is a fan of science fiction, this project may never move beyond the planning stage. The greater significance is the apparently universal agreement among billionaires that radical libertarianism is the one and only way to run a country, a free, completely unregulated market will govern itself through the miraculous powers of the invisible hand of competition. Thiel, along with fellow billionaires Marc Andreesen, Mark Zuckerberg, and David and Charles Koch may or may not believe in God, but they definitely believe in the divinity of the unregulated market, a kind of "market fundamentalism" that includes freedom from safety regulations, and they believe in their own divinity, at least in our social-psychological sense if not in a theological sense.[17] But that said, many of these leaders are quite intelligent and many are beginning to fear that the effects of growing inequality, stagnation, and the national decline we've been talking about may precipitate violent protests of many types. And so they are ready to board their private planes or yachts and escape the wrath of the angry masses.

The Rise of Predatory Banksters

In order to rescue the country from the Great Depression, government needed to enact substantial overhauls to regulate the flow of capital, which meant substantial transformations of the banking system. Implemented in 1933 in response to the Great Depression, the Glass-Steagall Act was far stronger than the recent and minimal Dodd-Frank legislation. Interestingly enough, conservative commentator George Will (2013) observed that Glass-Steagall was a mere 37 pages and managed US prosperity successfully for nearly 50 years. In contrast, Dodd-Frank was 848 pages, with hundreds of supplements, as for example the so-called Volcker Rule that banned banks from gambling with

---

17   Market fundamentalism, much like the theologies that engendered it, strongly believes that the short-term pain and suffering of unregulated markets, privatization, debt repayment, and retrenchments of social benefits will eventually bring great rewards. It's sort of like religiously based sexual abstention in which guilt and frustration eventually guarantee a place in heaven for the truly virtuous yet horny. In neither case has compelling evidence of this assertion been brought to bear.

federally insured deposits came in at an additional 298 pages. (It was later revoked by the legislation of December 13, 2014). The scant but clear and decisive pages of Glass-Steagall regulated nearly every aspect of banking and for several decades, these regulations and controls created a stable economic system of relatively predictable and sustained growth and an unprecedented rise of the middle-class from 1945 to 1980. Widespread prosperity made many things once reserved for a wealthy few now affordable to many more. Larger segments of the population could now afford college educations, home ownership and retirement security. Starting in 1980, three key acts of Congress and signed by Democratic as well as Republican Presidents undid Glass-Steagall and consequently transformed stable and shared prosperity into the speculative boom and bust cycles characteristic of the mid-late 1900s.

Firstly, the Depository Institutions Deregulation and Monetary Control Act (DIDMCA) of 1980 allowed banks to set their own interest rates as well as to freely merge without federal approval. This meant that banks could grow in size without any oversight and radically drop or spike interest rates. Of course, people will not take out loans or use credit cards if the interest rates are initially high. Banks needed a certain degree of deceit to scam borrowers, they discovered that teaser rates, previously prohibited under Glass-Steagall, would entice many to borrow ostensibly cheap money, just as they did prior to 1929. Once the teaser rates expired, the consumer then discovered the standard rate, now applied to the entire balance, and often augmented by punish rates surpassed 30% interest. Beginning in the 1980s, debt has fueled growth more than real earnings, which creates periodic spikes in spending and a subsequent crash as debt reaches maximum levels. Property values fall, businesses fail, workers suffer layoffs and capital consolidates in fewer and fewer hands. Secondly, the Garn-St. Germain Depository Institutions Act of 1982 allowed both banks and savings and loans to issue adjustable rate mortgages, and to issue mortgages without regard to assets, income, or other typical means of assessing repayment probability. Although variable rate mortgages, balloons, and interest-only loans of all types had always existed, they were limited to people who received income periodically (such as through a commission or bonus system) or seasonally, such as farmers. They would pay interest-only for a while and then pay down the principle in periodic big chunks, or make smaller payments for a few years and then pay off the entire balloon. For the mainstream borrower however, this made much higher levels of debt seem affordable. This has and still creates another path to boom and bust, as households take on far more debt than they can afford, and with high interest rates that suddenly spike or balloon (the entire remaining balance) due all at once. Thirdly, the Gramm-Leach-Bliley Act, also known as the Financial Services Modernization

Act of 1999, allowed commercial and investment banks, securities firms, and insurance companies to consolidate. One large financial corporation could now sell, insure, and even speculate against (hedge) their own financial assets. By 2007, the investment bank Goldman-Sachs had mastered this sort of revenue stream by bundling a number of perhaps risky sub-prime mortgages to one customer and then selling bets (hedges) against it to another customer (McLean and Nocera, 2010). Since they had already made their money on the sub-prime bundle when they sold it, Goldman-Sachs then lobbied Congress, the Federal Reserve Bank, and Sallie Mae to take no action on sub-prime mortgages, to make sure they failed, and thus ensure that the hedge bets would also payoff for Goldman-Sachs. While not a Ponzi scheme, it was a heads I win, tails you lose situation. How long could they sell toxic assets? As long as buyers believed they were healthy assets. The Gramm-Leach-Bliley Act also allowed the rating of packaged assets by only the highest quality assets in a package, even if the majority of the package consisted of high-risk junk bonds and sub-prime mortgages. This undid the final regulations of Glass-Steagall.

As a result, these three measures, which passed with overwhelming support from both Democrats and Republicans, allowed finance capital to conduct any type of transaction, and any on terms they wished. Oversight of such transactions passed from government regulators to the financial corporations themselves. With no regulation or supervision, sub-prime and adjustable rate mortgages from the housing sector became the basis of more mysterious artifices such as credit default swaps, collateralized debt obligations, and various derivatives (McLean and Nocera, 2010). Basically, a derivative is a type of contract, the value of which is based on, that is, *derived* from some future outcome. Typical derivatives are call (buy), put (sell), hedge (insurance), and speculation (bet). For example, an investor can place a call order to buy a stock if it hits a certain price. Or, an investor can hedge an investment against losses by taking out an insurance policy on it. An investor can speculate that prices of a commodity, let's say, wheat, will go higher in the future, and thus bet that buying now will pay off in the future when prices go higher. While such financial transactions are not inherently damaging to the economy and society, and are often necessary to some extent in order to balance supply and demand of essential commodities, they readily become damaging when the same bank owns all aspects of the deal, including oversight (see Ferguson, 2012; Taibbi, 2010, for extensive and clear explanations).

Other derivatives, illegal under Glass-Steagall, have recently reached a kind of hip and fashionable status, everyone is doing it, everyone is getting rich, and only a namby-pamby dumbass could lose money. Municipality and retirement funds, formerly prohibited from high-risk investments, were now free to gamble with public money and pensions. Like all other publicly available derivatives, the Credit/Debit/Income/Interest-rate swaps became the drug of choice including the painful bankruptcy-induced withdrawal. Basically, a swap deal means that someone swaps something now for (hopefully) better terms later.

Too Big to Fail, Too Powerful to Jail

The financial sector, rescued by the taxpayers, is again free to gamble with the assurance that public money will cover their losses. The banks are too big to fail and the leaders are too powerful to jail. Fossil fuels have minimal regulation. Rich individuals pay the lowest taxes since 1953 (Fieldhouse, 2013). Unlike regulated industries such as automomobiles and consumer appliances, financial and energy executives lack a similar commitment to reliability and personal health and safety, or in terms more appropriate to corporate business, they lack any commitment to social externalities. There is increasing evidence that fracking causes earthquakes and poisons aquifers. As we will shortly discuss, this creates a Hobbesian environment of war of each against all, and this sort of environment creates and rewards particular types of social character.

Congress and the President decided to further insure the financial sector with public money. On December 13, 2014, the United States Senate (with encouragement from President Obama) passed a 1.1 trillion spending bill. Thereby approving a bill already passed in the House of Representatives on December 11, this was allegedly a budget act to keep the government running. More than that, it revealed the big money players who really run the government. It also reveals the social character of the rich and powerful, as well as the social character of the people who vote for them or celebrate their wealth and power. Billionaire Jamie Dimon, CEO of JP Morgan Chase, presented President Obama and members of Congress with provisions to include in the bill to reverse the mild Dodd-Frank oversight on investment banks and guarantee government bailout money, should any risky financial bets fail in the future (Cassidy, 2014). The President and Congress complied. Finance capital is one of the big money players that now run the US government. Other provisions reduce funding for the Environmental Protection Agency, prohibit listing certain species as endangered (even if they are), reduce the reach of the Clean Water Act, eliminates many energy-saving mandates, such as carbon taxes, and even remove a ban on incandescent light bulbs (Pear, 2014), enacted during the George W. Bush administration. The fossil fuel industry is one of the big money player that runs the US government.

The European Community (EC) has initiated a two-year ban on neonic-otinoid pesticides, known to kill bees and other beneficial insects. The US has about half the total number of honeybees as it did in 1990 (Pettis et al., 2013). In contrast, recent legislation in the US specifically forbids regulation that curtails pesticides and GMO's. Most recently, the FDA approved Monsanto's GMO soybeans and cotton, which tolerate higher levels of the her-bicide glyphosate and a new biocide called dicamba, which kills everything with which it comes in contact (RT News, 2015). While dicamba is deadly to all life, glyphosate is known to cause a wide range of illnesses in humans, includ-ing ADHD, Alzheimer's, and autism (Cattani et al., 2014), birth defects (Garry et al., 2002; Paganelli et al., 2010) and various forms of cancer (Schinasi and Leon, 2014; Shim et al., 2009; Thongprakaisanga et al., 2013). It also contributes to obesity (Samsel and Seneff, 2013), gluten intolerance (Samsel and Seneff, 2013a), and internal organ damage (Seralini, et al., 2011). Whether alone or in combination with common agricultural pesticides, glyphosate causes a wide variety of harm to non-human animal species, which can be magnified over 100-fold depending on the exact environmental conditions of exposure (Roustan et al., 2014). Glyphosate is only one of several hundred herbicides and pesticides. Dichlorophenol pesticides cause a range of food allergies, immune dysfunction, and asthma (Jerschow et al., 2012) and brain damage in children (Rauh et al., 2012). Despite this obvious public harm (and Monsanto is only one of several such corporations and we have only mentioned the effects of one herbicide and one pesticide), agribusiness is one of the big money players.

Spoiled by Success

Bellah et al. (1992 [1975]) lamented the unbridled individualism that emerged when the covenant was broken, shattered by economic gain. Resting upon Protestant based individualism, commercial individualism was enshrined in the colonies, and the importance of the moral community eroded. The same factors fostered a long enduring "taboo upon socialism," which given neo-liberalism, has given us a number of taboos on critique that have succored an underlying social character that disdains government as a threat to some vague notion of freedom. That disdain is of course very situational, because the government should always defend the interests of private property, support military investments, and prisons to house the underclass. As George Lakoff (2009) argues, much in line with our analysis, the "strict father" orientation, quite similar to what we've called the authoritarian social dominator, is very supportive of the punitive and aggressive roles of government just as the strict father tends to be aggressive and punitive in his family relationships in order to instill toughness and independence so that his children may well function in a hostile world. On the other hand, the same character type believes that government largesse, welfare, health care, food and housing benefits for the poor, as the "nurturing parent" or "nanny state" renders people passive, emasculated, weak, dependent and ultimately a burden that the good, "hard-working folks" wind up supporting. Often heard is the lament of working and lower middle class folks who complain about breaking their asses so that the undeserving_____ (fill in racial, ethnic or gender orientation) can sit on theirs. Again we see the consequences of "motivated reasoning" in that the taxes most people pay support the defense and intelligence department and related industries, relatively very little spending goes to welfare recipients. Moreover, most of what goes to welfare recipients is quickly redistributed to agribusiness, landlords and merchants. Finally it might be noted that many recipients of government programs are members of what is generally been called the "working poor" that would include vast numbers of poorly paid retail employees so that employers like Walmart that can thus afford to keep wages low. A large number of adjunct professors often making $3,000 per course, lucky to get 10 course/year, burdened by student loans, must rely on food stamps in order to survive.

A number of Republican politicians, well-funded and supported by their reactionary constituencies, would like to end or vastly reduce a variety of entitlement and/or redistribution programs which are not only seen as socialism, but supporting a class of undeserving bums, parasites and moochers. When Romney privately noted that 47% of the voters that were getting "free stuff," therefore, they would never vote Republican. When his private feelings were made public his fate was sealed. It is worth noting the that one major category of the named parasites are Social Security recipients that given their age tend to vote Republican; the other recipients of such benefits include students in college and a vast number of people working in retail, fast food, and services whose minimum wages entitle them to food stamps and often housing support. Ironically enough, many Americans support ending the very same programs that brought and/or bring them benefits. As one-time speaker of the House Tip O'Neill once said, the Democrats enabled people to go to college, start small businesses, buy homes and get medical insurance. And how did they show their gratitude? They become Republicans and vote to end these programs. How does this happen?

Once again we suggest the legacy of American character remains salient. The power of individualism is such that people feel that their success is due to their own hard work, unaided by government programs, like schools or infrastructure, housing loans, SBA loans, subsidies, or even the labor of employees or co-workers. The power of underlying social character is such that people cannot see the contradictions between their political beliefs and the reality of government programs. As we noted in our preface, many government organizations and programs are clearly socialist, that is, paid for by the taxpayers to benefit everyone, such as the military, the post office, public schools and universities, Social Security, Medicare, highways, airports, libraries, fire departments and police departments. To reiterate, right populism in America reflects aspects of its Puritan inspired social character and deplores the aspects of government which they believe supports "immorality," weakness and dependency such as welfare, food stamps, and housing assistance—which are a small part of the budget. Social welfare programs are about 3% of the federal budget, corporate welfare about 5%, and the military gets about 55% of the discretionary budget. Insofar as individualism and beliefs in self-reliance rests upon fears of weakness and dependency, between motivated reasoning, cognitive dissonance and denial, many people would cut off or reduce their own medical insurance (Medicare) and let the defunct Lehmann Brothers or triumphant Goldman Sachs and various hedge funds and private equity firms gamble it away rather than admit that they depend on the very government programs they would dismantle.

It seems as if America embraced the narcissism that Christopher Lasch described that we noted in Chapter 1. America gave up commitments of work and community, and reduced life to a series of strategic moves with no ties to people or place (Lasch, 1979 p. 220). It gets worse. We have become narcissistic in two ways. First, we love our celebrities, our beautiful people—the movie stars, rock stars, athletes, and rich socialites such as Kim Kardashian and Paris Hilton who are famous for being famous. Celebrity is one of the few avenues in which narcissism is a real asset (Pinsky and Young, 2009). They thrive on public attention, and set the styles and codes of behavior for the masses who adore them, and increasingly, try to emulate them (Lasch, 1979: p, 232; see also Pinsky and Young, 2009). Party like a rock star! Celebrities seem to have it all: good looks, fame, wealth and hot sex lives, and thus become desirable role models (Rojek, 2001). Narcissism may function for the celebrity seeking fame and adulation, but pathological narcissism is quite dysfunctional for ordinary people who do not get the adulation and extravagances of material success. While Americans have always enjoyed gossip about the rich and famous, the middle-class life style based on home, family and work was also a valid and meaningful life, even if a bit constricted intellectually and culturally. By the early 1970s, Lasch realized that the broad middle-class affluence of the 1950s undermined the commitment to collective organizations and instead rewarded individual satisfaction through ostentatious consumption. Marcuse (1964) and Fromm

(1990 [1955]) similarly charted and lamented the consequence of consumerism and the turn towards privatized hedonism that weakened social ties, and indeed fostered the loss of genuine selfhood as it was colonized by consumerism.

Secondly then, "modern capitalist society not only elevates narcissists to prominence, it elicits and reinforces narcissistic traits in everyone" (Lasch, 1979 p. 232). It does this by offering a vast array of consumer goods that provide, or promise, the fulfillment of every desire both subtle and gross, and by making people dependent on external, official, and manufactured sources of satisfaction. Degrees, titles, licenses, certification, legally recognized affiliation and all manner of formal procedures are all required to do anything. Brand names on clothing project the good taste, cultural capital and consumer power for the individual's branded identity (Klein, 2000). Selfhood within certain subcultures became tied to brands that signified certain consumer based identities. Much like religious differences, The North Face fans deplore the American Eagle Outfitters people, and neither has any use for Abercrombie and Fitch, while Patagonia fans advertise their moral superiority over all. The ease of pre-packaged foods and the microwave oven not only replaced culinary skill, but separated the consumer from the social relations of production. The sweat shops and feed lots where clothing and food are produced are rendered invisible. Further, with packaged, microwavable foods, family meals have become rare as each of the multiple inhabitants of a household, once called a family, pass through the kitchen at different times, grab a packaged food, zap it in the microwave, gulp it down and move to another solitary activity like Facebook where people have lots of "friends" to compensate for fewer actual social ties. Consequently, even as a person draws momentary comforts from consumer spending, it disempowers them internally as basic conveniences such as quick fixes of food replace basic accomplishments such as cooking, while the social interaction spent around the dinner table has all but vanished. Eternally reliant on external recognition, praise and most importantly, outward signs of success, the individual loses both ability and autonomy.

What is a narcissist and social dominator to do in a society that expects collective commitments to work and community? Simple. Allow other narcissists and dominators to unwind collective commitments. Nowhere has this been more dramatic than in the economic sphere. As mentioned, major corporations give and take away the livelihood of thousands at a time, whether relocating facilities to low-wage countries or raiding and stripping assets. Even major cities can be pillaged to satisfy the longings of powerful narcissists who equate wealth with human value while oblivious to the human consequences of such decisions. Let's take a look at how the security and certainty of the post-War period was disassembled.

Detroit Falls to the Bankster Hordes

What is a city? A collection of individuals? Wealth to plunder? A complex network of personal and collective social ties? Human lives, or revenue generators? When the city of Detroit declared bankruptcy on July 18, 2013, the national media sold the story as decades of municipal mismanagement, serially bad business decisions at GM, Ford, and Chrysler, and lazy, hedonistic lifestyles of its predominantly Black population. In truth, the city's over-reliance on the domestic automotive business played a part, but the racial and ethnic composition of the city and their alleged lifestyle played no part. As for the city's management, changing political-economic forces gradually closed in and compelled increasingly unfavorable decisions. Yet, the bankruptcy might never have happened. Still unfolding, the real story is more complex and more scary.

Although the requirement of managing long term pension funds with dwindling revenue was the central difficulty, hipster finance was the far more immediate cause, itself a symptom of civil desperation. Over several decades, the American auto industry replaced workers with automation and cheaper labor, first moving from to the right to work states of the South, then abroad, mostly in Mexico. Starting in the 1970s, spikes in oil prices and foreign competition forced the Detroit Three to speed-up development of new models and technology, which also required cuts in quality. While mismanagement definitely played a part during this period (Lutz, 2011), so did high interest on the capital necessary for major transformation to a more competitive automotive market and innovative emissions technology (Rattner, 2010). Other durable goods manufacturers suffered similar fates, especially appliance makers like Whirlpool in Michigan and Maytag in Iowa that did not have a military division (like General Electric). Detroit's population and prosperity gradually declined after 1960, even as the city faced rising pension costs relative to income. By 2005, Detroit was scheduled to pay almost a billion dollars on bonds, notes, and other debts, including nearly $366 million for interest payments alone. The mayor at the time, Kwame Kilpatrick, floated $1.4 billion in municipal bonds to meet obligations to the city's underfunded pensions. This forced Detroit into a downward spiral of constantly issuing more debt to cover older debt, all of which also involved huge banking transaction fees and unpredictable interest rates.

UBS Financial Services and other banks collected 46.4 million dollars in upfront fees for a package deal that would allegedly save 13 million a year by lowering interest rates on the city's debt. The following year, the city paid another $61.8 million, including insurance costs, for UBS to sell $948.5 million in bonds replacing two-thirds of the debt sold the previous year. In two years, the city paid 74.8 million in fees for transactions that never delivered as promised. Since 2005, Bank of America, Merrill Lynch, JP Morgan Chase, UBS and other global banks have executed about $3.7 billion in bond sales for the city to cover deficits, pension shortfalls and debt payments. Detroit officials then entered into swaps to hedge against increases in interest rates and thus insure themselves against default on $800 million in pension debt and $1.6 billion in water department bonds.

The next move was an asset for credit swap. Already burdened with about two billion in debt and millions in yearly budget deficits and pension commitments, what did Detroit have left to swap? Detroit paid for these financial services by swapping its income. This involved entering into contractual agreements with "swap counterparties" including Zurich-based UBS and their subsidiary, Siebert, Brandford, Shank & Co. One agreement required the city's casino revenue—which was $181 million in 2012—to be sent directly to a trust and held as collateral for quarterly payments and termination payments owed to the swap partners. Total debt from bonds and swaps rose from less than 1 billion in 2005 to 20 billion by 2013 (Helms, Kaffer, and Henderson 2013).

The City then discovered what happens if they bet wrong on hedges and income declines while debt rates increase. Wrong bets cost Detroit $474 million in 2013 alone, and included payments for underwriting expenses and bond-insurance premiums. Just prior to bankruptcy, the single largest part of the city's budget was 350 million a year to pay for hedge fund derivatives that were supposed to guard against variable-interest debt, but instead only added expenses (Preston and Christoff, 2013).

As if that weren't enough, foreclosures in Detroit intensified as subprime mortgages collapsed. "Sub-prime" refers to mortgages given to borrowers who lack typical financial means to pay back the mortgage (called NINJA's—No Income, No Job, or Assets), or they are given terms that make it difficult to pay back even with decent employment. This raised the number of foreclosures well beyond those that resulted directly from economic downturn. The subprime meltdown in Detroit resulted from policy decisions at Morgan Stanley and New Century Mortgage, which colluded to systematically sell as many subprime mortgages as possible, and then sell those mortgages as bundles to investors before the mortgages defaulted (Gallagher, 2015). E-mails and other documents show that New Century (now bankrupt) informed Morgan Stanley of the impossible nature of the loans; they expected almost all of them to default. As Morgan Stanley traders remarked, "a bunch of scaaaarrryyyy loans!!!!!!," "crap," and "like a trash novel." Beginning in 2005, two years before the crash, a mid-level loan staffer, Rob Travis, notified his superiors that these loans were highly problematic. He was ignored. Morgan Stanley told New

Century to keep selling bad mortgages, and for Morgan Stanley officers to keep buying them since they could easily sell them before default (Gallagher, 2015). Morgan Stanley and New Century colluded to pump up the value of sub-prime loan bundles by selling them amongst their own subsidiaries, and then dumping them on some unsuspecting third-party, often government pension funds for teachers, fire fighters, police and government employees. Large investments in sub-prime bundles and other allegedly solid but actually toxic assets bankrupted Jefferson County, Alabama, the largest municipal bankruptcy before Detroit (Wilkinson, 2011).

Meanwhile, New Century sold and Morgan Stanley bought and then resold sub-prime mortgages in great numbers. Even when the borrowers had credible income and repayment potential, 90% of all mortgages to Black people included high-risk terms, such as variable interest and balloon payments. Although somewhat more favorable, 79% of loans to white people also included such terms (Gallagher, 2015). Consequently, the credible borrowers went into default and homelessness right alongside the truly risky ones. New Century loan officers aggressively scoured the city, often trailing potential borrowers to their place of work, or even siding up to them on the street and signing papers on a car hood (Gallagher, 2015). While we may fault the people of Detroit for their eagerness to own their own homes and claim a piece of the American Dream, and that we should all be suspicious of deals that seem too good to be true, we should also remember that at the time, New Century was (and Morgan Stanley still is) among the largest and presumably most respectable banks in the business. These were not small-time operations, but global corporations of formidable reputation.

Overall then, the bankruptcy of Detroit was the outcome of two historical forces. The historical decline of American manufacturing, including the forces of outsourcing and downsizing began the process, and as jobs went, so did the people. Detroit has half the population of 1960. At the same time, the rise of financial capital, quite apart from industry and other productive investments has, created a predatory form of finance that does not invest in productive value, but rather, extracts value out of productive (or formerly productive) enterprise and public investments. In other words, financial capital, based on speculation, is generally separated from productive capital, and from public investment (Chang, 2010). Whether this marks the beginning of the end for modern capitalism or not, it definitely marks a transition away from the Fordism of the mid-twentieth Century as a kind of truce period between labor and capital, and into a period where financial predation appropriates and then hordes vast amounts of wealth while making no productive investments in return.

Rich individuals do not create jobs. They typically place their fortunes in secure government bonds and simply collect the interest (Clinch, 2014). Even worse, as rich financial institutions extract wealth, they bet it all on risky speculation, what Susan Strange (1997) called "casino capitalism." The main difference between financial speculation and a casino game is that big banks are now guaranteed government bailouts to financial firms, whereas a high roller at a casino table merely craps out. Big banks and rich individuals, usually through private equity companies, take home the winnings, and the rest of the population get stuck paying for the losses. Jobs disappear, investment capital dries up, people move away, social ties diminish, and society dies a little more.

As billions of dollars flowed out of Detroit, the city laid off police, fire, and maintenance workers. The infrastructure decayed, more people left, property depreciated, and yet costs for services increased as the city attempted to pay for bad bonds. Water rates increased so dramatically while incomes fell so sharply that nearly half the population, including many businesses, were unable to pay for water. The city shut off water to several thousand households after bankruptcy, before activism from various organizations and even the United Nations pressured the bankruptcy manager, Kevin Orr, to place a moratorium on shut offs (Anderson, 2014).

As the outcome of social forces, Detroit is not alone. Bankruptcy is not the only possible outcome. We have done better in the past. From the collapse of the financial sector in 1929 to the election of Ronald Reagan in 1980, the United States moved away from patrician domination to a new prosperity facilitated by public investment in education and infrastructure that produced an emerging middle-class of unionized wage-workers earning greater pay and benefits, and a rising professional class especially after WWII. To pay for massive public investment as well as for World War II, the government increased taxes heavily on the richest .01%, who from 1948 to 1960 paid a 90% income tax rate. Corporate taxes paid for K-12 education. Today, a 90% tax rate would mean that, for example, Bill Gates would only take home about 1.2 billion a year. How is he supposed to live on such meager income?

With its first budget in 1981, the Reagan administration, with the support of a democratic Congress, rolled back the highest tax rate to 36%. In addition to the rollback of Glass-Steagall, and subsequent changes under George W. Bush and policy decisions under Clinton, Bush II, and Obama ensured minimal oversight and numerous loopholes for individuals to avoid taxes on massive income. Mitt Romney's mere 13.9% tax rate on 22 million in income in 2011 is only one of many such examples. According to the Buffet rule calculator on the White House website, at least 33,400 people with incomes of 1 million or more paid a lower effective tax rate than most households in the 60–90 thousand range. The top 400 richest people have seen their effective tax rate drop from 30% to 17% in the last 20 years. This same group makes about one-third of the contributions to the presidential campaigns.

Hostile Takeovers—The Social Dominators at Work

Suffering brings great opportunity for those willing to feed on the misery of others. This is what Naomi Klein (2008) called the "shock doctrine" in which the chaos of aftermaths of disasters from wars, revolutions, hurricanes and earthquakes leave people disaster shocked and before they know it, large corporations impose economic shock therapy, privatizing or appropriating assets or changing the terms of existing debt. The first cataclysm of deregulation was the collapse of the Savings and Loan industry in the early 1990s. The government paid 500 billion to cover deposits that the S&L managers had gambled away. Meanwhile, the leveraged buyout, also known as the hostile takeover or corporate raid, become the new means of rapid progress, along with a corresponding reckless risk of failure. In essence, a bank or investment company uses leverage (debt) to buyout a much larger company. They have the target company buy the debt and use the funds to pay off the borrowed money. The massive new debt forces the target company to lay off employees and sell any assets of value, which often means selling off pieces of the company until nothing is left. This typically wrecks the target company, people lose employment, and the raider walks away with all the value. One of the earliest such raids that become the model for subsequent leveraged buyouts was Kohlberg Kravis Roberts (KKR's) takeover of RJR-Nabisco in 1988. To make a long story short, a company of 180 employees took over a global corporation with 25 billion in borrowed money (leverage), had RJR-Nabisco buy the debt, used that transfer to pay off creditors, and then extracted several billion more in profit by laying off 20,000 employees, selling off assets and then extracting large management fees (Burrough and Helyar, 1990). Many of the major banks and private equity companies made money from the raid, including Morgan Stanley, Goldman Sachs, Salomon Brothers, First Boston, Wasserstein Perella & Co., Forstmann Little, Shearson Lehman Hutton, and Merrill Lynch. Unable to manage such massive debt, the company broke apart in 1999 (Legomsky, 1999). By the late 1990s, raids had destabilized much of the industrial and retail sector, and financial pirates searched for new treasure galleons to plunder.

With no such targets available, they devised means to build their own artificial galleons. There were two models that the subprime bubble patterned. One was the dot.com bubble. During the late 90s, the stock value of dot-com businesses, many of which were nothing more than a name and a web address, was bid high and then dumped, the so-called pump and dump method. This scheme ran out of pump in early 2001. Around the same time, one of the most famous and infamous companies of all time rose and fell—Enron. Widely proclaiming their own brilliance, the Enron Corporation pioneered a new trading sector based on energy futures. Enron neither produced nor delivered energy, but rather, they traded futures contracts on energy, which simply means they sold bets on what might or might not happen with energy prices in the future. In principle, it is the same as any other form of gambling such as betting on which number a craps shooter will roll next. Like all gamblers, Enron lost more than it won, so they fabricated revenue and hid losses in phony subsidiaries. In January 2001, Enron claimed total yearly revenue of 101 billion, with 63.4 billion in positive assets, and 26 billion in profits, all of which earned *Fortune* magazine's Best Company of the Year award. A few months later in September of 2001, the company collapsed when the market realized that, far from the officially reported 26 billion in profit, Enron in fact had 23 billion in losses (McLean and Elkind, 2003). Enron had crapped out.

Enron was just the beginning. On July 21, 2002, Worldcom filed for bankruptcy and surpassed Enron's losses. Lehman Brothers then surpassed Worldcom in 2008, followed shortly by the even larger Washington Mutual bankruptcy in the same year. Many other banks and insurance companies reported record losses, but the government saved them (except for Lehman, in which case the government paid for the toxic liabilities and turned over the valuable assets to a foreign bank—Barclay's) with the well-known 550 billion of free money under the TARP bailout (Taibbi, 2010). In retrospect, these massive failures were entirely predictable, and indeed, engineered to occur by individuals hedging heavily against their own companies. With Enron, the CEO Jeffrey Skilling, CFO Andrew Fastow, and many lower-ranking executives were prosecuted, fined, and sentenced to jail time. President Ken Lay died while awaiting prosecution. Ever since the Enron fiasco, not a single executive from a major bank has even faced investigation, much less prosecution.

Failure, fraud, and the rare prosecution are no reason to give up on new financial scams. At worst, a bankster can expect corporate—not personal— fines, but that is just part of the calculation of the scam, not a deterrent. For the 2000s, banks used CDOs (collateralized debt obligations), credit-default swaps, and other means to pump up the value of subprime mortgages as well as regular mortgages which they bundled in tiers with various other assets. Exploiting a regulatory change, the entire bundle could now be rated solely on the highest quality assets in the bundle, not an average of all of them. At the same time, another regulatory change allowed rating agencies, namely Fitch, Moody's, and Standard and Poors, to charge their fee to the seller, not the buyer. This meant that the seller of toxic assets paid ratings firms to give them high ratings, often rating junk bonds and subprime mortgage bundles as AAA or AA+ (the highest and second-highest, respectively) (McLean and Nocera, 2010). Detroit and other municipalities fell victim to toxic asset bundles, which were no longer illegal. Deceptive and unethical, but not illegal.

Simultaneously, other regulatory changes allowed speculators to buy and sell freely in formerly regulated markets—energy, food, and raw materials. This practice continues today, and since, 2010, speculation has increased food, energy, and materials prices by at least 200 billion dollars beyond what they would have been in a regulated market. As one oil industry analyst put it, "open speculation is great for investors, but it makes energy prices goddamn expensive for the consumer" (McLean and Elkind, 2003). In California, open energy speculation created sky-high prices for business and households, as well as rolling blackouts in 2000–2001 when Enron and other energy trading companies sent power out of the state or shut-down generating plants. In an environment that rewards the most ruthless self-interest, greed, and lust for power, only the most ruthless will triumph. They will lay waste to social relations and institutions in the process.

What ever happened to the checks and balances in government and the alleged self-regulatory interests of the financial (or any) business sector? These concepts are meaningless today. Capitalist enterprises only self-regulate to avoid governmental regulation. If the threat of government oversight is nonexistent, or even complicit with corporate interests over and against the people or the nation, then there is no need for self-regulation. As for the checks and balances in government, corporate executives currently run every regulatory agency, including the EPA, Energy Regulatory Commission, FDA, and SEC. The role of big money in campaigns, ongoing political advertisements by dark money organizations, perpetual involvement of big money at every level, moves political authority from democratic control to corporate, and often, individual control. If the only two candidates both represent finance or other big money interests, voting makes little difference. The US Federal Government has chosen sides, and they side resolutely with big business in general and it most powerful players in particular, many of whom circulate between corporate and government positions. This kind of ruthless political-economic climate encourages and rewards certain personality types who thrive on scheming, exploitation, and relentless self-interest with no regard for social consequences. In general terms, this is a sociopathic personality. In the environment of big business and politics specifically, it is the social dominator.

The Social Dominator

Only in comic books and movies do villains loudly and proudly proclaim themselves as evil and announce how they will seek to cause vast pain and destruction, usually followed by an evil cackle. Back in the day, they might twirl their moustache and chortle about their evil plots and nefarious ways. As we have seen, people like Charlie Luciano, Voldemort, Dick Cheney, Chris Kyle, Jamie Dimon, and most people in positions of power believe that their actions are fully justified. In real life there is no evil Red Skull who leads the evil Hydra organization, and we have no Captain America or S.H.I.E.L.D. (Strategic Hazard Intervention Espionage Logistics Directorate) to oppose them. Some, like Lloyd Blankfein, CEO of Goldman Sachs even claim they are "doing God's work" (Carney, 2009). It wasn't God that rescued his company in 2009, however, but the US government, which in one year enabled Goldman Sachs to go from absolutely broke to handing out 16 billion in year-end bonuses of government money for bankrupting the company during the previous year. If their business was illegal, we would call them racketeers or gangsters, like Charlie Luciano. If their business is legal, we call them entrepreneurs and investors, financiers, perhaps job creators (which is patently not true) maybe even financial geniuses. Whatever name we apply, they all share the same sense of inherent superiority insofar as whatever they think and do is inherently correct and should never be questioned. However, overt old-world haughtiness and condescension doesn't sell well in today's casual culture, so social domination requires some pretense of common association.

Billionaire Stephen Schwartzman, whom we previously noted, became known to the public when he announced to the world that he was ready for the "shared sacrifice" that it would take for the US to recover from the financial collapse he helped to orchestrate through his private equity group Blackstone. He was ready to "share the pain." Before he could share the pain he helped to create, he needed to spend 125 million dollars on five estates around the world, and as we earlier mentioned, a humble three million party to celebrate his 60th birthday (Tasini, 2011). Admiring fans in numerous media outlets, and people like Maria Di Mento (2014) in *The Chronicle of Philanthropy*, lauded him as the 23rd most generous person in the world, and celebrated his benevolence when he donated 100 million dollars to Tsinghua University in Beijing for 200 US students to attend college in China. This seems to have cost an apparent 500,000/student. Is China really that expensive, or is he buying something more than the enrollment of 200 students? He also donated another apparently impressive 100 million to various organizations. According to Forbes Online, as of 9:30 pm ET 9-24-2014, his net worth was 10.4 billion. With this in mind, his generosity amounts to about 1.9% of his current wealth each year, which is well below the national median of $2,974 in contributions (Giving USA Foundation, 2013), from those with median incomes of 51,017 (CNN Money 2014), or about 5.8% for a typical middle-class household. If we reckon generosity this way, Schwarzman would be a few million down the list of most generous people. Schwarzman's stinginess and attempts to manipulate public opinion are not just shrewd business decisions, but a manifestation of the social dominance orientation (SDO). He takes what he wants regardless of the consequences. Truth and lie are merely semantic distinctions that only matter if they benefit or hinder the social dominator.

Another popular billionaire, Bill Gates, argues that scientific calculation can solve all our problems and he has the money to prove it. The Gates Foundation funds the initiative to establish the Common Core standards in public schools. Not only do they mandate what must be taught, but what should not be taught, especially art, literature, philosophy, and the social sciences. After all, such things do not serve the interests of profit, which Gates and others regard as the only measurable standard of success. Since the calculation of profit and loss is considered the only viable measure of success or failure, the only viable orientation to education is a coldly calculating instrumental rationality:

> The instrumental rationality [is] being pushed by billionaires such as Bill Gates, Amazon's Jeff Bezos, Facebook's Mark Zuckerberg and Netflix's Reed Hastings. In this world, all human problems are essentially technical in nature and can be solved through technical means ... As a result, we now live in a world in which the politics of dis-imagination dominates; public discourses that bears witness to a critical and alternative sense of the world are often dismissed because they do not advance economic interests.
>
> GIROUX, 2014 p. 33

Many people are happy to join with Gates to bring business principles and profit-seeking into the classroom, such that Gates' billions have inspired numerous start-ups that sell elegant and mysterious products to facilitate education, such as design thinking, and innumerable assessment rubrics, protocols, goals, objectives, and outcomes. Whether any of these are successful in any way is secondary to the fact that rich individuals are now rich enough to bend the entire educational system to their personal will. Even with billions of dollars at their disposal, one person could not much alter entire social systems, but their money buys a lot of interest and loyalty from politicians, administrators, and grant-hungry professors. Social dominators may not seek admirers, but they often attract plenty of authoritarians willing to submit to, and often actively serve, their lust for dominance.

The lust for dominance may sometimes appear benign, even progressive on the surface. George Packer (2013) traced the lives of various individuals, each of whom contributes to the unwinding of America through the pursuit of individual self-interest. Some of them, such as Peter Thiel, are quite imaginative. Thiel loved fantasy and science fiction novels as a teenager and subsequently believes that technology is a kind of modern magic that will empower the United States into a golden era of wealth and ease. Thiel grew up in the Valley in California, which shaped his idealism. Back in 1977, the Valley was "egalitarian, educated, and comfortable ... more than almost anywhere else, ethnicity and religion and even class tended to bleach out in the golden sunlight. ... Almost all the children, even ones from the few wealthy families, went to the public schools—California was ranked number one in the country" in public education (Packer, 2013 p. 122).

Thiel embraced the heroes in Tolkien's *Lord of the Rings*, and rejected the entirety of Ayn Rand's *Atlas Shrugged* and *The Fountainhead*, in which the heroes were "implausibly righteous, the villains excessively evil, the outlook too Manichaean and pessimistic ..." (Packer 2013 p. 123). No, Thiel saw the future in terms of optimism and hope that technology could bring people together in new ways and create a global human community. Among his other works on the way to becoming a billionaire, he created PayPal (which he envisioned as a means for the common people to escape the control of global banks) and the Facebook online. Filled with egalitarian and humanitarian ideals, Thiel shunned backroom maneuvering, and assumed that others in the new tech economy shared his values. He was wrong. Other, much less egalitarian-minded people seized both companies in the old-fashioned way: back-room deals, payoffs, and stock manipulation. Thiel believed that technology had a life of its own, and that it transcended the decisions of people. Thiel was also no socialist. His sense of commitment to humanity was libertarian, where the best and brightest would rise to the top if business provided the public resources necessary for those from the lowest backgrounds to make the most of their abilities. In 2012, Thiel hosted a dinner party for the latest and greatest of Silicon Valley. The menu of organic and mostly vegan culinary masterpieces delighted the guests. Thiel offered the best wines, but they talked far more than they drank, and they all agreed on two things, (1), the superiority of the entrepreneurs and (2), the worthlessness of higher education (Packer, 2013 p. 397). Thiel believed that higher education was an utter failure, and only for-profit business could liberate the masses. He hoped that other rich people would support his idea of Thiel Fellowships which would scientifically and strategically promote those from disadvantaged backgrounds and "allow them to become entrepreneurs before they had a chance to lose their way or be snuffed out by the establishment" (Packer, 2013 p. 397). For the best and brightest, social and especially public institutions only inhibit greatness; private business expands freedom and opportunity.

We argue that Thiel failed to understand either American social character or modern capitalism. While he was able to make billions for himself, he, like most of the very rich, never realized that personal gain and vast hordes of money means a loss for someone else, often thousands or millions of others as competitors fail, while people lose their jobs and retirement funds as businesses and communities collapse. Thiel also never realized his own self-centeredness, nor that of other radical individualists. In our terms, he remained oblivious to the social dominance character that pervades entrepreneurial capitalists. Despite his good intentions, his lack of higher education (and that of many of his Silicon Valley associates who often dropped out of college, if they attended at all) limited his perspective to personal experiences. What worked for him would surely work for everyone, he imagined, and for all of American society and really, for the entire world. Consequently, Thiel contributed to social unwinding in his own libertarian way. Given his familiarity with science fiction and fantasy literature, we suspect that he may have a sense of irony about his life, that his own practices and the policies he advocates will not save the world, but rather lead the world straight to the chaos, injustice, and violence he hopes to avoid. The undoing of public education and decline of government oversight can only weaken social ties. Smart, but arrogant and broadly ignorant social dominators like Peter Thiel will not save the world. They will further unravel it as surely as did their more overtly predatory associates in finance capital, where Thiel, not coincidentally, also spent time. NB! Thiel, openly gay, became a Trump supporter.

Summary

As de Tocqueville noted, the fate of America was cast when the first Puritan set foot upon the shores of what would become Massachusetts. A number of Puritanical values from its theological positions remain as "unacknowledged" social ethics that intersected with a verdant land far from European conflicts and rivalries, and shaped a distinct culture, nation, national character and its underlying social character. The new nation eventually become the richest, most powerful nation in the world-a land where both its citizens and immigrants from afar would seek the pots of gold at the end of the American rainbows.

How and why? First and foremost, the emigrants would be among the more individualistic, more risk taking and most truly dedicated to their faith, qualities that would eventually morph into America's distinct social character. Of course, they often came from the poorest areas of their home countries or fled various forms of persecution, especially religious.

Protestantism arose as the rise of market society unshackled people from the bonds of traditional feudal society in which the majority of people were either peasants living on manors, or in small villages and towns where they practiced as artisans, tradesmen and shopkeepers. As market society grew, social bonds and attachments became attenuated while the economic security of relatively stable feudal life eroded. Individual effort became more and more salient for one's survival and indeed success. These changes also brought anxiety and uncertainty which prompted attempts to "escape from freedom" as Fromm put it, as well as foster characterological change as the typical "receptive character" of the feudal period, one who passively accepted the social arrangements faded and a new, hoarding (or acquisitive) character emerged to take center stage. For many people, especially those in vulnerable class positions, one of the major ways they chose to alleviate their anxieties and uncertainties was through authoritarian submission, in this case, to a Protestantism and its powerful God with whom the person might have an individual, unmediated relationship, mirroring the relationships typical of the market.

Although such submission to powerful leaders, organizations or ideologies might alleviate one set of anxieties, Protestantism, especially its Calvinist forms, created another set of anxieties, the uncertainty of predestined salvation in the next world was not all that different from the uncertainty of the market and one's economic future in this world. But nevertheless, Protestantism, having rendered work a "moral calling," valorized asceticism (austere living premised on rational practical outcomes) which transformed all of life into a relentless achievement-oriented career as opposed to a series of episodic moments. For the hoarding character, for whom economic success was more likely, that "success" was perhaps a wink from God that one was chosen, and hence that wink might somewhat alleviate anxieties and uncertainties about salvation. This of course suggested that some people, the more industrious or hard-working, were blessed by God. Moreover, they were likely to be fellow Protestants. Meanwhile others were likely to be lazy, hedonistic and self-indulgent, and not infrequently members of minority groups were not so blessed. This Manichean world view of wealth as good, poverty as bad, yet persists as "producerism," a view that the world consists of makers and takers which has been an important factor in a variety of right populist movements from the Know Nothing Party of the 19th Century to the Tea Party or Trumpsters of today.

The founding fathers of the country, Franklin, Madison, Jefferson, Washington and others attempted to create a democratic republic that granted freedom of, if not from, religion, freedom of the press, assembly and perhaps most important, freedom of capital. They nevertheless attempted to limit actual political power to the highly moral, educated, guardian classes meaning rich white men like themselves, many of whom were Southern aristocrats whose wealth depended on land and slavery. A number of conditions came together and the new nation slowly but surely prospered, pushed its frontiers ever westward, and as it did so, following its Civil War, a new class of financial and industrial elites supplanted the landowning elites. Industrialization brought a new kind of prosperity and new class relations because the factories needed more and more proletariat labor. Vast numbers of immigrants from all over Europe flocked to the United States, a land of milk and honey, where the streets were paved with gold, the same gold that filled the pots at the end of the rainbow. And so too some of these immigrants also prospered. While on the one hand, the new elites, the "captains of industry" clearly embodied certain aspects of America's social character, its individualism, industriousness and determination, unlike the founding fathers however, they were less and less committed to the public good and the maintenance of domestic peace and prosperity. Instead, they were more concerned with their private fortunes and opulent, ostentatious life styles. Moreover, they used their economic power to not only ensure that the government maintained the laissez-faire practices that enabled their fortunes, but they used the State's monopolization of the means of violence to control, dominate and limit the unrest, resistance and mobilizations of exploited workers who might resist their exploitation. To an extent, they succeeded, at least until the contradictions of financial system that they had created imploded in 1929.

Given the ineptitude of Herbert Hoover, businessman turned president, perhaps the tragedy that anticipated the farcical George W. Bush, the election of FDR reoriented government to actively invest in economic development through a variety of government programs. While the results were hit or miss, these various programs built roads, dams, public schools, and electricity to Appalachia and other impoverished regions. WWII fostered vast amounts of military spending. America's vast industrial base changed from peacetime consumer goods to military hardware. One of the major legacies of World War II was thus the growth of the defense and defense related industries. Notwithstanding the warnings of President Eisenhower, the military budgets rose and fell in conjunction with military ventures such as the Korean War and Vietnam, but the election of Ronald Reagan more firmly united politics, military spending and Wall Street. The era of endless war (and endless war spending) had begun. To this day, conservatives really believe that the fall of the Soviet Union was due to its inability to compete with the United States in terms of its expenditures on weapons and then Reagan's bold entreaty to "tear down this wall." This of course is total nonsense, but Reagan's domestic voodoo economics (tax cuts pay for themselves, everyone gets richer when the money flows to the top) reinforced the outflow of jobs and capital to the third world where cheap labor and lax controls were typical, especially China. This was the emerging age of globalization and neoliberalism that closed factories and de-industrialized the old centers of industry which in turn led to lower wages, and consequently diminished economic security, diminished buying power and the quality of life declined for many Americans. This more ruthless world created the openings for a new cadre of social dominators in finance and banking who created vast speculative bets, the so-called economic bubbles of false earnings and phantom profits based on speculation, trading currency, mergers and acquisitions, and hedge funds and derivatives. A new realm of commerce, computers and computer-based communication, this thing called the Internet began to flourish and generate vast profits (often as part of the speculative bubbles) along with instant and dot.com millionaires, often billionaires. Further, robots in vast numbers began working in factories to manufacture, assemble, paint and package consumer goods, except for clothing, which uses impoverished workers in sweatshops, and agriculture, which relies on illegal and easily exploited immigrant labor. More sophisticated computers track inventories, handle monetary transactions, route data, and even handle customer service complaints.

Starting in the late 1970s, three important economic trends were evident: globalization and the expansion of finance capital, computerized automation, and the Internet. Vast fortunes were created (again, often through financial manipulation and the illusion of profit rather than through the manufacture and sale of commodities). For the majority, especially blue collar workers, many well-paying jobs were lost, incomes began to stagnate and in many cases even decline. At the same time however new cultural values arose, not the least of which were civil rights, feminism and the widespread embrace of sex, drugs, and rock "n" roll, which offended the moral sensibilities of many Americans. Cultural realignment led many working-class Democrats to support more conservative Republican presidents such as Tricky Dick Nixon whose racist dog whistles appealed to white Southerners while at the same time, he promised to clamp down on the unwashed traitors of the anti-war movement—some of whom were rumored to be having sex outside of marriage. This trend was especially clear in 1980 when a number of traditionally blue-collar Democrats, facing economic pressures as well as dealing with the consequences of the civil rights movement, more women in the labor force, and the growing acceptance of the counterculture, supported Reagan. The Reagan Democrats have voted Republican ever since, and thus a large segment of the American working-class consistently votes against its own economic interests.

Secondly, Reagan and his successors, including the Democrat Bill Clinton, dismantled the social interventionist government policies of the New Deal. Government would no longer step in as needed to maintain widespread prosperity. Retrenchments in government social spending and eternal increases in the military industrial complex mobilized a vast army of lobbyists, consultants and neo-conservative think tanks to dream up reasons for military interventions against all those who were supposedly jealous and wanted to destroy our freedom. This call to arms appealed to the paranoid and authoritarian aspects of American character, as if we were still living in marginal settlement colonies or on an isolated homestead on the Western frontier. Vast sums have been spent on useless weapon systems from the Reagan Star Wars antimissile projects to the F-35 fighter of today—the ultimate fighter to combat aggression from a Soviet empire that collapsed decades ago. Trillions were spent on interventions and invasions such as in Iraq and Syria, which produced yet another enemy, the Islamic State.

Let's refashion the American mythology. The pots of gold at the end of the rainbows were emptied to make high-risk speculative bets, inflate executive salaries, automate and move production facilities abroad. In its place, the gold of Silicon Valley and Wall Street is more like that of the leprechaun—it shines from a distance but, like the derivatives, pump and dump economic bubbles, and CDOs, vanishes as soon as you get close. Like leprechauns, the banksters and high-tech "entrepreneurs" hide their gold away in remote redoubts and then venture forth to scheme more away from earnest but naïve commoners.

American society is now controlled by a small class of Über-rich who not only become wealthy beyond imagination, but whose lavish spending in opulent ostentation such as $10 million dollar birthday parties has made the robber barons of the early 20th Century seem like paupers. But this new class, quite unlike the founding fathers, the New Dealers, or even the robber barons (who after all did actually build things) are not simply indifferent to the vast majority of Americans who find it more and more difficult to survive economically. These Über-rich are in many ways hostile to the very ideas of popular democracy and that elected governments should serve the people in general. Instead, the new elites have given us *Citizens United* and an "inverted totalitarianism." Welcome to the brave new world, where at least the use of marijuana, the soma drug of our day is being decriminalized.

Guns: Violence, Gender and American Character

Violence is a part of America's culture. It is as American as cherry pie.

H. RAP BROWN

• • •

The essential American soul is hard, isolate, stoic, and a killer.

D.H. LAWRENCE

∴

Various progressives and left wing political commentators and humorists like John Stewart and Steven Colbert have enjoyed making fun at the contradictions between right wing conservatives who are typically religious Christians, and their miserly irrational hostility to the poor that we have seen was rooted in Protestant notions of moral purity and predestination. And while Christ's messages were of peace, generosity and forgiveness, love thy neighbor, give them clothes, food and shelter to all in need, many "good Christians" are quite hostile to the poor and quite often, "good" conservative Christians extoll violence toward them, especially if their skin is a bit darker. As we've tried to show, what may seem quite contradictory to some people is that certain other people might be both highly religious and yet hateful, intolerant and without compassion for others-especially members of ethnic, religious, racial or gender orientation outgroups.[1] But there is an underlying emotional consistency between authoritarianism and the "motivated reasoning" that enables a fusion of authoritarian submission to a strict God and aggression toward outgroups that can range from crude jokes to actual violence and indeed calls for genocide. So some of the more liberal minded humorously ask if Jesus would have treated sick people who did not have insurance or if they had pre-existing conditions?

---

1   One of us, Lauren Langman, teaches at a Jesuit University and here the social justice message of the Sermon on the Mount, of sharing and caring, is the dominant value, not the hating, smiting and stoning of the Other. Pope Francis from Argentina, once a bastion of liberation theology, has been as critical of capitalism as we.

The conservative logic, anchored within America's underlying social character, much like the "strict father" framework described by Lakoff (2009) condemns any person who might need government-sponsored or other aid of any kind, including healthcare insurance, as lazy, indulgent, dependent, irresponsible and morally unworthy of receiving such benefits paid for by good, decent hardworking folks. People should be independent and self-sufficient rather than weak, dependent parasites. At one Tea Party rally where Rand Paul was speaking, Wolf Blitzer asked a hypothetical about what to do with a 30 year old man without insurance who was in the ER in a coma. A number of the tea parties shouted "let him die."[2] Why was his poor condition physically and financially, the target of rage? What did Winthrop say about Christian charity?

In a similar way, we wonder, what kind of heat would Jesus pack? Let's try to answer that. The AK-47 is a Soviet design and Christ would never touch that legacy of the commies. Glock pistols are also foreign-made (Austrian) and often tied to urban street gangs (read African-American or Spanish-speaking) so they are out as well. The Colt 45 is a trusty revolver and still kicks ass after 150 years. The Winchester 1873 lever-action rifle played a major role on the frontier and in Western movies. For assault power, the AR-15 is a civilian version of the fully automatic Colt M-16, the current rifle of the US military. Assault rifles can be inelegant and cumbersome though; we are not without a sense of taste and style. So, for our money, you can't beat the Smith and Wesson Model 29 .44 magnum revolver with its classic styling, and the favorite gun of "Dirty" Harry Callahan (played by the very manly Clint Eastwood). It will fire through car windshields rather than ricochet and hit innocent bystanders. Most of the time, the baddies will flinch first and run away at the very sight of it. While the juxtaposition of Jesus and firearms may seem humorous, this humor however reveals that within American social character there is an interwinging of conservative Christian theology, religiosity, guns, hegemonic masculinity and propensities toward violence.

Former Arkansas Governor Mike Huckabee, an ordained Baptist minister, running for the GOP presidential nomination in 2015, stated that there should be no limitations on the kinds of weapons people can buy including military weapons. Does that include tanks, rocket launchers, Stinger missiles? What about howitzers, cruise missiles and tactical nukes while we're at it? Recently, the Texas legislature, as a response to university shootings throughout the country, allowed weapons on University of Texas campuses. And ironically enough, there was a student protest at the University of Texas, Austin that

---

2   http://abcnews.go.com/blogs/politics/2011/09/tea-party-debate-audience-cheered-idea-of
    -letting-uninsured-patients-die/.

took the form of publicly displaying dildos and chanting "cocks not Glocks." Furthermore, while Texas law now allows open-carry guns on its campuses, in Texas, the public display of sex toys is illegal. By now the reader should easily understand how phallic aggression is often associated with sexual repression. That is why the 60's generation articulated their resistance and claimed that we should "make love not war." Quite unlike many conservative religionists, most of these youth practiced what they preached. Of course they paved the way for the current "hookup culture," the personal sections of Craig's Lists, Backstage. com and Tinder, but, given the narcissism of the current era, the 60s generation gets no thanks, no recognition, nor appreciation from the more sexually open youth for the hard fought struggles of their parents or grandparents.[3]

Today, many people are worried about the intertwining of conservative Christian religion and phallic aggression as there are now many evangelical ministers in the armed forces that would suggest that the US military is there to serve God-by killing heathens, infidels and perhaps fornicators. Many of these military chaplains, especially in the Air Force, have largely become proselytizers of Protestant fundamentalism and some are clearly Dominionists (Weinstein and Seay, 2006). Many such chaplains and military officers, including generals, see the wars in the Middle East as a Holy War against Islam, a war blessed by God, Jesus, and probably both.[4] This was especially clear when General William Boykin, a born again Christian, former Undersecretary of State, proclaimed that Islamic extremists hate the United States because we're a Christian nation, because our foundation and our roots are Judeo-Christian. According to general Boykin, "The enemy is a guy named Satan" (Jehl, 2005). However, this notion of the right of the superior, white Christians to find "moral redemption" in violence is not a new phenomenon.

Guns deserve serious consideration because if Jesus would carefully select a firearm, the government should likewise advise citizens how to make appropriate choices so people can defend themselves against evils such as ISIS or Taliban jihadi showing up at their barbecues and picnics. Many states do have an "official" firearm, as in Utah where the official gun is the Browning Model

---

3   Most of what is called the hook up culture is of word and not deed, that while most young people are OK with a casual fling, it happens much more rarely than one might think if watching *Sex and the City*, or later, *Girls* and assumed the shows portray typical frequency and recklessness, which they don't really.

4   See the Military Religious Freedom Foundation for more information on how the military has become infused with Christian fundamentalists who fundamentally believe that killing Moslems is doing God's work. The founder and leader, Mickey Weinstein, an Air Force veteran, was a White House counsel for president Reagan. Http://www.militaryreligiousfreedom .org/.

1911 .45 caliber. Arizona's state gun is the Colt .45 caliber Single Action Army revolver, known popularly as "the gun that won the West" or in other words, killed many Mexicans, Spanish, and Native-Americans during its initial production run from 1873 to 1941. It therefore seems like a perfect choice for Governor Jan Brewer, Sherriff Joe Arpaio and other white politicians in Arizona. As state Senator Ron Gould gleefully remarked, "Any time you see a Western movie, the revolver in John Wayne's hand is a Colt single action." In contrast, Native-American state Senator and former President of the Navajo nation Albert Hale responded that yes, "If you want to symbolize something and shove that something in their faces, this gun symbolized the extinction, the extermination of those Indians who were here" (Schwartz, 2011).

The gun has a long tradition as an essential part of national character—especially for men. It has almost always been part of rural American social/family life (Bageant 2008). The United States has almost as many guns as people. The "freedom" to own guns is a salient moment of traditional identity and for many rural gun owners, guns are often intertwined with conservative/fundamentalist religion.

God, Guns and the Colonizer

If God blessed the Puritan colonists as a "chosen people," the only "evidence" seems to be faith, scripture, intuition, and folklore. But what is clearly evident, is that ever since Columbus landed in the Caribbean and Cortez marched upon Tenochtitlan, gunpowder based weaponry, either the pistol, arquebus (an early rifle), musket (rifle) or cannon gave Europeans a decided military advantage over the indigenous peoples. The first man off the Mayflower held an Italian blunderbuss, now enshrined in an NRA museum. In North America, as more and more European settlers arrived and moved from the settled East to the Western frontiers, they displaced the indigenous peoples and began a legacy of violence and murder that endures unabated.[5] In this way, unworthy immigrant invaders, minority group criminals and others threaten white male privilege from without and within, so a real American needs guns for self-defense against the hordes coming to steal their land, homes, and take their women. How did that happen?

The early colonies that would become the United States were much like other "new" settler colonies, especially Australia, New Zealand, South Africa and even modern Israel. Settler colonialism was based on more than simply

---

5   This was a fundamental aspect of Turner's "frontier thesis" in which underlying what he called dynamism was an aggressive quality, which we discuss below.

taking the natural or agricultural resources of another people and using force to defend that theft. Settler colonies also meant territorial occupation by immigrants from the home country who claimed political sovereignty and the right to take the land and dispossess the indigenous people. Since the colonizers made the laws and wielded superior firepower, dispossession could take any form they wanted. As Frantz Fanon (2004 [1961]) made so clear, colonialism and imperialism are inherently forms of violence, not only through the physical coercion by the better armed colonizer, but the ability of the colonizers to valorize their own culture and in turn dominate and denigrate the cultures and identities of the indigenous people, who in turn internalize a sense of their own inferiority, valorize the "superior" and then attempt to mimic the qualities of the colonizer in order to survive. As Fanon summarized it, putting a white mask on Black skins (2008 [1952]). Colonized people first surrender to force, and then denigrate themselves into servitude. It is at this point where in the America, Puritan religion and available land, aided by a few muskets, fostered a new identity as we discussed in detail in Chapter 2. Indigenous people, as allegedly inferior or unblessed subhumans, can be dispossessed by any mean available. For example, British General Amherst, who bequeathed his name to Amherst, Massachusetts, ordered the distribution of malaria infested blankets to the indigenous peoples and thus began the first known instance of biological warfare in the New World.

While guns eventually became the preferred weapons of war, and even became the ideal weapons for hunting, in few other nations did they become such an integral part of national character, social character and identity by valorizing the underlying assertive, phallic aggressive masculinity. In other words, many cultures embrace patriarchal domination, and many also have widespread gun ownership, but very few so closely connect guns as being intrinsic aspects of masculine identity as in the United States. In the national mythology, the gun first enabled the expansion of America and the removal and dispossession of native peoples from their ancestral lands, and the defense of that land from reclamation by the displaced. Similarly there is a very deeply enshrined, enduring myth that the widespread possession of guns enabled a ragtag colonial army of backwoods sharp shooters to defeat the most powerful empire at that time. Like most myths however this is not borne out by the facts, hunting muskets were not very useful in military combat at that time. It took longer to reload a hunting gun then did a military musket. Further, bayonets were easily affixed to military muskets and much of the combat at that era was in close quarter combat or distant artillery—not the long range musket fire from afar as portrayed in myth and movie. One is not likely to need a bayonet if hunting deer or squirrel, and when hunting bear, if you get close enough to need a bayonet you likely won't survive to pass on your failed technique to others. Also, most of the weapons and munitions used in the Revolutionary War were supplied by France which then declared war on England in 1778, and we already mentioned how the French navy blockaded Cornwallis at Yorktown to finally defeat the British, and talented officers such as Lafayette, Rochambeau, and the Prussian Friedrich Wilhelm von Steuben and others contributed vital training and leadership, without which the unprofessional colonial army would likely never have won. But giving the French, Prussians, and other foreigners due credit is not the stuff of self-aggrandizing myth, especially national myths of creation in which farmer soldiers and their guns enabled freedom and democracy. Yet that still informs conservative opposition to any and all gun control. Although no enemy yet draws breath in the United States, many Americans still worship the idolatrous power of the gun, many believe it will grant them personal safety and domestic tranquility, notwithstanding overwhelming evidence that ownership is more likely to perpetuate violence, early deaths, accidents and wrongful death to owners than to criminals.[6] Far more die from these accidents than are protected from harm. As automobile deaths have declined since 2006, gun deaths have steadily increased since 2004, and more rapidly since 2005 (VPC Report, 2015). Gun deaths outpace vehicle fatalities in 17 states, and if present trends continue, gun deaths will outnumber vehicular deaths in the US as a whole by 2018. This becomes all the more salient considering that over 90% of all households own at least one car, but only 29.7% own at least one gun. Americans spend vastly more time driving than handling guns, so it appears that guns have become far more life-threatening than cars (VPC Report, 2015). The gun, as both a symbol of assertive masculinity and a violent weapon remains a salient feature of American character and identity, and has become a central feature of American daily life that has not seen since the colonial era.

From the Seaboard Colonies to the Western Frontier

One of the major attempts to understand American character, especially individualism, democracy and its dynamism has been the "frontier thesis" in

---

6   It seems that tragic gun accidents are becoming more frequent, children killing each other or their parents, and accidental discharges. Hidden holsters in bras and underwear have taken a toll and men do sometimes shoot their own penises. So much for phallic aggression. Perhaps in the hyper reality of today's world, the symbol, or perhaps simulation of masculinity becomes so much more important than the actual reality.

which Frederick Jackson Turner (1921) saw the frontier as the defining feature of America that made it distinctly different than Europe with its legacies of deference to aristocratic hierarchies; the frontier attenuated such qualities. The existence of an area of free land, its continuous recession, and the advance of American settlement westward, explain American development. But that "free land," or "surplus land" was a misnomer because it was of course already inhabited by a large Native American population whose "rights" to the land were negated (Rojek, 2016). Turner's thesis has been criticized on a number of accounts, but the central point for Turner was his defense, if not celebration of the expansion of White Civilization that justified whatever violence needed. As Rojek argues:

> This portrait depicts racially superior frontier settlers bravely facing wilderness and the hostility of native barbarians and triumphing through principled commitment to self-government and adroit military conquest. Roosevelt understands history along classical Social Darwinian lines as a perpetual struggle between rivals for survival. The racially superior type (white settlers) seize the frontier "wasteland" and, through industry and enterprise, till and build upon it to produce prosperity. Turner is no closet racist. Nonetheless, he shares the evolutionist doctrine that it is the manifest destiny of the white race to prevail in the West and remake the world in their own image.
>
> ROJEK, 2016 p. 57

Turner argued that the frontier environment had been the primary factor shaping American character, egalitarian democracy was necessary to establish laws while toughness, independence and self-reliance were necessary for survival in the frontiers, especially given hostile enemies.

Turner's frontier did not include women, but as we know, wherever you had populations of single men such as cowboys, prospectors or miners, there followed women of the night. Meanwhile, slighting the "uncivilized" native population says little about how the expansion required the displacement and often deaths of vast numbers of Native Americans. Every hard working white man had the right to own the land, even if the original occupants did not think so. The cavalry came to the rescue! And they most often came with the Colts, Springfields and Gatlings we mentioned. The American military made the frontier safe for settlers. Thus Turner's view of "dynamism" sanitizes the underlying characterological aggression that was characteristic of the frontiersman.

Moreover, as Rojek also noted, the image of the "decent," civilized American seeking peace, freedom and economic security became transformed into an aspect of America's "celebrity culture" beginning with the "Wild West" shows of Buffalo Bill Cody that became enshrined in mass mediated mythic representations of the cowboy as a hero, the good guy in the white hat from Zane Gray novels, early Hollywood silent movies, then talking movies and finally television series as the monomyth we discussed earlier.In his majestic three-volume opus, Richard Slotkin (1998 [1992]; 1998 [1985]; 2000[1973]), speaking to the "frontier thesis" shows how the gun framed the American experience as a struggle for moral redemption. As a moral instrument, the gun transcends any practical need and becomes part of identity and character that believes violent solutions are the first and best choice to resolve any disagreement or conflict whether between settler and natives, cowboys and Indians, farmers and ranchers, or today, real Americans versus minority group criminals.

While our focus of this chapter is largely on the phallic aggressive aspects of American culture, this is only part of the story. The other part of the story tells of the more benevolent relations between people based on long histories of cooperation, mutual support, and philanthropy, but that doesn't make for great novels, movies, or TV series. There is a good deal of historic evidence that the mythic Wild West was not really as wild and lawless as its mythic representations; governors typically succeeded in enforcing private property rights (Anderson and Hill, 2004). Many of the settlers of the West were veterans, especially after the civil war. They were armed and trained in the use of firearms and hardly the helpless simple folks portrayed in movies or TV shows selling the American Monomyth wherein the good, but helpless decent folks needed a well-armed, quick on the draw hero to protect them. John Smith married Pocahontas, and as we will see, so did many other whites whose names have been lost to history. Just as slavery was a form of violence, there was also an abolitionist movement and Underground Railroad—often supported by Christians, especially Quakers who were just as religious as the slaveholders, but with a different take. This dialectic will be noted in our conclusion.

Slotkin was primarily concerned with the transformation from the actual West of history into the mythical West of the American imagination as expressed in popular culture songs, books, and movies, and in more recent years, television and even some video games. While perhaps less popular among today's millennials, several generations of Americans grew up watching John Wayne, Tom Mix, Hopalong Cassidy, Clayton Moore (the Lone Ranger) and Gene Autry battle the often mustachioed, "bad guys" in black hats who were the racialized Mexican Others, and Native Americans quite typically were depicted as wild savages. Much like *American Sniper*, the violence of the Other, in this case the Iraqi Muslim, is generally a sign of his or her utter depravity and evil. The context that is the American military occupying peoples land and those Others are not happy, is generally ignored. And yet the American Revolution itself was to rid the land of foreign occupation and control enforced by a military. A "chosen people," of course, like the Americans had every right to wage war on England. Seventy five years after the American Revolution, Canada gained its independence from England without firing a single shot. For Lipset (1990), this difference in origin explains why Canada is far less violent and far more respecting of laws and governmental authority than the US.

Many of the same themes of individualism, phallic aggression, and moral redemption were reproduced in the various cop and robber genres in which the tough cop ignores protocol and the law, but gets the bad guy(s). Dirty Harry, holding the .44 Magnum we just discussed, challenged a Black male to "make his day," as any excuse would justify blowing away a Black man. After Dirty Harry retired from the police force he became a film director and is surely no accident that he turned the sniper Chris Kyle, who killed more Iraqi men, women, and children than any other sniper in any other war into a folk hero, at least among the Southern and Western audiences.

Slotkin began his trilogy of the West by discussing the anxiety of the early settlers in the New World that led to the demonization and denigration of the indigenous peoples as violent, irrational "savages." Historically this was not always the case and indeed most of the violent conflicts took place long after the colonial era. He then traced persistence and changes in this central mythology of the evil, inferiority of the racialized Other as seen in literature, popular spectacles (the Buffalo Bill "Wild West shows") and most importantly in politics. The mythical West of good guys in white hats versus bad guys in black hats and swarthy complexions, became the frame through which many Americans interpreted the clearly imperialistic Spanish-American war (including the rebellion by the Filipinos). Then came the new Other, the "Jap," the monkeyman of WWII whose homeland was appropriately nuked as retaliation for Pearl Harbor and the Bataan death march, as if the women, children and old men of Hiroshima and Nagasaki were part of Tojo's war cabinet. Then the godless commies during the Cold War with the USSR, the gooks and slopes during Vietnam, then Chris Kyle killing as many evil savages as he could spy through the scope of his rifle. In other words, the same myth of good people, typically God-fearing Christian Americans, pitted against evil savages continues undiminished from the earliest colonial days to the present, the same cultural logic justifying redemptive violence, morally justified phallic aggression, that turns mass murderers into heroes.

In the American cultural imaginary, moral righteousness undergirds the "us" as sacred and "them" as evil. Indeed, the investigations of Turse (2013) and Scahill (2013) have shown how the mass slaughter of innocents, whether the slaughter of the Sioux at Wounded Knee, the victims of Operation Phoenix, My Lai, Bagram or Fallujah, were not the random acts of deviant rogues, but the expressions of a long-standing cultural logic in which a Manichaean understanding of good and evil justifies mass murder, torture and violence as the means of moral redemption.[7] Let there be no equivocation. This was rooted in the early colonial experiences and expulsions, slavery and a long history of interventionism. This legacy has persisted in many ways. While a comprehensive analysis might well constitute volumes, as for example Slotkin or Wilkinson (1986) have shown, the cultural tropes of guns, violence and moral redemption shaped a major aspect of the American (mostly male) social character structure that embodies and articulates a privileged and assertive, indeed phallic aggressive masculinity that is still highly evident.

Let's us only note the frequency of mass shootings that are almost entirely a male activity. Jeb Bush, while campaigning for the 2016 presidency proclaimed that "stuff happens" while not to be outdone, Ben Carson, a neurologist said the thought of gun control was more repugnant than a bullet filled body in the ER. Bush's claim is factually wrong. Stuff does not happen. In no other country with comparable gun ownership such as Canada or Switzerland do we see "stuff" like the endless numbers of murdered innocents. In the USA, it becomes clearly evident how the legacy of gun ownership rooted in the colonial era, as defense against the Indian "savages" or controlling the "primitive" Black slaves has endured to this very day. Moreover, the NRA, well-funded by gun makers, is one of the most effective lobbies in Washington. Thus gun ownership, often an essential part of the phallic aggressive social character, typically intertwined with individualism, endures as a significant aspect of many, but surely not all Americans.

In general, the mass media constructs mass shooters as the irrational actions of "deranged" individuals; mentally ill deviants are to blame for school, mall and theater shootings, never the culture of violence that is compounded by readily available guns. Yes, while many of the spree shooters may be psychologically disturbed, individualistic explanations serve to exonerate the cultural toleration for violence that is essential part of traditional American character. The overt expressions of psychopathology as violence were shaped by the combination of long-standing cultural legacies intertwined with the ready availability of weapons that make a mass shooting a desirable and

---

7 In the 2016 Republican primary campaign, when Donald Trump said he would bring back waterboarding or worse, he was cheered on, much like Ted Cruz who said he would carpet bomb ISIL and find out if sand would glow. Again, many conservative Republicans cheered them on.

available means to express severe anger and frustration. And while the shoot-ings at schools and movie theaters are deplorable, each year many thousands of people more die from gun "accidents" or criminal behavior, especially gang warfare.

Like Jeb Bush, elected leaders of the country quite "rationally" see violence as necessary to both thwart crime and deviance within. Of course the US also needs a strong military, and a long history of interventions to protect the coun-try from threats abroad. No real American would ever question such basic truths, whether that leader may be a kick-ass conservative like John McCain who sings "bomb, bomb, Iran," or, Noble Peace Prize winner Obama, the "Drone Ranger" who created and uses his own Praetorian Guard, JSOC (Joint Special Operations Command) in over 100 countries, the result is the same, the slaugh-ter of innocent civilians justified as moral redemption as if following the will of God. How did all this happen?

In Real America, Real Men Shoot, Kill, and Destroy

Toughness, rugged individualism was an essential quality for survival in the early years of colonial life and westward expansion. It was as essential for the early Puritan village as the later frontier town. Of course it was and is essential for the frequent military actions. Between Puritanism and the historical condi-tions of the colonizer in lands occupied by others, a cultural ideal of assertive (aggressive) hegemonic masculinity emerged as coarseness and toughness, expressed in the celebrations of guns and violence that was blessed by God. Fighting in the colonies began in 1622 with an Indian attack on Jamestown, then came the Pequot War, King Phillip's War, four imperial wars between 1689 and 1693, major rebellions, the War for Independence, the War of 1812, the 1848 war with Mexico to seize Texas, Arizona, and New Mexico from Mexico, the Civil War, the Spanish-American War. Genocidal war against Native-Americans was the first battle and continued for about 300 years. Founded in 1607, the colony of Jamestown, VA faced starvation in the winters of 1608 and 1609, saved only by gifts of food primarily from the Paspahegh Indians, led by chief Wowincha-puncke who were part of the Algonquin chiefdom. The chief of the Algonquin, Powhatan (or in his language, Wahunsunacock) then suggested that the colonists remove themselves from his territory and settle in an unoccupied vil-lage not far away where the Pospahegh would help them establish houses and farmland. In thanks for Wowinchapuncke's aid and Powhatan's diplomacy, the new governor, Thomas West, the Baron of De La Warr ordered the Paspahegh annihilated in 1610. The gun became the favorite instrument of death. After slaughtering the village, De La Warr's lieutenant reported that they captured Wowinchapuncke's wife, whom they raped and then stabbed to death. They then turned to his children, whom they threw into a river and "blewe out their Braynes in the Water" (Rountree, 1990). For the next 301 years, the colonies and then the United States carried out a genocidal war that reduced the indigenous population from about 12 million in 1610 to about 235,000 in 1911 when the genocide finally ended with the Obliteration of the Yahi on August 29, 1911 (Dunbar-Ortiz, 2015).

Beyond North America, there have been hundreds of military actions and interventions throughout South and Central America as well as the Caribbean, and this does not even include the "covert" interventions. The German attack on the Lusitania which precipitated the US joining World War I was based on its military cargo headed toward England. The Japanese attack on Pearl Harbor came after FDR had threatened to embargo oil and other materials to Japan. The many military victories and numerous other not so covert interventions that overthrew governments were "proof" of God's blessing of the winning side and God did not seem to fret all about millions of indigenous peoples getting killed.

These economic, cultural and political legacies disposed a uniquely American aspect of character, the "American Tough." Wilkinson (1986) argues that American toughness, a combination of masculine strength and bravery, if not bravado is a very American quality. Compare fictional American detectives like Dirty Harry with British counterparts like Sherlock Holmes or the French Hercule Poirot. This "toughness" is not simply an aggressive predisposition, but a resolute form of strength as much based on self-assurance and conviction as on one's physical power. It suggests that the person cannot only express aggression, but endure pain at the hand of a brutal enemy, that he can take it like a "real man," but the enemy's aggression will be avenged. This toughness is associated with individualism, the tough guy can handle himself, and he doesn't need anyone to tell him what to do. Conversely, nobody can push him around. As Humphrey Bogart so clearly put it in *The Treasure of Sierra Madre*:

> ... nobody tells Fred C Dobbs what to do. "You can't catch me sleepin' ... Don't you ever believe that. I'm not that dumb. The day you try to put anything over on me will be a costly one for both of you ... Any more lip out of ya and I'll pull off and let ya have it. If ya know what's good for ya, ya won't monkey around with Fred C. Dobbs!"

Strength is better than smarts. Whenever power has threatened or challenged us, the American response was likely to tough it out, to remain resolute in face of adversity. This "tough it out" aspect of American masculinity meant that we would not give up in Vietnam, or Iraq, nor Afghanistan, even when it has been long evident that the "Custer last stand" mentality means that many young men and now women die for lost causes that endured because leaders did not want to appear weak. We are speaking of Presidents Johnson, Nixon, Bush II and Obama.

Ironically, those who oppose the needless loss of lives of Americans as well as the "enemies" are denigrated as either anti-American traitors, cowards, pussies without balls or some combination thereof. As a result of the amalgamation of Puritanism, survival and almost endless military victories, "moral masculinity" *as articulated in redemptive violence* has been enshrined in our popular culture as part of the "American monomyth" discussed in Chapter 1. As a result, American character embraced a fusion of morally justified, religiously sanctioned, redemptive violence that was intertwined with essentialist notions of gender, sustaining, indeed celebrating a phallic aggressive male "toughness" and power sustained by female subordination along with an intolerance to either assertive women or "passive" men, based on the presumption that homosexual men are weak and effeminate. The long enduring social-psychological admixture of guns, violence and an aggressive masculinity in America social character still inspires both killers and their worshippers.

Chris Kyle—Mass Killer and American Hero

In the course of writing our analysis of the dialectical nature of American character, specifically this chapter on guns, violence and social character, Hollywood released a blockbuster movie, *American Sniper*. Based on the book with the same name, both of which generated a great deal of public and indeed private debate and discussion, it tells the personal story of Chris Kyle, an American sniper in Iraq who scored the greatest number of kills in military history—160 officially observed kills and he claimed many more were not counted. Kyle's is a personal story and not a political analysis, which of course is really the most important point. The story does not tell us why the United States invaded Iraq, nor why the Iraqis would resist foreign invaders who devastated their country, occupied their lands, broke into their homes, raped their women, tortured their men, and installed a corrupt government that began a sectarian civil war which finally opened the door for the rise of the Islamic State. What's not to like?

Instead, the story and the movie simply reduced the invasion of Iraq to another version of the Monomyth, good versus evil, the brave and valiant

Christian soldiers of the United States versus the vile, evil sadistic Muslim "savages" that include women and children (Kyle's first kill was a child). Just like the early colonists, he "blewe out their Braynes" with righteous might. As one acute observer, Chris Hedges put it:

> American Sniper lionizes the most despicable aspects of u.s. society—the gun culture, the blind adoration of the military, the belief that we have an innate right as a "Christian" nation to exterminate the "lesser breeds" of the earth, a grotesque hypermasculinity that banishes compassion and pity, a denial of inconvenient facts and historical truth, and a belittling of critical thinking and artistic expression.[8]

In a phone conversation with Hedges, combat veteran Michael Weinstein says that

> The movie never asks the seminal question as to why the people of Iraq are fighting back against us in the very first place ... It made me physically ill with its twisted, totally one-sided distortions of wartime combat ethics and justice woven into the fabric of Chris Kyle's personal and primal justification mantra of "God-Country-Family." It is nothing less than an odious homage, indeed a literal horrific hagiography to wholesale slaughter ... The embrace of extreme right-wing Christian chauvinism, or Dominionism, which calls for the creation of a theocratic "Christian" America, is especially acute among elite units such as the SEALs and the Army Special Forces.[9]

And as Chris Kyle tells us in his own words:

> We're here and we want to fuck with you. ... You see us? We're the people kicking your ass. Fear us because we will kill you, motherfucker. I wish I could kill all of you fucking savages. None of you deserve to live. I only wish I had killed more. I loved what I did. I still do, it was fun. I had the time of my life being a SEAL ... I never once fought for the Iraqis. They're all a bunch of raghead savages and shit on my boot. I could give a flying fuck about them.
>
> KYLE, 2012 pp. 4–6, 332

---

8 http://www.truthdig.com/report/item/killing_ragheads_for_jesus_20150125 Accessed 07/23, 2015.

9 http://www.truthdig.com/report/item/killing_ragheads_for_jesus_20150125 Accessed 07/23, 2015.

Our heroes are happy when they can invade a foreign country, and kill as many men, women, and children as they can. They enjoy it. They love killing. Everything else, the claims of bringing democracy, the love of freedom, are no more than rationalization and afterthoughts. As we previously noted, for D.H. Lawrence, the essential part of the American soul is hard, isolate, stoic, and a killer. It has never yet melted.

As we claimed in the first chapter, this clearly illustrates what Fromm (1967) called the necrophilic character for whom the love of death and/or destruction is one of the darker, more sinister aspects of American character.[10] Not only did the book *American Sniper* become a best-seller, but the movie was the #2 movie in 2015 battling with *The Hunger Games: Mockingjay*, a righteous revenge movie of its own, and the 32nd highest grossing movie of all time, and rising.[11] Righteous, redemptive violence sells in the United States because it appeals to deeply rooted aspects of American social character in which violence elicits powerful emotional gratifications and a sense of completion. Justice has been served. The wicked have been punished in the strongest way possible and even the socially weakest person feels empowered through association with authority and servants of authority who wield the power of death and extinguish life with no more thought or compassion than turning off a light.

Violence justifies itself, and killing the enemy, whether in war or otherwise, requires no justification at all. It is most troubling that despite the supposed rule of law, the heroes of the American monomyth, both in fiction and in the valorized version of Chris Kyle, are vigilantes. The hero alone has the guts to break the laws and moral standards and even kill children if necessary in order to save the otherwise impotent community. But as mentioned in Chapter 1, the American hero seeks personal glory or redemption first and foremost. The community is an afterthought. After Paul Kersey (Charles Bronson), the hero of the movies *Death Wish*, finds his wife assaulted, raped and murdered, he acquires a gun and goes about shooting the various thugs, thieves and low lives in New York and becomes a folk hero. Dirty Harry finds Miranda laws too confining to save the moral order from the nameless street thugs. He makes himself the judge, jury and executioner. Chris Kyle has no regard for the Iraqis (apparently not even the ones he is supposedly liberating). He has decided that they all deserve to die, and his only regret is that he didn't get to kill them all.

---

10 Some readers may remember the classical scene in Stanley Kubrick's, Dr. Strangelove (modeled after Henry Kissinger) where Major Kong, a western cowboy replete with a ten-gallon hat, straddles a nuclear bomb and rides it to its detonation point, screaming "yahoooo!" as if having an orgasm. Perhaps the thought of killing many people made that happen. See https://www.youtube.com/watch?v=JlSQAZEp3PA.

11 http://boxofficemojo.com/yearly/chart/past365.htm March 6, 2015.

Other white-supremacists that preceded Kyle felt similarly. On April 19, 1995, Timothy McVeigh and Terry Nichols blew up the Murrah Federal Building in Oklahoma City. To McVeigh's delight, they killed 168 people, including 19 children, all under the age of six. They purposely targeted a federal building with a daycare center, and exploded the bomb when they knew it would be filled with children (Serrano, 1998). The alleged enemy consisting of Jews, Blacks, and foreigners that control the government must receive no mercy. Regardless of what other people might think, real American men take matters into their own hands, because ultimately, they are answerable only to God. McVeigh and Nichols didn't use guns, but they drew on the same sense of moral righteousness, cleansing and redemptive violence that permeates American culture. In this culture, self-proclaimed normal citizens have the right and responsibility to destroy the evil enemy by any means necessary. Not Muslims in this case, but the ZOG, that is, the Zionist Occupation Government that allegedly controls the United States. For McVeigh, the ZOG is part of an international conspiracy through which Jews, namely the Rothschilds, use the Federal Reserve, the United Nations, the IMF, the World Bank, and other global institutions like the Bilderberg to rule the world. Nichols and McVeigh hoped to wake up all the white Christian Americans to this ominous threat that had already enslaved the country. Such an ominous and nearly omnipotent force requires good people to become monsters in order to combat such a monstrous enemy in turn. The hero does what must be done. Whether the country does wake up or not is secondary to their own righteousness.

Their actions didn't wake up the country as they planned. Many of the victims were white, and the sight of two-year old Baylee Almon dying on TV in the arms of firefighter Chris Fields turned much of the nation against Nichols and McVeigh—but not everyone. Rush Limbaugh said that "this is a terrible tragedy, but the government had it coming. They were asking for it. This is the first blow against tyranny in the United States. ... if the government doesn't change its ways, there will be a second violent revolution in this country" (Neiwert, 2009). Violence and imperialism have a long history and antedate the very emergence of the new nation, and still resonates with many people, especially when the targets are non-white. Kyle, McVeigh, Nichols, and Limbaugh and his many fans may follow somewhat different ideological codes, but the characterological core is the same: the enemy must die by any means necessary. Violence is the best way to solve any problem. Even when it has been shown time after time that in the contemporary world military force, even when spearheaded by tough, aggressive masculine guys, and in today's world tough gals as well, cannot defeat ideologies and deeply held cultural values. Nevertheless, America today is generally disposed toward electing such leaders. Ducat (2005) has argued that American politics has valued the phallic aggressive male such as Ronald Reagan, and then George W. Bush of the flight suit with a sock in the jock fame were seen as "real men" that can wield a "big stick" and stick it to others. When it was obvious that President Clinton was doing what real men gotta do with Monica, his popularity swelled and kept going up when he ordered Serbia bombed. Had not the economy tanked, John McCain, the tough Navy pilot in Vietnam veteran who spent a great deal of time in the Hanoi Hilton enduring torture would probably have beaten the metro-sexual Obama who nevertheless has himself dispatched many people to the next world and pursued his own form of gun violence, the drone. Finally, at the time of this writing, Hillary Clinton, the Democratic nominee for President, is a notorious war hawk who seemingly has the phallus and balls (characterologi-cally speaking) it takes to pursue any and all military challenges, especially the ones that don't exist or are unwinnable, such as in Syria and maybe, if the neo-cons get their way, in Iran. She celebrates the ruthless Henry Kissinger as her mentor, the Secretary of State who promoted endless escalation in Vietnam, Laos and Cambodia that concluded with carpet-bombing defenseless peasants and massive deforestation using agent orange, which also poisoned American soldiers and persists as a neurotoxin for years. Go Hillary! You can top the three million or so dead that Kissinger achieved. She convinced Obama to bomb Libya, so should we start her body count?

Big Balls and the Phallus in American Sport

The gun is not just a gun. It represents privilege and hegemonic masculinity. It represents aggression, power, autonomy, and control over life and death. In other words, the gun is the embodiment of phallocentric power in a society that idolizes and worships the phallus and the sexualization of killing as an inversion of sexuality as procreation or love. A gun culture is the inversion of life-affirming masculinity into a death-loving masculinity. So, the gun is as much about gender identity as is hunting or combat, which are also often aspects of phallic aggression. We have already seen several expressions of masculine toughness and violence wrapped in moral justifications especially among those that join patriotism with God's will. Its expressions will vary in every historical epoch. From the early frontiersman to the future captains of Federation starships, aggressive masculinity, skilled in the use of violence, typi-cally in the service of a higher "moral cause" has been and will remain a salient aspect of American character. In recent years, with the advent of feminism, we have seen more and more women showing these patterns, although with some important differences as noted in Chapter 1. Even as we write, Walmart has refused to sell the autobiography of Rhonda Rousey, a popular mixed martial arts fighter, on the grounds that the book is too violent. However, they are glad to sell *American Sniper* but they apparently see fighting and violence as inappropriate for a woman, although MMA's main audience overlaps significantly with Walmart shoppers. Nobody can accuse Walmart management of progressive sensibilities. Nevertheless, given these legacies, it is not surprising that football would eventually become the most popular team sport in the country and the contemporary Superbowl the most popular collective ritual in the United States, eclipsing Independence Day and even Christmas.

Football first began in the late 19th Century, the era that gave rise to modern industry and large scale economic organizations. Based on the British game of rugby, it valorized a heroic, assertive masculinity for college men who, many feared, might go "soft" and lose their masculine virility due to too much intellectual reading and thinking. The rise of football coincided with the muscular Christianity movement that similarly feared men would become soft and thus open to temptation. Baden Powell created the Boy Scouts to ensure that boys would become men and men would be tough and ready for war. Real men must never go soft. As the popular preacher Billy Sunday raved:

> You men have a chance to show your manhood. Then in the name of your pure mother, in the name of your manhood, in the name of your wife and the poor innocent children that climb up on your lap and put their arms around your neck, in the name of all that is good and noble, fight the curse. I want every man to say, "God, you can count on me to protect my wife, my home, my mother and my children and the manhood of America." By the mercy of God, which has given to you the unshaken and unshakable confidence of her you love, I beseech you, make a fight for the women who wait until the saloons spew out their husbands and their sons, and send them home maudlin, brutish, devilish, stinking, blear-eyed, bloated-faced drunkards ([1919] 2005 p. 67).

A major figure of the temperance movement, Sunday was a former baseball player who believed that sports and physical labor constituted the manliest Christian life, and although he did not advocate violence as such, he definitely advocated toughness and a fighting spirit.

As a working-class sport based loosely on the popular British game Cricket, baseball followed a different trajectory and developed a very different ethos than football. The field has variable dimensions, there is no clock, and much of the time, nothing happens. In football, the clock and detailed official rules govern the game from beginning to end. Action stops so the head coach and his command and control staff can send in orders to the quarterback who has the role of a field general. The offense bombards the defense with passes in conjunction with a hard ground attack to penetrate and grind down resistance until the final climax when the ball shoots into the end zone. In contrast, the leisurely pace and minimal structure of baseball appealed to factory workers and manual laborers who submitted to the clock and the overseer all day. The structured teamwork of football appealed to rich kids whose lives were otherwise individualistic, free, and sometimes reckless. Both sports remain popular, along with basketball, invented by Pastor James Naismith as a proper Christian sport. In the original conception, basketball allowed no contact at all between players. Naismith emphasized teamwork and especially, self-control. Today, basketball has become much more aggressive and violent, and although far from the violence of football, individual toughness and muscling for position in the paint has nevertheless replaced the no-contact rules of the original game. Sports in general, and football in particular remains a distinct articulation of American identity and values, especially the celebration of masculinity and rituals of male toughness and superiority. Men gather in living rooms, dens, game rooms and man-caves to cheer, curse, eat, and drink. They watch other men do battle, suffer injuries, so that otherwise subdued, moderate men, watching the game with others, realize the ordinarily submerged aggressive identities of the testosterone-driven, violent macho male hero offers vicarious satisfaction, even if indulged only once in a while.

Over time, football and other sports have created their own mythology tied to history and place. Lambeau Field in Green Bay, Wisconsin, holds great allure and mystery, and various university fields, such as The Big House at the University of Michigan and The Swamp at the University of Florida inspire memories and emotions. Perhaps no team evokes more reverence than the Fighting Irish of Notre Dame. It was here that the legendary George Gipp played for the equally legendary coach Knute Rockne. Gipp was out past curfew one night, and unable to gain access to his dormitory, he slept outside, contracted pneumonia, and died soon after, on December 14, 1920. Rockne claimed that Gipp's last words were:

> I've got to go, Rock. It's all right. I'm not afraid. Some time, Rock, when the team is up against it, when things are wrong and the breaks are beating the boys, tell them to go in there with all they've got and win just one for

the Gipper. I don't know where I'll be then, Rock. But I'll know about it, and I'll be happy.

QUOTED IN CAVANAUGH, 2010 p. 117

Although possibly fictional, such legends reinforce the sacredness of the game, which Notre Dame as a Catholic university further amplifies and brings into closer contact with religion. Although not intended as part of football, the large mural of Jesus on the side of Hesburgh Library overlooks the field. Entitled "The Word of Life," the mural depicts a resurrected Jesus with arms uplifted—a pose that looks very similar to the football sign for a touchdown, hence the nickname, Touchdown Jesus.

The religious aspect appears prominently at the University of Kansas (KU) in association with the men's basketball team. Among the most famous venues is the Allen Fieldhouse, the basketball arena at KU. Dedicated in 1955, the building is named after the legendary Forrest C. "Phog" Allen, who was a player and coach under James Naismith, and who coached the men's team at Kansas for 37 years (1908–1909, 1920–1956) and for 49 years total. At Kansas, Allen won a total of 590 games (771 total career), a record surpassed by only five other coaches as of this writing, two of whom learned the game as assistant coaches under Allen—Adolph Rupp at the University of Kentucky and Dean Smith at the University of North Carolina (UNC). The three others are Bobby Knight, Eddie Sutton, and Mike Krzyzewski. Rupp and Smith each in turn produced protégés of great accomplishment, including former KU and current UNC coach Roy Williams and current KU coach Bill Self. In terms of both history and legacy, all roads lead to the Allen Fieldhouse in men's college basketball. Allen is known as the "grandfather of basketball coaches," and can there be any more explicit connection between religion and sports than his first book, *My Basketball Bible*, in which he explains his devotion to the game as both an athletic competition and a religious devotion? In the Allen Fieldhouse, a banner above the stands reads "Pay Heed, All Who Enter," an ominous reference to the inscription over the gates of hell in Dante's Inferno, "Abandon All Hope, Ye Who Enter Here." Just beneath, the facility accords reverence to the local demigod, Phog Allen, and warns the opposition, "Beware of the Phog." Following 150 years of tradition, fans join arms and sing the alma mater, then the rock chalk chant, and finally wave the wheat (arms extended overhead and swaying like a field of wheat in the wind). President Teddy Roosevelt declared the Kansas Rock Chalk chant to be the best college cheer ever.

Success has been long and continuous. In recent years, the Jayhawks (men's team) is 206–9 in the Allen Fieldhouse under the current coach, Bill

Self. Kansas won the national championship in 2008, and finished second in 2003 and 2012. Kansas has the longest current streak of consecutive NCAA tournament appearances at 27, and the second longest streak of winning seasons at 32. The most winning seasons in Division I history at 101, the most conference championships in Division I history (60), the most First Team All Americans in Division I history (23), and the most First Team All American Selections in Division I history (30). The team is third in Division I all-time winning percentage (.722) and is second in Division I all-time wins (2,180). In 2012, ESPN ranked Kansas as the #2 most prestigious program (Duke as #1). Quite extensive achievements in competitive sports for an institution of higher learning.

Kansas basketball illustrates the heroic in the fantastic world of sport—a world of its own with nearly perfect justice where violators suffer fouls (or penalties in football) and the best almost always triumph based solely on their ability and commitment—the very embodiment of America as the land of hard-working truth, justice, and liberty! The religious-social-political nexus of American sports reinforces in ritualized celebration the "exceptional" identity, based on the intertwining of national character, Puritan religion and cultural consumption. Much like religious rituals or sporting events in general, football in particular forms a collective solidarity ritual that celebrates a distinctive collective identity—which is we have argued is anchored within a social character whose roots were nascent in the colonial era. Football is a violent competition between teams of males seeking territorial power and control as foretold in the earliest moments of American culture. American identity draws aggressive aspects embedded deep in the Puritan sensibility: a hostility to untamed nature, unrelenting self-control, submission to authority, and a relentless pace without rest.

Work and Sport

In the colonial period and early years of the Republic, the increasing economic power of the male as an individual economic actor superseded membership in a clan, family or guild. However, by the later 19th Century, his economic power came at the price of highly disciplined behavior in the marketplace or in the now growing bureaucracies where a managerial class was emerging. Protestantism reflected the world of masculine asceticism that displaced female emotionality. With growing urbanization and industrialization, as men left farms and small businesses for cities, the nature of work changed. Despite the values of rugged individualism, teamwork became more and more important, especially as more and more men worked in bureaucracies and vast assembly lines. So too did greater numbers of women enter college and the work force. The "New Women," more assertive and androgynous, raised new questions and rekindled old anxieties about gender identity and passivity (Oriard, 1991; Dworkin and Wachs, 2001). There arose a growing fear of "effeminacy," (castration anxiety) among the upper middle and elite classes of male. Among the attempts to valorize masculinity were the Boy Scout movement, "muscular Christianity" and the rise of football as a means of preserving assertive masculinity among the elite males. In the 1990s, the Promise Keepers, founded by the former football coach at the University of Colorado, Bill McCartney, filled stadiums with men all over the United States and drew more than a million men to a rally in Washington DC. Ostensibly to bring men closer to God, the PK revived the legacy of muscular Christianity, bringing together physical purity and vigor, and the longstanding evangelical concept of servant-leadership (servant to God, leader to the family).

After industrialization and the factory system severed work from home and craft, people increasingly turned to sports for a positive sense of self (Pronger, 1990). Amateur athletics promoted the values of discipline, teamwork and aggressiveness that were required by the industrial order—as well as a strong, masculine identity necessary to exploit and later lay off workers and to maintain a culture of militaristic toughness (Mangan, 2012). Football became organized into a college team sport with formal rules for the elite few who went to universities like Harvard, Princeton, Columbia or Yale where college football served to affirm a "heroic masculinity" by fighting as a team. It was believed that young, college educated, football players would become the business, professional, and political leaders of the future (Oriard, 1991 p. 211). The growing popularity of football as a sport for the elites was aided by the efforts of one of the first Yale players, Walter Camp who saw football and corporate life as essentially equivalent with the same principles of management in which player positions are organized on the basis of function and ability. By the end of the nineteenth Century, football, as a "gentlemen's" sport, had quickly spread throughout the country from Eastern colleges to urban sandlots (Falk, 2011). Thus, it is not surprising that football first emerged among the new national elites as they were attempting to forge an inclusive national identity that would valorize aspects of traditional masculine aggression when industrialization and modernity moved men from manual labor to the office or the mechanized factory floor.

Industrialization and the expansion of leisure time as well as the growth and commodification of spectator sports brought large crowds together for sporting events. For much of the 20th Century baseball, as mentioned earlier, was a working class game and the original national pastime. By the late 1960s, football's popularity grew among audiences who were not college educated. American football eventually became a lucrative business, the culmination of which is the Superbowl, the most widely celebrated annual event of American popular culture with over 100 million viewers, for which major global corporations pay some $500,000 or more for a thirty second TV commercial spot. To achieve such popularity, the Superbowl taps longstanding cultural legacies and deeply rooted desires. It both draws upon and reproduces the historical construction and performance of hegemonic masculine identities, now honed for an age of globalized consumption. The Superbowl has become both a reflection of American culture and a unique expression of American (male) identity, or as Mariah Nelson (1995) sees it, "the stronger women get, the more men love football." The identity of the fan (short for fanatic) is invested in the team to which he owes allegiance. As McBride (1995) notes, "Fans thrill to the moves of players with whom they identify ... and find euphoria in victory ... humiliation in defeat" (p. 85). McBride further argues that the euphoria-humiliation experience shapes all masculine encounters and turns gender relations into aggressive sporting contests. Hence, this tends to equate aggressive contact sports and aggressive contact gender relations such as domestic battering because the emotions are the same.

The devotion to football and its cultural power derives from the collision of the modern and anti-modern with a dialectical embrace of competing notions of manliness. For middle class males in the nineteenth Century, the new industrial and commercial order meant a redefinition of work in terms of mental rather than physical activity, and thus there was ambivalence and uncertainty about the "masculinity" of mental work. Physical prowess and power became a mark of the lower classes, while rationality in industry became linked to middle class definitions of masculinity. Football represented a union of the physical and the mental that was difficult for middle and upper class men to find elsewhere in modern America (Oriard, 1991 p. 201). Boxing was too much tied to the "lower" classes. Whether in football or in war, the violence of men in modern combat is not irrational, but clearly requires discipline and teamwork. It is oriented toward specific goals and bound by rules. Well-planned strategies and practiced tactics serve to bond males together and provide them with recognition and a sense of empowerment. The planned yet still mystical bonding of males through the pain and violence of war or football celebrates their heroic masculinities as they struggle for victory, overcome separation and alienation, and for brief moments provides wholeness and completion. Violence transcends the mundane through a descent into excess and degradation. Football acts as a catharsis in which the domination over and symbolic castration of the Other displaces violence from everyday life and preserves the social order.

By the late 20th Century, low-income and minority men do almost all the actual combat of the many wars the US starts. Masculine gratification for economically and culturally higher men take either a vicarious form through sports, or as with the Promise Keepers, a carnival experience that simulates a kind of football-battlefield intensity without the rigorous training or risk. As Lundskow (2002) shows, the PK advocated a milder form of patriarchy in which the man still presides over the household, but puts the interests of his family before his own. The PK appealed to mid-level professionals and office workers (Bartkowski, 2004) who felt alienated and unfulfilled (Lundskow, 2002). Copying the cheering, singing, and even tailgating and grilling of football games (but no alcohol) the PK rallies connected the energy of a sporting contest with the ascetic patriarchy of old-time Christianity revival meetings in a way that still allowed emotional exuberance and the comforts of middle-class life. In other words, the PK reinforced middle-class consumerism joined to a somewhat milder patriarchy for men who needed a vibrant sense of fulfillment without having to live like Puritans or risk their lives on the battlefield, or even to devote any volunteer time to missions, shelters, food banks, or poverty relief of any kind as a regular church might expect. Although the PK have dropped out of the mass media news, the evangelical model they created allows middle-class professionals and bureaucrats to feel like real men right with God, and just go on earning and consuming in comfortable suburban subdivisions far away from combat or poverty.

Instrumental Aggression and Character

In football, the players use instrumental aggression to combat each other, while cheerleaders foster male bonding and solidarity through the shared male gaze of the team of powerful warriors, the males who identify with them, and the women who desire them, thereby reproducing gender domination. Thus while most men are not overtly violent to each other and do not abuse their partners, wives or children, domination through violence is valorized through the football player who acts out the erotic/aggressive fantasy desires of many spectators and implicitly reinforces the gender privileges of males, their monetary advantages, institutional power, and feelings of superiority. Football and other sports can be seen as a "will to violence" and refusal of bourgeois civility that remains encapsulated within the substantive rationality of society that must release repressed violence which otherwise would return as self-hate. In other words, if a man (or woman) cannot release emotions that produce feelings of powerlessness, then the person will eventually hate themselves for always feeling weak. More intensely than other sports, football violence is subjected to rules that make it a site between "the unreason of desire and the rational order of civilized society ... As a form of character ethics, football inculcates a virile asceticism of fortitude and discipline that will serve men well in the society at large in much the same way as does the military (McBride, 1995 p. 82)." Football in consumer capitalism is both an economic enterprise and an ideological mirror of the system that reveals deeper unconscious aspects of American social character, especially its phallic aggressive forms of hegemonic masculinity. In most of our lives, there are few clear winners and losers in the short term. However, in sports there are clear winners at the end of almost every game. In this sense, football is an alternative realm of male territorial competitive violence that stands in dialectical opposition to the bland and passionless environment of corporate life. Thus football is more than an athletic competition; it is also a boundary that maintains a male subculture and mythically glorifies hypermasculine identities. For players, managers, owners and of course fans, football is an occasion for "real men" to get together and express who they truly are.

Patrice Oppliger (2004) sees wrestling similarly as an allegory of good versus evil that frames real men as white Americans who are tough to the core, compared to the evil and phony males whose masculinity fades when confronted by the good guys. Similarly, American football can be seen as an ideologically constructed myth of disciplined, instrumentally-oriented warriors ready to go to war into a crucible that will plainly reveal the true winners and losers. Teams are like platoons; lines engage in hand to hand combat; generals in the form of coaches issue commands from the sideline or in the present day, from on high in skyboxes that allow surveillance and analysis of the entire theater of combat. The groans, screams, blood and injuries, stretchers and medics simulate a battlefield. War and commerce as rationalized combat find their ultimate ritual performance in the Superbowl that celebrates the male warrior/spectator and affirms that they are "real" men who enjoy violence and power (McBride, 1995). Football valorizes the phallic aggression of war but without its death and destruction. Whereas wars eventually end, but the Superbowl constantly renews and reaffirms aggressive identities in celebrations of violent male performances, much like the aboriginal tribes of Australia who gather together on a yearly basis to enact the rituals and affirm the beliefs that bind them together based on a common totemic ancestor. In the American case, the totemic ancestor may be the owner of the "Mayflower gun," or another Puritan settler, or perhaps the unknown soldier who first "blewe the Braynes out" of a Native-American.

Connected to the monomyth, the Superbowl allows the taboos against in-group violence to be sustained while the ritual sacrifice of the outside enemy enables both the experience of the taboo and its transgressions. Even as American football can be seen as a hyper masculine war game over territory in which primitive violence is subsumed under rational codes that carefully locate combat within a clearly measured site, the game also allows women to enter into the more general conflict of in-group versus outgroup, and it occurs at definite times and places, regulated by strict rules that provide a degree of security for women in a highly masculinized environment that otherwise victimizes women. For example, the shoulder motion that throws the ball mimics the use of the club, battle axe, sword or spear. In modern armies the shoulder supports the rifle and rocket launcher, while in football it throws the "bomb" or "missile."

The ideal football hero is a hyper-real male warrior in armor who joins a long legacy of warriors fighting over territory. The football player moves from civilian to warrior as he dons his helmet, massive padded shoulders, and extensive body armor—icons of masculinity that exaggerate male angularity and musculature (Oriard, 1993). He joins with the Centurion, the gladiator, the armored knight and the samurai warrior, seeking victory in violent combat on the field of battle. At the same time, football spares the spectator the unpleasant reality of war while simulating its primary emotions in the safer spectacle of sports. The teams with their totemic emblems (uniforms, mascots, names) enact rituals of solidarity that draw the spectators in and bring all together to affirm an inclusive group identity of warrior males and their cheering consorts.

Pom-Poms and Male Power

As mentioned, women also have a role to play. As the men do battle on the field of truth and justice, these warriors with big shoulders and squared features are juxtaposed against the slight, but highly curved bodies of female cheerleaders. Whatever else, football affirms that men are not the women they both fear and desire (McBride, 1995). Masculine power reigns over and subordinates female compassion and thus the spectacle affirms phallic identity, and sustains male bonding and solidarity. Violent combat cements male bonds through misogynist denigrations of women and the conversion of the enemy into "pussies." Players and fans have a simultaneously ambivalent obsession with bouncing breasts under skimpy outfits as well as their exaggerated, simulations of breasts as the large, jiggling pom-poms of the cheerleaders. These exaggerated simulations of breasts as pom-poms are not there for warmth or nurturance or even intimacy, connection or relationship, but rather the pom-poms and public displays of female sexuality must be understood as exaggerated simulations that affirm hyper-masculinity as valorized difference. Unlike the real equipment the men wear, all the body armor and the helmet, the woman's skimpy outfit and pom-poms are trivial and useless, just as her social position compared to the players is trivial and useless. The men decide the outcome of the game, not the women. Yes, men love busty and scantily-clad cheerleaders. However, the hyper-masculinity of football valorizes women's breasts and outfits to reinforce gender differences and affirm the superiority of his assertive masculinity. The larger the breast the greater the visual difference between "real men" and "real women." Breasts are objects of a male gaze that empowers the male voyeur through visual domination. In much the same way, the short skirts of the cheerleaders that flies up as they descend from a jump reveals that she lacks the essence of masculinity, the balls of the tough male players. Her shaved legs and underarms provide visual verification of a decisively feminine and young body, the body of the Other who can never be a true and equal buddy who bonds through violent territorial games, but she does serve as the perpetual anti-fetish whose very existence as a curvy *castrata* celebrates the superiority of penis power (Irigaray, 1985). A woman is not a complete, unified person but a pastiche of breasts to be viewed and fondled and orifices to be penetrated, dominated and denigrated, thereby dramatizing masculinity as superior. While some women may find male violence erotic and submission to the 50 shades of warriors appealing, the female Other can never enter the sacred temple of the phallus and join as an equal comrade in its rituals of violence.

Phallic Worship

Football celebrates the phallic aggressive masculinity engrained in America's traditional gender ideology, some of which was rooted in early colonial America. As a cultural fiction that recreates the psychological dynamics of war, football is a male struggle for the exclusive possession of the phallus. It reiterates the boundaries of the homoerotic community by defining sexual differences based on victorious winners and vanquished losers. Whereas the defense attempts to sack the quarterback and strip the ball, the quarterback attempts to penetrate the defense through the use of his surrogates, the ball carriers and receivers. When the defense is either successful in stopping the offense's drive or in forcing a fumble of the ball/phallus, the siege undergoes a transformation. The offense becomes the defense (ball-less) and the defense is now the offense in possession of the ball/phallus. Although the defense is in the more vulnerable position, as if a female, the defensive players attempt to reverse this disadvantage by acting with even greater aggression, trying to do to the other team's offense what has already been done to their own.

More so than most societies, American individualism frustrates the more feminine values of community, attachment and dependency and thus abhors those who embody these qualities, for example, women and traditional peoples. And thus as we have noted, a central theme of American character, observed by de Tocqueville and a central issue of contemporary social research is the loneliness of a society in which social ties are not only attenuated, but violence always threatens to move from the background to the foreground. Especially for women, the apparent peace and security of public places can turn violent, often at the hands of male acquaintances and family members. As mentioned, the spectacle venue of football offers a degree of security often better than the real world that the spectacle mimics. This energized yet safe masculine environment allows relaxed, easy communication between males, whether they are bosses and workers or sales clerks and customers so that even total strangers can relate to each other. In the mundane world of deskilled work in impersonal organizations, male knowledge of sports and discussions in "sportuguese" demonstrate shared "stocks of knowledge" and individual expertise that become realms of sociality and recognition. Sports knowledge has become a central trope of identity for "real men," which differentiates them from women, children and "effete intellectuals." Typically, males gather around the television set, bond through the consumption of intoxicants and the exchange of "sports talk" laden with frequent obscenities and a sexual imagery of phallic power and domination by penetration and degradation.

Football is played as a male war game, and while the "enemy" is the other team, there is a subtext of female subordination. While women as cheerleaders are on the one hand highly erotized while subordinated by the male gaze to celebrate hegemonic masculinity, there is another trope, the denigration and control of women and their sexuality that "needs" to be controlled by men, whether serving their sexual needs when they are sluts and hos, or when they remain pristine virgins whose "purity" serves to sustain their subordination. In either case, virgin or whore, female sexuality "needs" to be regulated and controlled by men—or so they would like to believe. When women claim the right to define themselves, craft their own identities and take control their own bodies and their own sexuality, there is a threat to male domination and such a threat to male power, rooted castration anxiety, fosters an aggressive counter attack. This has especially been the case since the 60's and as more and more women, indeed now that the majority have become sexuality active before marriage, if they even want to marry, are quite OK with recreational sex. But there are still many older, typically religious, conservative men, culturally and characterologically descended from the Puritan colonials and plantation owners who are not comfortable with women as equals and even less comfortable with women who give up or their purity which is then a danger to both gender hierarchies of status and sexual repression as a defining aspect of authoritarian submission. As we previously noted, Mike Huckabee somehow thinks that more rural, church going women are classy while secular, urban women are trashy. We would suggest that he look at stats, as Megan Kelly told him, ain't true no more, Guv. But we also know that facts, figures and empirical evidence does not change minds nor sway opinions. For many who still typify the traditional American social character, especially its religiously conservative variants, especially older white people, the growing economic power of women and their claims to control their own bodies has led to a vehemently denied "war on women," though assault might be a better term. Of course, many conservative women join in this battle. Ever since Roe v. Wade, moral conservatives, the "values voters," have tried to overturn the decision, and when that proved unlikely, they have made it more and more difficult for women to control their own bodies, regulate their fertility and have freedom to choose parenthood. Now of course as we have said, there are often major gaps between proclaimed words and deed, between values and actual behavior, and the power of sexual and gender repression is such the many lapses of conservative religionists is too numerous to enumerate. Just as we enjoy the *schadenfreude* when we see conservative family values leaders caught breaking the moral rules they loudly proclaim, for example, when the Governor of South Carolina Mark Sanford disappeared, supposedly on a hike along the Appalachian Trail, but was in fact in Argentina with his girlfriend, Maria Belén Chapur, an Argentine journalist. This affair led to divorce, but that allowed him to marry Chapur, so apparently family values and hypocrisy can co-exist.

God Bless American Violence

Why does this concern with football matter for understanding American social character? Aside from reinforcement of the aggressive man as the "normal" human, and demur, submissive woman as the Other, we see three additional reasons. First, the mythic nature of moral redemption is an important part of the socialization of social character, especially the phallic aggressive forms of male character. The captain of the football team generally has higher status among his peers than the nerdy winner of the science fair, who ten years later may become another digital billionaire. The captain of the team is also more likely to be "popular" with young women, that is, he is more likely to have a richer sex life. It is hardly an accident that a disproportionate number of college athletes and/or fraternity members perpetrate sexual assault (Harding, 2015; Sanday, 2007).

Second, while the geopolitics of alliances, conflicts and wars is for the most part based on the intertwining of economic factors and political power, the cultural realm and its underlying social character nevertheless can act as a catalyst or barrier for mass support for certain policies of the elites. Thus as we have often said, the colonial crucible of character bequeathed a disposition toward phallic aggression legitimated as moral redemption when vanquishing enemies. But in many cases, it is those in power that "decide" just who are the friends and are who the enemies.[12] Consider how shortly after 9/11, as we discussed earlier, how 80% of Americans quickly and easily supported the clearly fraudulent claims of WMDs that the Bush administration used as an excuse to attack Iraq, even though most of the funding and perpetrators came from Saudi Arabia, an official ally of the US. Large numbers of Americans, mostly males of course, endlessly gathered to shout USA, USA, at least for the first few years until Iraq became an endless quagmire. Then John McCain sang "bomb, bomb Iran" to the tune of "Barbara Ann" by the Beach Boys. The main point for us however is that the dominant ideology of God-ordained "exceptionalism" resonates with the dominant social character, so the leaders of the State can pursue their geopolitical goals with a high level of popular support, even if those goals make no logical sense.

Although no single factor is responsible, as many have noted, the vast amounts of money and allocations of human effort that support the defense industries that could be otherwise invested for the common domestic good is one of the major reasons for the waning of the infrastructure, the contraction of research and decline of American wealth and power.[13] This is clearly evident in the decline of innovation, the deterioration of our infrastructure,

---

12   We might recall that when France declined to join our fiascos in Iraq, there were hence enemies and the salty, fatty deep fried potatoes served in government buildings were renamed "Freedom Fries." But after they joined us, or we joined them in the Libyan fiasco, they were again "friends," and this "friendship" was further cemented after Charlie Hebdo and then the November 13 attacks in Paris. And yes, we can again enjoy the carcinogenic artery blocking French Fries. By the way, nations don't have friends, they have interests.

13   The defense industries locate facilities in every state to garner legislative support for the "many" jobs brought to each State. Even Bernie Sanders has supported most military appropriation bills.

bridges and highways need repairs, our antiquated rail transportation does not have a single mile of high-speed transit, outdated water and sewer lines often burst. We have an educational system that is being privatized and in the process, are performing far worse for American students, but quite well for owner/investors (Ravitch, 2014, 2010). The United States is now a country in decline economically, politically and culturally, and the fascination with vicarious and escapist spectacles in sports, film, and TV draw upon a long cultural history of redemptive violence yet now softened by consumerism. Escapist violence reinforces the morality of violence yet with none of the risks of actual death or dismemberment. Real men don't worry about complex issues like infrastructure or global economics. Only a clear sense of might makes right matters. Let the geeks and losers worry about infrastructure. Meanwhile, the ascendant power today is of course China that is rapidly developing a modern infrastructure with over 6000 miles of high-speed trains and of course, they are putting huge investments into their educational system.[14]

Third, aggressive masculinity has had an "elective affinity" with theologically based ideological positions resting on populist sentiments in which the political became intertwined with these often unstated religious justifications for certain policies. Arthur Schlesinger (2004) traces the connection of war and purity in American culture that began with the Calvinist pioneers who saw America as the Redeemer nation. It persevered in the 18th Century in Jonathan Edwards theology of Providence, in the 19th Century as Calhoun's theology of slavery, in the 20th Century in Woodrow Wilson's vision of a rationally and morally managed world order, and in John Foster Dulles summons to a holy war against Godless Communism. To this litany we would update this analysis and add the "war" against Islamic terrorism and the invasions of Iraq and Afghanistan where the US was not only engaged in defending its "interests," namely hegemonic control of the world economy, but defending the good Christian God against the evil Allah of the Muslims.

The growth of its economic power, and eventually having the most powerful military in the world, confirmed the messianic vision of those who believed in America's divine appointment. The United States, as a happy empire of perfect wisdom and perfect virtue, was divinely commissioned to save all mankind. The overt religious message of Christian redemption is often disguised as "universal" or "higher" values as the implicit telos of existence. When foreign policies are guided by moral ideologies they are not only dangerous, but to

---

14   http://www.nationofchange.org/2015/03/01/china-accelerates-into-the-future-racing
      -past-america/ accessed February 28, 2015.

the extent these ideologies frames the world incorrectly, they typically distorts reality and leads to ill-advised strategies and hence disastrous outcomes, not only from a stance of *realpolitik*, but think of all the deaths, wounds, destruction and devastation that might have been avoided had not "reality" been refracted through an ideological prism.[15] Ideology summons the true believer to a *jihad,* a crusade of extermination against any people who proclaimed as the enemy. Perhaps two million Cambodians died after we destabilized Sihanouk's fragile coalition. Perhaps just as many Vietnamese died in the course of the bombings and free fire zones and perhaps as many were wounded or tortured. Then our support of Suharto in Indonesia, and Marcos in the Philippines led to another million deaths, and then of course are the small-change numbers of just a few thousands of Latin and Central Americans who died in Argentina, Brazil, Nicaragua, Honduras, El Salvador and Guatemala at the hands of American supported and often trained dictators who helped US companies exploit their own lands and people for profit. Moreover, a foreign policy shaped by ideology, and a religiously informed one at that, often becomes a self-fulfilling prophecy. The attempts to stem Islamic extremists, typically through military means, often through support of repressive governments, has more often than not fostered greater resentment and fueled even greater hatred for the United States and swelled the ranks of radical jihadi militias and terrorist organizations, who appear to be the only ones who can successfully defy US power. Officials call this "blowback," the process by which we create our own worst enemies (Johnson, 2000).

As was earlier noted, America has had an affinity to war and violence long before the colonials declared their independence. The colonists at Jamestown didn't need diplomacy when they could and did simply obliterate the Paspahegh Indians. With its ascendant power as a major player on the world stage in the 20th Century, various external "Others" have been constructed as an enemy, beginning with the Axis of World War I and II, to the Communists of the Cold War and the Islamic terrorists of today. While all of these present(ed) a real threat to the US, these "enemies" have also fulfilled a larger purpose— they provided real-life proof that there is evil is in the world and the US must lead the way to righteous victory as God's chosen country. Through war and the power of the gun, we can defeat enemies on the battlefield and purify our souls in the baptism of mortal combat. God wills it!

---

15   If the fusion of moralism, individualism and phallic aggression had not led to an irrational anti-communism, anti-socialism, the governments of Iraq would not have been overthrown, nor Iraq, nor Chile. Vietnam would not have been invaded nor Cuba blockaded. We could go on but let's just say, give peace a chance.

Summary

When traveling to other countries, perhaps as near as Canada to the north, or as far as Japan halfway around the world, one aspect of the United States that becomes so blatantly noticeable is its level of poverty, infrastructure decay, violence, its high rates of imprisonment and prevalence of gun ownership. As we noted in the previous chapter, de Tocqueville noted that the first Puritan to set foot upon the shores of New England had within him certain attributes of Protestantism that would eventually shape America's destiny. But let us not forget that aboard the Mayflower were a few flintlocks and Wheelocks—one of which, an elaborate Italian model belonging to one John Alden, sometimes called the "Mayflower gun," is now said to rest in a National Rifle Association Museum in Virginia—how fitting to frame American history between the Mayflower and NRA.

As we have noted, the Puritan teachings included two highly important moments, first the domination of men over women and privileging certain notions of what might be typically masculine, e.g. strong, tough, assertive and powerful, yet using that power for benevolent reasons, primarily to defend against enemies and/or hunt for food. Even in Winthrop's sermon on Christian charity, he noted how ten of them armed with faith and commitment could defeat 1,000 of their enemies. Given the time it would take to reload a colonial era musket, and repeater rifles would not be around till more than 200 years later, we are not quite sure how this might happen, but we are surely open to the notions that myths may express profound truths—or at least people behave as if it's true, if they believe the myth, it is in fact true. Closely intertwined with gun ownership and masculinity was the notion of the appropriate use of violence to stem or thwart evil, and the early settlers faced a great deal of evil. Firstly were the enemies from without, primarily native Americans who resented displacement from their ancestral lands, and knowing of the frequent slaughters of other tribes, chose to fight the encroachments of the colonizers. The authoritarian character of that age, as with most ages, is equally fearful of evil from within and that such evil warrants violence. As we previously mentioned, this is especially clear in the Salem witch trials in which the evil Others, especially marginal women, had cavorted with Satan, the "Evil One," who allegedly seduced women in a way unique to women—their sinful sexual natures. And of course how might they glean evidence of such liaisons? As we noted, certain "experts" could find evidence of a woman's sex life and the identity of her partners by poking her vagina and other body parts with sharp objects. If she (and occasionally he) were guilty, witch hunters embraced the true Christian tradition of mercy and forgiveness with public humiliation, torture, and execution.

As we have seen, the passionate fanaticism of gun ownership in the United States not only has a very long history, but gun ownership is an intertwined moment of a complex of phallic aggressive masculinity, violence as a means of moral redemption and an essential part of certain collective identities especially in more rural areas, and even more so in the states of the old Confederacy and "Wild West." Notwithstanding the recent epidemics of shooting sprees at schools, malls or theaters, there is very little political support for gun control. Among the almost paranoid fears of the more extreme right in America is that Obama was hell-bent on confiscating the guns of Americans and several organizations, for example the "Oathers" have pledged to use their guns against anyone who challenged their constitutional right to own and bear arms.

As the early colonies began to thrive, guns became especially important and useful. Along the Western frontiers, they were very helpful in battles with native Indian populations that attempted to defend themselves from the onslaughts. Meanwhile as the plantation system developed in the Antebellum South, gun ownership became an important aspect of maintaining the pacification of slaves and deterring any thoughts of escape.

Although there are many other societies with high rates of gun ownership, for example our northern neighbors, in no other society have we seen the intertwined complex of a phallic aggressive masculinity, a religiously inspired Manichaean worldview in which it becomes the duty of the good to willingly use violence as a form of moral redemption against evil, while that aggressive masculinity also provided a personal and cultural narrative valorizing the tough guy, who has long been a hero in American literature and of late, popular culture. The American hero, embodied within its Monomyth, may change his outfits over time, from buckskins to spacesuits, and his weapons may change from muskets to machineguns or even phasers, disruptors, and photon torpedoes. While a few women such as Calamity Jane and Annie Oakley had mastered the skills of shooting guns, the changes in gender roles seen in recent popular culture have seen the rise of various women warriors from Xena to Katniss Eberdeed (heroine of Hunger Games) to Captain Janeway, Buffy Summers, and even Mullins and Ashburn in *The Heat* (this movie challenges many gender stereotypes even as it reinforces the hero of the monomyth) have gained the same skills as men and willingness to spill the blood of evil enemies.

As we have noted, the hero of American literature has typically been the tough guy, who more often than not, uses violence for the sake of moral redemption. It was not an accident that Turner's celebration of the frontier was published as motion pictures were about to become a major element of American popular culture and as a result, the cowboy, typically an uneducated, rather crude and aggressive type was sanitized and elevated to heroic status as the protector of virtue, saving decent folks from harm whether by ambush or crime, or perhaps untying the heroine from the railroad tracks just before the express train barreled through.

The tough guy, and of late tough gal was somehow magically transformed into a basis of celebrity of the Western genre, but that monomythic hero has also assumed many other similar personas as cop or detective, spy or counter-spy, soldier or sailor or superhero. Moreover, the same hero/heroine has even been projected into the future where the good hero, or heroine, battles vile alien Others often quite ugly to boot, hell bent on destroying decent humans, or perhaps dangerous forces such as asteroids headed to earth, maybe time warps or some other threat that he, she or they, our heroes and heroine thwart, quite often with fantastic weapons that more often than not, resemble the long barreled guns that first came over on the Mayflower. Phallic symbols?

An essential part of the cultural imaginary of America has been the cel-ebrations of the phallic aggressive forms of hegemonic masculinity who employ violence for both practical reasons of survival and moral reasons of every generation, especially when defending against evil enemies, or perhaps in the service of territorial expansion, or perhaps in the service of maintain-ing control over subordinates. But in the latter part of the 19th Century, with the growth of industry, expansions of trade, and increasingly sedentary office/managerial work as a career paths for elite men, there was growing anxiety over the demise of male strength and toughness. Perhaps men of every era fear getting soft. As the frontier settled and men moved off the farm and out of the factories and into office jobs, the fear of softness intensified.

Enter masculine athletics. A number of organizations and programs emerged to valorize, socialize, and train masculine toughness. These would be as varied as the Boy Scout movements, various expressions of "muscular Chris-tianity" and for our purposes, the emergence of college football as the training ground for corporate capitalism and the expression of masculine aggression within the context of a highly rationalized rule bound game premised on pub-lic displays of strength, valor, and competition that may and often does involve a degree of violence. Thus it is no accident that football was first introduced on the elite campuses of the East coast where the sons of the affluent would not only get an education in the arts and sciences but learn team-based competi-tion and hone the skills of a simulated combat that affirms masculine strength, toughness and willingness to fight even if that combat might cause injury. While a football game is not quite a gladiator match that ends with one win-ner and one mutilated body slain at the bequest of the crowd with downward thumbs, football injuries are common. "Real men" can take it as well as dish it out. Like warriors ever since the Bronze Age, they don helmets and armor to do battle against the evil enemy.

Football celebrates a phallic aggressive masculinity through the juxtaposition of the angled and muscled male with the rounded and soft female, the cheerleader (and scantily-clad women in commercials) who not only inspires the team and the fans, but in terms of body and motion, highlights the differences between the strong man and the softer woman. Most notably, as she makes herself the object of the male gaze, her large pom-poms jiggle up and down and from side to side. And meanwhile, revealing outfits most of all reveal that she is a woman and her femininity highlights the phallic aggressive nature of the football player who in many ways represents the wish fulfillments of many traditional male notions that are aspects of social character.

While football games are "fun" (Lundskow is a long-time football fan), we should note that the most important secular holiday in America is the Super Bowl in which perhaps half of American households watch the game and in so doing reproduce the gender relationships of the game especially in so far as the male viewers watch, scream at the players and coaches, utter endless profanities, and stuff themselves with beer, dutifully brought in by their wives or partners that also provide endless bowls of guacamole, salsa, chicken wings and then after halftime with its magnificent commercials, comes either chili or pizza and in some cases both (Lundskow's wife does not wait on him). And more beer. However frivolous but indeed playful and joyous might the Superbowl party well be, our more sociological standpoint is one side of the important concerns its celebrations of the fusion of phallic aggressive masculinity, the celebrations of male violence, the implicit preparation for a particular kind of predatory, winner take all form of capitalism that reached it apogee in the 20's when the robber barons ascended their pinnacles of wealth, replete with the ostentation of the Gilded Age. The contradictions of capitalism of course ushered in the Depression, but that same class, perhaps whose actors were even more predatory and aggressive, ascended to domination after WWII, especially by the 70's, a time in which football became more popular than baseball. Finally, given what we have said about the Puritan influence on social character, and given that the festive partying as the most popular collective celebration of the nation held in parking lots, living rooms and sports bars throughout the country, there is a quasi-religious aspect in which as a collective ritual acts as an aspect of American civil religion celebrating the "exceptional" nature of its society, to which we turn in the next chapter, one element of which is its tough, aggressive men. And as we have pointed out, it is no accident that the military has become intertwined with football games.

For reasons that we cannot explain, most reports of national crime rates have shown that crime has dropped precipitously in the last several decades, although there still exist certain pockets of urban violence that are typically limited to areas where urban street gangs compete for exclusive marketing rights for distributing various goods and services. But here the use of violence is primarily based on commercial concerns, the maximization of profits, quite peripheral to the celebrations of masculinity and moral redemption through violence, which may be present, but are not central to the questions of social character.

While given current realities, especially the domination of the Congress by conservative Republicans, indeed many are reactionaries from Southern or Western states, or rural part of Blue states, we see no chance of any kind of meaningful gun control in the next decade, especially since we are not so much dealing with the facts and figures of crime, accidents and spree shootings, but a deeply ingrained aspect of American social character. Once again we choose not to wallow in gloom, doom and pessimism, but as we have mentioned and will conclude, one of our central points is that American social character is in the process of major transformation and the emergent configuration, more empathic and compassionate than tough, aggressive, destructive and necrophilic. As Tupac calls to us, Let's change the way we eat. Let's change the way we live. Let's change the way we treat each other.

Glory: The Rise and Fall of American Exceptionalism

From Chosen to Exceptional

The Puritan founders, escaping the decadence and religious intolerance of Europe (especially intolerance toward them), came to the New World and settled where they were free to practice their own version of Christian religion which of course they regarded as a purer religion, "superior" to the corrupt Catholic or Anglican Churches as well as other Protestant denominations. And of course their Christianity was "superior" to the heathen beliefs of Native-American "savages". Many of the colonial settlers thought of themselves as a special, "chosen" people, a lost tribe of Israelites coming to the Promised Land. The early settlers felt a unique "calling" to build a "moral community" in America, blessed by God that would be the "new Jerusalem" unfettered by the corrupt and decadent Europe with its scurrilous and immoral nobles and clergy. In the New World, the land was fertile, abundant and there for the taking from the native populations. The colonies were thus beacons for supposedly "unclaimed" and thus available land and natural resources of water and forests. Eventually the raw materials that would be needed for industry were abundant. The colonies were more or less protected by the most powerful empire at that time. As we discussed earlier, the Puritan settlers brought with them a religiously based individualism and piety based on their direct relation to God.

The notion of being a "special people," being "chosen" by God to fulfill a holy mission is as good as it gets. Notwithstanding a precarious beginning, they nevertheless survived and after a while, even prospered, becoming a "people of plenty" (Potter, 1954). As America's economic and military power grew, interpreted as signs of Divine providence, religiously based feelings of moral superiority became integrated with its political revolution, its democracy and its capitalism which fused into an integral aspect of American character as its "exceptionalism" and superiority to all others. Citing the glory and "superiority" of its values of freedom, equality and democracy, its economic and political accomplishments, America's political elites, religious leaders, and everyday people interpreted this success as God's blessing, which, as we have argued, was integral part of America's underlying social character and manifests as a strong ambivalence. Both confidence and insecurity arise from the same conflict between individualism and expectations of service to authority. Only a special relationship with God can resolve this inherent ambivalence.

While the founding fathers eschewed any particular denomination, they avoided the sectarian conflicts typical of Europe, and as we previously noted, without a State religion, Americans voluntarily embraced various denominations. Indeed, shortly after his inauguration, Washington went to a Jewish Synagogue and Catholic Church where he proclaimed that all were welcome to pray as they might, Christian, Jew or Mohammedan (the term used for Muslims at that time). America's uniqueness and specialness, before the term exceptionalism became common, was its blessing by a God of all faiths that proclaimed that America was and is the greatest and best country in the history of the world. Moreover, its general prosperity, at least compared to feudal Europe, and its long history of military victories starting with 200 years of genocide against Native-Americans, then its war of independence and 1812, subsequent victories against Mexico and Spain, triumphs in World War I, World War II and the "Cold War" gave further testimony to the uniqueness and specialness that proved American exceptionalism.

For Perry Miller and Jackson Turner, the "unsettled" wilderness and the frontier set America apart from Europe and played a considerable role in fostering the individualism that would be so important in shaping of American culture and character. We have repeatedly noted that a fundamental aspect of America's cultural values, noted by its observers and citizens alike is the notion of its exceptionalism and an essential aspect of its collective identity as well as its social character. As we earlier noted, from the earliest days of colonial settlements, Americans have seen themselves as "chosen" as "special," and over time, that specialness morphed into exceptionalism, the notion that the United States was a unique nation with a special destiny. God had favored America and everything America does is righteous. Americans see themselves as virtuous, the major force for good in the world, spreading peace, freedom and democracy. Exceptionalism as a "chosen people," a "city on the hill" to radiate its goodness as model for all to emulate, became a central moment of a America's collective self-image, indeed this cultural imaginary, became highly intertwined with its narcissism, often bordering on pathological grandiosity. As such, the slightest critique or challenge, evokes narcissistic rage and destructive urges directed to "traitors" within and/or enemies from without.

Most social groups, from families and clans with enduring and direct face to face ties, to large, modern Nation States, "imagined communities," with indirect, mediated ties, demark social, cultural and often spatial boundaries between the in-group, "we," and outgroup "they." In most cases, the in-group is seen as inherently special, unique and different, typically "better" than any other group or society. A collective narcissism typically valorizes the in-group and its qualities and denigrates the out group-especially when they are darker, and may have different religions.

Puritan Co-existence?

The early colonists were also committed to a collective transformation of the New World into the community of God, except their independent and autonomous congregations couldn't agree on exactly what God wanted. Some, like Roger Williams, believed that Native-Americans should be respected and left free to pursue their own way of life (Barry, 2012), although more commonly, New Englanders assimilated Native Americans aggressively—forcing them to renounce their indigenous belief, language, dress, and way of life (Bailey, 2011; Vaughan, 1995). Interestingly, people on both sides who lived in close proximity on the frontier actually blended their cultures more than they fought. As Russell Bourne (2002) argues, the Puritan leadership represented both economic interests that required removal of Native-American livelihood, and also ideological interests that would not tolerate corruption of Christian beliefs with Native beliefs. Common people were much more flexible and practical. Why fight when we can peacefully co-exist? Or can we co-exist with each other?

What was especially problematic was the generally much greater freedom for women in Native tribal communities, and the fact that many white women preferred life among the Natives. Kirsten Fischer (2002) documents how white colonials, Natives, and Africans had all manner of diverse sexual relations, especially on the frontier. Free of church, government, and patriarchal oversight, everyone had sex with everyone else, as they pleased. Since the authorities couldn't be everywhere at once, they often relied on terror to maintain racial and gender order. As Sharon Block (2006) found, rape was a favorite tool to keep colonial women subdued, and consequently, white women were not always "kidnapped" by Native-Americans as white men claimed; the women ran away and sought sanctuary among the Native-Americans. In general, Native women lived generally easier lives and received much more respect (Ulrich, 1991). John Demos (1995) documented the life of Eunice Williams, who in the early 1700s decided to marry a Mohawk man and spend her life with his people. Apparently, her father's promise of a proper life, that is, a life of restrictive morality and oppressive drudgery under patriarchal domination did not win her back from the relaxed and open life in a Mohawk community. The threat of female emancipation was already too ominous for the "anxious patriarchs" of early New England as Kathleen Brown (1996) calls them, so the possibility of Native-American coexistence decisively overwhelmed Puritan sensibilities. The patriarchs were so anxious and insecure that the laws of the time allowed for the persecution of witches and whores, but protected wife-beaters (Crane, 2012). Hoping that terror and brutality could accomplish what their charming personality could not, the men of God were free to clear the land for ample lumber and cultivate vast fields of cash crops to further develop their capital-intensive businesses in whaling, shipping, and shipbuilding. The Natives had to either assimilate and submit completely, move away, or be destroyed.

De Tocqueville: On Americans as Exceptional

Long before the term exceptional was used, the early settlers, and eventually many American people saw themselves as chosen by God, a truly "exceptional" people. As we noted, this was already foretold in Winthrop's "city on the hill" sermon. American "exceptionalism" was already evident to de Tocqueville who observed the virtues of its republican form of democratic government, American's intense devotion to work, their preference for the practical over abstract ideas, the persistence of religion when attendance was voluntary, and the community spirit expressed in "civic activism."[1] For De Tocqueville, there were five aspects of American society that he saw as distinctive, indeed exceptional: (1) There was general freedom from legal control and mildness of its laws, (2) They were egalitarianism and with few differences of rank between people, (3) They had a strong sense of individualism and self-reliance. (4) There was local political engagement and autonomy, or populism, and finally, (5) The laissez-faire economy promoted entrepreneurialism. For De Tocqueville, these features constituted Americans as an "exceptional" people and society, previously unknown in the history of the world and while yet in the 1820s early Americas was a rural backwater quite marginal to the European world, he predicted its future greatness.

Unlike most European societies of the 19th Century, America provided for equality of opportunity in that in theory anyone could become rich or the President, or whatever they wanted, if they worked hard enough and long enough.[2]

---

1   We should recall his books, were titled *Democracy in America*. De Tocqueville, 1945 [1840]

2   To be sure, anyone needed to be a white, property owning male (slaves were property), but compared to Europe, it was a place where a growing economy did enable more upward mobility.

In its laissez fare economy, individual rights allowed various people to break from their family history, or hereditarily based social rank, or whatever past they needed to escape, and in so doing, they could "get ahead" in America. Opportunities to start life anew were unknown in many of their home countries. By the early 1800s, we find that immigrants owned many small businesses that produced success and social mobility not possible in their own countries. As De Tocqueville described it:

> ... the position of the Americans is therefore quite exceptional, and it may be believed that no other democratic people will ever be placed in a similar one. Their strictly Puritanical origin, their exclusively commercial habits, even the country they inhabit, which seems to divert their minds from the pursuit of science, literature, and the arts, the proximity of Europe, which allows them to neglect these pursuits without relapsing into barbarism, a thousand special causes, of which I have only been able to point out the most important, have singularly concurred to fix the mind of the American upon purely practical objects. His passions, his wants, his education, and everything about him seem to unite in drawing the native of the United States earthward; his religion alone bids him turn, from time to time, a transient and distracted glance to heaven. Let us cease, then, to view all democratic nations under the example of the American people.
>
> DE TOCQUEVILLE, 1945 [1840] p. 40

At the same time, De Tocqueville was critical of the disjunction between how Americans thought their country was so wonderful, the freest, most democratic and wealthiest in the world, but without any real knowledge or experience of other countries to make such judgments and comparisons. Many had never been more than 25 miles from the farms where they were born. This limited awareness of the rest of the world, but strong opinions about other countries and cultures endures to this day when for example, only 25% of Americans have passports and have had any real experiences in other countries. The seven-day, nine-nation guided tour of Europe from a bus window does not provide much sense of the life, the people or the culture of other people, nor even exposure to languages other than English. Consequently, with very little knowledge and even less experience outside their own country, Americans have no reason to question their own assumptions that their nation was divinely inspired, better than any other, and should therefore "naturally" lead the world. As we seen, deployment of military force that can freely employ "redemptive violence" to secure peace, freedom and the American way throughout the world, readily proves US greatness. Political power and corporate profits along the way are justified rewards for bringing freedom and democracy to the world.

After De Tocqueville, various commentators in the 1920's but mostly and ironically the Communist Party and then Stalin attempted to explain why Americans did not broadly embrace socialism, was it "false consciousness?" no, they used the term, exceptionalism.

The Land of the Free-for White Males

Meanwhile, back at the plantation, whips, guns, and rape maintained levels of terror against slaves (Rosen, 2009). Slavery contributed strongly to the construction of whiteness and blackness (Allen, 1994; Battalora, 2013). A central theme was the construction and valorization of white virtues of hard-working fortitude and integrity, and the otherness of blackness which was laziness and wildness (Molina, 2014; Pinder, 2013). The valorization of whiteness and the demonization of darkness (both Native and Black) through myth and imagined history began in the early colonies and continued into the mid-twentieth Century (Smedley and Smedley, 2012), by which time it had become systematic and institutionalized (Cohen, 1991; Hale, 1999). For our purposes, this pervasive culture and institutionalization of racism created a racist character (Sue, 2004) that not only permeated white culture but white science as well (Frosh, 2013). By the mid-Twentieth Century, race had become a central aspect of white identity and character, such that racism became colorblind; the white worldview and character became hegemonic and defined mainstream "normalcy" (Bonilla-Silva, 2013; Rodriguez, 2011). An essential part of American exceptionalism was its economic opportunities. However, we might note that the "exceptional" people were hardworking white men, and perhaps to an extent, especially recently, hardworking white women. The American Way was the identity and values of white men, which included a strong sense of entitlement, the world was there for the taking, but not for non-whites (or women) who were lazy, self-indulgent and hoped to live off the labors of others or so rich white men like Mitt Romney, believe. White Christian males were and are the chosen and exceptional people who make and break laws as they go, and settle any conflict with violence. American exceptionalism also means that not everyone is like us (which is true of course) but "Others" are also inferior and wrong.

In the past, many immigrants did find prosperity in the United States and got to the pot of gold. But most did not, at least within the first generation or two, and they soon discovered that only Anglo-Saxon males were "exceptional" enough to enjoy full rights and privileges. The rich easily gained access to higher education, especially the professions, readily received loans to start businesses, readily hired for trade apprenticeships, and even secured union membership as the means to gain employment. Until the mid-late 20th Century, the leading universities, typically with professional schools, limited admissions to white, Protestant Anglo-Saxon males (except for the "token" minority to prove their merit-based admissions). Until the 50's, many universities had quotas for Jews. Indeed the growth of Catholic universities was based on the fact that Catholics were just as likely to get sick or need lawyers or accountants as Protestants, but the restrictive policies of the mainstream universities limited admission. As for women, what did a housewife or wealthy trophy wife need with a professional education? Today, overt racism and sexism have waned, but cultural factors, poor quality urban public education and poor test scores typically limit the number of African-Americans and other brown people in higher education. We should also note, although outside our current topic, certain ethnic minorities, Jews being the classical example, and more recently Asians, especially Indians, Chinese, Thai and Vietnamese, given both class origins and their own cultural traditions valuing scholarship, have been quite successful in the pursuit of higher education in America as well as an entrepreneurial or corporate careers. They achieved this success separately from the mainstream by establishing ethic communities, New Delhis, Chinatowns, little Saigons, Koreatowns and so on where locally owned banks helped to build the community of stores, restaurants, and affordable housing. From there the children avidly studied, did their homework and found mobility through education.

Some ethnic groups such as Italians, Poles, Irish, and other Europeans only became "white" after decades of time (Ignatiev, 1995; Roediger, 2005). Some Chinese, Japanese, Indians and Pacific Islanders, and other Asians have become partially exceptional, while Black people and Hispanics are still working hard at the lower ends of the economic and status ladder.[3] In general, whites found the American Dream waiting for them to seize, some marginal whites worked a generation or more to achieve it, and non-whites still struggle mightily for minimal prosperity and relief from arbitrary or racially targeted law enforcement (Taibbi 2014). Today as we have often noted, the American dream has become more of a nightmare—and increasingly for whites as well.

Meanwhile, women and people of color became the objects of domination and terror, reinforced through cultural traditions and myth, violence itself gained mythical status. In his detailed trilogy of American frontier mythology,

---

3 Many Afro-Caribbeans take great pains to differentiate themselves from African-Americans, such as retaining their accents. In general, they live in more stable communities, do better in school and tend to be more upwardly mobile.

Richard Slotkin argues that violence not only purifies and rectifies all types of corruption and injustice (1998 [1992]) in the American vision, but also renews the American soul (2000 [1973]) as we have argued; it is never too late to set one's life and the life of the nation back on the path of righteousness (1985) by stomping the enemy. In short, gunfights and wars settled the land, exacted justice and ensured the progress of civilization. Conventional understanding of the Old West, has nothing to do with the actual political-economic history of mass slaughter of Native-Americans, buffalo, whales, and others, or the quiet farming life that most people sought, but rather, a mythology of righteous conquest and a violence of moral redemption. The legends of the Old West teach us that we must be fierce and noble, righteous and humble, and always finish a fight. More than anything else, American violence proves the righteousness of the American Way, and thus of American exceptionalism.

Perhaps cognizant of the actual realities of crime, racism, sexism, social decay, economic disparity, the waning of mobility and a history of aggression including imperialism, genocide and torture, far fewer people today see the US as exceptional. According to a recent Pew Research Center (2014) report, only 28% of the US population sees the US as "above all other countries in the world." Only three years earlier, that number was 38%. Indeed, a recent Pew Research Center (2015) report found that the biggest recent change was that 52% believe we need a stronger military to defend the country, up from 41% in 2013. Exceptionalism also teaches that everyone should be like the US, and if they don't recognize that truth, then we need to show it to them by force if necessary. Before the US invasion of Iraq on March 19th, 2003, Dick Cheney and Donald Rumsfeld believed that the Iraqis would welcome US troops and tanks, they would throw flowers at the liberating heroes, which, predictably, was not the case. How dare they resist the foreign invader? It seems that the American public has learned that a series of failed wars, including Vietnam, Iraq, and Afghanistan will not repair potholed roads, their antiqued bridges and sewer systems, nor improve education and career opportunity. Nevertheless, this does not contradict our thesis, but rather supports it—Americans are a highly ambivalent people.

Manifest Destiny—Exceptionalism as Political Doctrine

Three intertwined moments, the persistence of Puritan religion, the celebration of guns, and its economic prosperity made America an "exceptional" country as studied by professional scholars as well how most of its people express immense collective pride and glory over its economic power and military successes that in turn became an important aspect of a distinct national character at the level of collective values as well as underlying social character. We have already noted how these conditions gave rise to a unique social character, a contradiction of individualism, devotion to authority, collective moralism, self-righteousness, valorized violence and material success that have long been shaped American consciousness, values, understandings, and identities. As the country expanded Westward, more and more areas were transformed from a colonial frontier life to a "settler nation" such that law and control, already emphasized in terms of gender and race, now increasingly applied to free white men as well. The nation needed a greater semblances of discipline and order, especially in the form of "duty" and "service" necessary to raise armies against Native-Americans and Mexico. A propensity toward violence as a solution to all problems, not just those of insubordinate women, slaves, and inconvenient Native-Americans, also fomented a violent war of independence against Britain, and a subsequent number of wars westward. The vast expansion of the Louisiana Purchase meant that large numbers of Native Americans would stand in the way of what came to be called America's "manifest destiny" which Andrew Jackson proclaimed demanded a westward expansion. American exceptionalism became intertwined with "manifest destiny," that much like the "invisible hand of the market" meant an activist God intervened in human history and graced the superiority of the American way of life which demanded expansion.

The westward expansion, both by purchase (Louisiana Purchase, Alaska, the Oregon territories) and conquest (Texas and the Southwest), justified by God's will, vastly enlarged its territory which attracted more immigrants and settlers that had government protection in the form of the cavalry. With military power combined with private investment, the USA soon became one of the wealthiest powers in the world and further proof that God blessed America. Following World War II, when the United States defeated the evil Nazi Germany (and we agree it was evil in every sense of the word) and emerged victorious with half of the world's intact manufacturing capacity, it would not only be a prosperous nation, but between its wealth, military power and global influence, it became a true superpower. Yes, this was God's will as well, manifest for the entire world to see.

Presidents from Washington to Obama speak of America as exceptional and indispensable in all of the world's affairs. Every US politician knows that a required part of any campaign speech is about the greatness of America as the chief force for good in the world and the ultimate defender of peace, freedom and prosperity. To this day, politicians reiterate the specialness of America as blessed by God. As Ronald Reagan once put it, America was made up of optimistic individualists, tough yet God-fearing, such that America was blessed with a special destiny:

> I believe that faith and religion play a critical role in the political life of our nation, and always has, and that the church—and by that I mean all churches, all denominations—has had a strong influence in the state. And this has worked to our benefit as a nation ... Those who created our country—the Founding Fathers and Mothers—understood that there is a divine order which transcends the human order. They saw the state, in fact, as a form of moral order and felt that the bedrock of moral order is religion ... Without God, democracy will not and cannot long endure. If we ever forget that we're one nation under God, then we will be a nation gone under. ... I, in my own mind, have always thought of America as a place in the divine scheme of things that was set aside as a promised land. It was set here and the price of admission was very simple: the means of selection was very simple as to how this land should be populated. Any place in the world and any person from those places; any person with the courage, with the desire to tear up their roots, to strive for freedom, to attempt and dare to live in a strange and foreign place, to travel halfway across the world was welcome here.[4]

And in much the same way, President Obama more recently stated:

> I believe in American exceptionalism with every fiber of my being. ... We have a core set of values that are enshrined in our Constitution, in our body of law, in our democratic practices, in our belief in free speech and equality, that, though imperfect, are exceptional. ... And I think that we have a core set of values that are enshrined in our Constitution, in our body of law, in our democratic practices, in our belief in free speech and equality, that, though imperfect, are exceptional ... I see no contradiction between believing that America has a continued extraordinary role in leading the world towards peace and prosperity and recognizing that leadership is incumbent, depends on, our ability to create partnerships because we can't solve these problems alone.[5]

---

4 Ronald Reagan, Remarks at an Ecumenical Prayer Breakfast in Dallas, Texas http://www.reagan .utexas.edu/archives/speeches/1984/82384a.htm Accessed 08/14/2015.

5 Barak Obama, American Exceptionalism http://www.factcheck.org/2015/02/obama-and -american-exceptionalism/.

Americans are the self-proclaimed and God-proclaimed "indispensable peo-ple" whose nation is not only the greatest in the history of the world, but who have a moral imperative to lead the entire world—even if many peoples throughout the world do not desire that leadership. Death and carnage are of-ten the terrible burden Americans must bear in order to teach the world of our righteousness.

If They are not Willing ...

Many still maintain that an ideology of exceptionalism governs US domestic and foreign policy. More than any other perspective except maybe corporate capitalism, exceptionalism resonates strongly with the American public, even if ever fewer people consciously believe we are the best as demonstrated ear-lier, the belief remains powerful, and if less than great, as Trump would prom-ise, he would "Make America Great Again." Notwithstanding the clear-cut evidence that the American government engaged in systematic torture, and revelations of genocide as a clear-cut policy in Vietnam, most Americans be-lieve they are highly moral and ignore past and present use of torture today and indiscriminate bombing campaigns.[6] The lives of hundreds of thousands of Japanese civilians incinerated in the nuclear destruction of Hiroshima and Nagasaki shouldn't cause too much moral discomforts as we demonstrated our righteous might to the "evil" Soviet empire. As Nick Turse (2013) showed, the military policies in Vietnam were under the simple order to "kill anything that moved" and many thousands of peasant villagers were arbitrarily murdered. As he points out, given the nature of many search and destroy missions, free fire zones, the evaluation of "effectiveness" and military "progress" based on body counts and the use of extremely destructive bombs and weaponry, that more explosives were dropped in Vietnam than in all of World War II, mass civil-ian deaths constitute an overkill or even genocide. The My Lai Massacre and Operation Phoenix were the norm, not the exceptions. Appy (2015) argues that the aggressive masculinity we have earlier noted produced a fear of weakness in US political leadership that consequently could never admit failure as a nec-essary first step to either changing tactics or leaving Vietnam completely. After

---

6   When the torture of Iraqi prisoners at Bagram became news, it was assumed that American would feel repulsed and there would be massive protests again Bush II and his war. From what we have said it was not so surprising that many Americans, especially Republicans, approved of torture. During the 2016 presidential campaign, when Trump promised to bring back waterboarding, and even worse, he was loudly cheered.

years of stalemate, Lyndon Johnson contemplated total war and a huge expansion of the draft, and only relented when J. Edgar Hoover (director of the FBI) informed him that this would lead to massive social upheaval and he could not guarantee the internal security of the United States (Barrett, 1993). Richard Nixon received a similar message when he contemplated nuclear weapons to force Ho Chi Minh to surrender that he gave up his little "plan" to end the war. Looks like Tricky Dick really was a tricky dick.

Across the board, American muscle is the order of the day for the American public. According to the PEW Research Center (2015), respondents indicated that their top concerns are getting tough on terrorists (76%), street criminals (57%), and moral breakdown (48%). Apparently, the fact that the US spends as much on the military as the next 14 nations combined (Macias 2015) is not enough, and the Bureau of Justice Statistics shows that white collar crime affects more people and accounts for billions more in losses than street crime just through cyber-attacks and identity theft (Truman and Langton, 2014) and not including things such as banking fraud or money laundering. Most white collar crime is regulated by, but (seldom) litigated through professional organizations such as the American Medical Association, or government oversight offices such as the Securities and Exchange Commission rather than criminal units such as the FBI (Barnett, 2013). As for moral breakdown, well, an immoral person is usually someone who has more fun than I do. This is all irrelevant, however, because only wussy intellectuals worry about the factual details. No matter what, the one simple fact is that the United States can't be great if we aren't strong and tough.

Religious sentiments undergirded the Cold War in which virtuous, decent, God fearing Americans confronted an evil, godless Soviet Union allegedly hell bent on world domination that would include destroying churches, arresting priests and ministers and massive atheistic indoctrination. While the conflict was typically cloaked in self-justifying, allegedly rational perspectives such as *Realpolitik* or the "domino theory" (if one country falls to communism, others will fall in quick succession), when the Soviet fell many interpreted this as a victory for the USA, and of course the implosion of the atheists that hated capitalism was blessed by God (Langman and Burke, 2006). For many Americans, the telling moment came when Ronald Reagan, himself often an actor in many B-grade mythic cowboy movies as we previously discussed, uttered, "tear down this wall." Again we see how motivated reasoning bends facts to suit preexisting frameworks. As usual, inconvenient facts don't matter. For one thing, it was very costly for Russia to subsidize living standards in its Eastern European satellites lest they revolt as did East Germany, Hungary, Poland and Czechoslovakia. The standard of living of the average person in the "satellites" was greater than the Russians. The vastly richer US spent the Soviet Union into bankruptcy, not exactly a clever plan, and bankrupted itself in the process. It was much "easier" to understand the fall of Russian communism as due to God's will, Reagan's rants, and the superiority of American capitalism than the complex historical, political and sociological factors involved. Furthermore, no one bothered to ask why so many countries would tumble into communism. Did it offer something appealing to regular people? Many of the anti-colonial, independence movements of the post WWII period were nationalist struggles that often used the collectivist language of socialism that was more likely to resonate with the various peoples, but as we have seen, when given the choice, few countries beside North Korea "embrace" the classical forms of Communism.

Various material conditions and cultural legacies gave rise to American Exceptionalism, the notion that America was a unique Nation, blessed by God to be an example and beacon to the world of the superior nature of constitutionally based personal and collective freedom, independence and democracy. Implicit in that notion is that a combination of Christianity and a "frontier spirit" enabled a colonial backwater to declare independence, establish the longest lasting government in the modern world, and create the most powerful Nation in history. American Exceptionalism has been transformed it into a hegemonic ideology, embraced as a civil religion. According to Bellah (1967)

> What we have, from the earliest years of the republic, is a collection of beliefs, symbols and rituals with respect to sacred things and institutionalized in a collectivity ... American civil religion has its own prophets and its own martyrs, its own sacred events and sacred places, its own solemn rituals and symbols. It is concerned that America be a society as perfectly in accord with the will of God as men can make it, and a light to all the nations.[7]

Much like a religion, its rituals and beliefs regarding the sacred and profane unite believers into a community. As a widespread belief, taught in schools, endlessly repeated in civic and patriotic rituals, constantly reinforced in the mass media, exceptionalism also inscribed an American character that was lionized and valorized into ideal-mythical expression. Instead of rational politics, American Exceptionalism became a cultural ideology that fused the moral salvation of a "chosen people" with an "assertive masculinity" that legitimated belief in "redemptive violence." The fusion between moral salvation, masculinity, economic success, and imperialist ambition became an enduring ideology

---

7   Civil Religion in America, Robert Bellah, http://www.robertbellah.com/articles_5.htm
    Accessed 8/23-2015.

deeply insinuated into the very psyche of American social character that sustained and legitimated both its political economy and geopolitics.

While these tendencies were first nascent with the victories in the colonial era wars against the French and the genocidal Indian wars against native populations, it was after the Revolution when imperialism, God's will, and and profit united, encoded as the Monroe Doctrine and other vast claims to territory, were enacted as the military conquest of Texas, the war against Mexico, the Spanish American war, numerous interventions into Central America, Korea, Vietnam, two wars against Iraq, and Afghanistan. And then there were dozens of coups and overthrows. Didn't the overthrow of Iran's progressive socialist, Mossadeq work out just fine? Ask the mullahs. Whether the military victory is decisive or not, the end result of these moments has been a glorification of America as the best, most decent country in history that has been blessed and guided by divine providence to lead the world. American Exceptionalism, intertwined with its civil religion and nationalism, legitimated a massive military machine to sustain America's imperialist ambitions and numerous interventionism in other countries, cloaked as securing peace, defending the "free world." The costs of this military would of course be quit costly to the taxpaying populations as well as the various young people who would pay with life and limbs for the sake of America-or at least the geopolitics of its elites. But as we have argued, while military expenses are consistent with America's social character, social welfare is not. But this is changing as will be seen.

Part of being the greatest is making sure that others learn how great you are, and we should teach that lesson to them by force if necessary. In response to the release of evidence of CIA's torture program that included forced rectal feeding and threats to rape prisoner's mothers, Fox news correspondent Andrea Tantaros commented, that the "The United States of America is awesome." Apparently, the public agrees that torture is awesome; 59% of respondents in a poll by the Washington Post-ABC News (2014) approved of torture, while only 39% disapproved. But narcissistic nations, like people, often lack either empathy for the pain of others outside their in group, nor can they make objective self-appraisals. Indeed the narcissistic gratifications of being the best, systematically distorts the fact that the USA is no longer the best. If the US uses the same torture as its enemies, or uses terror (in the form of drone strikes) how are we better? As Friedrich Nietzsche argued, "whoever fights monsters should see to it that in the process he does not become a monster" (Nietzsche, (1989 [1886] p. 89)). American politicians never cite philosophers or any other thoughtful person. We should also be careful not to create more monsters. Many of the truly barbaric and vile executions of the Islamic State, the burnings, and beheadings were carried out by Iraqis who had been tortured by Americans at Abu Ghraib, and the larger Islamic State militia army draws from former Iraqi army personnel thrown out by the US occupation managers (Chengu 2014).

Exceptional ... How Exactly?

The United States is the wealthiest country in the world, but also the most highly indebted country in the world. From 2003 to 2015, pay for the bottom 70% of workers, including college graduates, remained stagnant or fell, and since 1973, median compensation (pay plus benefits) increased by only 7.9%, while productivity increased a wondrous 64.9%, by far the best in the world. In other words, businesses keep the vast majority of the profits that increasing productivity creates. As incomes fell, but growing productivity meant greater corporate profits, capital found a new way to exploit its workers; credit cards became easily available so that economically burdened families could still maintain their standards of living (Wolff, 2013). But shock soon came to the card users when the bills came due and they saw how easily they lost track of how much they spent. And when they saw that the banks were charging Mafia-like interest rates and exorbitant late fees, it was then too late to tear them up.

The growing disparity of compensation between the rich and the rest creates even greater disparities in wealth, and today, inequality in the US is quite literally off the charts. The top 1% earns nearly 36% of all the income and controls almost 50% of the nation's wealth. The six Walton heirs have as much wealth as the bottom 30% of the country, in round numbers, that's 100 million people. Twenty four hedge fund managers make over $1 billion a year. Steven Cohen, the manager of SAC capital, made approximately $2.4 billion in 2014 giving him a net worth of over $11 billion. Meanwhile 46 million Americans are on food stamps, and about 20% are working minimum wage jobs for a yearly income (full-time) of about $17,160 with no paid vacation, healthcare, or retirement (Bivens and Mishel, 2015; Economic Policy Institute, 2014). This level of inequality is extreme even by the standards of most advanced capitalist countries. Currently, the United States ranks fourth in *average* net worth at $330,000, but 19th in *median* net worth, at $45,000. In other words, the extreme wealth of a few individuals at the top skews the average much higher compared to the midpoint, such that half the US population has a net worth below 45K, dead last among the developed nations—and in fact, about 24% of the population has negative net worth (Shorrocks, Davies and Lluberas, 2015). As this shows, averages can be misleading as the familiar joke illustrates: billionaire Bill Gates goes into a bar with nine other people and suddenly everyone's average income is 100 million dollars a year. In the other developed countries, especially the Nordic countries, labor unions and social democratic parties, representing the people and not the economic elites, act as a counterforce to the radical individualism and unrestrained interests of big business in America. Iceland jailed the criminal bankers that led to its financial collapse, but in the US, where the bankers control the government, they got multi-million dollar bonuses and major pay raises for the "good work" of accepting the largess of the taxpayers who covered their malfeasance (Carney, 2010).

While most Americans think they have the best health care system in the world, and its medical technologies may well be, between the American diet that promotes obesity and diabetes, heart disease and cancer, and a lack of accessibility to health care for many, we are not the healthiest. The US is 70th overall in health, 49th in life expectancy, and 178th in infant mortality. We have one of the highest rates of child poverty. We spend 18% of our GNP on healthcare, much more than any other country, yet with middling outcomes at best. The US spends almost twice as much per person as Canada or the European Union who have much better health outcomes. Japan spends 8.5% of its GDP and they too have much better outcomes. They eat a much healthier diet of fish and vegetables, and have more equitable access to healthcare, they live longer, healthier lives. We are 69th in ecosystem sustainability. Once upon a time the United States had the highest literacy rate in the world and was a leader in mass public education. Today we are 39th in basic education. We're seventh in literacy, 27th in math, 22nd in science. Teenagers in the U.S. woefully rank about 36th in the world in math, reading and science. The US is 34th in access to water and sanitation and 31st in personal safety. Even in its access to cellphones and the Internet, the United States ranks a disappointing 23rd, partly because one American in five lacks Internet access and we have the slowest speeds among all first-world nations (Leopold, 2012). We do have the highest percentage of our population in jail, a tribute to the legacy of traditions of violence, intertwined with inequality, compounded by unequal access to education and jobs, and to be sure, a big helping of racism and differential enforcement of laws such that nearly 80% of the prison population consists of racial/ethnic minorities. As a legacy of Puritan asceticism, e.g. the moral damnation, condemnation and criminalization of hedonist indulges such as drugs and sex has meant that the majority of prisoners in the US penal system are drug related, namely, dealing and possessing. Most of the incarcerated tend to be poor minorities. Rich white folks can easily snort some blow or smoke some weed without any fears. But if one is Black or Spanish speaking, there is a good chance that if the arresting officer doesn't shoot you in alleged self-defense, you may get a doobie planted in your pocket. Supposedly, marijuana is harmful, habit forming, and the gateway to hard drug addiction. Moreover,

its associations with African American music, from jazz to rap, its known pleasurable association with sex and pints of Ben and Jerry's ice cream seems like
a clear and present threat to the Republic. After legalization, tax revenues in
Colorado increased, and Mexican production dropped. More and more states
are noting the huge costs of policing and incarceration and the tremendous
growth of tax revenues, thus there are more and more pressures for decriminalization. The Federal government has not shown any willingness to act on
this issue, even though Obama has been open about having a joint or two, at
least in his youth.

The American infrastructure is rapidly deteriorating. Highways are in dis-
repair. 61,000 bridges are now structurally deficient and in need of urgent repair. In many cases gas, water and sewer lines that are over 100 years old spring
leaks. Meanwhile, the American Congress, dominated by Republicans, refuses
to allocate the necessary funding for the reconstruction of our transportation
networks. China now has the world's largest high-speed rail network, 5,600
miles with trains that generally travel over 200 miles an hour, while the maglev
(magnetic levitation) train between the Shanghai airport and the city hits 300
miles an hour on its 50 mile run—comparable to short-haul jet service, but
using only 20% as much fuel. Japan's experimental maglev just hit 375 mph.
Italy has the fastest regular rail service in the world and nowhere in the US do
we have anything comparable. In Germany, passenger cars regularly attain 200
miles per hour on unrestricted segments of the autobahn. Not only are speed
limits set much lower in the US, where speeding tickets are a major source of
revenue, but our roads are engineered to 1950s standards even when they are
new construction or complete rebuilds (Vande Bunte 2015). Even if the roads
were engineered to 21st Century standards, collision with an American-style
pothole at 200 miles per hour would result in catastrophic suspension and
steering failure.

To repeat our basic argument. If American exceptionalism, anchored by its
particular social character once facilitated the rise of American economic and
political power, the same characterological traits now limit self-awareness, obscure objective considerations, discourage self-examination and indeed fore-
close the possibilities of changing directions to halt the downward spiral of
the great Colossus that is now tipping toward its collapse. As Todd Leopold
(2012) pointed out in his CNN discussion, if businesses don't evolve, they go
out of business. Former sector leaders like Atari, Pan Am, Montgomery Ward,
Radio Shack and Woolworth's all crashed against the rocks of strategy, innovation and competition. Why then is it so hard for the United States to admit its
shortcomings and change its policies?

As we argue, the combination of American exceptionalism as an ideology intertwined with its social character and elements of its self-acclaimed superiority, its self-righteousness, its "motivated reasoning" and denial, filter and indeed, grossly distort reality. An interesting example of this denial, "motivated reasoning" has been over the 2008 implosion of the financial market. For conservative Republicans, the underlying character structure not only exonerates Bush and blames Obama for the crash, but does not admit how the limited bailout by Obama was quite successful, as seen by both the CBO and academic economists like Krugman, Stieglitz, and Baker. Further, the Republican "solutions," meaning do nothing, just obstruct, hurts the economy and directly intensifies overall social decline. As a culture, the American people have a characterologically limited capacity for self-reflection, and cannot see or comprehend the complex nature of realty. As we have seen, the majority of the country thinks we are on the wrong course, but yet they vote for the same incumbents they claim to hate. Since 1964, Congressional approval ranged between 35–52% earlier in the period, and roughly 33 to the current 11% approval recently. Yet, incumbents retain their seats 80–91% of the time, even with only 11% approval (Mataconis 2012). The current year 2016 may prove different as the outsider Donald Trump has become the Republican nominee, and Bernie Sanders nearly won on the Democratic side. Whether their success brings sweeping change to government remains to be seen.

The Sorrows of American Exceptionalism

In his now classical three volume series, Chalmers Johnson (2000, 2004, 2006) has traced the rise of the American Empire in which America has gone from the "exceptional nation" to a superpower that has now become the lone wolf sheriff who was created, valorized and celebrated in the American monomyth of the valiant hero who saves the good people through the skilled use of redemptive violence. With its vast wealth and post WWII gargantuan military machine spread across the world, the US has intervened in the affairs of many of countries. For Johnson, the adverse consequences include dictatorships friendly to the United States but whom the local population despises. Second, the best laid plans of the CIA and the American military have a funny habit of fostering "blowback" that turns local resentment against our dictators into anti-US movements and full-scale revolutions, as in the Philippines (Marcos), Indonesia (Suharto), Cuba (Batista), Nicaragua (Samoza), Chile (Pinochet), El Salvador (Duarte), Haiti (Duvalier and "Baby Doc" Duvalier) and Iran

(Shah Pahlavi). Then there are the dictators that we long supported but then removed because they exercised a little too much independence such as in Panama (Noriega) and Iraq (Hussein). And let us not forget unqualified support for our current friends the present-day Kingdom of Saudi Arabia, a major candidate along with North Korea for the most repressive government in the world. They are now doing about 1,000 public beheadings a year, far more that ISIS, and women still cannot legally drive cars among other restrictions. Let's not ignore how they have funded Wahhabi madrassas throughout the Muslim world that teach a highly repressive fundamentalism, along with hatred toward the West and any other Muslims who believe and live differently. Osama bin Laden, the Saudi Arabian, late of Al Qaeda, who once worked with the CIA fighting against the Soviet invasion of Afghanistan, felt betrayed when the US placed bases in Saudi Arabia, and so he organized various terrorist actions against the US that culminated on the infamous day of September 11, 2001.

When the US proconsul of Iraq Paul Bremer dismissed the entire Iraqi army officer corps who were members of the Baathist party (a job requirement), about 500,000 men were suddenly unemployed, and many of them were easily recruited to join a new organization, the Islamic State in Syria, ISIS, which gained many more willing recruits when the US continued to imprison and torture people and then celebrated that abuse by posting images on the Internet of nude, hooded, threatened and humiliated Iraqi prisoners. The self-appointed Caliph, Abu Bakr al-Baghdadi, a sadistic, psychopathic killer, had spent time in Camp Bucca where he and others were tortured. We have described many examples of resistance, revolution, and terrorism that were inspired by pervasive hatred of US military occupation and political support for oppressive regimes. As we noted in the earlier discussion of Chris Kyle, who killed so many Iraqi "ragheads," "camel jockeys" and "savages," including women and children, few Americans asked why so many Iraqis hate the US with such intensity.

Today, every Latin American and most Caribbean countries have moved toward open defiance against US domination. On December 3, 2011, 34 Latin American and Caribbean nations created the Community of Latin American and Caribbean States—and specifically excluded The United States, Canada, and all territories currently held by Britain, France, the Netherlands, and Denmark. Mexico hosted the first organizational meeting in Cancun in 2010, where the President of Mexico Felipe Calderon said that "it is time for Latin Americans and Caribbeans to unite." Evo Morales, the President of Bolivia went even further:

> A union of Latin American countries is the weapon against imperialism. It is necessary to create a regional body that excludes the United States and Canada. Where there are u.s. military bases that do not respect

democracy, where there is a political empire with his blackmailers, with its constraints, there is no development for that country, and especially there is no social peace and, therefore, it is the best time for prime ministers of Latin America and the Caribbean to gestate this great new organization without the United States to free our peoples in Latin America and the Caribbean.

WILKINSON, 2010

This new union makes the US-led Organization of American States, or OAS, effectively defunct. Secondly, in order to sustain a massive military machine and dispatch armed forces throughout the world, the move from exceptionalism to Empire has meant a fundamental loss of democracy. Johnson (2004) compared contemporary America to Rome, when Caesar led the move from the Republic to an Empire, not only did Rome lose its democracy, but at the same time, a number of processes were set in motion that would ultimately lead to its fall. As he traced the decline of Rome, its parallels to the present United States are to say the least, quite scary. With the fall of the Republic, Roman civilization fragmented into various regions, each of which served as a power base for various men who wanted to be emperor. Each successive emperor could only hold the empire together with ever increasing force and public investment. In other words, they had to partially force, and partially buy loyalty because the fall of the Republic also destroyed any sense of legitimacy or social cohesion. The US definitely lays out the money for its military, police, and surveillance, but less and less for those social investments. This will of course only accelerate collapse from within. We have noted how the high cost of maintaining its military, which includes extremely expensive, highly advanced weapons systems, has meant less money for infrastructure, education, and social programs.

To repeat what we said in our prefaces, Sheldon Wolin (2008) has gone so far as to claim that indeed we no longer have a genuine democracy, but a "managed democracy," an "inverted totalitarianism" in which a plutocracy dominated by the financial sector, which now includes the military-industrial complex, completely controls all three branches of government in order to enact, adjudicate and execute policies with little or no input from the electorate. In fact, using multivariate analysis on a massive dataset from a meta-analysis, Gilens and Page (2014) show that, in terms of how our institutions actually function, the US is a "nominal" democracy, and of four models tested, the vast majority of governmental institutions function according to Economic-Elite domination. Of the other models, a few agencies still function according to Biased Pluralism (biased in favor of elite groups), while Majoritarian Electoral Democracy and Majoritarian Pluralism no longer applies to any governmental institutions in the dataset at the federal, state, or local levels. In short, the US is now dominated by elite groups as C. Wright Mills (1956 [2000]) feared would happen from his vantage point in the 1950s, and increasingly by elite individuals. Thus we have a government controlled by an unelected plutocracy with charades of democratic government by a clearly dysfunctional Congress in which a small cadre of right wing fanatics can undermine governance. Even conservative critics like Ornstein and Mann (2012) fear the rising extremism on the right and its threat to the US Republic.

The Unwinding of Exceptionalism

How did America lose its long standing history of economic growth and improved standards of living for most of its people? What happened to its premier leadership in science and education, how did it lose its position as the foremost educational system in the world. What happened to the nation that pioneered the skyscraper? What happened to the state-of-the-art infrastructure? After all it was the United States that invented the airplane and first mass-produced automobiles, then it built highways and then expressways that spanned the nation. We built such world famous bridges of the times as the Brooklyn Bridge and Golden Gate Bridge. The TVA system of hydrolelectric dams brought electricity to many areas of Appalachia for the first time, and the Hoover and Grand Cooley dams brought water and power to the West. Given such grand achievements and the seeming invincibility of the US war machine at the end of WWII, the sight of American choppers evacuating the last people they could carry form the rooftop of the US embassy in Saigon revealed the futility of military power against a population determined to resist foreign domination. Iraq and Afghanistan followed in this new pattern of popular resistance, that no conqueror can sustain their occupation indefinitely, and that military conquest in recent decades ultimately creates more problems and enemies than it solves or defeats.

Today, the nature of neoliberalism has resulted in a conjoining of the massive financial power of corporations, especially in certain industries like banking/finance, defense, pharmaceuticals, and energy, with traditional forms of individualism and democratic populism, "civic activism." In turn, an essential part of American values has long been a disdain toward government. This was already evident in the American Revolution, Shay's Rebellion, and the Whiskey Rebellion. Many people have noted that American patriotism is such that many people "love their country" but hate their

government and disdain any and everything that the government might do-
completely unware of the number of things the government does. It seems
like the only thing that excites a majority of Americans and rallies them
around the government is killing an enemy, whether real or imagined, as long
as other people, poor minorities, do the fighting. While this current blend
of corporate interests with long enduring right wing populism may well provide corporate profits and succor the individualism of its social character,
this is no way to run a government that at least in theory claims to be representative. It is largely representative of corporate interests, not the welfare
of the population.

American Exceptionalism is Really Authoritarianism

Aside from the federal government, what could oppose the mighty power of
big business? Who or what will stop the export of jobs to low-wage countries?
Who will invest the many needed trillions (yes, trillions) to rebuild our infrastructure? Who will pay for school and college? Aside from the government,
who or what can oppose the menacing expansion of surveillance, stop the
militarization of the police, and end racially targeted law enforcement? The
will of the people, perhaps? Which people? As we have argued, an intrinsic
aspect of American social character is such that many people identify with
the power and glory of military might. Polls show that many support the torture and annihilation of people in foreign countries and the imprisonment of
Black and brown people at home (Taibbi, 2014). The majority of whites (65%)
even approve of gunning down unarmed Black men in the street if police think
it is appropriate (Pew Research Center 2014a). A heroic leader? God perhaps?
While it may seem amusing to rely on supernatural forces to correct fundamentally social problems, Nietzsche's pessimism seems like an appropriate
response:

> As much now as any other times, there have always been a very few hu-
> man beings, and great herds of people ... nothing has been more condi-
> tioned in the masses than obedience, the unconditional acceptance of
> authority as a kind of formal conscience that commands to uncondition-
> ally do something or other ... thus they need a leader to follow without
> question, and the herd person quakes at the frightening danger that one
> might fail to appear ... but our real worry and gloom, my free spirits, is
> that we know they always do.
>
> NIETZSCHE, 1989 [1886] pp. 110–117

We have however argued that Americans distrust the government, so if we now argue that they long for governmental authority, how can we reconcile this apparent contradiction? The answer rests upon the nature of authoritarianism as discussed in Chapter 1. This is a central aspect of American exceptionalism. For an authoritarian, not just any authority will do. The authority must be righteous, powerful, and evoke emotions that connect the social character of the individual to the authority figure. Today, that authority is not really God, or a hero. The tragedy of American decline is the fusion of individualism and big business, or in other words, the structural power of capital has united with the psychic anchoring of individualism to limit support for government as an independent actor that can initiate the kinds of changes necessary for a more benevolent, humane society. There is support for the coercive, punitive functions of armies, police and jails, but disdain for the social improvement functions that provide people with healthcare, education, housing, unemployment and/comfortable retirement. The type of hero required seems impossible today, namely one who embodies the power of corporate hegemony, as well as individual masculine strength, yet somehow directs his authority towards progressive change on a national scale using tax money extracted from the same corporations and rich individuals he embodies. Could a woman embody this kind of heroic status? Maybe, but given our argument, she would need to be both attractively feminine but also assertively masculine, or in other words, embody the American ideals of both femininity and masculinity at the same time.

Thus, the massive and fundamental changes that are necessary for a humane society with expanding social programs, universal healthcare, quality education for all and rebuilding a deteriorating infrastructure collide with a barrier of characterologically anchored individualism and its resistance to the expansion of any government programs (except the police and military). This begins with a long standing resistance toward any increased taxation or regulation on the corporate gods, although many large corporations gladly seek government tax abatements and free bailouts while parking their huge taxable profits in off shore banks to protect those profits. For example, the defense industries are more than willing to amass great profits producing extremely expensive highly advanced weapons of questionable value against militia armies that rarely fight a set battle and terrorist cells that have no central command, formal structure, or fixed location.[8] The current US approach is something like bombing all of New Jersey just to get Tony Soprano.

---

8 The nuclear weapons in the American arsenal and the delivery systems are provided by major, for-profit corporations, for example Boeing, Northrop Grumman, General Dynamics,

Following World War II, and especially during the Reagan and Bush II administrations, the military-industrial complex mushroomed and became increasingly intertwined with the autonomous corporate sector. This diverted vast amounts of money to the military machine, money taken away from various benefits, social programs, and infrastructural improvements. While the country could sustain spending for both the military and civilian developments for a while, the government needed to vastly increase debt loads left from the Vietnam War and thereafter. In the 21st Century, the country must now choose one or the other—a massive military or greater investment in civilian society. The assertive, phallic aggressive masculinity symbolized by the gun and undergirded by theocratic based notions of morally redemptive violence, tends to view the world as a very threatening place and believes that the only way to deal with threats is military power and total annihilation of the enemy, just to be sure we got all of them because even one enemy left alive will fester over time. In other words, the authoritarian expressions of social character view military force as the best way to deal with any problem, which simultaneously assents to the geopolitical agendas of the elites. Since World War II, none of the US military interventions have produced the desired results and actually intensified the very threats they sought to prevent. North Korea remains a bizarre, hereditary dictatorship with nuclear weapons. A united Vietnam has embraced the socialist reforms that would supposedly domino throughout the region. Iran became a theocratic dictatorship. Jihadists flock to any anti-American militia armies in the Middle East and there are many to choose from. Afghanistan is in shambles and we turned Iraq and Iran from bitter enemies to best friends, with Iraq distrustful at best towards the United States and Iran ranging from deeply resentful to hostile.

Despite the clear historical record against a unity of religion and State, most conservatives still insist, without any evidence, that the founding fathers were devout Christians and that America and its constitution were was based on Christian principles. As we saw in Chapter 2, this is simply not true, no matter how "motivated" the reasoning. Quite the opposite. In fact, the founding

---

GenCorp Aerojet, Huntington Ingalls, and Lockheed Martin, Babcock & Wilcox, Bechtel, Honeywell International, and URS Corporation, Aecom, Flour, Jacobs Engineering, SAIC, Alliant Techsystems and Rockwell Collins. Needless to say, these are generally based on cost plus profit contracts and there are always overruns. Finally as private corporations, these "merchants of death," employee small armies of lobbyists, typically retired military officers and or congressional representatives as lobbyists that can easily dull out the vast campaign contributions. We recall Eisenhower's warning about the military-industrial complex. See: https://www.thenation.com/article/meet-the-private-corporations-building-our-nuclear-arsenal/ accessed September 25, 2015.

fathers, actively sought to prevent the extremely bloody history of Europe's religious wars from continuing in the New World. Many were also aware of the Enlightenment thinkers and their critiques of theologically legitimated dynastic rule. Thus they vehemently opposed the notion that the US was founded upon any religious principle or that it should in any way be a Christian nation, but rather its freedom of religion enabled people of all faiths to share in accepting America's civil religion, but they could not foresee nor overcome all possibilities of oppression. "Christian" principles have justified slavery and patriarchy, and continue to justify various aspects of white, male, heteronormative, identities and/or esteem.

Another interesting aspect of American exceptionalism remains its attitudes toward sexuality. While most European countries provide realistic sex education in their schools that includes accurate information on contraception, the early Puritan legacy teaches an irrational sexual ambivalence in America. Conservative moralists condemn all things sexual as forms of "licentiousness" and perfidy in deed, in print, in pictures, rock music videos and most recently, the Internet, especially the proliferation of more than 300 thousand porn sites. With smartphones, people can send highly revealing selfies, sexts and share other provocative images as they happen. Hook-up apps like Tinder, or Grinder for gays connect nearby strangers to each other, show pictures and let the folks decide upon an immediate "connection." Casual sexual liaisons and pornography of every genre is a mouse click away, so while many "conservative" leaders preach abstinence and still teach that all sexuality outside of marriage automatically leads to all manner of STD infections and death, while marriage somehow magically shields the man and woman (hetero couples only) from disease, emotional stress, and any other problem. Ever fewer heed this learned wisdom from ages past. Despite the efforts of abstinence-only sex education, the "conservative" states and regions have the highest rates of unwed parenthood and STD transmission while the bastions of liberalism have the lowest (Lewis 2014).

Meanwhile, the constant discovery that the most militant evangelical ministers or conservative leaders who proclaim the sanctity of sexual purity, extoll "family values," frequently have extramarital affairs and same-sex liaisons.[9] In other words, they quite often practice for themselves what they condemn for others. Quite recently, the former Speaker of the House, ex Representative Dennis Hastert was found guilty of paying millions of dollars of hush money to cover up liaisons he had with young male students when he was a gym coach. For those too young to remember, Hastert was the Speaker of the House

---

9 See http://www.ranker.com/list/republican-sex-scandals/web-infoguy for a list of Republican hypocrites, Accessed Nov 2, 2015.

during the Monicagate impeachment proceedings of Bill Clinton, and along with Henry Hyde, Newt Gingrich and Robert Livingston, Hastert championed the prosecution of Bill Clinton for the so-called blow job heard around the world. While any number of Democratic leaders may also have transgressive liaisons, FDR, JFK, LBJ, and who can forget Anthony Weiner sexting images of his penis, seemingly to nearly every female for whom he had a phone number, one major difference is that most liberals don't preach the glories of purity, the virtues of virginity, extoll premarital abstinence and marital fidelity, or pry into the relationships of others.

Throughout the country, 40 + years since Roe versus Wade, women's choice and agency remains under assault. Conservative males and many of the conservative females that love them have attempted to preserve traditional gender roles and utilize religious appeals that deny women the right to control their own bodies which includes their own sexuality and fertility. Thus we see typically authoritarian forms of denigration, such as slut shaming and the obdurate belief held by 39% of men believe that women ask to be raped (ACWS, 2012). In fact, 31% of men would rape an intoxicated woman if they thought they could get away with it (Edwards, Bradshaw, and Hinsz, 2014). This testifies to the enduring mythology of patriarchal norms and phallocentric power. Like a hierarchy of wealth, gender hierarchy makes sense to people in an authoritarian subculture that ranks nearly everything.

In the USA, the intrusion of traditional religion into the political or scientific realm causes still other problem. As medical and biological sciences make rapid advances, especially with various genetic therapies, nanotechnologies and robotic surgeries, religious curricula teach millions of young people that the theory of evolution violates the biblical stories of creation. As we earlier mentioned, the Creation Museum in Petersburg, Kentucky features 70,000 square feet of the latest animatronic scenes of humans riding dinosaurs, as well as a botanical garden, petting zoo, "educational" theater shows, "history" classes, and a planetarium. While this might well delight little children, the rejection of evolution, as well as geology, biochemistry, and nuclear and astrophysics which are crucial for the radiocarbon and other means of dating fossil remains, as well as the earth and the universe, means that hundreds of thousands of young people are diverted from studying science at a time when the various fields are most in need of technicians, researchers and practitioners. China however, unburdened by such nonsense, now produces more engineers and scientists than does the USA.

As Europe races to expand renewable energy, Germany went from nearly zero renewable in 1983 to a world-leading 74% today as well as seeing major reductions in carbon emissions and industrial pollution (Kroh, 2014).

The legacy of its religious based exceptionalism leads the US toward a different course. Climate change deniers, aided and financially abetted by major fossil fuel energy firms use religion or simply their political authority to forbid any public mention of climate change or global warming as did Rick Scott, the governor of Florida.[10] He was soon followed by Scott Walker, the governor of Wisconsin (Roston, 2015). No state employee may use the terms "climate change," "global warming" or "sustainability" in any public context. This won't change the fact that human use of hydrocarbon fuels, as well as the methane produced by ever larger herds of cattle destined for the hamburger franchises of the world, may be the most serious problem of our age in conjunction with toxification of the environment through industrial pollution and massive application of artificial fertilizers, herbicides, and biocides. Extreme weather, droughts, melting glaciers, rising sea levels, poisoned drinking water, fracking based earthquakes, dead zones in the Gulf of Mexico and elsewhere all foretell major ecological disasters. As we have said, certain aspects of America's social character, for example certain conservative religions, dispose the embrace of social and political beliefs that become intertwined with and support for big money interests that are quite contrary to their own self interests. For example, a small but extremely wealthy segment of the population like the Koch brothers whose oil fortunes support and finance politicians redefine climate change/global warming and industrially based toxification as a "debate" rather than as empirical facts, the very possibility of moving toward alternative energy source becomes impossible. If the truth will set us free, then it is also necessary to develop practical solutions to real-life problems.

Anti-intellectualism is also an integral expression of American authoritarianism. Anti-intellectualism in America was a direct legacy of Puritanism religion and culture fused authoritarianism as a personality factor together with religious beliefs which then serves as highly effective, seamless barrier against facts, logic, reason and scientific evidence. Hofstadter (1963) saw this anti-intellectualism as disdain for intellectual life and for those people who are devoted to ideas and the life of the mind as an essential aspect of American society. The emphasis on techniques and practicality leads to a mediocre sameness that dumbs people down and entraps them in a "cult of practicality." This has been more recently developed by Susan Jacoby (2009) who notes the resurgence of anti-intellectualism especially evident with the rise of the Tea

---

10   A very serious problem for Broward County where Miami Beach is located, has been the migration of sea water into the fresh water aquifers. While it may take 100 year until rising sea levels put southern Florida underwater, they may not have drinking water in the very near future.

Party. Chris Mooney, drawing upon much of the social science that we ourselves have used, has charted what he called the "Republican brain" which became programmed to wage a war on science (2012, 2006). Today, the fossil fuel companies, much like Big Brother, are watching and no Republican candidate for elected office dare utter the words "global warming" except as a joke. Like good authoritarian toadies, they fall into place and chuckle accordingly as the world dies a little more.

Strangely enough, no other country has had more faith in education as an instrument of social mobility. No other country in the West democratized education earlier, but no country has been more suspicious of too much education. We've always thought of education as good if it gets you a better job, but bad if it makes you think too much. With minimal critical reflection and imagination, faith readily overcomes reason, so that not only is the US likely exempted from the laws of physics, but blind to the detrimental effects of climate change, indifferent to pollution and domineering toward people who see the world differently. Many Americans are isolated from the usual standards of logic and evidence. It's not that Americans are stupid, but rather that American culture has always valued ingenuity and practical knowledge over abstract and contemplative, imaginative inquiry, which discourages the psychological dispositions and the academic training necessary for serious social critique as well as the desire for imaginative thinking about alternatives.[11] One area where this has become noticeable is how many American universities are emphasizing the STEM (Science, Technology, Engineering and Math) curricula and retrenching from humanities and social sciences, especially philosophy and sociology that are most likely to foster critical thought. As we mentioned, back in the 1950's, Eisenhower wanted strong support for the sciences, but equally for the arts and humanities because he did not want a nation of coldly-calculating technocrats. Today, that seems to be all we want. American inventiveness only applies to the moment, the immediate desire to solve an immediate problem or devise the next great money-maker, as we saw with Peter Thiel in Chapter 3, who already knows all the answers to the world's problems and it's time for elite entrepreneurs to just take charge and do it. Long before Marx wrote about ideology, or Gramsci wrote about hegemony or Marcuse (1991 [1964]) described "one dimensional thought," traditions of critique and self-examination have had little purchase outside rarefied academic settings in the United States. Thus

---

11   Some of our readers may get bored with our constant uses of data and evidence to buttress our arguments about income growth, inequality, comparative health figures, sexual behavior etc. And while our work is interpretive and moralistic, we do think the evidence supports our views.

for example, referring back to the creationist myths of the earth being created around 6000 BCE, most such believers know nothing about or simply reject the very notion of radioactive decay, carbon dating, geological formations, the life of stars, or the motion of celestial bodies. This also entails rejection of nuclear physics as well as astronomy, and even the ancients knew the movement of celestial bodies can be used to establish dates. Pierce (2010) put it quite succinctly in his analysis of how and why America, has had a long history of the preference for faith and feeling over facts and reason:

> American idiocy is a huge and expensive demonstration of Hofstadter's argument: The case against intellect is founded on a set of fictional and wholly abstract antagonisms. Intellect is pitted against feeling, on the ground that it is somehow inconsistent with warm emotion. It is pitted against character, because it is widely believed that intellect stands for mere cleverness, which transmutes easily into the sly and diabolical. It is pitted against practicality, since theory is held to be opposed to practice. It is pitted against democracy, since intellect is felt to be a form of distinction that defies egalitarianism. ... Once the validity of these antagonisms is accepted, then the case for intellect is lost.
>
> PIERCE, 2010 p. 88

One of the sorriest places where this anti-intellectualism is evident is an understanding of the world outside the United States. If one values force above all, this precludes any need for understanding. Furthermore, authoritarians generally blindly accept the decisions of people in positions of power. Foreign people just need to learn that the American way is best. For the first 150 years or so, the United States was separated from Europe or Asia by vast oceans where only a few affluent travelers, government/military officials, seafarers, whalers and merchants were likely to go. That isolation rapidly changed in the 20th Century with the development of mass communication, global travel and the globalization of the world economy. But for the most part, the political interests of the now transnational capitalist class is to reduce any and all national barriers in order to more efficiently garner resources, cheaply manufacture products, manage shipping and other commerce. Lesser Americans are generally quite limited in their knowledge of the current world and how it functions. For example, most Americans do not have passports and have not traveled outside the country and this includes the majority of senators and congressmen who supported the Vietnam War based on clear fabrications of a Tonkin Bay attack on US patrol boats. Most Americans know nothing of the Middle East, its history, culture, languages or religions, and overwhelmingly believed that Saddam Hussein was in league with Osama bin Laden on 9/11, and that he had weapons of mass destruction, some of which were loaded on ships getting ready to attack the United States. Anyone with the most cursory knowledge of the Middle East would know that Saddam Hussein ruthlessly persecuted religious fundamentalists, and that Iraq's dismantled weapons programs were under constant surveillance by UN inspectors. The idea that Hussein, a secular, heavy drinker and insatiable womanizer, might find any common grounds with a Wahhabi religious fanatic was nothing more than an absurd fiction invented to justify the invasion of Iraq, and besides, dictators do not share power with stateless religious zealots like Al Qaeda, or with anyone else.

Similarly, many if not most Americans believe that Iran is developing nuclear weapons, even though the government's own evidence has shown that such programs were dropped many years ago. Even the Mossad, Israel's version of the CIA reported in a document leaked to Al Jazeera states that "Iran at this stage is not performing the activity necessary to produce weapons" (Mossad Report, 2012). Iran completed negotiations with the United States and other powers and agreed to very strict demands. Nevertheless, many conservatives in Congress, naturally suspicious and fearful as authoritarians tend to be, tried to scuttle the treaty, but it managed to squeak through. For many of the more conservative Americans, given what we've said about social character, a war with Iran as phallic aggression and moral redemption, was the only acceptable outcome for most Republicans in the Senate, and several Democrats as well (Everett, 2015). By the way, Iran had deactivated its heavy water reactor, shipped most of its enriched uranium to Russia and deactivated most of its centrifuges. Further, Iran agreed to a prisoner exchange and when 2 US navy patrol boats entered Iranian waters, the boats and sailors were returned within 24 hours. Yes, sometimes the soft power of negotiation works and prevents wars.

Nevertheless, authoritarians don't deny all logic and evidence, only the logic and evidence they don't like. As Lundskow (2012) argues, authoritarians are happy to make up information that better suits their temperament and tastes, which allows acceptance of absurd nonsense without critique. At the time of this writing, FOX News reporter and self-proclaimed expert on Islamic extremism Steven Emerson reported that Birmingham, England had been taken over by Muslim fanatics (Adamczyk, 2015). The then Prime Minister of Britain David Cameron publicly called the Fox News reporter "a complete idiot." Meanwhile, another crack team at Fox reported that multiple districts in Paris were controlled by Muslim extremists who had imposed Sharia Law. The Fox team claimed that some parts of Paris were more dangerous than Damascus, Baghdad or Kabul (BBC News, 2015). A French news team visited the areas and shock and surprise, the local residents were flabbergasted at such outlandish assertions. The mayor of Paris, Anne Hidalgo threatened to sue Fox News. In a rare acknowledgement of actual reality, Fox News did apologize, and curiously, Fox has scrubbed all references to both events from their internet pages. Let's not forget the ban on climate change discussion we mentioned earlier. Inconvenient facts have a way of disappearing.

We could go on and expand the litany of the denial of facts and reason and the simultaneous acceptance of the absurd, the ridiculous, and the preposterous. Of course the immediate reaction of more sensible segments of the population is to regard such people as stupid, willfully ignorant, or crazy. At the same time, many politicians and their staff, as well as Fox News agents and others are highly educated or experienced, and should be able to readily distinguish fact from fiction—and most likely they do. Truth and falsehood are merely instruments for personal gratification, political influence, and social domination. More specifically, anti-intellectualism is an integral part of the authoritarianism and social dominance undersides of American social character—although for different reasons—the authoritarian believes whatever their conventional culture and authority figure tells them, and the SDO only uses truth and falsehood as tools for personal gain. One nexus between authoritarianism and SDO is narcissism.

Cultural Narcissism

American social character has internalized the values, beliefs, and most of all the mythologies of American exceptionalism and except for a few progressive academics and social activists, most Americans basically support American exceptionalism and regard the United States as a benevolent force in the world. This is generally true for liberals and conservatives alike, for Republicans or Democrats, for believers and atheists—even if the atheists may question the role of God in American society. Since this belief relies on emotion and myth, rather than at rational assessment of factual comparative data, any sort of conceptual analysis, or even personal experience given the high levels of dissatisfaction we cited earlier, it appears that the belief of exceptionalism is really cultural narcissism. Like a narcissistic pathology at the individual level, there is little capacity for self-examination, self-awareness and self-criticism nor any capacity to tolerate differences or critiques either from within or without. Similarly, like a narcissistic pathology, exceptionalism obliterates any capacity for empathy, and turns perception of the world into simplistic us versus them, you're either with us or with the terrorists dichotomies. Narcissists perceive any critique of America or American policy as an insult, which in turn fosters intense narcissistic rage.

Those who would criticize from within are labeled as traitors, deviants, sinners or terrorists. The glorification of self-worth both individually and collectively, in this case the grandiose overestimation of America and simultaneous underestimation and denial of its shortcomings makes for a starkly authoritarian and narcissistic social character. Not only are many such characters in positions of power, even if that powers to support the economic elites, they are supported by much larger numbers of people with similar character structures who fundamentally agree with and support those kinds of positions and policies.

Summary

Exceptionalism began when the first English settlers arrived in the New World. They saw themselves as a people chosen by God to create heaven on earth, to conquer the Promised Land and, like the ancient Israelites, they would face and defeat numerous heathens such as the Catholic French and Spanish, as well as some Native American tribes who opposed colonization and displacement from their lands. But they did survive, prosper and began to see their good fate as God's Will, and themselves as God's chosen people and anointed to serve God's Will upon others. These were the roots of as the belief of American exceptionalism.

Given both the growing economic system, unhindered by the legacies and barriers of a feudal system, and an almost endless stream of military victories, including its own War for Independence from England, (although The British exacted revenge and various treaty conditions in the War of 1812), the US came out on top once again in 1846–1848 in its war against a weak Mexico, and the newly emergent American people once again felt "exceptional." De Tocqueville noted these qualities, and quite presciently saw that this country was headed toward greatness. Some 70 years later, by the end of the 19th Century, as the United States began to enter the world as a major power, Jackson Turner echoed de Tocqueville's observation of Americans, but saw that the unique qualities of America had been shaped by the frontier. As the nation prospered, and expanded through both purchase and imperialist conquest, it moved from a rural society to an urban industrial society. Economic growth and military victories reinforced the notion of exceptional accomplishment and the mythology grew as a central part of American character. Anyone willing to work and fight can prosper, and as long as the nation is willing to work and fight, the nation will prosper. There is no defeat or failure as long as Americans are determined to succeed. At the end of the 19th Century, a class of wealthy capitalists emerged whose business ethics were of a highly flexible variety, and hardly distinguishable from people who acquire wealth through illegal means. President, business owner, mafia boss—what's the difference? All make money through perseverance. Even the working men (and some women) can earn a decent living if they are willing to work. Capitalist robber barons and industrialists led the country to a Gilded Age, the towering skyscrapers of success that reminded everyone at home and abroad of American greatness.

In the 1930s a world-wide depression led to a variety of political conflicts and transitions. Hitler, Mussolini, Franco and FDR rose to power on the basis of platforms that promised major reform or perhaps radical change. German fascism, allied with Japanese Imperialism led to World War II, the most destructive conflict in the history of the world. In the aftermath, the economically unscathed United States became a superpower as did the Soviet Union. Untouched by the war, American industry and politics ascended to unchallenged leadership of the "free world," and the dollar displace the Pound Sterling as the new global currency, all with God's blessing of course. The middle-classes rapidly expanded and prospered, again with God's blessing and perhaps some government programs, at least until the 1980s. It was at that moment that automation, globalization, and the growing powers of corporations to control the political process and growing corporate profits and the flow of capital out of the country meant that ever more wealth would be concentrated at the top and less would be invested domestically. Middle-class incomes began to stagnate and decline while unionized industrial workers fared the worst. The continued deindustrialization, coupled with sophisticated forms of strike breaking, union decertification and multi-tiered pay and benefits for new workers meant declining incomes (Wolff, 2013) and less job security. Elites in the financial sector now had ever greater revenue and were able to "lend" the middle classes as much money as they needed to sustain their standard of living. Enter the proliferation of credit cards which meant that banks could charge as much as 20% interest on their "loans" while various fees, membership dues, and the use of ATM machines added ever more profits to the banking industries.

Moreover, the utter impunity of the terrorist attack on the World Trade Centers on 9/11/2001 revealed how hollow and fragile the American Colossus had become. On a practical level, the massive US military was helpless against clandestine terrorist and militia enemies that had no fixed army or specific locations. The counterattack and retaliation for 9/11, misdirected toward Iraq, and an exercise in futility in Afghanistan, the graveyard of empires, has left the Middle East in far worse condition. Yes, Osama bin Laden was found and executed and perhaps Al Qaeda may be less powerful today, but instead, The Islamic State and numerous other groups have become a far more serious threat to Middle Eastern peace.

The costs of the Middle Eastern wars further weakened the American economy while the indifference of the Republican administration to any hint of regulating the booming financial markets meant that any fiscal shock threatened to collapse the economy. And indeed this is exactly what happened in 2007 when the subprime mortgage market imploded, as many economists such as Nouriel Roubini (2004) predicted at least three years in advance. As the earlier Asian banking crisis foretold, as well as the dot.com crisis and the collapse of Enron, WorldCom, Global Crossings, and Washington Mutual, all of which fabricated earnings and hid billions in losses, the lack of regulation and oversight made the banking bubble and implosion inevitable. The highly regulated Canadian banking system suffered no losses. The US has yet to fully recover and now has two trillion dollars of household debt, nineteen trillion dollars of federal debt and its cities and states have reached or are approaching bankruptcy. At this point, we see how many of the long-standing and enduring social psychological aspects of American character—the religiosity, the propensity for violence, the exaltation of wealth by any means, often shaded by authoritarianism—led disparate colonies to incredible success and now lead the country to decline and ruin. Political, economic, and religious leaders and large portions of the population are psychologically disposed to embrace a variety of social, cultural, and political positions that thwart adaptive transformations to the changing realities of the world, and instead pursue policies that hasten the erosion of US society from within. America is surely no longer an egalitarian society, and its one-time leadership in education, industry, architecture, and many aspects of industry has waned as finance capital has become ascendant and so many investment banks pay far higher and much quicker returns by manipulating stocks, currency, and speculative contracts in the global marketplace than by investing capital in productive industry or local business. This leads to systemic failure. Compared to other European nations, the US healthcare system is the most expensive in the world, yet does not cover millions of its citizens. The so-called Obamacare overhaul, officially called the Affordable Care Act, does nothing to control costs which still prohibits millions from buying insurance, despite the new law that forces them to do so. The university system increasingly serves government and corporate interests at the expense of undergraduate education and innovative research in areas that don't lead directly to profit. What is to be done? In the next chapters, our conclusions, again indebted to the Frankfurt School tradition in general and Erich Fromm in particular suggest the emergence, or perhaps more accurately the reemergence of a submerged constellation of American character better adapted to the conditions of the 21st Century.

The Sorrows of American Character

The Rise, Fall and Transformation of American Character

We have now sketched a psychodynamically informed, socio-historical picture of the emergence, rise, flourishing, and consequences of a relatively unique American character and its underlying social character. We have looked at four qualities of American culture that shaped the American experience, its identity and its underlying social character, namely God, Guns, Gold and Glory. We first noted the power of religion that has endured to this day. Most Americans tend to believe in God and are somewhat religious, though for younger generations, support for institutional religion is now rapidly waning, while they do remain spiritual. Compared to most other industrial societies, America has been and remains a violent country in which phallic aggressive toughness, symbolized by the love of guns, is a central trope. Mass shootings at schools, universities, malls and/or theaters and armed turf wars between gangs have become almost commonplace. The US has 4.4% of the world's population, and about 25% of the imprisoned population of the world (Yee Hee Lee 2015). But it has also been a country in which individualism flourished and migrated from its religious roots to a worldly economic motivation and the quest for economic gain and prosperity. This not only contributed to its national growth, but encouraged immigration from other lands as their poor sought "pots of gold." Ever since Winthrop envisioned the "city on the hill" as a beacon to all mankind, a model for all the world that all should emulate, Americans have seen themselves as chosen, special, and in a word—exceptional people. This sense ofAmerican exceptionalism has endured as central aspect of its collective identity that is constantly reiterated as a sound bite in the politics of today and is often cited to justify any course of action, no matter how irrational or contradictory. The laws of civilization and nature and the reason of logic and science just don't apply to the United States. Indeed, American exceptionalism is an integral part of America's civil religion, its collective identity and its narcissism.

Genesis: The Rise of the American Character

The English colonization of North America began at roughly the same time as did the Spanish and Portuguese colonization of South America which was also a vast land with great natural resources, yet it never developed the economic level of the US. Why then did the United States become the preeminent world power while most of Latin America still consists of developing countries including Brazil? We would suggest that these different trajectories were the consequences of the cultural/religious and political factors that shaped its social character. More specifically the Spanish and Portuguese colonizers attempted to reproduce the neo-feudal system of their home countries primarily through the creation of the *latifundas* (vast landed estates) that were first evident in Rome that more or less endured as the manorial system of feudal Europe. Moreover, such lands were often worked by slaves as was the case in both Rome and South America, especially Brazil. Given the wealth produced by these neo feudal systems, and the persistence of ascriptive status systems, there was very little incentive for either mercantile capitalism or industrialization to flourish. Indeed, industrialization at least in other parts of the world, led to demands for many of South America's abundant natural resources such as copper, tin and especially rubber, as well as its agricultural products. That led to dependency based economies more geared to exporting resources. This has of course changed in recent decades and Brazil is now a major industrial power producing cars, commercial airplanes and other products.

Secondly, and closely allied to this form of a patrimonial, patron-client system, Catholic religion played a major role in Latin America where it fostered neither the individualism, nor asceticism, nor the salvation anxiety that were more typical of Protestantism with its work ethic. Indeed, between the economic and political powers of the landowning classes, closely allied to the Church, South American politics has often had a highly authoritarian streak. This is not to ignore the more recent democratization or the developing economies of Argentina, Chile or Brazil. Rather, we are highlighting the importance of a nation's social character in fostering different trajectories.

As we have seen, the Puritan settlers were seeking religious freedom in a land without a propertied aristocracy and/or a compulsory state religion. Meanwhile, the land provided economic opportunities and benefits for both England and the settlers. The colonies of New England eventually gave rise to a distinct American social character and collective identity. The pious early Puritans settlers of New England, the rugged colonial mountain folks of Appalachia and the gracious Old Southern landowning aristocracy, as well as the frontiersmen, cowboys, sheriffs, marshals, gamblers, desperados and prospectors, and let us not forget the women of easy virtue, named after the eminent General Hooker whose camps they followed, are all long gone, but the their contributions to American social character, both real and mythical still influence our society in ways that impact our collective identities and how people today act, think and interpret the events of the day, both cognitively and emotionally. We should also remember that while the early settlers were fleeing the Mother country, as has often been the case, later generations of colonial elites often returned for a short while for education in the Mother country and thus many of our early founding fathers ultimately forged a synthesis between Puritanism, Republicanism and liberalism. However contradictory these qualities, they enabled the rise of commercial classes and eventual prosperity. Thus Protestant individualism and agency in relationship to God, with a bit of "salvation anxiety" and asceticism thrown in for good measure, facilitated self-interested economic behavior that eventually became detached from its religious roots such that consumerism replaced asceticism. As a result, the US became the richest nation, but also the most indebted. For most of the time from the earliest settlement to the latter part of the 19th Century, the country was primarily rural and many of the immigrants migrated to the territories to the West where land was "freely available." With the explosion of industrialization in the 19th Century, a new breed of economic leaders, the "captains of industry," as they called themselves or as "robber barons" as the popular press called them, began to amass huge fortunes, often through the most ruthless means of destroying competition, suppressing worker requests and violently repressing worker organizations and protests.

The Fall

By most measures, the rapid economic growth and greater equality of wealth and income of the post WWII boom years peaked by the 1980s as the impact of deindustrialization early neoliberal globalization turned the productive industrial cities of the Midwest into the "rustbelt." Recent research confirms that US economic growth following WWII was much higher than normal in the history of global capitalism, such that by the end of the 1970s, the typical pattern of lower and slower growth had become evident (Piketty, 2014). Following this "typical" pattern, the degree of inequality ever since the 1980s has grown to a level unprecedented since the "Gilded Age."

By 1980s, given the general stagnation after rising prosperity, frustrated populations in Britain elected Margaret Thatcher Prime Minister, while in the US, Ronald Reagan was elected president, and the conservative Helmut Kohl became Chancellor of Germany. All three promised to change directions, and change they did, unleashing the emerging neoliberal globalization that quickly began to remove or dilute regulations of businesses and lowered corporate taxes. Massive privatization of services such as telephones, utilities, and most important, education began, all much more strongly in the US than elsewhere.

They similarly retrenched benefits and entitlements. Many state enterprises were transferred to private ownership. Although the economy grew, most of the newly gained wealth went to the upper classes—a new pattern that undid the middle-classes of the 1950–1970s and spread beyond the US to other nations as well. We now witness similar trajectories of middle-class decline present in all major national economies (Bershidsky 2016).

If the US leads the way to economic totalitarianism, other democratic countries follow, and not because they made some kind of fair and just collective decision to wreck the middle class, but because the structure of neoliberal capitalism compels them. Many industries increase their productivity through improvements and advances in technology, even among the higher professional middle-class just as much among the higher-paid working class. For example, CAD/CAM design vastly increased the productivity of, and reduced the number of jobs for architects and engineers. Similarly, robotics and in turn automation greatly increase productivity and eliminate workers to produce far greater quantities of steel, automobiles or appliances. In the "dark factories," robots work 24/7, ask for no wages and make no complaints. Given these advances, as well as development of containerized shipping and many other ways to make design and production bigger, better, and faster with fewer workers. Several decades ago, Stanley Aronowitz (1990) predicted a "jobless future," as many highly skilled unionized blue-collar workers and professional white-collar designers, engineers, clerical, and data-entry workers lost their jobs to the newer technologies. The list goes on. ATM machines replaced most tellers and computers run the access to banks. On line merchants (Amazon, E-Bay) now sell practically everything—which reduces jobs in retail sales. Online computers decide your insurance rates and what kind of mortgage you qualify for. Similarly, travel sites on the web enable people to not only make their own travel arrangements (air, lodging and car rentals), but also shop around for the best prices. Technological advances have replaced some doctors as well. A radiologist in India or China can read digital x-rays and CAT scans as well as a doctor in the US. Although the Da Vinci robotic surgery machine requires a doctor to provide commands, the robot does all the work. Autonomous surgery robots are in development, as are autonomous cars and passenger planes. Surely Jeff Bezos will equip his Amazon.com delivery drones with robo-doc functions so they can both deliver packages and perform surgery—all within fifteen minutes if you sign up for Amazon-Prime.

As capital seeks to maximize its profits, manufacturers either moved a number of their facilities overseas or increasingly imported components cheaply made abroad. As Apple likes to brag, their devices are designed in California and assembled in China. Globalization, as a seamless, de-territorialized world market has produced vast amounts of wealth, moved hundreds of millions of poor peasants from subsistence living levels to the lower rungs of the middle classes with enough disposable income to begin to enjoy modest levels of consumerism where they can enjoy a better standard of living that includes using more fossil fuels in their cars and eating more meat. In the process, this has created unprecedented numbers of billionaires. These trends have of course led to the emergence of a transnational capitalist class that discards any sense of devotion to people, city, state, or nation, and instead embraces neoliberalism as an ideology to cut taxes, eliminate public investment, and remove governmental regulations on wages, product safety, and pollution (Robinson, 2004; Sklair, 2001). For us the essential point has been the diffusion of neoliberal values from the economic sectors to society in general, which we suggest, has depended upon the already existing "elective affinity" of these values with American social character. For our purposes there were several main consequences of the rapid embrace of neoliberalism. Firstly, given what was already noted about the increasing use of automation, computerization and manufacturing services, there was also a concerted effort on the part of American employers to dismantle unions whose struggles had secured decent wages, benefits and working conditions that enabled middle class life styles for workers. Highly sophisticated "union busting" firms, using psychological persuasion replaced the crude, pipe wielding violent goon squads of the past. Many companies moved manufacturing facilities to "right to work states" and we can easily trace these moves from the North and Midwest, to the American South and then into Mexico and finally to China. Secondly, given the globalization of markets, many corporations parked their profits offshore and not only reduced their domestic taxes, but similarly, reduced amount of money that had been typically contributed to the public good such as schools, museums and parks. A general migration of capital from manufacturing and retailing to the vast expansion of the FIRE industries (finance, insurance and real estate) ushered in varieties of speculation, and this financialization led to the concentration of various financial, legal and technical skills that in turn led to the rise of "global cities" that fostered massive reconfigurations of urban space and class relationships through gentrification. Urban mini-mansions and high-end condos displaced the poor while there has been a proliferation of poorly paid service work for outsourcing domestic help through childcare workers, food preparation, and janitorial services (Sassen, 2014). But many, perhaps most lower paid service workers can no longer afford to live in the cities where they work.

As a result of automation, globalization, privatization, financialization and neo-liberalism, we have witnessed a "great divide" in wealth that resulted from shifts to finance, high tech industries, and online retail, that employ few workers, and for many of the rest, huge improvements in productivity increased profits for corporations and the shareholders but laid-off millions of workers (See Stieglitz, 2015; Wolff, 2013). Finally, shrinking taxes and anti-government sentiments reduced investment in public works and infrastructure.

The founding fathers of the United States were of course more affluent, more educated, and more experienced politically than most of the people. After the American Revolution, when English laws were no longer in effect, George Washington became the richest man in America due to land speculation. Moreover, at that time an important measure of wealth was the ownership of slaves and indeed many of our early presidents were wealthy slave owners. These same political-economic elites wrote and ratified the American Constitution. Although it legitimated the sovereignty of the ruling classes, it has also provided some response to popular demands, including various rights and liberties to sustain governmental legitimacy. In contrast, financial elites today now have unprecedented economic power that in turn enables near total control of the government and the mass media. This has led to the erosion of a number social contracts and has rendered personal ambition and ruthlessness highly valued qualities. Meanwhile, questions of fairness, equality, and the public good are not even open for discussion. Not only does corporate money typically control elections, especially since corporations became people in the minds of the Supreme Court, but there are revolving doors between corporation elites and governmental agencies that supposedly "regulate" the corporations. As we have seen, dozens of top Citibank and Goldman-Sachs executives work for a short while in Treasury and Commerce departments and then return to their seven-figure salaries. Finally, when elected representatives leave the Congress, they typically go directly to corporate boards or lobbying firms in which their congressional connections play a vital role in further securing corporate wealth by favoring defense, pharmaceutical, energy and financial firms. Tax laws, tariffs, trade agreements like NAFTA, CAFTA and TPP, wage laws, product safety standards and regulations including agricultural products, working conditions, liability, and environmental laws privilege the rich because they control the governments.

As we noted, Reagan began a process of tax changes and deregulation that benefited the corporations that continued through the subsequent Bush I, Clinton, Bush II and even the Obama administration. Obama's former Attorney General, Erich Holder, had been deputy attorney general for Clinton where he had had already been concerned that aggressive prosecution of big banks could destabilize the economy. He had also worked for Covington and Burling, a law firm that specializes in corporate tax avoidance and deregulation lobbying. As Attorney General, Holder blocked all efforts to investigate the financial collapse of 2007–2009. As Matt Taibbi (2014) documents, the case of Barclay's bank and Lehmann Brothers was especially telling because the federal government provided money and regulatory cover for a small group of foreign banksters at Barclay's to transfer Lehman's assets to their personal accounts while the government took on billions of Lehman's debt. The banksters got all the cash while all the other investors lost everything, and the American public got stuck with all the debt. Such backroom deals are now quite common throughout the banking/investment/hedge fund industries. In response to the great collapse, Holder produced no indictments, but millions of poor Blacks and Hispanics did go to jail on minor drug charges. One major outcome of neoliberalism is that legal systems lock up petty criminals and leave the billionaire thugs untouched.

Some liberal economists like Paul Krugman have wandered into our social psychological territory to note how conservative ideologues have been wrong on neoliberalism, wrong on austerity, wrong on Iraq and wrong on the impact of the ACA (Obamacare). Although schooled in facts, figures and actuarial data, liberals like Krugman have trouble understanding how little impact facts have on people's opinions. Nevertheless, given the combination of "motivated reasoning" and economic support from certain people, authoritarian conservatives can ignore facts and evidence and zealousy defend failed policies, and rewrite history to blame liberals and poor immigrants for their own failures. We hope that Krugman soon understands how ideologies that appeal to America's unconscious social character, anchored by powerful emotions, therefore resist change regardless of facts and evidence. That said, a growing population, especially of the young, especially those born after the demise of the dreaded "red menace," now saddled with debt, facing an insecure economic future, are increasingly critical of neoliberalism and its elites, such that about 85% of millennials flocked to the democratic socialism of Bernie Sanders, and the rest to Donald Trump. Either way, they will no longer accept business as usual.

The Crises of Empire

The growing trifurcation of the American economy into the haves, the have nots and the haves with obscene wealth is not simply due to the economic policies of the government as such, but the huge costs of maintaining "imperial overreach," the inherent flaw that brings down all empires that at one time seemed eternal. Yet the overconfidence of the elites, coupled with the absence of an objective self-appraisal, makes weakness and decline inevitable. Our political class, which is generally dysfunctional on most issues, well serves corporate

capital in general, especially the FIRE (finance, insurance, real estate) industries, energy, pharma, agribusiness and a defense industries that enables aggressive interventionist policies that endure long after they have failed. An
important aspect of our politics has been erosion of any trace of an organized
left, what Hedges (2010) called the *"Death of the Liberal Class"* that "fights for
nothing, stands for nothing and is a useless appendage to the corporate state.
It exists not to make possible incremental or piecemeal reform, as it originally
did in a functional capitalist democracy; instead it has devolved into an instrument of personal vanity, burnishing the hollow morality of its adherents."[1]
Where is the anger and the outrage that we have so often seen in US history?
Endless war, mass bombings, torture, police violence at home, while Black
Lives don't matter to racist police, wealth inequality, racism, sexism, nothing
inspires us except celebrity worship (voyeurism), escapism and sensationalism
while avoiding real news or serious analysis in favor of "infotainment" packaged as news talk shows. Moreover, the guest "experts" are for the most part
the older, white men who quite often have very little real knowledge or expertise. When "guests" either deny, fabricate, prevaricate or downright lie, they
are rarely challenged, pressed and instead, questioning turns to their favorite
pasta or political celebrity gossip. How often do we see leading antiwar critics
with either research or first-hand experience such as Noam Chomsky, Seymour
Hersh, Tom Hayden, Juan Cole, Tom Engelhard, Nick Turse or Jeremy Scahill
appear and offer not just critical assessments of America's war machine, but
supply abundant evidence of the lies, distortions and calumny of the elites,
as well as recount the grisly deaths, wounds, injuries, destruction and massive displacements of people? How about ... never? That's right! Although their
works and critiques are easily found on the web, those who are likely to seek
this information have already learned that corporate owned mass media is little more than the mouthpiece of power, the real-world Ministry of Truth, and
the that the US government perpetrates and supports death all over the world.

Coming Soon: Election 2016: POTUS as American Character

In the 1990s, Bill Clinton abandoned the working classes and moved the
Democratic Party into the political space that had been occupied by socially
moderate Wall Street Republicans who had become an extinct species, seen
only in history books or perhaps as wax reproductions in history museums.

---

1 Hedges, Chris. Death of the liberal class http://www.truthdig.com/report/item/once
  again--_death_of_the_liberal_class_20121112 Accessed August 27, 2015.

It is worth recalling that Clinton pressed for the passage of NAFTA and signed the overturning of Glass-Steagall, both of which adversely impacted the working classes. He cut welfare bigtime. Surely, with the election of Bill Clinton and the move of the Democratic Party from a party representing workers and minorities to a center-right supporter of Wall Street business interests, the domination of corporate capital over both political parties was completed. As noted, union membership is minimal, and as recent analysis shows, American workers don't miss manufacturing jobs as such, but rather, they miss the benefits of *unionized* manufacturing jobs and unions in general (Casselman 2016). Today, the few remaining union workers in the private sector tend to support conservative causes and/or politicians (Phillips, Curtis, and Lundskow, 2010). Aside from the United Steel Workers and possibly the SEIU service workers, labor no longer (and can longer) offer much resistance to corporate capital. Central to our argument of the power of emotions and feelings, the Democrats usually resist passionate expressions of any kind, and instead maintain the erroneous belief that facts, figures, evidence and logic, stoically presented via power points with bar graphs and pie charts inspire and sway voters away from the hard-right politics of the Republican party and toward the republican-lite of the Democratic Party.

It is however interesting to note that in the primary presidential campaigns of 2016, the right populist xenophobic campaign of Donald Trump who defeated the establishment candidates and won the nomination, the silly homilies of Ben Carson, and the Democratic socialism of Bernie Sanders, all demonstrated the widespread dissatisfaction voters had toward the established figures of both parties and business as usual. The elites of each wing of the capitalist parties were quite isolated from the realities that most Americans were struggling financially, especially working class drawn to Trump and youth drawn to Sanders. The initial heirs apparent, Hillary Clinton and Jeb Bush, had assumed it was "their turn" to be president. The right-wing corporate butt kissers such as Scott Walker and John Kasich engendered little real passion from the Republican voters. Trump bushwhacked Jeb! as low-energy, but he could have called him slow-witted and that would have fit just as well. Even his mother and brother couldn't save him. Jeb! never recovered and dropped out after the South Carolina primary. Marco Rubio next tried to claim the standard for the capitalist class, but he only offered a pretty face, robotic speeches and a flaccid refugee "rags to riches" biography that included a history of financial irregularities that just didn't stand up to Trump's claims of having a big penis (Shapiro 2016).[2]

---

2   Yes, Donald Trump really did brag about the size of his penis. Rubio attempted to demonstrate his own masculine prowess with a joke that Trump has small hands, "and you know

Although quite passionate, and perhaps sincere, the messages of religious cranks like Rick Santorum and Mike Huckabee who called for a racially pure Christian in-group committed to a return to Puritan sexual asceticism and un-limited access to guns no longer resonated with many people younger than about 70. They soon tanked. Dominionist Ted Cruz appealed to the most con-servative, evangelical voters, but even with God on his side, between his erratic personality and unpleasant looks reminding many of the Addams family, he failed to rally his natural constituency.

The openly racist, sexist, ethnocentric and rude reality TV star and bil-lionaire Donald Trump talks like a Brooklyn tough guy, with his in-your-face persona, represents a fusion of the classical American social character that we described which took different overt forms historically. Trump, the social dominator is individualistic, phallic aggressive tough with a streak of sadism, narcissism, authoritarianism, xenophobia, and anti-intellectualism. What's not to like? Much like his buddy Vince McMahon of World Wrestling Enter-tainment, his style of self-presentation equally channels American elements of the carnival barker, the snake oil salesman and the itinerant tent revival preacher. These elements were fused together as reality TV spectacle and as Trump insults women and immigrants, he incites the angry voters who feel betrayed by politics as usual, meaning the Republican leadership. So too do many angry, fearful phallocentric working class white males and the women who love them, who have been genuinely adversely impacted by the econom-ic changes we have discussed and who have felt abandoned by the political parties. They think that a tough, strong businessman, an iconic figure in the American imagination, can make the deals to "get things done." And the death rate for many of these white working class men is rising due to drinking, drugs and suicide.[3] Insofar as neither wing of the Wall Street party has addressed the conditions of the vast numbers of factory workers or bakers, truck driv-ers and barbers, plumbers and carpenters or the exterminators and repairper-sons whose annual earnings, roughly $35,000/year represent about an hour's income for the elites. Trump offers the classical menu of right populism, blame

---

what they say about men with small hands" Rubio chuckled. In response, Trump held up his hands at the next debate and declared "Look at those hands. Are they small hands? And he referred to my hands—if they are small, something else must be small. I guarantee you there is no problem," Trump affirmed. "I guarantee you."

3   Andrew Cherlin suggested that such men saw their own families as a reference group, and in comparison to their dads and moms, they were not doing as well, whereas for African American and Mexican American men, given the harshness of the conditions of their family lives, they are doing better. http://www.nytimes.com/2016/02/22/opinion/why-are-white-death -rates-rising.html?_r=0 accessed 02/23/2016.

the least powerful. Today it's the Mexicans, African-Americans and Muslim refugees who provide suitable scapegoats. Disempowered people with different languages or skin color seem like more real threats to an authoritarian than the complex, abstract discussion of structural weakness, the role of the upper classes and the dysfunctions of the government in a global economic system. Nor does Trump proffer the bizarre prescriptions of austerity and retrenchments for the masses and tax cuts for the rich that appealed to certain qualities of traditional American social character as well as the coffers of the very rich who fund such nonsense. Rather some of his demeanor of rough and tough with popular appeal echoes Andrew Jackson, the proud killer of Brits and Native-Americans who issued blood-curdling oaths of violence and bullied political opponents into submission. Meanwhile, his strong condemnation of Bush II's Iraqi war was not well received by more traditional Republicans who prefer solemn and insincere reverence for the soldiers they sent to fight in wars of corporate interests. By violating this solemn insincerity, Trump reinforced his position as a powerful outsider who says what he wants, doesn't play the usual games, and doesn't care if it hurts some feelings along the way.

Meanwhile in the run-up to the nomination, Doctor Ben Carson, a very prominent and successful neurosurgeon became the unlikely front-runner for a while. Not only was he an outsider at a time of anger toward the insiders, but an outsider to facts, logic, history and reason. On the one hand, Ben Carson's life story, from ghetto poverty, living on food stamps and "toughness" as a teenager who then went to elite schools and eventually became the chair of pediatric neurosurgery at Johns Hopkins School of medicine is indeed an inspiring tale, Horatio Alger for the 21st Century. Further, by supporting an African-American, Republicans could show that they were really not racists (and in truth, many are not). Carson's complete lack of understanding of government wavered between ignorance and insanity. Clearly, brain surgeons don't necessarily know anything beyond brain surgery, and his ignorance of history matches his ignorance of government. For example, his views that Jewish gun ownership could have stopped Hitler, or we should replace income taxes with tithing, and instead of gun control, potential victims should rush mass shooters because they can't get all of us. He suggested the way to deal with global warming and rising sea levels is to build arks while he also said that Joseph, not the pharaohs, built the pyramids to store grain. Yes, huge pyramids with very small rooms to store grain next to dead people, and the story of Joseph took place 500 years before the pyramids were built. He claimed that the signers of the Declaration of Independence had no electoral experience, and yet most had spent many years as elected representatives of their state parliaments and Houses of Burgesses where they came to resent the appointment of the colonial governor by the throne. Carson told the world that that the major threat to Israel came from hummus (garbanzos, garlic and sesame tahini). Maybe he meant Hamas. Carson has also warned that the socialists and atheists of the world were the forces behind the "New World Order" that was seeking world domination to impose socialism and atheism. While he never really had a chance to get the nomination, the appeal of his fabricated biography, his actual ascent from poverty, and given the power of "motivated reasoning" in America, his message had enormous appeal to either devout evangelical Christians or the very seriously deranged. His appeal to conservatives was based less on his command of facts, being quite generous as to the fairy tales and delusions he made up and called facts, or any proposed policies and agendas. Instead, supporters found inspiration in his biography and character. He claims that he was a wild teenager with a quick temper who got into fights and tried to stab his friend but the knife conveniently hit the belt buckle and no harm was done. As a teenager, he allegedly had dinner with General Westmoreland who supposedly promised him admission to West Point, yet the General was nowhere in or near Detroit anytime close to when Carson alleges (Livengood and Burke, 2015). Great stories that appeal to traditional American social character, but clearly false. None of his childhood friends seem to remember him as violent, or even as problematic (Glover and Reston 2015). Still, Carson maintains that everything changed when he accepted Jesus into his life, who gave him both his intelligence and gifted hands. Hallelujah, praise the Lord.

On the Democratic side, the Democratic socialistic message of Bernie Sanders, who like Trump has a brash, assertive New York City style and accent, offered a clearly progressive agenda, a new New Deal that passionately resonated with many people, especially young people who were unemployed or underemployed, saddled with debt, fed up with endless war, appalled by racism, sexism and homophobia, and looking for a more hopeful future. He also drew many working class voters and many Trump supporters actually said Bernie was their second choice. In other words, Sanders was the inclusive and progressive left populist, while Trump was the bigoted and reactionary right populist. The elites of both parties struggled energetically to keep Trump and Sanders out. Through the chicanery of the DNC, revealed by hacked emails, Debbi Wasserman Schultz and the Democratic party elite managed to swing the candidacy to the ultimate insider, Hillary Clinton, while Trump successfully claimed the Republican candidacy. Our concern is really not so much the outcome of a particular election as such, but rather how the presidential race speaks to the issues of social character we've raised. American social character that we've described is facing several social psychological, as well as demographic challenges and changes. One, the traditional American social character that we've described is more frequent among aging, older, whiter, more religiously conservative populations, especially where they are more entrenched in the Southern and Western states where gerrymandering and restrictive voting laws have given Republican certain structural advantages in state and local elections, but except for Texas, most large states tend to vote Democratic and are likely too again.

The conservative bearers of the traditional American character we have described are both frightened and angry to see their economic security problematic and their futures tenuous. Their sexist, racial and cultural hegemony that has been attacked s waning, their admixed Puritanism and hypocrisy is under assault, along with a relative decline in their social status based on their race, religiosity, patriarchy and heteronormativity. Moreover, and what particularly fuels many of the more extremists, for example the Tea Party, their hitherto strong support of conservative Republican candidates, has little impact on the changing demographics and/or cultural shifts taking place, especially since there is ever more support for liberal social values. Roe v. Wade stands, gays can now marry, straight people openly live in sin, more and more states are decriminalizing pot and pornography is freely available. The conservatives know this is true because porn consumption, about 35% of Internet traffic, is much higher in Red states than Blue states and the highest per capita porn consumption is in Utah. We suppose that if Mormons can now only have one wife, they at least want to see what they're missing.

Secondly, the ethnic composition of the United States has been rapidly changing and much of its growth consists of Spanish speakers from Mexico and Central America, as well as Asians and East Indians, most of whom have been completely and thoroughly rebuffed by the ethnocentrism of the Republican Party and are quite unlikely to vote for them. These demographic trends are continuing, and there is nothing that conservatives can do to stop it. Even if a president Trump persuaded Mexico to pay for a wall along the border, that would have little effect on the nature of demographic changes within the US, such as growing minorities, ever more liberal cohorts and the ever more important women's vote. Women voters outnumber men voters and single women are now the largest single electoral bloc in the United States. The bloc consists of single women who have either never married, divorced women with children and/or the widowed. Given the Republican "war on women," clearly evident in their positions on contraception, abortion, and sex education, requirements for transvaginal ultrasound probes before abortions, restricting or privatizing healthcare, deteriorating public schools and attacks on Social Security, we expect that in the next election, even more women will vote for Democrats than did for Obama who garnered 56% of their vote.[4] Finally, many

---

4   In the Democratic primary of 2016, Bernie Sanders has attracted far more young women that has Hillary.

of the young people who had seen Obama as the symbol of hope and change were quite disappointed with his timid centrism and retreated from politics. But nevertheless, given how many of the young are facing financial pressures, we believe that whatever else the Sanders campaign may do, having moved the Democratic Party to the left, inspiring young voters to join his progressive revolution will bring many younger voters to the polls and as such, given that political identities are typically established when people are young, we do see a progressive shift in the political arena consistent with the changing social character we will discuss in the next chapter.

It's the Economy Stupid

We have charted the growing inequality within the USA, the massive indebtedness of the nation as a whole that is financed by about $19 trillion worth of bonds as well as its massive balance of payment deficits. Similarly, there has been an explosion of personal debt and many of its people are burdened by maxed out credit cards, mortgages, car loans and student debt. The trends toward greater inequality which means greater hardships and more suffering cannot be sustained in a country whose national character, identity and sense of exceptionalism was based on seemingly limitless economic opportunities and ever improving standards of living. With stagnation and decline, alienation, and anger, outrage and indignation become powerful emotions and when such powerful emotions are widely shared and become intertwined with hope and visions of alternatives, quite often this fosters mobilizations from below.[5] Moreover, we see these as more than economic movements, but as an intertwining of economic, cultural and social psychological forces that constitute mobilizations for dignity, such as the diverse groups who rallied in Raleigh we noted back in Chapter 2.

As we have pointed out, the typical social character structure found among the corporate and political elites today often takes a pathological form, especially among those with the social dominance orientation (SDO) that now control the economy. Politicians and their supporters, mostly conservatives, manifest strong authoritarian-destructive traits. In other words, the corporate and political elites possess certain qualities that are not typical, and are not just odious, but given what we earlier said about splitting and denial, for many traditional Americans the economically successful who have gamed the

---

5   We have already noted how this inequality has led to support for outsider candidates for the 2016 presidential race.

system are generally celebrated as esteemed and valuable members of the society. They are called "job creators" which is completely opposite to what they do. Company success does not equate with job or wage growth. In face of the plunging prices of crude oil, for example, Paal Kibsgaard the CEO of Schlumberger, an oil service firm, fired one-fifth of the workforce, 25,000 workers, and for his good work, the stock price went up, so he gave himself a bonus on top of his 18 million dollar salary.

Many social dominators tend to be highly narcissistic, lacking any trace of empathy or concern with others. They can often fake it, but they never feel it. Moreover they are psychologically unable to see the adverse consequences of the policies that bring them personal advantage whether by destroying unions, firing workers, suppressing wages, closing plants or creating pollution that is spewed into the air or dumped into rivers, and rigging the system to reduce their taxes while garnering a variety of subsidies and/or bailouts from the government-and then putting profits in off shore banks. Rather they take pride in expanding the bottom line, while filling their own coffers, for which they regard themselves as benevolent endeavors. Lloyd Blankfein, the CEO of Goldman Sachs, claimed they were "doing God's work," which now consists of mergers and acquisitions, the management of hedge funds and speculative investments. God as an investment banker and hedge fund manager?

Given their narcissism, elite billionaires such as Jamie Dimon, Lloyd Blankfein, Steven Schwarzman, Donald Trump, and even the so-called liberal Bill Gates regard themselves as a "better class" of people and "deserving" of their fortunes which they claim were due entirely to their own efforts. Elizabeth Warren, along with many sociologists, have shown that these fortunes have depended on government provided infrastructure, courts, schools etc. Techie billionaires such as Steve Jobs, Mark Zuckerberg or Michael Dell have all depended on government supported research that enabled the development of computers and perhaps equally important, the Internet began as a government project, ARAPNET to share scientific knowledge and ensure military communication following an atomic attack. Oblivious to the roles of race, gender, class, the cultural capital that enables access to education, along with a bit of help stemming from their parent's wealth, they assume that whatever worked for them will work for anyone. Meanwhile, as a legacy of the Puritanism that shaped American character, they have nothing but disdain and contempt for the poor, who "choose their poverty." This was clearly articulated in 2012 when Mitt Romney noted that 47% of the Americans would never vote for him because they were bums, parasites and moochers getting food stamps, Obamacare and free Obama phones and who just wanted to live off the government dole, paid for by the "hardworking," hard-pressed taxpayers. Romney applied the phrase "moochers and parasites" rather broadly, however, and in so doing, alienated many potential voters since the recipients of government aid includes students with Pell grants, the unemployed, retirees, Medicare recipients and disabled veterans. Moreover, most of the food stamps actually go to working families whose poverty level wages leave them hard-pressed to purchase food. Insofar as many of these workers are found in retail sales, think Walmart or fast food, think McDonalds. And thus the American taxpayers subsidize poorly paid workers so that the employers might keep more of their profits. And of course the employers especially in the fast food and lower and retail businesses vehemently oppose raising the minimum wages that enable their profits. Furthermore by virtue of their occupational locations, residential choices and the locations and costs of their exclusive leisure and recreational pursuits, the rich have become more and more isolated from the lives of ordinary people. Many of the social dominators who ascend to the pinnacles of power could not care less about the impacts of their agendas on the masses-nor are they likely to see the consequences of their policies.

For the most part Americans have rarely felt anger, animosity or resentment toward the rich since they aspired to join them and reach into the pot of gold (See Chapter 3). But the current and projected economic trends, stagnation and decline of living standards, bode ill for the masses, especially younger cohorts. Collective attitudes are beginning to slowly, but surely change, and we believe such changes reflect a changing social character. As we previously pointed out, certain enlightened conservatives such as Mike Lofgren and John Dean, along with progressives like Chris Hedges are becoming especially critical of the greed and indifference of the rich, whom he saw are different from the rest of us since with all their money, human beings become disposable, and even friends and family become disposable and easily replaced. When they get absolute power, even citizens become disposable, which is exactly what happened.

For those who concerned with the health of the nation or the rights and health of people, the growing inequality and "hollowing out of the middle class" is now being seen as the basis of a great deal of personal and collective suffering. Furthermore, this kind of deprivation thwarts creativity and personal fulfillment and when prolonged, becomes the basis for anger, nihilism, violence and destructiveness. As we previously noted, for Fromm, the love of death and destruction comes from thwarted self-fulfillment, and anger and shame over a "failed life." Similarly, poverty has adverse consequences on mental, physical and social health (Abramsky 2014; Acemoglu and Robinson 2013). In much the same way, demographic research has shown that income inequality is associated with a number of physical and social pathologies, for example obesity, diabetes infant mortality and heart problems, as well as high crime rates, social bullying, divorce, mental health, school dropout rates, unwanted pregnancies, and juvenile delinquency (Wilkinson and Pikett, 2009) As the research shows, alienation and pessimistic fatalism in the American population has intensified as inequality increased. Paul Krugman argues that "the darkness of economic malaise and early death is spreading over the middle classes."[6] It is not surprising that this group has been especially hard hit by the economic downturn and with the end of the American Dream, they have lost the narrative of their lives. They are far too old to begin new careers, especially with just high school educations and limited techie skills. Yet they are far too young to retire, and quite often, they might have little or no retirement plans nor much money in social security accounts. The grim realities of political economy assault the Appalachian elements of American social character we saw in Chapter 2, proud, tough, and individualistic and with a notion of personal honor that never complains, but can no longer thrive either. These are the men becoming addicted to opioids and dying at earlier ages.

Small cadres of ever wealthier and more powerful financial elites control the dissemination of information as well as political and other decision-making processes, which closes off public discussion on vital issues and perpetuates economic exploitation and hopelessness. Whatever else one might say about the Occupy movements, they did articulate a growing resentment toward the elites, naming the 1%, who engineered and profited from these conditions. This has been especially the case among younger people, some with huge burdens of debt, facing daunting job prospects. And this is equally true for the many working-class youth impacted by the waning of well-paid, relatively secure manufacturing jobs. If the Occupy movement expressed the alienation and fatalism that many feel and Wilkinson and Pikett (2009) empirically measured, nevertheless the OWS movement did not change the political-economic order that generates negative feelings. The nature of the occupy movement was such that it avoided the establishment of an organization with clear-cut leadership, tactics, and goals with visions of a better alternative (Langman, 2013). Despite its short duration, we see Occupy as the tip of an iceberg, and remember that the iceberg that sank the Titanic was not visible to the crew—until it was too late. Just like the Titanic, Americans like to think that the United States is "unsinkable."

---

6 Paul Krugman, *Despair American Style*, http://www.nytimes.com/2015/11/09/opinion/despair-american-style.html?_r=0 Accessed November 09, 2015.

It's Not Just the Economy Stupid

One of the fundamental problems for progressives ranging from Orthodox Marxists to liberal Democrats is the assumption of the primacy of the economic, the notion that people vote their pocketbooks. But as we have noted, for Thomas Frank (2004), the people of Kansas voted on the basis of their conservative religious sentiments and feelings about abortion and sexuality-that sustain male patriarchy. Similarly, as Joe Bageant (2008) noted, the generally poor working folks born in his small Virginia town vehemently support the Republicans whose antiunion efforts were believed to protect their jobs while the Republican/NRA agendas would enable them to keep their guns. But as many people have noted not only are the Southern and Mountain states among the poorest, but they are also among the most religiously and politically conservative who consistently support Republicans whose policies keep them trapped in poverty and enhance the riches of the rich.[7] Many of these governors have rejected any and all money from Washington that might have provided medical insurance or aid to the poor.

In our understanding of the Tea Party, the crucial issues are the defense of highly traditional identities and values regarding race, gender, patriarchy and heteronormativity (Langman, 2012; Lundskow, 2012). The Partiers were shocked and angry that an African American had been elected president. For many Tea Partiers, there was an anger toward the government for supporting bailouts to the big corporations and impending expansions of healthcare benefits that were seen as steps toward socialism and the loss of some kind of amorphous freedom that would be restored when the Tea Party took their country back. As we earlier noted, as legacy of Puritanism, there endure a "producerism" that sees aid recipients as parasites living off the hard earned wages of the makers and doers.

As it happens, but of course quite denied by conservatives of all stripes, the Obama bailouts and subsequent quantitative easing of the Fed, saved the jobs and businesses of many of the Tea Partiers, especially in now booming

---

7   The poverty of the old Confederate States has endured since the antebellum period. A good illustration can be seen in the following map: Accessed September 23, 2015 http://www.nytimes.com/2014/06/26/upshot/where-are-the-hardest-places-to-live-in-the-us.html?WT.mc_id=D-E-Keywee-SOC-MOD-LABORDAYSALE-NWS-0828-0905&WT.mc_ev=click&bicmp=AD&bicmlukp=WT.mc_id&bicmst=1409247693000&bicmet=1410025293000&kwp_0=3113&kwp_1=67870&kwp_4=22072&_r=4&abt=0002&abg=0&utm_source=Sightline+Newsletters&utm_campaign=dc10eaobb1-SightlineWeekly&utm_medium=email&utm_term=0_18df351f8f-dc10eaobb1-291863981.

construction industries, housing markets and auto sales. Even many conservatives have found that the ACA provides better and lower-cost insurance, especially when covering pre-existing conditions that most insurance companies would have never allowed. Thus, it is quite naïve to believe in the *Homo economis* who acts in a rational way to maximize his/her economic self-interests. Yet as we made abundantly clear, people act on the basis of feelings and emotions that are characterologically anchored, not rational, self-interested maximization. For Max Weber, the accumulation of wealth was not the goal of Protestant asceticism but rather its unintended consequence. We might similarly note that for Freud happiness was the gratification of childhood wishes, and children seek love, attention and recognition. The quest for money is not a primary motive, but a social motive learned much later:

> Economic self-interest is not, in fact, the foundation of the human psyche. It coexists and interacts with multiple other needs and interests, themselves every bit as important as Maslow's survival needs. The failure to understand the complexity of human motivation is a blind spot for liberals and progressives, making it exceedingly difficult to inspire and move people at levels deep enough to create sustaining institutions and a movement based on people's deepest passions.
>
> BADER 2015 p. 19

As we argued in Chapter 3, an integral aspect of American social character has been seeking money which of course is quite typical in a capitalist society. In the American context, the pursuit of wealth has been as much for self-esteem, power, and recognition to assuage problematic "status anxiety" and overcome phallocentric insecurities about perceived weakness. Since the accumulation of money is unlimited, the insatiable passion feeds upon itself. The pursuit of wealth is quite prominent among the pathological social dominators we've previously noted who see the size of their fortune as proof of their inherent superiority, often expressed in mega-mansions, mega yachts, and private planes. But size is not everything, and while such people seek any accumulation of fortunes, they will never have enough. Similarly, people often seek wealth in order to afford various aspects of consumerism that might have an underlying sexual motivation. Little did Marcuse anticipate in 1964 that using a "new and improved" washday detergent or synthetic motor oil might elicit the same gleeful sounds and facial expressions typical of the "money shot" in current pornography. Consumer products not only elicit the same superficial gratifications, but also reproduce the superficial and often oppressive and exploitative forms of social relations in modern consumer culture, much as Marcuse predicted. Similarly, many "successful" men, and today even some women, purchase expensive sports cars, muscle cars and motorcycles to compensate for waning sexuality.[8]

As we have noted, political preferences, allegiances, and in turn sociopolitical changes are based on a number of factors, typically beginning with class, race, gender and what is important for the current analysis, the collective values and shared understandings of the world that are typically anchored within the typical social character. Thus people are likely to either vote, or not vote, or otherwise mobilize for or against social change on the basis of a number of factors. As we just noted, it is often a matter of economic self-interest. But that of course is a gross simplification in so far as some affluent people, Warren Buffett for example, think that taxes should be raised. For our analysis, it is extremely important to note that the more conservative, traditional social values of America, especially the intertwining of radical individualism and the pursuit of wealth, typically upheld by older and whiter, typically suburban and exurban voters, especially in Southern States, hold little allure for younger, browner, more likely urban and multicultural youth who are more likely to seek meaning and community.

The extent to which Republican conservatives are entrenched in many states can easily lead one to believe their views are more widely accepted than is the case. In the 2014 midterm elections, for example, Republicans won control of both the US House and the Senate, even though Senate Democrats received millions more votes than did the Republicans while House Democrats got about 2 million more votes.[9] Beyond economic issues, many contemporary youth feel more and more alienated and estranged from the conservative social attitudes and values that have long been aspects of American society and character. Many feel anger and indignation at attempts to suppress or even deny women, minorities or gays their rights especially when conservatives complain that their discrimination is an expression of their "religious freedom." Conservatives always seem to find a way to view themselves as the victims. In any event, while many conservative social values that were typical of Puritan New England remain strongly embraced (even if not followed) by various fundamentalist Christian congregations especially among the Southern Baptists in the more rural South and West. But many of these values can also

---

8   For the sake of full disclosure, GL drives a 525 horsepower Dodge Charger he lightly modified himself, and he is content to not pursue the 700 HP Hellcat model. Meanwhile LL gave up his Porsche Targa for a Honda American Classic motorcycle—a far more dependable bike than either a Harley or even a BMW that C.W. Mills preferred.

9   http://www.fairvoteblog.com/2014/12/with-louisianas-senate-runoff-election.html Accessed 11/21/2014.

be found in some of the mega churches of the exurbs throughout America. Based upon hierarchical, authoritarian social relationships, legitimated by literal interpretations of the Bible and the alleged inerrancy of Scripture, fundamentalism is for the most part a modern phenomenon which many scholars of religion see as a form of anti-modernism that resisting long-standing secular trends in greater toleration, inclusion, equality, freedom of choice and lifestyle and the waning of traditional ways of life. Accordingly, authoritarian beliefs and practices, rooted in early Judeo-Christian teachings that sustain patriarchy, punitive childrearing practices, unquestioned obedience to authority, puritanical and repressive sexual values that require female subordination to male dictates, also stress in-group loyalty, ethnocentrism and an intense xenophobia toward outgroups. There can only be one real church of God.

Variations on a Theme

The US has never had one and only one church. Religious schisms, dissenters and social differentiation have long been part of American society. Among the earliest schism was the Antinomian Controversy of 1636–1638, in which a number of people embraced John Cotton, Anne Hutchinson, and others who taught free grace theology, namely that everyone is saved the moment they accept Jesus as their savior (and live like the Good Samaritan, as Christ said, "go and do likewise"). John Winthrop ousted the antinomian governor Henry Vane, placed himself in office, and then banished the antinomians to Rhode Island. In little more than 100 years after the first colonialists had arrived, there were already cultural and religious differences between the towns and the hinterlands.

Despite the apparent Puritanism of the Puritans, a number of historians have claimed that they were not as dour and repressed as we sometimes think. Rather, they were indeed a randy lot. In many of the seaport cities, a widespread working class tavern culture prospered among the abstemiously hard-drinking colonials. Workers and sailors, pirates, prostitutes and libertines, freed slaves, Native Americans and many others might freely interact with white Americans in egalitarian realms apart from the "official" worlds of hierarchy and domination where they indulged a vigorous hedonism of music and dancing, overt public debauchery, and sexuality that was in some cases inter-racial. There were even homosexual encounters (Thompson, 1999). Taverns also hosted various official government committees because they were so thoroughly integrated into public life (Conroy, 1995). This was a matter of concern for the founding fathers in so far as some neighborhoods around Independence Hall in Philadelphia were teeming with working-class decadence such as the drinking, singing, dancing and sexuality we noted. (Like many other aspects of American history, this aspect of social history is usually not taught.)

In general, however, the dominant values and practices of early America strongly embraced religion, primarily it's more authoritarian forms. Nevertheless, the non-hierarchical theologies such as the Quakers and Shakers still abstained from alcohol, and the Shakers could only gain new members through conversion because they also abstained from sex, even within marriage. Whether hierarchical and formal or non-hierarchical and customary, domination fosters resistance and dissent that have been as much a part of American history as its economic growth and political power. For example, the beginning of the modern civil rights movement goes back to the emancipation movement prior to the Civil War. Emancipation movements go back to the Quaker efforts to end the slave trade. Given the economic power of the South, many of our first presidents were wealthy slave owners. Slavery was not just a lucrative economic practice, but a strong cultural norm, consistent with biblical teachings. It acted as a mechanism of social stability that reminded poor whites that life could be even worse if they were Black. Yet dissent arose anyway, and growing abolitionist sentiments especially in the North culminated in the Civil War. Similarly, the women's movement traces its roots to the dissenting women who gathered together in Seneca Falls, New York in 1844, that meeting became the basis of the suffrage movement, and sometime later, evolved into the Mother's Day movement to oppose US involvement in World War I.

The current "culture wars" harken back to the radical views on lifestyle and politics that were limited to the Bohemian subcultures of the 1950s that disdained the flatness, asceticism, sexual repression, shallowness, superficiality, inauthenticity and blind conformity of the dominant culture.[10] This gave rise to the Beat generation writers and critics who lamented the shallowness and conformity of the times, and extolled the virtues of drugs and various kinds of sensuality and sexuality. Their critiques morphed into the flourishing countercultures of the 1960s that extolling drugs and sex and rock "n" roll, also posed political and cultural challenges to racism, patriarchy, and the military-industrial

---

10   Many of the beat writers were influenced by existentialism and Heidegger's critiques of Das Mann, and/or Sartre's critiques of "bad faith," inauthenticity and conformity. That the beat generation writers became a significant part of American literature, and their critiques of both the culture and economic system were widely embraced in the 60s, reminds us that quite often below the surface, the smiles of the "cheerful robots" mask a suppressed humanity condemned to seek wealth, power or both and ignoring needs for community, caring, meaning and self-fulfillment. Mephistopheles may have won for now, but the battle for the American soul is not over.

complex. For some people, these were the best of times, this was an era when young people who are most amenable to social changes, dissented from the status quo, and in turn embraced and mobilized for "desirable" moral changes, or perhaps more accurately, they discarded the hypocrisy of their elders and celebrated the hedonism of the times which of course was a reaction against the waning, hypocritical Puritanism and blind patriotism of earlier times.

It would take is too far afield to offer a comprehensive explanation for the major changes in cultural values that have taken place since the latter part of the 20th Century beginning of course with changing nature of gender relations and sexual values. This actually began in the 1920s when more and more women began attending college, and more college men had fathers who could afford to buy them automobiles while still in school. The Stutz Bearcat offered style and power at a price many could afford and allowed young couples freedom from the panopticons called chaperones or "house mothers." Cars gave young people a time and place to partake of "prohibited" alcohol, while parked in "lover's lanes" and enjoying all the "comforts" of the backseats from the earliest days of the automobile (Heitmann, 2009).

Given the early association with sex, booze, and personal freedom, advertisers learned that the car culture, celebrating phallic power, and providing privacy for the amorous, is what sells products. Advertising and public relations began to appeal to unconscious sexual desires. Edward Bernays, Sigmund Freud's nephew, turned his uncle's social-psychology into marketing schemes. One of the more famous was the parade of "upscale" women holding up cigarettes (penises) dubbed "torches of liberty." In a short time, smoking for women took on air of respectability and tobacco sales doubled. Although the Depression put a damper on things erotic, with World War II, millions of American GIs found themselves in other cultures that were more sexually open than the United States where Puritan values were still generally unchallenged, even if actions did not always coincide with values.[11] Notwithstanding the 1873 Comstock Act that prohibited the distribution of contraceptive devices, the American military provided soldiers with millions of condoms and warnings about STDs, or VD (venereal disease) as they were called it back then.

Rosie the Riveter personified millions of the women back on the home front who entered the workforce during World War II. Given how many men were serving in the military, single women vastly outnumbered single men, so many women relaxed their moral constraints in order to gain a "competitive advantage" in the dating/marriage markets and the few men who were still around,

---

11   Since time immemorial, victorious armies freely raped the women they conquered.

happily seized upon opportunities.[12] Following the war, the G.I. bill enabled millions of men and women to attend college and in general college education, especially courses in the humanities, philosophy, and critical social sciences exposed people to wider views and more often than not, college education led to more liberal social values.

After WWII, as the mass production of weapons and munitions ended. Given both pent-up demands since all production had been for the war effort, and people had chunks of available cash, consumerism exploded. Laden with subliminal sexual messages in mass media, namely magazines, radio, and soon television, and today the constant spam and adverts on the Internet, have diminished the restraints on consumption. The changing rules and roles and of men and women, the growth of consumerism, and greater opportunities for young people to find privacy, and the commercial colonization of sexuality encouraged impulse buying and experiences tied to products that also conveyed a sense of status and identity with perhaps a naughty innuendo as is often evident in advertisements and commercials cars, fashions, accessories and makeup. Carl Jr. is notorious for their erotized commercials for example the scantily clad Paris Hilton in a car wash eating the barbecue burger as if it were her male lover. Not to be outdone, the Hardee's Patty melt commercial again turned a burger ad into soft core porn. Commercialized toleration of the erotic directed pleasure towards commodities as "repressive desublimation" had been very successful at incorporating the masses into the new forms of administered, "one dimensional" consumer society in which privatized hedonism joins with uncritical "one-dimensional thought" to serve hegemonic purposes (Cf. Marcuse 1964). Commodification, requires mass production and mass markets to be profitable. Thus various tabooed topics and/or things have been mass marketed for the mainstream and their very ubiquity leads to the normalization of what had been transgressive. Consider the rise of *Playboy* in 1953 as a harbinger of things to come. In 1972, a sexually explicit movie *Deep Throat* was shown in theaters across the nation and suddenly oral sex was on everyone's lips. *Deep Throat* initiated what is been called "porn chic" in which pornography first entered into the mainstreams of popular culture. The grainy, highly amateur 8mm stag movies of the silent era have now morphed to over 300,000 web sites that produce more revenue than football, baseball and basketball combined. *Deep Throat* was soon followed by the *Rocky Horror Picture Show*, the cult classic of sensuality, sexuality and gender bending when two "innocent" white-bread, suburban kids, Brad and Janet embarked on a journey of

---

12   And we need remember that in 1947 the famous Kinsey report revealed that over half of American women had lost their virginity before marriage.

sexual transgression and polymorphous perversions, more or less orchestrated by Dr. Frank N Furter, an alien transvestite. The porn film *Debbie Does Dallas* clearly linked the phallic aggressive football player with a vaginally and orally receptive cheer leader. Porn is double-edged. It challenges Puritanical bourgeois repression, it relaxes moral standards, undermines guilt and repression and makes sex, sexuality, nudity and the body more acceptable. But like the porn industry in general, *Deep Throat* and *Debbie does Dallas* both perpetuated the objectification and degradation of women. In contrast, *The Rocky Horror Picture Show* depicted gender bending, gay and bisexuality in ways that mainstream audiences could appreciate, but also makes the bisexual alien transvestite into a tragic (if farcical) hero. Sexual immorality, flagrant nudity, blasphemous music, recreational drugs, rejection of religion—turns out they aren't necessarily so harmful after all.

Battles Today

Not all Americans were particularly happy about the social, cultural and political changes that directly challenged their traditional identities and values regarding gender, sexuality, asceticism and an unqualified patriotism that meant supporting American foreign policies right or wrong. And for progressives like us, these interventions are not only morally wrong, but inordinately destructive of human life, sanctioning of torture and wasting vast sums of money on losing causes is just plain unacceptable. Liberals, progressives and radicals typically look askance at the religious folks who sustain authoritarian values, resist social change, sustain intolerance and support a variety of political leaders and positions that not only ill-serve the nation, but hasten the very decline that ill serves themselves as well. Nevertheless, as social scientists have long known, religion has a number of appeals to many believers and is not simply an anachronistic set of beliefs or delusions. For our purposes, religion integrates people into people identity granting and recognizing cohesive communities of meaning and solidarity. Collective identity and solidarity based upon religion typically takes one of two forms stressing love or hate. Love creates and sustains empathic communities of inclusion, mutual respect and dignity for all. Hate creates communities of hierarchy and domination and exclusion of vile Others, sinners, infidels and heathens worthy of hate if not elimination. Such religions require an enemy to give them meaning and purpose. As America has become more socially liberal in the last several decades, the many blatant challenges, dismissals and rejections of the traditional, authoritarian, norms and values that conservatives hold dear, have inspired the massive conservative counter mobilizations that have attempted to reverse the liberal values of toleration and inclusion that have become enshrined in the last 50 years. They would preserve patriarchal authority, insure the chastity of young women so they might stay in the kitchens where they would remain subordinated, barefoot, and ever pregnant. When so constrained and socially isolated within submissive housewife roles, women could not challenge male power and hence for traditional conservatives, we see that the vehement opposition to female choice arises from a threat to patriarchal values, male power and authoritarian relationships.[13] The defenders of traditional values such as Mike Huckabee, Rick Santorum, Sam Brownback and The Family Research Council, are desperately fighting a rearguard action against cultural change. While surely the conservative forces have failed to reverse the trends toward female equality and sexual freedom, they have not given up, as Mike Huckabee attests. And with enough votes in conservative state legislatures, they still have enough power to inflict a great deal of pain and suffering upon women.

Between economic stagnation and decline that we mentioned that fosters insecurity, fear, anxiety and anger, together with the liberalization of social values that not only challenge traditional values identities and social relationships, but laws and court decisions have upheld many progressive changes. Consider only the support for gay marriage and/or legalizing marijuana use. One of the primary defensive responses of traditional American social character has been reactionary social movements that seek to "restore" the mythical monolithic perfection and purity of a bucolic small town replete with a renewed and newly aggressive, empowered white male identity heralding the restoration of patriarchy, renewed sexual repression, homophobia, racism, ethnocentrism, and global domination espoused by conservative politicians and clergy. Fantasies of restoration might temporarily alleviate the fears, anxieties and anger brought about by the loss of white male power over women and minorities, as well as the power to define moral values and impose them on others. The condemnations of the government as the usurper of freedom is little more than a misplaced attempt to find a blameworthy target, especially when that government is headed by an African American. Thus for example the death panels that the ACA would allegedly establish, the FEMA detention camps to imprison conservatives, the Jade 11 military exercise preparing to hand Texas over to the Chinese and the impending draconian restriction

---

13   We should note that given the current economic realities, very few American families could survive on a single income. Many families depend on 4 incomes, eg each partner has a regular and part time job. But yes they do communicate with each other and their children text messages.

on firearms represent little more than the age-old paranoid style in American politics tinged with racism directed at the African American President.[14] As we earlier mentioned the various open carry and/or concealed weapons programs may provide short-term feelings of agency and empowered masculinity but will have no effect whatsoever on reversing the decried social changes.

But these conservative agendas that might otherwise wither and go softly into the night are nevertheless well supported by certain movement conservatives typically economic elites, billionaire sugar daddies who want and need the masses of conservative "values voters" to support conservative, if not reactionary legislators who will minimize regulations on production and transportation, maintain low wages and low taxes and protect unlimited freedom to pollute in order to maximize profits. This story was played out in Kansas as chronicled 12 years ago by Frank (2004). And what did that get them? Economic decline, retrenchments in education, road repair and so on. The Koch Brothers and others have therefore supported the conservative moral and family agendas of the "values voters" in order to gain their support for their own economic agendas. These "values voters" have surely slowed the process of cultural change but for all intents and purposes, notwithstanding many small victories over limiting women's health care issues, restricting access to birth control and abortion, excluding and/or demonizing minorities, marginalizing gays, and attempting to end premarital/extramarital sex, nevertheless, they lost the culture war.

Growing numbers of nonwhite minorities, more liberal youth and many of the not so youthful liberals, have challenged the social privileges of older, whiter, more religious conservatives. This *resentment* over growing social liberalization was abundantly clear when an African-American was elected president and that synecdoche was a major animus of the Tea Party movement (Langman, 2012; Lundskow, 2012).[15] As we saw earlier with the conservative Fox news commentator Megyn Kelly's smack down of the aging Mike Huckabee,

---

14   As much as paranoid thought is a part of American culture, there are some claims that yet baffle us. Why would the Chinese want Texas? Surely not oil at a time of glut, and surely their Beijing Duck is as good as any Texan BBQ.

15   In our writings we were quite clear about the racism of the Tea Party. Many mainstream scholars and researchers were reluctant to note the racist side of the Tea Party mobilization and preferred to simply look at the mechanics of mobilization, for example, the particular ways that people organize, such as whether they use a cell phone or e-mail more. If one did follow the events, the early rallies included abundant images of Obama as an African witch doctor in a grass skirt with a bone in his nose, or portrayed him as a monkey. But the TP folks are not stupid and they quickly learned that overt racism would undermine support for their movement.

his gender role ideals are both old and old-fashioned and relevant only to older and ever shrinking, smaller constituencies. Very few younger people of any political persuasion today will seriously postpone their sexuality until marriage or advocate that women return to domestic labor and do nothing else but have and raise children and serve men.

By themselves, liberal values regarding race, class, sex, sexuality, gender, gender orientation and other identity issues as well as environmental movements, do not fundamentally alter the economic system, its class relations and the nature of power. Although many corporations may resist, especially those in oil or coal industries, a green capitalism can do quite well. At present, solar power is the fastest growing source of energy in the United States, increasing at 30% a year, because photovoltaic technology has achieved much greater efficiency at a much lower price (Cusick, 2015). There goes the fracking, drilling, pipelines and oil spills, as well as earthquakes and tap water that bursts into flames. Ditto for the coal mines, especially the strip mines and the pollution of the waters, the air and nearby land. Most progressive social movements have relatively specific goals, inclusion, toleration of social differences, democratization of the political system and a better environment. but most of these movements have very little coordination with each other, very little formal affiliations with a political party, and thus do not aim at major structural transformations. Besides becoming less costly, the rise of solar power is partly the result of tax benefits to promote it, so its success remains within the capitalist economic system. Nevertheless, these developments create social spaces and open-mindedness to initiate more challenges to established power that become the gateways to contesting the system itself. For the authoritarian moralists, the departure from the stage of world history is clearly marked, and they should be sure to take their authoritarianism, their intolerance, narrow mindedness, and hostilities to Others along with them to the deserts of history where the desiccated skeletons of their failed worldview can bleach in the sun of Enlightenment. Have a safe trip, but don't call when you get there!

History, Social Change and Social Character

Following Erich Fromm's study of social and characterological change we discussed in Chapter 1, we have seen that there is an ever-changing relationship between a society, its political economy and cultural values on the one hand and the kind of social character that is best able to adapt to changing circumstances which typically becomes the most frequent type in any society. It is also important to note that less common types exist alongside of the predominant types. They may become more numerous; indeed, they may become the modal type of social character. Although most histories focus on events and persons, leaders, battles and wars, conquests or particular histories of industries, workers, criminals and jails, our concern is less with the day-to-day or even year-to-year events than with the major changes of underlying social character that take place over time in response to changing economic or cultural conditions. Conversely, changes in character become reflected in changes in the nature of nation.[16] For our purposes, having discussed the historical changes in social character that took place as the colonies grew and became the "first new nation," as well as noting a remarkable degree of continuity in social character, our concern is that given the social conditions of our times, what, if any, factors are leading to the changes that are taking place today before very eyes? Given what we have often said, there are two primary forces fostering, indeed demanding major social and characterological changes. In the last several decades radical changes have taken place in the economic system as well as radical changes in cultural norms.

The Transforming of American Character

Social character, as the most typical constellation of desires, internalized values, and narratives of self-definition and frameworks of understanding found within a particular population is the bedrock upon which collective values, perceptions and understandings of reality and modes of relationships rest. But social character is not simply formed in early childhood and thereupon carved in stone and unchanged by later experience. Insofar as the majority of people fall close to the middle ranges of distributions of various social psychological qualities such as authoritarianism, religiosity or dogmatism, inclusiveness or exclusiveness, depending on circumstances, people may go either way and shift their views. Social character can be thought of as setting the limits or parameters of choices and most people remain within these limits. Yes, our history is filled with dissenters, yes there are numbers of people who may shift from highly religious to highly secular, or politically conservative to politically liberal. But for most people, the acorns fall close to the tree. Although this may be most evident in the case of authoritarianism, authoritarianism is not

---

16   After wwii, the usa prohibited physical punishment of any kind in Germany, everything from spanking, the most frequent means of fostering authoritarianism, to the death penalty. Today, Germany is one of the least authoritarian, most cosmopolitan countries, a favorite destination for progressive Israelis and Syrian refugees.

distinctively American which is not to say that the United States does not have a relatively sizable population of authoritarians. Perhaps about 20 to 25% of the population might be considered highly authoritarian, and fully 49% of Republican voters (MacWilliams 2016). Given our concern with the formation of American social character, given discontinuities and capacities to change views of changing circumstances, perhaps one of the most important aspects of authoritarianism is openness to change and openness to new ideas. Some people are typically highly dogmatic, which is a correlate of authoritarianism. When faced with disconfirming facts, evidence or information that challenges their beliefs, they become even more adamant, intransigent and recalcitrant to change. But many people apart from the extremes of authoritarianism, do in fact change their views and beliefs—consider only how in face of overwhelming evidence of the link to cancer, cigarette smoking has plummeted.

Some kinds of changes have a considerable impact upon social character, especially the ways people socialize their children and the kinds of role models their children internalize. Consider only the use of physical punishment. Between "expert opinion," greater levels of college education that may include a psychology class or two, and public agencies concerned with child abuse, spanking children is far less frequent today than a few generations ago. The use of physical punishment as a primary form of discipline is typically only found only among highly religious conservatives like the Family Research Foundation who still believe that to "spare the rod" is to spoil the child. And every so often, the news reports tell of a child, or children, who have been punished to the point of abuse and even on rare occasion, death.[17]

Further, as we've already noted, adolescence, as a critical period in the development of one's personality, is a time when people achieve their cognitive maturity. But at the same time, older teen-agers/young adults are still especially flexible and, given the circumstances of the times when this is crucial, they are open to change especially the crafting of one's identity. We've already mentioned how the millennial generation of today is leaving institutional religion and swelling the ranks of the "nones," atheists, agnostics, Wiccans and others. Similarly, generations growing up after the Soviet Union had fallen, knowing little of the gulags, purges or the inefficiency the authoritarian version of State Capitalism that labeled itself socialism. Facing economic pressures, a slight majority of the young favor socialism over capitalism. This would have been unthinkable in the past.

---

17   There is now overwhelming evidence gathered over the last 50+ years that has shown how harmful physical punishment is in terms of bullying, various measures of psychopathology, and even slower and lower cognitive development.

Despite massive socio-economic changes such as the influx of large numbers of immigrants, the radical changes in technology since the early colonists used horses to plow their fields and travel, different stages of industrialization and now digitalization/computerization, the primacy of urban over rural life, there has been a great deal of continuity between contemporary American social character and its early expressions as described by Crevecoeur and de Tocqueville. There are many ways we can understand and explain this continuity across generations beginning with the importance of early identification within a family that, shaped by the conditions of the larger economy, foster certain authority relations within the family that become internalized via identification with parents. The intergenerational transmission of values, mediated through early identifications as well as cultural memes often persist for several generations after material conditions that engendered certain patterns may change. Social character can act as either a barrier to social change/ changing values as well as a catalyst for change. On the one hand, older people especially those who still embody the traditional American social character, who are most likely members of authoritarian religious communities, are generally not only resistant to change, but certain changes that impact values, beliefs and identities, may evoke powerful emotions that dispose people toward joining or supporting reactionary social mobilizations that seek to stop or perhaps even reverse social change. This was very much the case with right populist movements such as the Know Nothing party, the Ku Klux Klan and more recently the Tea Party-all fearing social change, all seeking to restore a past that is more imagined than real. The rise of feminism in the 60s provides a very good case in point. Although many feminist leaders had been involved in various progressive struggles for a long time, it was not until the 60s when large numbers of younger women were more likely to pursue higher education and careers that critical masses of progressive women obtained. Having attained that education, they found that the promises of marriage, family and suburban living fell remarkably short of expectations. Thus when Betty Freidan published the *Feminine Mystique* in 1963, her critique resonated with millions of young and frustrated housewives as well as large numbers of young women college students. This sparked the modern, second generation, feminist movement. More and more women began to seek occupational careers and the ranks of feminist organizations swelled with young women, most of whom were college-educated and for the most part, their educations were in humanities and social sciences, disciplines that stressed and critiqued various forms of domination and quite often, envisioned alternatives. Once a critical mass of activists and a larger mass of sympathizers emerges that can pressure political leadership, social changes takes place, or perhaps more accurately, become accepted. An important legacy of this era has been the academic recognition of African-American studies, women's studies and queer theory. As progressive organizations grew in strength, social and political power, two often overlapping groups fundamentally opposed the rise of feminism and its challenges to traditional male patriarchy.

When large number of women entered the labor force, where they gain not only incomes but independence, many blue-collar male workers resented "women taking their jobs" and forgetting their "proper" place. Similarly, various conservative clergy and/or political leaders holding highly patriarchal views toward women, often justified by certain religious beliefs, were angry, fearful and anxious about the demise of their male privilege and power. One of the places where mail power was expressed was in the attempt to control female bodies, sexuality and fertility. Similarly, for many women, their primary identities as wives, mothers and caretakers were equally outraged by other women who might combine motherhood with careers in business, the military and politics, up to and including the presidency.

How do people respond to changing values? For example, many youths grow up expecting that they will almost automatically attain if not surpass the standard of living of their parents. Until the millennial generation in the US, for the most part, this was true. Today however, most millennials will fall short of their parents standards of living (Taylor 2016); this financial decline undermines feelings of self-worth, self-esteem and basic human dignity. Similarly, real-world experiences that contradict expectations, as for example when Americans get to Denmark or Sweden, especially for extended times in work or school, they discover that poverty is not an inherent part of modern society but a product of unregulated, predatory capitalism joined with ideologies and practices that thwart popular resistance. Similarly, many Americans are quite surprised to find out that Europeans really do have much more relaxed attitudes about teenage sexuality or the human body at the beach where topless sunning and/or tanning are the norm. We must then reconsider our uptight notions about the body or beliefs about the poor. In modern times, people from politically or religiously conservative backgrounds face several challenges and contradictions. When people with restrictive values see other people engaging in prohibited behavior, enjoying it, and yet not suffering the wrath of God, they may engage in the prohibited behavior. This is especially the case when young people go off to the more permissive atmospheres of college where free of surveillance of parents, they quite often become sexually active before marriage. And surprising enough, this even happens at the evangelical universities that condemn such transgressions.

There are three possible ways to resolve the cognitive dissonance. First, some may repent the transgression and return to the fold. Second, people may embrace newer, more permissive values and abandon previous positions, which as we have seen is very much the case today especially insofar as many youths raised in conservative households leave institutional religion when they grow up and leave home. Finally, some people may compartmentalize their behaviors and values and aided by powerful defenses of denial or splitting, maintain certain values in one context, often publically, while discarding them all together in another, more private context. This can range from simple insincerity to outright hypocrisy.

As we previously noted, liberal websites delight in exposing the total hypocrisy of those conservative ministers or politicians who proclaim support for "traditional" family values, condemn sex outside of marriage, yet then have secret affairs. After Ashley Madison, the adultery website was hacked and its patrons exposed, 400 clergymen immediately resigned. Consider for example, from 2015, Michigan republican representatives Todd Courser and Cindy Gamrat, both far-right and married "family values" and anti-gay conservatives, had an affair with each other. They enlisted their staffers to cover up the affair by asking them to spread rumors and post fake messages on his Facebook page that Courser was addicted to drugs and often paid for sex with men in order to make it look like he was the victim of a radical gay smear campaign. Courser hoped this would draw attention away from the real affair with Gamrat. The staffers refused and instead went to the media with the true story. Courser then claimed that his staffers were part of the gay conspiracy and were trying to blackmail him, until the staffers produced a mountain of e-mails, paper documents, and an audio recording on which Courser tells his staffers, among other things: "The way to handle this is a controlled burn that is so over-the-top that people will say holy shit! It's a little truth mixed with a lot of lies." In response, Courser now says that he is truly sorry for the indiscretion, and eventually resigned his seat rather than be expelled, as was Gamrat (Gray, 2015). Similarly, conservative pastor Ted Haggard relentlessly expounded homophobic diatribes, until a male prostitute testified that he often had sex with Haggard and they smoked crack together. After initially denying it, Haggard later admitted it was true (AP/NBC News 2006).

In short, emotional pain and suffering rooted in either economic factors or normative contradictions impact an individual's character as well as the social character typical of the society. Facing social and psychological pressure, a person or group may move from one side of the contradiction to the other, for example, from abstinence, to hedonistic indulgence. When there are shifts among a large number of people there are changes in the nature of the social character that foretell changes in the society. Much as Fromm described the characterological changes in traditional European society or as he observed in the Mexican Village, we are suggesting that this is now happening in American society.

Dynamic Character Change

For Freud, character structure was fixed with the resolution of the Oedipus complex at about age five. One of the most important concepts advanced by Erich Fromm, yet given too little attention was the notion of dynamic change that character can and does take place throughout life and indeed, social factors foster generational changes. How and why did social character change over time? Fromm makes the point that for an American, learning how to use chopsticks is a relatively simple mechanical task that does not change one's character or identity very much. Today, about 75 years later, almost every city, town and village in the United States has a Chinese or other Asian restaurant where many of the American patrons use chopsticks. But we should note that the use of chopsticks by itself or appreciation of Asian food has not made any American more cosmopolitan or liberal.

Characterological change occurs in conjunction with more meaningful personal experiences as part of broader social change. For Fromm, the historical conditions of every epoch fostered a particular social character "best adapted," that is, motivated to embrace the dominant values and motives to enact the required social roles of work and engage in the social relationships required by the existing socio-economic conditions and class arrangements. As Lundskow discovered when he first went to Germany as an exchange student in high school, not only are topless women at public pools common, but both men and women are sometimes entirely nude—but otherwise completely normative. True, some European men, for aesthetic reasons, might want to rethink bikini-brief swimsuits, so not all American notions of normativity related to the human body derive from our uptight Puritan history. Still, exposure to more open and relaxed notions of the body allowed Lundskow to drop some of his Midwestern puritanism in general, not just about what to wear at swimming pools, and adopt more relaxed attitudes overall. Either that, or risk not fitting in to the more relaxed social relations in Germany. As the US becomes more relaxed, uptight types no longer fit in, and even stand out as old-fashioned and irrelevant—remember Mike Hukabee and Megyn Kelly. Broader experiences often make a person's character broader.

For Fromm each historic epic has its own typical social character, its own discontents and its own "mechanisms of escape," ways of adapting to the world that alleviate anxiety and uncertainty. While each character type may be well "adapted" to its particular socio-economic/cultural milieu, each type rested on contradictions between the self and the society that fostered various kinds of malaise and discontents:

> In the 19th Century inhumanity meant cruelty; in the 20th Century it means schizoid self-alienation. The danger of the past was that men became slaves. The danger of the future is that men may become robots. True enough, robots do not rebel. But given man's nature, robots cannot live and remain sane, they become "Golems"; they will destroy their world and themselves because they cannot stand any longer the boredom of a meaningless life ... In spite of increasing production and comfort, man loses more and more the sense of self, feels that his life is meaningless, even though such a feeling is largely unconscious. In the nineteenth Century the problem was that God is dead; in the twentieth Century the problem is that man is dead.
>
> FROMM, 1990 [1955] pp. 102, 360

But how did social character change in face of economic change, Fromm:

> Social character results from the dynamic adaptation of human nature to the structure of society. Changing social conditions result in changes of the social character, that is, in new needs and anxieties. These new needs give rise to new ideas and, as it were, make men susceptible to them; these new ideas in their turn tend to stabilize and intensify the new social character and to determine man's actions. In other words, social conditions influence ideological phenomena through the medium of character; character, on the other hand, is not the result of passive adaptation to social conditions but of a dynamic adaptation on the basis of elements that either are biologically inherent in human nature or have become inherent as the result of historic evolution.
>
> FROMM, (1992 [1973]). p. 296

Social character, the most frequently found type within in the population is perhaps the most likely to be well "adapted" to the demands of a particular economic system at a particular moment-this it's socio-cultural niche. In this view, while a given social character may the best adapted at a particular time, things change, a market society develops. The early market society of small

tradesmen and shopkeepers later became an industrial and bureaucratic society and with the growth of affluence, a consumer society. Then American
capitalism morphs from mass production to financial services and digital
products and services. But again with major socioeconomic and/or cultural
changes the heretofore typical social character becomes less adaptive and faces stress, strains and anxieties specific to the times. But as we will argue, and
new social character is nascent and growing in numbers.

There are two levels of dynamic change, individual and collective. Within
a particular individual, any number of personality characteristics, traits and
talents may or may not be salient or realized depending on the situations and
opportunities available in the social and economic system at a particular time.
In this way we might look at selfhood and self-presentations as the expressions of an underlying constellation in which individuals have a number of
potentials of self-expression, self-presentation and even particular identities
that might opt for realization depending on what might be most adaptive the
specific circumstances, opportunities of the system and nature of one's social character. Furthermore, individual subjectivity includes various modes of
selfhood, some of which may indeed be quite contradictory, but certain aspects of self may be more relevant at particular times or contexts than others.
Certain kinds of motives may be articulated in some circumstances but not
others. As we have so often seen, at moments of rapid change, if not revolutions, certain people have hitherto unrealized talents and abilities that enable rapid adaptation to the new circumstances. What is evident to us is that
as a result of dynamic change a new social character is emerging today with
several salient features, with a shifting of the polarities from one side to the
other. Secondly, this type is much less authoritarian, meaning more open to
what is new, more experimental. Ogilvy (1979) suggested that authoritarian,
hierarchal societies foster a unitary self that without contradictions (ambivalence) from within that went along with the authoritarian society-much like
the "receptive character" Fromm described. But he claimed that we were now
seeing the emergence of the "many dimensional character," more flexible, tolerant, democratic and open to change. The notion of selfhood as a plurality
has a very long history beginning with William James. More recently, Lifton
(1993) has claimed that there is an emerging "Protean self" that can take a
variety of forms which is highly adaptive to our times. This protean self stands
diametrically opposed to what he calls the "fundamentalist self that we have
seen as authoritarian. However, it might be termed, an emerging social character, is more pluralistic, democratic and more likely to seek self-fulfillment
than subordination of self to another person or ideology. And more likely to
resist domination.

In any given population for most personality characteristics, most people tend to cluster in the middle. Long traditions of research on authoritarianism, introversion, extroversion, narcissism, anxiety levels or depression, show more or less bell curve distributions and it's only a minority of people that are at the extremes and incapable of change. People who tend to be highly authoritarian and/or dogmatic are less open to change and in fact, they may often strongly resist change even to the point of embracing violence to maintain a status quo that nevertheless provides a variety of gratifications. Given different character types, with a variety of personality characteristics and/or talents, some of which may or may not be realized depending on the opportunities available in the economic system. Thus some of the less frequently found types, already present in a society with multimodal distribution of character types, may well differ from the most common type (also called the normative type). One may have initially a bit "unusual" or "deviant," yet, perhaps prompted by stress and strains, might in fact prove be better able to adapt to new and changing circumstances and opportunities. "Social selection" suggests that certain individuals, groups or classes of people, who are not necessarily the most typical may nevertheless possess certain characterological qualities that enable them to more readily adapt to changing circumstances (Fromm and Maccoby, 1996 [1972]; LeVine, 1973). Over time, that type becomes more numerous, acceptable and successful "variants."[18] Consequently, social norms, attitudes, and eventually policies more actively foster the more adaptive social character patterns that may have been present in the group, but were infrequently found. When a previously rare character structure enables better adaptation to a new social-historical context, such as with the rise of high-tech and instantaneous communication compared to mechanical technology and snail-mail, expectations and attitudes also change. Over time, each new generation moves though the life cycle and manifests the traits that better match the newer social conditions. What had been rare and perhaps deviant becomes normative. The new, now more adaptive, social character type is then more likely to command various resources, including the control of culture, childrearing, schooling and other institutions of socialization now including mass media (which includes the Internet) which enables them to foster a number of structural and cultural changes in values, family structures, dynamics, values, and socialization practices that cumulatively leads to changes in the frequency of the dominant

18   Think of how Bill Gates or Steve Jobs may have been nerds in high school, neither the "popular kids" nor the jocks. And then personal computers came on board. Where are the popular kids now? Some are managers at McDonalds, and the jocks, trainers at the local gym, and the nerds, among the richest men in America.

social character from rare and deviant to an acceptable variant and then to the most frequent constellation.

Thus for example, the nature of the political economy, namely how wealth is produced and owned, gained and distributed, who benefits, who controls and/or is controlled by the government, and who sets the dominant cultural values, many of which may be the legacies of previous generations are such that certain character types are likely to be ascendant. Social "selection" is dependent on thought, language and cognitive processes that disposes characterological adaptation to changing environments. Given what we previously said, the major impetus for characterological change comes from crises and contradictions rooted in the political economy that foster a certain amount of distress that prompts people to make adaptive behavioral changes that become habitual and impact social character. Similarly, changes in a value system due to economic changes, technical changes, and perhaps exposure to alternatives often lead people to change. This is especially true for young people who have not yet established a firm identity and sense of self, this allows for freedom and experimentation.

People think and behave differently in different social contexts and crises often provoke change. In World War II, however, millions of Americans quickly adapted to the war effort and quickly become soldiers, sailors, and pilots, including women. Yes, many women and minorities became pilots, quite contrary to social expectations that neither African-Americans nor women were intellectually, emotionally, or physically capable of mastering complex flight skills.[19] The experiences of leadership, the acquisition of a variety of skills, and exposure to different cultures impacted what has been called "the greatest generation." Following the war many veterans took advantage of the GI. Bill, attended college, and soon find employment in the large corporations that then flourished. The cumulative effect of military service, technical or college education, corporate careers, upward mobility and the "comforts" of suburban life had a major impact on social character and enabled, if not encouraged different aspects of selfhood to emerge. While the greatest generation did not become the most progressive generation, they created new social realities that opened the door for their children, the baby boomers, who pushed social boundaries well beyond any previous generation, and Gen-Xers broke even farther conventionalism, to open the door for the Millennials who are writing their history today.

---

19   The African American Tuskegee pilots had a stellar record protecting bombers from German interceptors. Given the short careers of most combat pilots, many bombers were flown from the factories to the battlefronts by women.

As we have suggested, despite America's history of macroeconomic success, capitalism no longer delivers an acceptable quality of life for many Americans, and many have lost hope that it ever will.

Sturm, Drang and the Bearers of Social Change

Historically, adolescence, as a socially constructed transitional stage in the life cycle between childhood and adulthood, is the result of a disjuncture between the family and the larger society that emerges when the family can no longer provide the kinds of secondary socialization experiences, job skills and world views needed for living in the larger society. In traditional agricultural societies, children learned everything they needed to know in their households. Today, the son or daughter of a farmer who may still want a family farm, but needs a college education that includes meteorology, biochemistry, agronomy, agronomics and computer science. And perhaps some accounting as well. Thus nearly all youth today must look outside the home to finish their social preparation for adulthood.

In most societies with a disjunction between the family and larger world, age graded youth cultures, perhaps tied to schools, monasteries or warrior training camps, separate the young from their families and serve as transitional groups to educate and socialize youth, often granting transitional identities, and thereby facilitate their transition from childhood to adulthood. In modern societies, major discontinuities between older and newer generations result from different social, cultural, political and economic realities, and new identities arise from this changing social character.

For much of the post war period, adolescent peer groups such as punks, bikers, geeks, jocks, metalheads, gearheads, stoners, bible thumpers, theater crowds, yearbook kids, the science club and/or Harry Potter Club and many more groups are "try ons" where young people try to find identities that enable a best fit with certain peer groups to provide then with friends, meaning and gratification. Adolescence peer groups provide a time and place in which young people explore many of the aspects of themselves and their surroundings to weave together a more or less coherent notion of selfhood, assembled from his or her past that will impact his/her current everyday life and surely impact the person's subsequent life course, often in unforeseen ways. Further, one's identity, or perhaps we might better say the constellations of identities, need a certain degree of emotional affinity with the social character of any particular group. The stoners won't have much in common with the bible thumpers-although perhaps we, the authors are too far away from our high school years to remember. In simple terms, people identify with a group, and the group recognizes the individual as a member. But at the same time, people can change their group memberships quite often and hold multiple memberships at the same time. Today, when thinking of the peer groups of yesterday, youth seemed to live in a simpler time more concerned with school, play, a rock concert or a motorcycle rally, or perhaps drugs and sex and rock "n" roll, which harken us back to the pleasant memories like a freshly baked brownie-especially if it was baked with a bit of hash. Thirty years ago, who could believe that most people would own a small handheld device that would enable them to communicate with others all over world, gather information about anything, or watch movies—that they or friends had just made. Only techie or sci-fi geeks who were into *Star Trek* and *Popular Science* could envision Captain Kirk's communicator as a smartphone and billions of people now have them. Back then, no-one could envision the predatory economy of today in which its vast wealth at top now means a bleak, uncertain and precarious future for many young people.[20] Most young people today are not so anchored within social and/or family roles and networks as to fully embrace the norms and values of the previous generation given the extent to which given the generational contexts that we have noted, the world today is so much different than when their parents were their age.

Adolescence has long been associated with "*Sturm und Drang*," the storm and stress associated with the transition from adolescence to adulthood. But today, there is the additional stress due to the economic conditions that make life uncertain and establishing closure of one's identity and thinking of any kind of future is difficult. As is well known, adolescence is now extending to early adulthood and perhaps for the millennial generation, may be prolonged even further. For many millennial's today, the attainment of cultural expectations of adulthood, a stable career, marriage and family are increasingly unattainable. As the Pew statistics revealed in Chapter 1 show, groups may be diverse, but taken together we see that many people have very little loyalty to the system that seems to them increasingly unjust and illegitimate.

Cohort flow intersects with the problem of establishing one's ego identity at a "critical period" in the life course when acquiring or crafting a sense of self that shapes the subsequent life course. Every generation, and units within the generation, establish the parameters of their identity, or identities, at a particular historical movement, as adolescence is a period of openness, flexibility and receptiveness to the impacts of the historical moment in which s/he forges a self. But today, in many ways, given the uncertainty of the future, this

---

20   The sci fi geeks authors might note that there is a long history of dystopian sci-fi depicting this bleak future, for example 1984, Brave New World, A Scanner Darkly, the many Planet of the Apes movies, various zombie apocalypse scenarios and the Mad Max series.

becomes a formidable task. Given what we have said about character change, the historical context, mediated through socialization and impacted by everyday life experiences, establishes ranges of what might be desirable and gratifying identity(ies) and insofar as people have ever more social space for crafting one's self rather than simply incorporating a role model; such an identity can reflux back upon the person and itself become a factor fostering a changing social character. The economic conditions of our age, coupled with the normative issues, impact people during their youth, a critical moment in the life cycle, and thus, through dynamic change, impacts one's character. Understanding the socially based transformations of social character thus requires us to the question of the establishment of one's identity, one's narrative of self, one's own constellation of group membership but also individual uniqueness based on personal choices of inclusion and differentiation. Thus on the one hand, establishing a clear cut identity and anticipated future is more difficult problem today. But on the on the hand, there is also a flexibility and openness to change that enables changes of social character-especially since given the cultural changes and great fluidity of emergent social character, there is greater openness to the kind of post capitalist sane society we envision.

The Social Psychology of Social Movements

If discontent is so widespread, why do we not see sustained, massive mobilizations recently? For one thing, the rhetoric and promises of neoliberalism yet resonate with significant numbers of Americans who still embody the traditional social character and retain the beliefs of their youth that hard work brings success, government aid makes poor people lazy, cutting the taxes and regulations of the elites brings wealth for all and free markets/low taxes are the best way to prosperity. This is especially the case when neoliberalism is presented in terms of a "level playing field" and "equal opportunity." Neoliberal economics seems fair and just to many Americans, especially those more conservative with a predominantly hoarding character, as described in Chapter 1. Many are older and yet financially secure and yet fear any redistribution programs would impact their wallets. Of course, the concept of equal opportunity in neoliberalism really means an equal opportunity to create inequality. In order to change the system, the underlying [traditional] social character of a large number of people needs to change, and that can in turn change the cultural systems and dismantle the existing political system. And as we have seen, this is precisely what happened in terms of civil rights, the sexual revolution, gay rights etc. But we should also note, that while certain segments of corporate capital support traditional social values, and while the vast majority of CEOs are white men, for the most part, capitalist elites who don't care if it's leading luminaries are gay, women, or African-American such as Tim Cook of Apple, Sheryl Sandburg of Facebook, and Kenneth Chenault of American Express respectively.

Gays, women, and minorities can create class inequality as well as heterosexual white males, and ideology—neoliberalism or any other—can only supersede reality for a while until real material and emotional needs demand actual fulfillment, not just abstract ideological promises that can't deliver the goods in the real world. While we should remember that many social movements took decades to accomplish their goals, and systemic transformations requires massive sustained efforts, we suggest the rumblings of discontent today may crash through the walls of the establishment tomorrow. Let's recall that the Czarist government easily suppressed the Revolution of 1905. By 1917, World War I had so enfeebled the Czarist government that it lost its legitimacy and another revolution began, major elements of the Army joined the Bolsheviks who overthrew the Czar, civil war ensued, and the Bolsheviks won.

In 2010, city officials and the police confiscated the cart and produce of Tarek al-Tayeb Mohamed Bouazizi, a poor street vendor in the city of Sidi Bouzid. Accustomed to police harassment and extortion for years, Bouazizi could stand it no more. In debt and with no means to earn a living, on December 17, 2010 around 11:30 am, Bouazizi doused himself with gasoline and lit himself on fire. This act of defiance set off protests across Tunisia. Bouazizi was not the only one upset about political oppression, corruption, poverty, and poor education. Mass protests and strikes ensued that shut down the capital, the airports and seaports. Demonstrators filled the streets. The Tunisian Army balked at using massive violence to suppress the demonstrations. President Zine El Abidine Ben Ali fled to Saudi Arabia on January 14, 2011 (with billions of dollars) only 28 days after the protests began. Bouazizi never knew that his protest worked so well and the government fell. He died on January 4, 2011. In place of the Ben Ali dictatorship, the Islamist Ennadha Movement along with two center-left progressive parties, Congress for the Republic and Ettakatol formed a coalition government. In less than a month, longstanding discontent exploded across the country and toppled a dictator who had been in power for 23 years.[21] This was not ye the end of social change. The Ennahda, an offshoot of the Muslim Brotherhood, with its conservative Islamic ideology and incompetent management attempted to impose religious laws in a fairly secular

---

21 Popular discontent had been building for years. Bouazizi's protest was a singular, dramatic and unpredictable moment, much like in 1956 when the police opened fire on occupiers at a radio station in Budapest, Hungary, a moment that turned a peaceful populace into freedom fighters that ultimately required a Soviet invasion to suppress.

Muslim society. In response, a female blogger gathered receipts from the hotel across from the presidential palace and revealed that Ennahda leaders were renting rooms at government expense to entertain their women friends. It went viral on the Internet. They resigned. More secular socialists took their place. Two important implications then: first, popular social movements can change governments, sometimes very quickly. Second, religious conservatives of all denominations show the repression-desire-transgression-hypocrisy pattern. Tunisia inspired other mobilizations, and popular uprisings overthrew the long-time dictators in Libya, Egypt, and Yemen in the Arab Spring of 2011. The Assad regime in Syria, backed by a massive Russian air campaign, clings to power in about half the country. Numerous militias vie for power in Libya, a military dictatorship seized power in Egypt, and Yemen suffers under an all-out civil war.

The spirit of revolution soon crossed the Mediterranean to Greece, Portugal and Spain, that in turn the Occupy Wall Street movements that began in Zuccotti Park in New York City that quickly spread throughout the country and into many other countries as well. Across the globe, millions of people took to the streets, squares, and parks to protest neoliberalism in general, its resulting inequality in particular, as well as elite corruption. Meanwhile, many people experienced pains and adversities that followed from European debt crises and the subsequent austerity programs that demanded debt repayment by reducing or eliminating government services, including education, healthcare, retirement pensions and by privatizing public utilities. For many people the costs of living went up while many became jobless and the economy declined. Thus in addition to job loss and rising prices, they faced sharply reduced benefits and pensions. However, these mobilizations were not the classical union-worker or socialist party mobilizations that simply fight for better wages, working conditions, benefits and job security, but the current social movement's demands for recognition as human beings with fundamental needs for dignity (Benski and Langman, 2013). Moreover, inspired by the World Social Forum they offered a direct challenge to the modern world order as a whole, not just a call for a better place in it, but through the hope that "another world was possible."

Beyond North Africa and the Middle East, a newly established, progressive leftist party called *Syriza* won the Greek elections by protesting the austerity programs demanded by the troika consisting of the EU, the ECB and the IMF. In Spain, *Podemos* and other New Leftist parties came into being and collectively hold nearly half the elected offices in Spain. Student protests in Chile as well as Québec with more modest goals of reversing tuition increases arose and succeeded. The Occupy movements drew a lot of attention, critique and praise, and while they may not have accomplished very much in the short run, they did articulate the widespread discontent and grievances of their generation. They also changed the national conversation from austerity and debt reduction to inequality, especially by labeling the elites as "the 1%." One of the major factors for the electoral success of *Syriza* was its ability to form a political party in the Greek parliamentary system. Even though eventually its leader Tsipras capitulated to the Troika and accepted their austerity terms as a condition for their loans, the party still garnered a great deal of popular support. Whereas in the American system, it would not be possible for Occupy to form a political party as such. They had some chances though. For example, Norman Solomon, a progressive journalist with a long history of exposing deceit and corruption, was extremely sympathetic and supportive of the Occupy movement. He ran for Congress in a relatively liberal California district but with almost no funding, his extremely well-funded opponent in the Democratic primary won the primary by less than 2,000 votes. If a few dozen Occupy activists had supported Solomon on the ground, and done some organizing, heavy lifting and knocking on doors, he may very well have won and Occupy would have had a voice in the Congress. Occupy was rightly quite critical of the Democratic Party, but this was a chance to confront the dominant political system and work from within. Social change is quite often a rather slow process and tangible results may often occur many years if not decades after initial mobilizations and often in ways few intended. Tunisia achieved a free and open democracy and a much more broadly democratic society. Egypt remains a military dictatorship while Libya, and Yemen are torn by civil war. Most importantly though, progressive political organizations emerged that are necessary to lay the groundwork for future political mobilizations.

In the United States, far less dramatic than systemic changes in government, popular pressure led to a worker take over and ownership of storm window factory and a successful teachers strike in Chicago, increased wages for Walmart workers, and for McDonald's and many fast food workers, minimum wage increases passed by wide popular margins in every state where they went on the ballot in 2014, including the conservative stronghold state of Arkansas. Seattle, with Kshama Sawant, an Indian-American socialist woman on the city council, raised the minimum wage to $15. In any event, the minimalist Keynesian policies of the Obama administration, slowly but surely stemmed the economic plunge and indeed the massive bailouts of the large banks, financial institutions and carmakers eventually "turned the economy around." As the economy appeared to be on the mend, as seen for example in growing GNP, rising stock markets, and a resurgent construction industry, along with lower official unemployment rates, the fervor for social mobilizations seeking structural change seemed to wane. Notwithstanding how these official figures belie the realities for many perhaps most Americans. The overt discontents have receded, but were surely expressed in the 2016 presidential primary where as we noted, outsiders did very well. But as we also suggested, the underlying discontents of economic stagnation and inequality will not soon go away as was evident in the Democratic presidential primary of Bernie Sanders. The Democratic socialist quite clearly challenged the billionaire classes, fueled by the enthusiasm of youth that were not only seeking change, but changes consistent with an emerging pattern of a progressive social character.

Needed: A War of Position

At this point, we would like to take a page from Antonio Gramsci who argued that political transformations require long "wars of position" in which various intellectuals, artists and activists who understand the nature of hegemony, the ideological control of culture that enables elite domination by acting as barrier to critique and/or resistance. Hegemony means that the dominant culture is accepted as "normal" and as such, it naturalizes the historically arbitrary to render class domination as natural, normal and in the best interests of all. It's "common sense," and anyone who might question the dominant system appears bizarre, pathological, immature or "crazy." Until they don't. in order to appear credible, they need to gain position in the hierarchy of values and ideas. These agents of change are "organic intellectuals". Coming from the subaltern classes, they understand the life experiences and emotional dispositions of the everyday people. Quite often trained in critical philosophy, "organics" attempt to launch "wars of position" to remove the cloak of common sense and expose dominant values as nothing more than the arbitrary and unfair self-serving interests of the ruling class. Once everyday people can reject these values, they can establish a new normal of more progressive and inclusive values (Langman, 2015). Indeed domination, buttressed by ideology, ill serves the people who remain alienated, dominated and dehumanized. The cultural barriers to social change further rest upon an underlying character structure that has generally internalized the hegemonic values of ruling class. Consequently, as we have seen, "motivated reasoning" means facts, figures, logic, and reasoned analysis and even pragmatic self-interest play little role in politics as Machiavelli observed long ago. At the same time, it should be noted, that for Habermas (1975) legitimation crises at the level of system migrate into the "life worlds" of emotions and identities, and trigger any number of negative emotions, including anger, hostility, resentment and indignation. At such times, people often withdraw their loyalties from the dominant, hegemonic system, such that crises offer critical periods of potential self-reflection and

openness to critiques that may envision alternatives. At such times large numbers of people often support, if not join social movements. Seemingly small
shifts of social character can produce significant social change. The leader
who seemed so powerful or so normal suddenly seems illegitimate and helpless, and in a matter of days or weeks a mass movement overthrows a dictator
who held power for decades.

Social Movement Organizations

The US currently lacks a progressive political party or even coalitions of such
parties, but many small SMOs (social movement organizations) and NGOs
(nongovernmental organizations) represent a wide range of dissatisfied, angry and indignant views about economic inequality as well as racist and patriarchal traditions and values, yet as of now they have not united for mutual
reinforcement and collective action to achieve structural change. For example, various environmentalists and preservationists worry about pollution,
global warming, climate change and the very viability of the human species.
Environmentalists have not typically supported gay rights movements and/or
marijuana reform. In much the same way, feminist groups are not typically
concerned with banking regulations. Nevertheless it is noteworthy that many
such movements tend to be successful over time and actually able to implement many parts of their agendas. In less than ten years, as noted earlier, public opinion changed from decisive opposition against to decisive support for
gay marriage and the legalization of marijuana.

While these various challenges and contestations change laws, these efforts leave unchanged the fundamental nature of the political economy which
requires major transformation. Corporate capitalism has little problem with
successful women like Sheryl Sandburg or the former Hewlett-Packard CEO,
turned Republican presidential primary candidate Carly Fiorina who encourage women to be assertive in the corporate world. Martha Stewart not only
heads a major fashion, publishing and gourmet cooking empire, but has publicly admitted that she has had three-way sex trysts and claims she can roll a
joint with one hand. This has not hurt her rep or cred. And then there's always
Oprah in a class by herself. Nor does corporate capitalism have any problems
with gays, indeed Tim Cook, the CEO of Apple, the world's richest corporation,
is quite openly gay. Apple may very well be a progressive company in some ways
and a good place for some of the workers, but let's remember that Apple has
grossly profited from technologies developed through government research
such as Defense, Energy, NASA, and typically manufactures its products in the

Chinese sweatshops of Foxconn. Apple sales persons make about $30,000 per year while generating about $600,000 per year per person, the largest profits of any company in the world, which are safely parked in offshore banks to limit taxation on the 203 billion dollars it currently holds in cash and a total market value of 700 billion dollars (La Monica, 2015). Tim Cook declares that Apple has a very strong moral compass—whatever that means. Apparently, he believes that making products with child labor in China is not immoral. This demonstrates why a radical transformation is necessary, and for that to happen, many and various social movements would need to challenge the poverty, environmental degradation, exploitation, and human trafficking that are all part of the global capitalist system.

One final requirement for social change requires goals and visions of viable, working and successful alternatives to globalized, neoliberal capitalism and its rule by the rich. Surely the Romans thought their Empire invincible until Alaric and the Visigoths arrived at their gates. The British Empire once controlled so vast a global empire that the sun never set upon it. Hitler and ardent Nazis wholeheartedly believed that The Third Reich would last 1000 years. Twelve years later Berlin and the rest of Germany were piles of rubble. Nuclear bombs brutally marked the end of The Japanese Empire. The USSR went bankrupt after a costly 10-year war in Afghanistan and the extensive social fragmentation that resulted from years of internal discontent. So too the internal contradictions and discontent of America dispose radical transformation. Economic change will not happen for practical or any other reasons unless there are also changes in underlying social character such that the bearers of a new social ethic are part and parcel of social mobilizations that envision a different kind of America as a credible possibility, which we consider in the next chapter.

Summary

Capitalism, by definition, is an economic system based on the ownership of private property and free markets in which owners invest capital (that is, money) in order to make more money. There are two fundamental classes, the capitalist who own the wealth and means of production, and the workers who sell their labor power to create that wealth. Owners and workers have the same and markedly different interests at the same time. Both sides agree that the business should be successful, because if it fails, the owner loses the investment and the workers lose their jobs. Both lose their livelihood. The same class relations also produce the conflicting interests. Capitalists want the most work for the least cost (namely, the lowest wages). The workers seek better wages, better working conditions and better benefits. In actual practice, class divisions are not so clear. For example, as businesses grew and prospered in the early 20th Century, more and more "ordinary" Americans sought to buy stock in the growing corporations. With almost no regulation, the inevitable happened; the stock market collapsed and the economy fell into a long, dark depression. As the new President, FDR instituted a myriad of government programs and projects, as well as a number of social reforms. The economy stumbled up and down for a few years despite the best efforts until World War II. Given the government's ability to print money and sell War Bonds, the idled factories again began to whir with the production of war goods and in a relatively short time the United States had built a huge war machine, vastly more productive than that of the Axis. The famous Willow Run factory, over a mile long, was able to produce B-24 bombers on an assembly line in record speed, giving it the name as the "arsenal of democracy." About one-third of its workers were women, including the iconic Rosie the Riveter. And as mentioned, women piloted these planes to combat zones.

After the United States and its allies won, several important consequences ensued. Between pent-up demand, huge savings accounts and the G.I. bill, the country finally prospered, consumerism flourished and suburban housing mushroomed a vast highway Interstate network that connected Maine to California and Florida to Oregon and along the way, enabled the explosion of suburbs around the major cities. Suburbs, like mass media, consistently foster stupidity but that's a different book. As the United States built up itself, it also rebuilt the shattered economies of Europe and Japan and in fact created the conditions that would enable global trade to proceed and eventually explode. In 1944, the Bretton Woods conference established the US dollar as the global currency, to replace the Pound Sterling. Secondarily, English replaced French as the language of global diplomacy and commerce. Bretton Woods laid the foundations for what would later become the World Bank, the IMF, and the WTO. It was thought that developing nations would build up their economies and collectively create a better more peaceful world-based on capitalism. Of course that "better world" is primarily better for capitalist profits, but also for US prosperity since the US was the only economy to emerge intact from World War II—another clear case of American exceptionalism. Ironically, the rebuilt economies of Europe and Japan brought cheaper imported goods to the US and began, slowly at first, the long trend toward offshoring and downsizing. The last but less noticed consequence of WWII was the institutionalization of military spending and the growth of what President Eisenhower warned as the danger of the military-industrial complex that would eventually become the "permanent war economy." Overall, we see that the distribution of wealth is not simply an outcome of cooperation and conflict between particular owners and their workers, but much more broadly a political and economic negotiation and struggle between the owner and worker classes as a whole. Government has historically played the role of arbiter (if mostly in favor of the capitalists) to enact policies that distribute wealth in various ways, such as public investment in education, infrastructure (highways, bridges, schools, utilities etc.) and defense. All classes benefit from such distributions of wealth even if the capitalists must pay more taxes now, the economy grows more reliably in the long run.

From 1945 through the 70s, all seemed well as growing corporations provided secure, stable, well-paying jobs with clear-cut career progressions for millions of (mostly male) managers who wore gray flannel suits along with the packaged smiles of "cheerful robots" who exchanged empty conformity and loyalty to the company for comfortable incomes. And the workers thrived. With unionization, workers could make decent incomes with decent benefits and they could buy houses, cars and some even managed to buy vacation homes and small boats. Perhaps best of all, both workers and managers could afford to schlep their families to Disneyland where they could frolic in simulated worlds of a magical kingdom, an animal kingdom, Hollywood, and experimental prototype communities. Consumerism flourished and thick steaks sizzled on backyard barbecues.

But soon the glorious outcomes of World War II would come back to haunt the nation. The terms of Bretton Woods meant that once the factories and mills of Europe and Japan were rebuilt, and given the exchange rates, slowly but surely more and more cheap imports came to the United States and as time went on, the quality of these imports, from steel ingots to cars, was often higher than what was domestically produced. Once the world standard for style and power and object of desire worldwide, American cars fell behind in both style and quality to European and Japanese cars that seemed to last two to three or many times longer than their American counterparts. By the late 70s, the globalization of the economy with its seamless, de-territorialized world market became more and more evident as more and more well paid jobs were lost through both automation and imports that began to impact the domestic job markets. 1980 conveniently marks the point when average incomes for most Americans began to stagnate, for some Americans jobs were becoming more and scarce and their incomes began to decline to precipitous levels. At the same time, the incomes of the elites began to grow many fold and indeed their wealth rocketed skyward faster than the space shuttle. Moreover, given the nature of globalization more and more wealth and profits were to be found in finance, speculation, currency trading, banking, insurance, mergers and acquisitions and hedge funds-none of which required many workers or an actual product. But another consequence of globalization was the shifting of profits to offshore banks that reduced the treasuries of both the nation and many local communities. Meanwhile, the ever growing, military-industrial complex enabled a very large, very well-equipped, powerful military and indeed foolhardy forms of military interventionism into Vietnam, Afghanistan, Iraq and Libya, and elsewhere along with close to 1,000 military bases throughout the world.

Following the election of Reagan, the simulation of the tough cowboy of the Monomyth who would save the endangered community, brought a number of changes, especially supply side economics that promised that tax cuts would make everyone rich. Meanwhile, the military grew, billions were wasted on his star wars anti-missile project and other military boondoggles, such as retrofitting the Iowa and North Carolina, two World War II battleships. Just the weapons we need for fighting guerillas and militias with no fixed location or even membership. The military now consumes more than half of the nation's income taxes. The result was a gradual deterioration of the infrastructure, rusting bridges, and deteriorating schools. By the early 21st Century, the invasion of Iraq exposed these legacies with a wasteful, immoral, unnecessary and pointless war. Nevertheless, by now a new class of millionaires and billionaires ascended to the pinnacles of economic power and accumulated more and more of the national wealth, some of which was used to consolidate political power. Just as businessman turned President Herbert Hoover had proven himself to be completely inept, so too would failed businessman Bush II preside over the greatest implosion of the economy since 1929.

It is now evident to almost anyone and everyone that the great Colossus of the United States is falling apart, its demise due not to a single cause or treacherous, foreign enemy, but death by 1,000 failures. Given that the plutocracy owns the government and cannot or will not manage it effectively, what is to be done?

49 Shades of Social Character and One More on the Way

American social character, as currently constructed, serves to reproduce and sustain a variety of contradictions of its political economy that not only engender considerable pain and suffering, but undermine America's capitalist system and at the same time, thwarts the very progressive change that might ameliorate economic and cultural adversities. But class conflicts may not be the moving force of history as such, those conflicts and contradictions need to foster actions and movements and as we have argued, underlying social character can serve as the switchman on the track of history, as a barrier or catalyst for change, and if a catalyst for change that enables social mobilizations, will they be progressive, reactionary, or both? As we have argued, certain fundamental polarities of American social character shaped by the early colonial and early national conditions and experiences not only undermine America and prompt its current descent, but act as barriers to prevent the changes that would set us on a different, progressive direction that would not only be better for most Americans, but the entire planet. A fundamental characterological shift is needed, and we have claimed, that shift is in process. We believe that individualism must give way to privileging the community and common good, the materially based needs for riches must be to be transformed to seek richness of needs, aggression and violence must be tempered by empathy and compassion, its authoritarian hellfire, damnation and hierarchal religions must fade to create spaces for humanistic, egalitarian inclusive communities of meaning. Meanwhile the notion of a divinely blessed, exceptional America must understand that in a multi polar world, the USA cannot afford its bloated military budgets, with forces spread throughout the world. The USA must end its self-designation as policemen, judge, jury and executioner, intervening everywhere, fostering hate, resentment and blowback. The beacon of the "city on the hill" must dim.

Can Reforms Reform?

Outside the miniscule community of the academic left, what little dissent and critique of the system today is a primarily a mixture of neo-Keynesian economics and calls for the expansions of the welfare state. These have been the mantras of Krugman, Reich or Galbraith for the last decade. For the most part, their analyses of what's wrong with neoliberalism and the extreme concentrations of wealth, the myths of austerity, the distorted views of Republican politicians are spot on, at least as far as they go, which is the reform of capitalism, namely better laws, more generous benefits and breaking up big banks. But they cannot get to the root of the problems that are inherent to capitalism, nor do they call for its transcendence. Moreover, as desirable as counter cyclic government spending (pump priming) may be, along with free college tuition, universal health care and increased benefits to the poor, such liberal reforms ultimately serve to sustain and reinforce the dominant capitalist system and thus repress and thwart emancipatory visions, and prevent the emergence of mass "mobilizations from below" that would transform property relationships and free human potential. Liberal critiques and reforms cannot address the fundamental problems that are inherent to capitalism, namely alienation, class domination/inequality, private property or ideological obfuscation etc. Indeed, such reforms quell and pacify and prevent change Yes, even the middle classes are suffering stagnation if not decline, and as much as we do favor such expansions of benefits, entitlements and redistributions of wealth through progressive taxation, and massive retrenchments of military spending and adventurism, liberal reforms essentially reproduce the system while they nearly guarantee the perpetuation of inequality while capital's economic crises will consistently reappear. The same vague dissatisfactions will continue as long as the same class war endures. Even with better pay and benefits, most workers would remain alienated. Meanwhile, the same corporate media will entertain, distract, and squelch or marginalize dissent. Liberal reforms, especially in modern consumer societies, more often than not dampen the sentiments for radical transformation of the system. In any case, they do not alleviate the inherent class contradictions of capitalism—workers want more of the profit and the owners want to keep it for themselves. Given the nature of contemporary reality, with the totalization of the digital panopticon and its highly armed and militarized police, a violent revolution such as 1917 or 1949 is not possible nor even desirable knowing its likely failure and massive loss of life even if successful. Rather, we suggest that widespread changes in social character that are taking place now can lead to the anger, indignation and outrage that erodes support for the system and create spaces for critiques of existing values and structures, as well as provides openness to alternative progressive visions, not just liberal reforms. Such failures of the system typically precede "great refusals" and growing embrace of counterhegemonic discourses from below that have been ignored by the culture while the longings for a better world remain repressed. We offer a truly radical approach for peaceful revolution, though we might suggest has been inspired by Marx, Reich, Marcuse and Fromm, the solutions to the contradictions of capitalism and its various discontents are not simply structural transformations, but inherently aspects of human emotions including quests for dignity and spirituality—the need for meaning and transcendence. As Fromm argued, only one reality applies to everyone, a reality that no one can escape. By the way, Benjamin Franklin was wrong—taxes are not universal. In the US, the richer someone is, the lower their tax rate. Death should be the one truth that unites people to celebrate life.

The Return of the Repressed

Perhaps the single and most important insight of psychoanalysis was the illumination of the multiple levels of consciousness and regions of the psyche. The ego (the I) was that which was conscious and of which we are self-aware, and what was especially important, the unconscious, or should we say unconscious processes within the id (It), namely desires, memories and even traumas, that are repressed and which, given the nature of repression, these thoughts and desires are not easily amenable to consciousness and self-awareness. Consciousness and overt behavior stand in marked contradiction to underlying unconscious; obsequious politeness might depend on the intense repression of aggression. We all know many authoritarians that seem like nice people, even fun, until certain topics come up and we have to say, how can they believe that shit? The brilliance of Freud was to understand the dynamics and dialectics of desire and repression that were not only were the basis of individual neuroses, but much of everyday life from love and work and the nature of religion, then on to dreams, slips of the tongue, forgetting, humor and group dynamics. Indeed Freud argued that civilization itself rested upon guilt based repression, lest uncontrolled desires were such that everyman would be a wolf to each other.

Freud described the "id" as a seething cauldron of contradictory desires. There resided archaic images and memories that had been suppressed, repressed and/or submerged by the demands of social life. These hidden depths of the psyche, its desires and defenses, played a major role in the individual's life as well as the being the repository of the typical social character that underpins and shapes the very nature of the society to provide assent or resistance to social, political or economic factors. There too are various wishes and dreams, and might we dare suggest, dreams and visions of a better, more gratifying society. But the main point is that there was more to personality than its overt manifestations; lurking below consciousness were prohibited sexual desires-often toward prohibited choices like mothers or fathers, and along with these erotic desires were the aggressive desires to slay the same sexed parent and take his/her place and most often, both such contradictory impulses existed side by side and were often mixed with guilt for just having such desires.

One of the primary functions of the rational ego (cognition), aided and abetted by the internalized voice of society, the superego, was to ward off the return of the repressed, to hold in check these powerful emotions and desires that had were tenuously controlled by social rules, but, whose potential eruption might threaten the stability of social order. Freud, like most cultural conservatives, regarded the poor as "irrational" and dangerous to the social order. The angry mobs of the irrational poor threatened the bourgeois social order in which conservatives see their inegalitarian society and privileged rank as natural, and normal, while the angry mobs threaten their status, power and wealth. But elites never see how their political-economic systems and resulting policies impact others and indeed foster the very "irrational mobs" and upheavals they disdain.[1] In sum, for Freud, for both the individual as well as civilization, one must be ever wary of the potential eruptions of powerful urges.

In this case, Freud made a major mistake. He conflated all of civilization with its capitalist forms. Thus what is repressed is not simply various destructive and antisocial desires, but American social character and its underlying polarities that emphasize individualism and competition and demand the repression of longings for attachment, meaning and community are specifically the requirements of capitalism, not civilization in general. Aggression and toughness must repress desires for empathy, kindness and compassion and a peaceful society. Authoritarian religious based moralities of hierarchy, repression and obedience must inhibit a more humanistic worldview and disdain the pleasures of wonder and awe. The human elements that capitalism in general, and its American form in particular represses are the very qualities of character that are essential to the psychosocial basis to imagine and enact an alternative society that is based on caring, sharing, empathy, cooperation, interdependence and democracy.

Individualism, especially its American forms, have required the repression of basic human desires for connection and attachments to others and indeed the inability to be dependent and simultaneously grateful for aid reinforces both narcissism and isolation. Philip Slater (1970) especially emphasized the

---

1   In social movement theory and research today, the angry mob theory has about as much value as might phrenology to neurology or the heliocentric view of the universe to astronomy.

need for connection to community, and saw that the nature of American individualism, its competition, materialism and compulsions to work in order to consume, has frustrated

> the desire for community. To live in trust, cooperation, and friendship; the desire for engagement, to come directly to grips with one's social and physical environment; and the desire for dependence, to share responsibility for the control of one's impulses and the direction of one's life.
> SLATER, 1970 p. 8

In short, George Carlin captures the same idea—I need a car, so I can get to work, so I can make payments on the car—there just isn't any time for meaningful connections in a routine that serves the interests of consumerism and profit. Moreover as we have also seen, between the valorization of individualism and changing nature of work in which jobs are now episodic in which people are constantly on the move, the fear that dependency on others is a sign of weakness, further mitigates against the establishment of community and group loyalty. This was a central aspect of what Sennett (1998) deemed the corrosion of character.

In a very similar way, as we have seen, the phallic aggressive nature of the tough American social character was deeply rooted in its Puritanism that required unchosen infidels and heathens be banished if not slain redemptive violence became essential to justify the conquests of other people and indeed, phallic aggression became a highly regarded, positive aspect of male self-esteem via kicking ass or taking pain. Christian Kyle took pride in "killing ragheads" while John McCain boasted of his having suffered as a tortured prisoner. But beneath the toughness and aggression of American phallic aggression is a masculinist response to the fear of death and annihilation, the ultimate fears of all humanity. Thus American masculinity requires the repression of what is considered weak and feminine, namely the softer, tender qualities of empathy, caring, nurturance, vulnerability, and sharing (all feminist responses to the fear of death) in phallocentric terms mean, passivity, dependency, and weakness. As we noted in our discussion of football, one of the greatest insults to an American man is to be called a pussy. "Real men" get pussy, they don't act like one. As the FBI UCR shows, and the national family surveys corroborate, violent crime in America is at a 40-some year low. Most criminologists are a bit stumped to explain the declining crime rates. The typical explanations of more severe punishments, better law enforcement, and surveillance generally fail to stand up to scientific scrutiny even if such "explanations" do resonate with large numbers of more conservative authoritarians who support these measures. We offer another interpretation, that dynamic character change now taking place has reduced the status of the phallic aggressive warrior, the monomythic hero appears less desirable especially for millennial youth who provide ever less support for aggressive militarism or gun ownership. At the same time, younger men reject the phallic aggressive male, typically quite patriarchal, as a desirable role model. In the same way, younger women prefer kindness, empathy, caring and tenderness rather than six-pack abs, bulging biceps, tremendous triceps and high definition deltoids and an open carry AR-15. Indeed we would suggest that the current fanaticism over gun ownership is much deeper than fear of crime, violence, terrorism/ISIS or Obama's goon squads coming to take away your "liberty," but an underlying fear of losing one's masculinity. In the 19th Century playing football did it, and today, having a gun makes you a tough guy. Given what we have seen about changing gender roles among younger men, we understand how packing heat is the sign of having a big dick—mostly for men over about 45. Sadly we must tell the various would be gunslingers, cowboys, sharp shooters and "patriots" of American society that having a gun or three won't preserve patriarchy nor make you more courageous or more attractive. Indeed when we look at the number of gun accidents, one's own gun is far more likely to do harm to one's own manhood than thwart any alleged attack from Islamic terrorists or Mexican rapists.

Historically, religion has provided solidarity and cohesion that has held groups together. As we earlier noted for de Tocqueville, anticipating Durkheim, this was one reason for the persistence of religion as a central quality of American character and that has been embedded within its social character. Moreover, religion provides a framework of explanations that gives one's life meaning, provides moral codes that would regulate behavior to insure tranquility, grants a collective identity and proffers explanations for the distributions of fortune. All of this tells us how to live, what's important, and why, so that life becomes more important than death.

Can we imagine some sort of broad religion today that incorporates all the many existing religions without diminishing any of them? What has been heretofore repressed for most of American history, we will simply call the "Commune." What American culture has suppressed and its social character has repressed are the unconscious longings for an egalitarian, democratic community that has been thwarted by individualism, materialism, and authoritarianism at both collective and individual levels. What has been repressed are desires for empathy, kindness, tenderness and compassion. What has been repressed, and indeed policed, is the freedom for self-fulfillment, to paraphrase Marx, the self-fulfillment of each must depend on the self-fulfillment of all. Thus we welcome that return of the repressed, that has been a part of American history, culture and social character that enables a progressive regression in the service of the ego.

Progressive Regression in the Service of Humanity

In classical psychoanalytic theory, regression was a defensive operation, an attempt to avoid dealing with a difficult present reality by psychologically regressing returning to an earlier, however immature stage of development that might well be repressed. It was seen as a pathological adaptation, an attempt to psychologically regress, to return to childhood to avoid painful adult realities. But with later developments in psychoanalytic theory, namely the rise of ego psychology, another, more positive view emerged, "regression in the service of the ego." In a pioneering psychoanalytic study of art, Ernst Kris et. al (1952) argue that certain forms of regression to childhood innocence provide a sense of security, love and trust by recapturing certain "lost" childhood aspirations and sincere experiences. Most importantly, such regressions enabled a recovery of untapped inner resources and creative potential. The critical question is whether or not a person can control the moments of regression and retain the mature emotions and intellect of an adult so that preverbal primary process imagery based on the repressed pleasure principle, along with archaic desires could provide inspiration that could be incorporated into creative processes in the real world. In other words, can we rediscover the unpretentious enthusiasm of youth and yet retain the wisdom of adulthood? Otherwise, regression would result in child-like states or escape into fantasy that contributes nothing to real life in the present. This moment of regression to recapture images and experiences of earlier development has been an essential aspect of certain genres of modern art as seen for example in Dada, surrealism, and a great deal of the resurrection of childhood experience can be evident in the work of Calder, Ernst, Klee, Miro, Dali, Man Ray, Kandinsky and Chagall. In literature, Proust's *Remembrance of Things Past* remains the gold standard. Walt Disney commodified the regressive processes to reap billions of dollars gratifying the wish fulfillments of children and adults regressing for a time to the simple pleasures and exuberance of childhood.

While such "regressions in the service of the ego" may well be quite salient for understanding artistic works and even useful in psychotherapy, social structures cannot exist without an alternative realm where the transgressive, the forbidden, the dangerous and impure are held in abeyance apart from the "normal" society. These betwixt and between "liminal zones" (Turner, 1995) usually sequester potentially disruptive challenges to the established order of society. Every society has some level of discontent, contradictions and repressed desires that seek gratification, so every society produces some degree of challenge to itself, but at the same time the liminal zones typically encapsulate them to preserve the norms and structures of the society. There are however, episodic moments such as carnivals that episodically tolerate if not celebrate the eruptions of the transgressive into the normative and migrations of the transgressive into the mainstreams for a few days. This can sometimes be seen in much more momentous events such as revolutions when heretofore suppressed economic and/or political transformations erupt, cast out the old and begin the new. Thus we would suggest that every society holds a forgotten, ignored, or submerged and repressed political history, a "political unconscious," while long banished from consciousness, although perhaps expressed as hopes, desires and dreams, that much like the muse for the individual artist, provide collective inspiration for creative social change. When those elements are progressive, when they contain hopes for a better saner, kinder world, a more humane, sane society, we call that "regression in the service of humanity," or what we can playfully call progressive regression. Needless to add, there are also reactionary regressions, convulsive moments of barbarism in the service of death, destruction and nihilism that culminate in the various expressions of genocide and mass destruction as for example in the Belgian Congo under King Leopold, in Nazi Germany—think *Kristallnacht* or the many spontaneous arrests and summary executions in Cambodia where about one fourth of the population was murdered under Pol Pot or in Rwanda, or on the island of East Timor when Indonesia invaded to suppress a popular democratic revolt, or the arbitrary beating, shooting, and strangulation of Black people by law enforcement in the United States today.

Many people, especially older authoritarians may employ "motivated reasoning" to deny, split, or simply reject any serious critique of American capitalism or imperialism. They are likely to celebrate, rather than castigate the ruthless social dominators who game the system or the authoritarians who kill Black people in the streets. But today the hopes for neo-liberalism are beginning to fade. Sooner or later the realities of national descent and growing inequality will force collective pressures of change to realize an alternative, a "sane society." When we began our argument, we claimed the "fault was not in our stars, but in ourselves." So too, buried in our past lie the outlines of alternatives, more fulfilling society are already here, deeply submerged within our history and repressed within our character.

For various reasons, the dominant intellectuals in any society, to sustain the ruling hegemony from which they benefit as leading "intellectuals," (who often accrue large paychecks or grants) must distort, deny, suppress or ignore certain legacies of their own culture and history that support dissent and which might rekindle those sentiments and, perish the thought, foster change. For example, the mainstream media with its hired political pundits who exemplify and extoll the mainstream, ignored the Sanders primary campaign until massive crowds indicated a great deal of support. They then belittled his campaign as an exercise in futility, notwithstanding that most Americans support his positions, at least when not linked to socialism. His progressive socialism would not just challenge the billionaire class and corporate domination and other big money interests that control our society, but large-scale political economic challenges and changes might reveal how the corporate mass media and leading educational institutions serve as purveyors of hegemonic ideologies that are essential parts of the current system of domination providing the "official" versions of the past, extolling glorious "memories" that are distorted and cleansed of perfidy while peddling biased reporting and distorted analyses of current events. At one point Donald Trump had 81 times the press coverage of Sanders. But when it became evident that Sanders' left populist message resonated with many Americans, and he did well in early primaries, not only did the media take notice and regard him more seriously and more kindly when there was a chance that he actually had a chance at the nomination. The last thing any mainstream news want is rejection of requests for face time with leaders—whoever they may be.

Meanwhile, the "elite" universities create and disseminate knowledge according to the canons, meaning to extol "one dimensional" thought that prepares students to assume positions of power and reproduce the systems of power. In our discipline of sociology, what is "significant" is not a critique of inequality and unbridled power, let alone capitalism, but the statistical model in which correlations are "significant" if at the .05 level, or better yet, .01. Whether those numbers show anything interesting is irrelevant. All that matters is that they were collected and analyzed with correct methodological technique. The liminal areas of dissent in higher education in the US are not located within the big name prestigious universities that train the next generations of social dominators, but the ones of lower status where marginalized professors depend far less on grants in service of power and can offer more trenchant critiques of current society.

For progressives, the political unconscious contains collective memories of dissent, conflict, resistance, and a number of victories against the forces of domination. Ralph Young (2015) presented a detailed history of dissent in America beginning as did we with Ann Hutchison and ending with the contemporary Tea Party and Occupy movements to show that far from the myths of a peaceful and harmonious society, from the colonial times to the present, dissent, conflict, contestation and change drive US history. Usually, the heroes and leaders on the progressive side are forgotten, demonized, or rewritten to serve established power. Recently, the right-wing Tea Party and religious conservatives tried to invoke Martin Luther King as their ally to start a war with

Iran, and use popular songs from the group REM as theme music. MLK strongly opposed the war in Vietnam as a war of imperialism. REM, which has stood for and played benefits for many progressive causes, including gay and transgender rights, issued a strong condemnation of the right-wing trying to turn their song "It's the end of the world as we know it" into a right-wing anthem. Michael Stipe, the lead singer, seems rather clear on the matter when he tweeted "Go fuck yourselves, the lot of you, you sad, attention grabbing, power hungry little men. Do not use our music or my voice for your moronic charade of a campaign." REM bandmate Mike Mills added succinctly, "cease and desist"—a clear legal warning (Krieg, 2015). Michael Stipe probably feels a lot less emotionally repressed. He also shows awareness of the type of argument that we are making. The Tea Party event featured Donald Trump, the new symbol of white supremacy and authoritarian power for the angry "little men," fearful of their waning power based on race and gender, who face economic uncertainty and seek reassurance and purpose through association with power they can never wield themselves. We use the term "little men" decidedly, since that term was used by Wilhelm Reich to describe the frightened "little men" who find solace in identification with and support of authoritarian power. For Reich, these are the ones who

> ... let the powerful demand power "for the little man." But you yourself are silent. You provide powerful men with more power or choose weak, malignant men to represent you. And you discover too late that you are always the dupe .... A little man does not know he is little and is afraid to know. He hides his pettiness and narrowness behind illusions of strength and greatness, someone else's strength and greatness. Hess proud of his great generals but not of himself. He admires an idea he has not had, and has few himself. The less he understands something, the more firmly he believes in it. And the better he understands an idea, the less he believes in it. ... a *little man does not know he is little and is afraid to know* ...
> REICH, (1990 [1946]) p. 141[2]

Reich does not blame the "little men" who are indeed victims of the system, but understands how the shaping of their authoritarian character structures disposes submission to power as a means of assuaging anxieties about one's powerlessness and isolation. Given the salience of phallic aggression for the

---

2 Reich was influenced by the novelist, Hans Fallada, whose novel, *Little Man What Now?* written in 1932 foretold the appeal and rise of Hitler.

authoritarian personality, the notion of powerless "little men" points to the underlying castration anxiety, a derivative of the fear of death and annihilation that prompts identification with the powerful. This is one form of "identification with the aggressor." Fromm saw "authoritarian" aggression as a mechanism of escape from powerlessness. We all need a sense of agency, recognition and respect. The various, mixes of evangelicals, white populists and Tea Partiers, seek that security, agency recognition and respect through submission and service to power. But this acquiescence to power is learned quite early in life (Tagar et al., 2014), and for many people, the initial submission to power is the submission to powerful males, starting with submission to the all-powerful father, God in Heaven and their own "strict father." Few values voters can or want to see how they were duped by the mega-rich to gain their votes to keep their taxes low, regulations few and incomes in the stratosphere. Again we would note that given the salience for their values, meanings and very identities, they could not tolerate the notion that they had been had.[3] Despite their best efforts, submission to authority does not replace or restore a sense of security; it only suppresses the feelings of anxiety and fear, which threaten to reappear if the authority figure ever appears weak or the authoritarian feels threatened by anyone or anything different or unfamiliar.

In place of submission to hierarchical power, we suggest a progressive alternative based on equality, democracy, freedom, sharing, caring and empathy to provide more gratifying social relationships and in turn, genuine security, agency and respect through egalitarian cooperation and service to the community. The growing economic, political and cultural adversities of our times, evoke strong emotions of fear, anger and indignation and promote what might be called the "escape from the present" and attempts to resurrect a mythical past. While we cannot return to the past, it may hold insights that are still useful. We need to re-examine our own history. different versions of American history and "memories" of the past teach different lessons for the present. Perhaps the most widely known is the authoritarian, conservative, often religiously tinged version in which the "imagined community" of Americans memory began when ardent Christians, aka the founding fathers, inspired by the Bible, crafted a constitution declaring America a Christian country. It's warm, loving communities were most often tied to a Church that was perhaps located in the

---

3   There are some journalistic and anecdotal accounts that during Bush II's presidency, when religious leaders like Falwell and Robertson departed from meetings, people like Cheney and Rove made fun of them. Similarly, when discussing a bill coming up in the House, and the Whitehouse was trying to figure out how to get popular support, Tom DeLay reportedly said, just get to their ministers, those dumb fucks will believe anything the ministers tell them.

central square that might also have an old cannon or tank. That community existed at a pristine time when there was economic security, moral decency, safety, harmony, conformity and cooperation. It was a time and place where everyone knew his or her place, accepted their roles and were happy with the way things were. Only despicable radicals, probably gay atheist commies and pussies, wished to change it. But that "constructed memory" is actually quite at variance from what was actually the case; such accounts are more fictional than historical. The frontier was not so pristine. Whire male authority exploited and oppressed women, Native-Americans, and slaves under very harsh conditions. The violence, bloodshed and subjugation of other peoples has been conveniently expunged, erased and "forgotten." Indeed in many states, Texas for example, school boards need to certify the "acceptability" of high school history texts, meaning they be cleansed of "uncomfortable" material like the genocide of the Native Americans, the oppression of slavery, slave revolts (how can slaves revolt if slavery never really existed?) labor struggles, or the civil rights movements. The more textbooks publishers sell, the more money they make, and sanitized texts sell the most because they offend the least number of people and pose no challenges to preconceived beliefs. It is of course always amazing that somehow thousands of students read subversive books like Howard Zinn's *A People's History of the United States.* Zinn and others chronicle the insurgent histories that recall moments of progressive mobilizations and changes in the past, the ones that we believe will serve us best in the present are those that arose from progressive solidarity, movements that fought for a common good. In other words, Zinn documents the moments of the "return of the repressed" that portends resistance, confrontation and in turn fundamental changes in social character that can in turn can transform the nature of the society.

And yes, we harken back to the ill-fated Paris Commune that remains an inspiring vision of an emancipatory political project, an example of what can be. When we talk about the repressed Commune, we're not suggesting that many Americans, even many progressive activists are aware of the events of Paris during three months of 1871. So here are the basics. When Prussia decisively defeated France in 1871, the Paris Commune arose in the capital city after the government and many business owners fled. The Commune provided a glimpse of a "sane society" with democratic, participatory commerce and governance. Workers were allowed to take over enterprises deserted by their owners, but the owners had the right to compensation. Pawn shops were required to return the tools of workers. The Commune ended night work in bakeries. The Commune insisted on the complete separation of Church and State and keeping religion out of schools. They would abolish standing armies in favor of people's armies, with democratic control of whether to make war and also over strategy. The communards set up schools and provided students with clothing, food and school materials. They established hospitals and canteens. In only one month, the Commune had rallied the ruined city and restored a decent standard of living.

The very success of the short-lived Commune would be its downfall. The very existence of a worker ruled community that functioned quite well without private property was a threat to capitalism. It needed to be mercilessly crushed because the disdain for socialism is not based on rational factors, but on the requirement of private property in order to amass private wealth. The workers stood alone. Eventually the central government, lounging in Versailles until the smoke of battle cleared, joined with their former Prussian enemy, retook Paris and ended the short life of the Commune. In the process, 30,000 unarmed men, women, and children were slaughtered in the streets to terrorize the population into submission, as well as warn other French cities of what happens after an insurrection. While the short lived Paris Commune moved from event to memory, it bequeathed some real notions of a better alternative. Its basic ideas: freedom, equality and brotherhood, already promised by the French Revolution of 1789, joined with an actual democracy, worker rule, worker ownership of enterprises and industries, syndicalism and participatory governance. This model of worker owned and managed enterprises repeated in Spain, especially Catalonia, the most industrialized part of the country. Following the principles of the Paris Commune, the self-management of enterprises extended to many sectors of the economy such as railways, streetcars, buses, taxicabs, shipping, electric light and power companies, gasworks and waterworks, engineering and automobile assembly plants, mines, mills, factories, food-processing plants, theaters, newspapers, bars, hotels, restaurants, department stores, and thousands of dwellings previously owned by the upper classes (Bolloten, 1991). The popular success of anarcho-syndicalism in Catalonia eventually led to growing political support. After several years of turmoil, in 1936 the people of Spain elected a coalition of Socialists and Anarchists, the Popular Front. But then, Francisco Franco led his fascist party and various monarchists into a rebellion, which became a Civil war between the Republicans and the Fascists. With far more popular support, the Republican coalition scored several military victories with only a volunteer army since most of the professional army had joined Franco's fascists. An iconic moment for the American left was the Abraham Lincoln brigade in which a number of Americans came to the aid of the Republicans. But meanwhile, the official US military blockaded Mexican ports to prevent Mexican troops and supplies from reaching the Republicans, and Hitler and Mussolini rallied to support their fellow fascist Franco. The *Luftwaffe* began its training in targeting civilians. Pablo Picasso immortalized the brutal carnage in his famous *Guernica*.

We cannot try to copy or restore the agendas of 1871 that existed for a brief moment 150 years or so ago in a very different cultural and historical context. Instead, the Paris Commune, like the Civil Rights and anti-war movements of the 1960s, and like the gay and transgender movements of today, and maybe the union movements of the early 1900s, endure as models and inspiration for the success of mobilizations from below and attempts to create an alternative society, or at least aspects of one. As we mentioned, what generally passes for the progressive left in the USA, consists of a number of highly fragmented, single-issue movements that lose much of their transformative energy when they fail to unite with other movements that challenge other elements of oppression. The kind of social movement that is needed for today requires an organized mass mobilization of various progressives that might seek to create a cohesive community that restores the Commons much like the citizens of Paris who claimed the resources and benefits that capitalists had appropriated and rendered what had been collective and communal into private ownership.

For us, the idea and ideals of the Commune revives those social psychological moment, qualities and institutional arrangements that emphasized democratic cooperation, sharing, and mutual support. We use the term Commune as a universal vision of a humanistic political economy that abolishes private property, overcomes alienated labor, establishes the egalitarian distribution of resources, and encourages the self-realization and dignity of all. But potentially subversive of slavery, domination, capitalism and elite domination, the notion of the Commons has been repressed and submerged by the rise of the traditional American social character which in turn facilitated the ascent of America to the pinnacle of power. Or did it? The Commune reminds us that the current system dominated by globalized financial organizations, depends on the ownership of private property which is the basis of the various forms of contemporary neo liberal globalization controlled by a small cadre of billionaire social dominators that however odious and nefarious, are given accolades and legitimacy by the media and generally accepted by many given its appeals to certain aspect of underlying social character.

As elite interests continue to shape the schools and cultural institutions to reproduce and valorize their hegemony, those institutions and values have repressed the nurturing aspects of social character, namely connections to others, mutual support, intimate caring, sharing and empathy. A vision of the Commune, recaptured by the "return of the repressed" hopefully provides the outlines and visions of a different kind of society that provides the social-psychological basis for a new kind of person living in a new kind of society, where locks on houses are no longer necessary and prisons nothing more than a phantom of a failed and long-abandoned system of domination.

The Commune as Moral Regeneration

Our notion of the Commune restores the community and a long tradition of concerns with the Commons. The Commune requires a participatory democracy in which ordinary citizens play a deciding role in the policies and practices of their government that impacts their lives. A number of cities, for example, now practice "participatory budgeting" where the citizens vote on fiscal allocations. The history and vision of the Commune suggests a moral regeneration with far more egalitarian distribution of resources, the overcoming of alienation, exploitation and domination. Alienation today is not simply based on wage labor. Political alienation is systematically produced in a "managed democracy" that primarily serves the elites and renders people powerless while providing "infotainment" ranging from electoral politics to political gossip all of which cloaks and mystifies the actual nature of contemporary capitalism and the power of its elite mendacious, narcissistic, self-proclaimed "masters of the universe" whose quests for grandiosity and power, are clearly indicated in exorbitant salaries and even more so exorbitant wealth that today has reached a level of obscene ostentation. Their attitudes toward the rest of the world is callous, indifferent and totally devoid of any capacity for empathy, caring or what might benefit the society. Today, in part due to the higher levels of education, the universality of the Internet, and despite their economic circumstances, many millennial's have traveled elsewhere in the world, perhaps as workers, and tourists, backpackers or volunteers in various philanthropic activities. One of the great benefits of such exposure to other societies is to give one a better perspective on one's own society. Spending time in Scandinavian and/or northern European cities makes one aware of the greater equality, the more generous the benefits social support programs, and the better conditions of work. Many surveys have shown that the Danish people are the happiest in the world, notwithstanding they are among the most highly taxed. There are clear-cut reasons why people living in the Scandinavian countries in which highly progressive taxes sustain a variety of government services that make people much happier. In contrast, our crass and unbridled individualism and associated materialism joined with neoliberal global capital undermine the system in so many ways that impact the everyday lives of most Americans, especially the millennial's, who are struggling. And while the USA provides among the miserly social benefits and entitlements, its reactionary conservatives would further reduce or privatize them. We noted that the fervor of American exceptionalism is waning along with the decline of its preeminence. Yes, we remain a desirable destination for many people, whether poor peasants seeking any kind of menial job, or students seeking advanced, technical or scientific educations, or refugees from war, poverty or discrimination. The US remains a magnet for various highly educated professionals who can still make much more money in the United States that in their home countries. But the immigration of many unskilled and a few highly skilled workers does very little to reverse the trends we have been discussing. Most important for our argument, is that the waning of American exceptionalism despite the constant proclamations and sound bites of its continued greatness from politicians of all stripes, masks a deeper change in social character and the growing desire by Americans is to become a country devoted more to the quality of life rather than costly military bases all over the world, along with vast amounts of resources dedicated to a perpetual state of war that benefits only the defense contractors.

Toward a Sane Society: Step One-Transforming the Political Economy

The American social character, normative values and political economic hierarchy reinforce each other. As Fromm (1990 [1955]) noted, in face of spreading markets, the "receptive character" was displaced by the "hoarding character" which in turn facilitated large scale industrial capitalism, and created the next type, the marketing character. This person seeks personal gain by telling everyone what they want to hear. The prototypical form is the salesperson who must sell him or herself in order to sell the product or service. The modern consumer is an expression of the marketing type, someone who shops for his or her identity, finding models of desirable selfhood, often from mass media and quite often celebrities, suggesting sexual gratifications, as we earlier mentioned. He or she then flocks to the malls, or more typically today goes to a favored website to purchase a "branded identity" (Klein, 2000). The American version of the hoarding type emerged from small businesses and farms, and quite readily morphed into the marketing character with the rise of industrialization, corporate capitalism, and, after mass mediated images and adverts, as asceticism was undermined, consumerism flourished while the pseudo-gratifications of false needs masked the alienation, ennui and emptiness of capitalism and incorporated people into the society. And for a while, many accepted financialized, neoliberal globalization-until its impacts were felt. Yet globalization further encouraged the marketing and consumer types, which requires ample pay and free time in order to shop for fulfillment. In the 1945–1980 period, this connection between the consumer and social rewards worked well enough. But as wages began to stagnate if not decline, not only did consumerism collapse, but it also revealed the vacuity of the system. Money buys almost everything, but not happiness. People need more than pay check to find friends, meaning and fulfillment. But this has been known by sages, philosophers and even religious leaders throughout history. In his later years, Erich Fromm became concerned with Zen Buddhism and one of the main principles of Zen is dispelling the illusions that material riches bring one happiness. Buddha himself, raised in a privileged family, abandoned the pursuit of material wealth for the sake of inner fulfillment.

Exploitation has existed for thousands of years. Most of the great civilizations of antiquity depended on slave labor, much as did the antebellum South. Under capitalism, the wage laborer gains no recognition or respect on the basis of what he or she produced, or the ancillary business services he or she provided (Sennett, 2006; 1998). In the process of work, the wage workers loses their uniquely human qualities so that their productive efforts not only make money for someone else, but most workers derive no gratification from the work they do that fills the coffers of others. In other words, alienated labor distorts, truncates and warps the self, negates a sense of agency and empowerment, erodes community and collective recognition of humanity and each other. Just as we have become objects at work just like the machines, now automated and computerized, we also view each other as objects. The nature of capitalism, resting upon alienated labor appropriated by the property owning class thwarts the unique capacity for humans to find dignity, understood as both a desire and the goal of that desire (Langman, 2015). Dignity differs from pride, self-esteem, or even self-realization because dignity only develops from social relations of mutual respect, from the various actions which not only provide dignity, but bring dignity to others. Mutual respect was fairly typical in pre-modern societies where giving away goods, e.g. the potlatch ceremony or sharing the results of the hunt, benefits the group as well as oneself.

In one of the most memorable scenes from the Wizard of Oz, Glinda the good witch told Dorothy that she had the power to return to Kansas all the time. Given what has happened to Kansas today, many people have been happy to leave (Mann, 2014) maybe as soon as they realized they were in fact free to go. Thus we would suggest that the elements of a humanistic, sane society have been present all the time. Howard Zinn (2005 [1980]) in *A People's History of the United States* illuminated the often overlooked if not ignored and denied history of ordinary people and their many struggles against the rich and powerful.

He provided us with a detailed history of the power of the rich to craft a self-serving Constitution, to foster territorial expansion and sustain imperialism that would bring them vast economic benefits. But at the same time frontiersmen and agrarian farmers joined populist uprisings /or worker strikes. Inspired by Zinn, Dunbar-Ortiz (2014) gives us a much more recent *Indigenous Peoples' History of the United States*. History texts rarely mention progressive uprisings, from Bacon's Rebellion in 1676 to Occupy (Loewen, 2009). Similarly, John Curl (2009) provides a history of the various kinds of communes, collectives and co-ops that have been present in the United States since the very beginning, indeed he notes that most of the Native American tribes were organized on the basis of communities that controlled their Commons. The early settlers had long shared housebuilding, barn raising, plowing and planting each other's fields, harvesting corn, quilting, sewing and other essential functions. Given the vagaries of health and death, families often helped widows and widowers raise their children. Curl further argues that cooperation, not competition re-sounded as the dominant chord across the continent. The real conflict symbolized in the Boston Tea Party was not directed against the Crown, but against the British East India Tea Company and its monopoly that forced cooperatives out of business. Benjamin Franklin organized the first community based subscription library as well as a mutual aid society. The Union Fire Company that was a forerunner of other mutual insurance companies.

One of the qualities that de Tocqueville admired about Americans was their ability to work together and collectively form various associations devoted to the common good, as well as the propensity for "civic activism" in which people took it upon themselves to work together for the good of community and build roads, bridges, and dams.[4] In Europe this required petitioning a distant government. Curl further documents the important role of various worker communes and co-ops in the 19th Century which led to the formation of labor unions that naturally the courts, part of the system of State coercion, deemed illegal restraints upon trade. When many co-ops such as stores, building associations, and banking associations actually became competitive with capitalist enterprises, the capitalists did everything they could to undermine them, denying them raw materials and services. Many abolitionists such as Horace Greeley and Frederick Douglass also supported co-op movements. With the westward expansion, especially after the Homestead Act of 1862, as farming

---

4   Like perhaps Jefferson or present day conservatives, he disdained central power as a threat to local power and autonomy. But in the 1820s, there was no need for airports, eight-lane bridges a mile long or mass transportation systems that cost billions of dollars and require armies of workers, specialized engineering, and heavy machinery.

moved West various cooperative movements arose, especially the Granges beginning in 1868 when the Minnesota Grange emerged as collective purchasing
and marketing agents. They operated a number of banks, warehouses, grain
elevators factories, brick yards, rail and ship transportation. These various mutual aid societies and co-ops proliferated throughout the farm belt.

As capitalist industries began to flourish after the Civil War, poorly paid
workers, toiling for long hours, under adverse conditions, began to organize
and unionize and confronted business. The radical history of the Knights of
Labor and the Wobblies (IWW-the Industrial Workers of the World) have faded into obscurity in the hands of most historians. Many such union activities
were successful, at least until 1878 when Rutherford B. Hayes turned Federal
troops on the strikers. One of the important strikes in American history, in
which hundreds of thousands of workers fighting for an eight hour day culminated in Haymarket Square where the police attempted to break up the rally, a
bomb went off leading to police violence throughout the country. Urban police
forces and private security companies such as the Pinkerton's and Wells Fargo
emerged to repress dissidents, strikers and radicals, and secure the property of
wealthy people and companies, rather than serve the people in general. Today
the passage of "right to work laws" as well as automation and import substitu-
tion have decimated the labor unions. Curl continued to note the importance
of co-ops during the New Deal in which the government attempted to provide
electricity (REA, TVA) to electricity cooperatives. In contrast to mainstream
accounts, the tapestry of US history is woven with the day-to-day struggles
of hundreds of millions of ordinary people for better lives. Mutual-aid organizations such as cooperatives and unions have always been near the heart of
those struggles.

Various forms of economic democracy have been part and parcel of American history, but for the reasons we have suggested, this part of history has been
denied, submerged, and repressed in order legitimate the dominant narrative
of heroic capitalists and triumphant armies crushing workers, taming the land,
and building the greatest nation on earth. Cooperatives, communes and worker owned enterprises are not simply historical curiosities. Little noted in either
classrooms or the mass media, over 120 million Americans belong to various
kinds of co-ops, over 30% of the population. Co-ops produce about 20% of
US electricity (Zeese and Flowers, 2013). The rise of co-ops is at the forefront
of challenging the domination of large corporations if not the very nature of
private property itself. This legacy of co-ops, cooperatives, mutual aid societies, and labor unions offers the foundations for a different future. Furthermore,
those submerged aspects of our economic history are quite compatible with
cooperative, sharing and caring aspects of social character that have also been

repressed and submerged. They directly challenge the dominant system of private banking and the usurpation of government power through which the top .01% control the nation.

Toward a Sane Society: Step 2-Democratizing Democracy

In place of forced servitude in order to generate profit, work should arise from voluntary organizations and social attachments to the Commons in order to attain collective prosperity rather than a private paycheck. This would also foster a more genuine democracy rather than the mere appearances of democracy such as its current system with illusory choices and options that obscures the ruling class domination of the State while providing vast rewards and emotional gratifications for individual success over and against others. As we have noted, social dominators, such as many of the as CEOs, may profit more from firing workers than from increasing sales, and will do so, ruining the lives and *communitas* of workers without a shred of empathy or remorse. Instead, coops and cooperatives celebrate collective success. Even when the economy tanked after 2008, the Mondragon cooperative may have cut hours and shifted worker-owners to other enterprises, but not a single one lost his/her job.

Emotional appeals to the underlying values of American social character may not be conscious. Ironically, the billionaire Donald Trump surged to the top of Republican candidates because he truthfully and openly speaks the language of power, domination, racism and sexism, which resonates with many angry white people with moderate to strong authoritarian character structures, but this also reveals how insincere and phony his rivals are. He dared tell the people that money buys politicians, which brought Bill and Hillary Clinton to his wedding. The other Republicans share Trump's commitment to corporate domination, of course, and he dared reveal their appeals to patriotism and moralism for the lies they are. Most politician are bought and paid for. While this has long been the case, in the last few years, especially since Citizens United, the purchase of politicians is now quite transparent. Similarly, Bernie Sanders revealed the same thing, pointing out how Hillary Clinton works closely with Wall Street, corporate America and the billionaire classes. Yes, she got hundreds of thousands of dollars from Goldman Sachs, but that did not impact her values. No, not at all. Despite her professed dislike for Wall Street, they sure do like her. Goldman-Sachs, the leader of the shadow banksters, paid her 675,000 for three speeches (Borchers, 2016). Either Goldman executives like to be lambasted, or Clinton tells them one thing and she tells the public something different. Whether Trump or Clinton wins the Presidency, their campaigns, in different ways, exposed the fact that our "democratic elections" are nothing more than shams, choices between two corporate-funded, wealthy candidates or those who would be sycophants to the wealthy. Deliberative democracy rests on a false understanding of the nature of human reason and the potentiality of rational forms of democratic debate, deliberation and discourse (Thompson, 2012). The problem is that people operate primarily from deeply ingrained value orientations and emotions that deliberative procedures cannot much address.

More specifically, small cadres of the capitalist elites occupy elected offices, such that the range of deliberation rarely goes beyond different strategies for growing wealth at the top. And many of the government offices concerned finance and commerce have revolving doors for executives from the big banks, especially Goldman-Sachs and Citibank. Yes, the Democratic Party is more open to progressive social reform and surely on social issues such as racial inclusion, gay rights or feminism (workplace discrimination or harassment, access to medical care, contraception or abortion). The inclusion of minorities, gay rights, are surely important reforms, and surely make lives better for many people. While such reforms are valuable they do not really have impact upon class relationships nor challenge fundamental interests of the ruling class and their accumulation of wealth and profit. Such reforms maintain the fragmentation of progressive movements, because it reduces activism to claims about who should and who shouldn't receive benefits and legal protection, in other words, who should or shouldn't receive some scraps from the master's table. It is ironic that in America, voting for one or the other faction of the ruling class is regarded as democracy when in fact such beliefs, resonant with an underlying character disposed to embrace authoritarian social relations that submit to and accept the wealth of powerful individuals as a natural condition and thus beyond the realm of debate. This more than anything else, prohibits real rule of, by and for the people.

The tradition of violent suppression of progressive worker organizations also became a policy of the United States as a long history of labor struggles has shown. We contend that these struggles are not just over wages and working conditions, but suppressing progressive tendencies that might empower workers who might then directly challenge political power of the elites. The highly authoritarian social dominators are as much concerned with maintaining their status and power as increasing their profits, and massive mobilizations of progressive organizations could make those challenges. This might also be seen in the many attempts to invade, overthrow and embargo Cuba that were ultimately based on the fear that Cuban style socialism might become a model for other South American countries and perhaps even inspire progressive mobilizations in the United States, which has in fact started, quite independently of Cuba. As we have shown, the new Community of Latin American and Caribbean States specifically excludes the United States and displaces the US outpost of colonial power, the Organization of American States. Cuba, however, is not the model. Although Cuba developed a laudable system of education, healthcare, and greatly reduced poverty, the model for the Cuban economy is really state capitalism of the Soviet Union that sharply limited democracy. Notwithstanding its progressive rhetoric Cuba is still a top down society. As we previously noted, the worked owned and manage model of Mondragon or the Spanish anarcho-syndicalists is far more democratic and fulfilling to its workers.

In the US, the police violence is used to suppress the radically democratic, indeed the violence toward the anarchist OWS movements was quite disproportionate to any threat they might have. Like the communards of Paris, or anarchists of Spain, democratic, communal alternatives to capital need to be quickly and violently suppressed, lest they become an inspiration for others and ignite widespread popular revolts. Again we are reminded of what Slater (1970) said about the vehemence directed against the counterculture who articulated and embraced community, engagement and dependency, while at the same time, articulate the free and open sexuality that the more traditional Americans so deeply desired, yet remained thwarted and repressed. The public expressions of such desires by others was met with violence and hatred. For example, the Civil Rights movement of the 1960s had many components, and conservative forces directed their malice and aggression against all of them. Martin Luther King, Malcolm X, Fred Hampton, Emmitt Till, and many more whose names we have forgotten died because they dared to defy white authority and publicly state that Black people should have equal rights. If the racial hierarchy should fall, how many other hierarchies might fall as well? Better to violently stomp the life out of freedom movements before capitalism and private wealth fall.

The decisions on just how to organize the society should be left to the people who would determine their own destinies. Nevertheless, the Paris Commune, the Spanish anarchists, and the many traditions buried within our own history provide numerous examples of alternative ways to organize a political economy that are more democratic, humanistic and fulfilling to all. The basic point is that the people should collectively and democratically make those economic and political decisions that impact their lives. And for us, dignity should be the goal. Dignity is not so much an emotional state as such but a condition, a state in which people have connections to others, realms of freedom for the expressions of agency, creativity and self-realization, recognition of their fundamental worth (Langman, 2015a). Dignity however depends on those acts in which one's own forms of self-esteem and self-realization and enhances the dignity of others. This may very well range from the empathic and nurturing of children to inspiring teaching and or to leading progressive social movements. But for us, the "good society" is not simply one that abolishes private property and wage labor. Stalinism did that, and the Soviet Union remained a harsh and oppressive police state. Nor is it simply tempering individualism as Bellah or Etzioni or other communitarians and would have it. Rather, the good society, the "sane society" is organized in ways to encourage fostering the conditions whereby the dignity of each depends on the dignity of all.

Toward a Sane Society: Step 3 After God What Comes Next?

Religions need not depend on an authoritarian father figure who imposes strict rules of oppression, repression and demands obedience to secular authority in which people gain entry to the afterlife if they are observed. Echoing Durkheim, Fromm saw one of the problems of modern society has been the failure, if not inability of capitalism, to provide a meaningful, humanistic framework that encouraged a community of shared meaning as well as providing caring, sharing and encouraging human fulfillment and yet provided a spiritual dimension to life. Fromm generally disliked organized religion, and advocated instead an alternative and more humanistic "spiritual view," sometime captured in aspects of Zen or Wicca or progressive forms of Christianity. As Rabbi Michael Lerner (2007) has put it, spirituality can be seen in the awe of nature, when the natural world is experienced as beauty rather than raw materials to be turned into commodities. While some people criticized Erich Fromm's later writings as pantheistic mysticism, today we find a great deal of empirical evidence that the sense of awe, in relationship to experiencing the splendors of nature has a variety of positive effects on people. We believe that a sane society must provide spiritual experiences apart from authoritarian religious institutions and instead cultivate a challenge to capitalist economic and political power and cultural domination. A newfound activist spirit of this type appears in certain strains of Christianity (Bruggemann, 2014; Rieder, 2009), Judaism (Lerner, 2007) and in Islam (Ramadan, 2009).

During World War II, the psychiatrist Victor Frankl, forgoing a chance to move to America was eventually sent to a concentration camp where he witnessed the most inhumane sadism, brutality and genocide in the history of the world. During those experiences, he noticed that a number of the people who had survived were people who were able to find some kind of meaning, some way to understand their suffering thereby endured it and afterwards, to overcome it. He then argued that the human search for meaning is one of the most fundamental of human desires. Simple happiness aims at personal gratification, or perhaps we should call it what it is: privatized and personal hedonism seeking to maximize one's advantages of wealth, status or power. In contrast, meaning is decisively social, and not a thing to control or own. As Frankl stated, "being human always points, and is directed, to something or someone, other than oneself—be it a purpose to fulfill or another human being to encounter. The more one forgets himself—by giving himself to a cause to serve or another person to love—the more human he is" (Frankl 1992 [1959]). In other words, the more social a person becomes, the more connected and fulfilled life becomes for the individual and the more sustainable society becomes.

As sociologists Peter Berger (1990 [1967]) concluded long ago, every religion offers answers to four central existential questions: who am I? Why am I here, how should I live, and what happens when I die? Taken together, the answers provide a sense of meaning for both the individual and, as Frankl argued, religion as a source of meaning is not a thing, but shared experience. These collective experiences may be inclusive or exclusive, reactionary or progressive. In earlier times, Puritan beliefs created this meaningful community of believers, as did the austere individualist beliefs of the Appalachians when they fought bouts of personal honor or labored in coal mines or opposed state and governmental regulation on whiskey. Whites in the Old South reinforced their supremacist beliefs and identity when they bought and sold human beings, lashed their backs with whips, scratched out a living on tenant farms, and fought side by side against the Union in the Civil War. Elements of these collective beliefs remain as central elements of American social character. In the past, they held communities together by providing people with meaningful identities and purpose, which enabled them to survive and prosper, even if that prosperity depended on exploitation and enslavement.

If Frankl is right, as we believe he is, then the search for meaning, as a necessary corollary for social justice, must involve progressive and inclusive spiritual experiences as a necessary cornerstone for a sane society. As civilization advances, one's obligations to community should become greater, not lesser. In places were democracy replaced dictators and the hereditary right of kings, it placed obligations on the rich and powerful to serve society more than themselves. Democracy increases the accountability of people to each other. Democratic societies rely on free and open discourse in order to unify people through discussion and compromise, to do the greatest good for the greatest number, yet also protect the rights of minority groups.

We still have religion. We have churches, synagogues, mosques and temples for nearly any belief system a person could want. Even Satanists have their own churches. Freedom of religion is a major freedom that not only reduces social conflict, but empowers people to live as they see fit. By itself, the freedom of religion in the United States was a crucial foundational right and a principle of an advanced civilization. At the same time, the great diversity of religious belief means that all of us collectively, the grand total of humanity, have no universal system of human rights, and therefore no basic and automatic respect for each other. No common moral basis exists to stop ourselves from running over each other. As Jonathon Haidt (2012) has shown, religious communities, especially conservative ones, highly value in group loyalty while remaining indifferent, if not hostile to outsiders. We highlight the differences, and fail to realize the similarities among the world's religions and the people who alive today. Even when religion is not the source of conflict, it cannot bring us together because we have lost a sense of obligation to people in general, and to society. This is not just a matter of sacrifice, for example, that we join the military in times of war. It means that, on a daily basis, we need only follow the rules, formal or informal, that we feel like following. We throw trash along the side of the road because it's convenient and we won't get caught. We tolerate torture of people "over there" somewhere, or as we have seen too often, we let the police shoot unarmed black men. We don't care about things that don't affect us personally because we identify as individuals, not as members of a society. If religion has lost its ability to unite humanity, only religion can restore this unity because nothing else can speak to a reality that transcends all people—the universal experience of death. The stark, inescapable reality of death could and should be the basis for making life better for everyone, because we all die and take nothing with us. Only in life can we think, feel, experience, love, grieve, celebrate friends and family. To the extent we reject collective obligations, we reject the possibility of universal religion and thus the possibility of global unity.

Does a transcendent God or a Divine power exist? We can't answer that. However, modern capitalism offers its own very tangible deities that are purely social creations. They do not exist in either nature, or in the heavens. Although some people have more than others, their pursuit is available to everyone, and perhaps constitute what we mean today by "the pursuit of happiness." The four gods of contemporary America are: money, fame, thrills, and power—all of which are inherently unlimited; there is always more of each to accumulate. Only society can set a limit on such socially created desires, which it has done historically through religion.

However, we need meaningful and legitimate limits on desires, not just formal limits. We must believe that limits are good and just, not just laws that forbid something or "steal our liberty." Institutions can force limits on people, but no institution or person can force meaningful limits. People must find satisfaction and fulfillment, not just barriers. They must accept limits willingly because they believe it is the right thing to do, and given the vision of the Commune that we advocate, the requirements and restrictions on behavior should be whether action or inaction helps or harms other people, harms society, or harms the natural world. Yes, this calls for downsizing our lives and requires a different kind of social character that embraces radical limits to inequality, consumerism and the despoliation of the environment and also actively seeks a saner, more humanistic society.

Durkheim pointed out that our biological desire were limited and easily gratified, our social desires are insatiable. We have no such meaningful expectations or limits today, at least none that we all accept. The special problem in modern society is unlimited desire. In contemporary capitalist society, more is always better. Bigger better and faster more so! However, "unlimited desires are insatiable by definition, and insatiability is rightly considered a sign of morbidity. Being unlimited ... they cannot be quenched. Inextinguishable thirst is constantly renewed torture" (Durkheim, 1951 [1897] p. 247). We find ourselves in a state of perpetual unhappiness, and "a thirst arises for novelties, unfamiliar pleasures, nameless sensations, all of which lose their savor once known" (Durkheim, 1951 [1897] p. 256). We want it all, and we want it now. The more we want, the more we seek. The more we get, the less satisfaction we find. This vicious circle produces feelings of desperation, despair, and self-destruction.

We accept no limits, instead, we have sanctified unlimited desires, "and by sanctifying them, this apotheosis of well-being has placed them above all human law. Their restraint seems like a sort of sacrilege" (Durkheim 1951, [1897] p. 255). Money, fame, thrills, and power are the new gods, and we worship them without limit. We celebrate them with every thought, every breath, and every effort to accumulate them, possess them, and gain ever more of them, any way we can and admire those who have amassed the most. Regulation of any kind becomes a kind of sacrilege, the demented ravings of a lunatic. Furthermore, do we ever talk about meaningful limits and boundaries on things that can be owned or consumed? On anything? No matter how useless, how futile, how destructive we may be towards ourselves, towards other people, towards animals and the environment, it seems that we never say no. Indeed, it is just the opposite, we have discarded the meaningful regulation of conduct that traditionally, more authoritarian religion once provided. Yet as Hedges (2010) lamented, the liberal Churches eschew taking moral positions. Thus we see a huge spiritual lacuna that makes it clear, empirically evident and morally justified to illustrate how humanity must reduce its inequalities, its standards of living and unbound consumerism to reduce is consumption of raw materials for the sake of generations not yet born.

As mentioned above, the release of sensual desires and the rise of cultural hedonism offers potential for broader challenges to the forces of domination, but by itself, hedonistic personal gratifications, such as sex and drugs and rock "n" roll, may be well enjoyed, and distract from the social, but will not much impact class, race, or gender inequality. The pain, suffering and existential malaise of our times, the discontents of American character are rooted in its capitalist economic system that now controls the political, is anchored within our social character. For contemporary youth, the economic uncertainties stagnation and decline, in face of growing inequality and an indifferent government, and being controlled by the elites has fostered both anxiety and anger. The nature of the existing system that privileges the wealthy is not simply based on their wealth and the power it brings, but is largely sustained by large numbers of people whose social character has been socialized to support ruling class interests that seemingly resonate within. One of the great mysteries of the political system is how and why the poorer working-class citizens become highly motivated to support conservative politicians who seek to maintain low wages, restrict benefits, and undermine union organization. This is really no different than poor white sharecroppers fighting to preserve the slave system of the Old South. As we have said, it is futile to look at rational, logical explanations but rather, most voters, respond to the emotional messages especially those that are seemingly consistent with their underlying character.

We believe that the need for a humanistic framework of meaning and devotion, based on the awe of nature is more essential today than when Fromm wrote *The Sane Society*. This has become especially salient the when American exceptionalism, an integral aspect of American civil religion, is accepted by most Americans and fervently embraced by about one fourth of the truly conservative Americans. But this notion of American exceptionalism, expressed in fanatic patriotism celebrates an "awesome" America, right or wrong, with an inability for any critical self-reflection provides mass support for military adventurism and political interventions including coups and overthrows the throughout the world.

What happens if a society loses the ability to integrate faith and reason? As the great Roman statesman Cicero (Marcus Tullius Cicero, 106–43 BCE) wrote, "the disappearance of piety towards the gods will entail the disappearance of loyalty and social union among men as well, and of justice itself—the highest of all virtues" (Cicero 1960 [c. 40 BCE]). One of the most effective politicians and orators in Rome, he cherished and celebrated the Republic as many would celebrate religious devotion, and indeed, Cicero connected public service and democracy to true religious faith. He could not prove that democracy was a divine form of government, but he believed it nevertheless. His faith would cost him his life. Although offered power in the emerging imperial system as a member of the new *triumvirate*, Cicero refused to compromise his devotion to democracy and justice under the law. Marcus Antonius (Mark Antony) ordered him assassinated and Cicero's alleged final words were, "There is nothing proper about what you are doing, soldier, but do try to kill me properly" (Dio 1987 [c. 229]). He could have saved himself by simply standing next to Antonius in the Senate and provide tacit approval. He would not throw away a life dedicated to principles of democracy and justice.

On Being and Having

One of the most important aspects of meaning for Fromm, essential for a sane society, is understanding the difference between being and having. For much of human history, one of the primary basis of meaning was being—a mode of experience more felt than easily described, fully experiencing life, oneself and others. For Fromm the having mode meant placing primary emphasis having things, material possessions that were fixed and easily described. The being mode depends on the very fact of existence, it is the basis of productive love and creative activity and leads to solidarity and joy. It means living spontaneously and productively and having the courage to be open to new experiences and new ideas. Capitalism changes people into commodities, and thus they become alienated, dehumanized things based on their abstract values, as workers or consumers and not as human beings. Thus humans became objects, reduced to things while the accumulation of capital encouraged people to accumulate many of these things that might seemingly provide one with power, self-esteem and status, and material displays of one's worth since inner, more human qualities had little or no real value. Slowly but surely, encouraged by modern advertising with its hidden and not so hidden messages equating buying things with power, admiration and even sexual gratification, we became a society where having things became the fundamental basis of meaning rather than being, the pursuit of fulfilling human experiences, enjoying life, other people and Nature as such. Surely the teachings of most religions and indeed philosophies, has taught us that the full gratification of life is not to be found through riches and possessions, but given the extent to which modern society in general, and the United States in particular, has fostered the false needs of consumerism, while colonizing consciousness such that we believe having things brings us happiness and fulfillment has done just the opposite, estranged ourselves from ourselves and other people. Moreover, hardly noted when Fromm was writing, but today, the frantic need to accumulate more and more, the latest model of the latest fashion, has irreparably damaged the ecosystem and some scientists suggest that the Anthropocene age in which we now live may well be the last stage of human history.

What is to be Done?

The works of David Schwiekert (2002), Gar Alperovitz (2013) and Rick Wolff (2012) among others, show the fundamental superiority of employee ownership and democratic self-management over the current system where billionaires and multimillionaires own or control most of the private property of the USA who are also part of a transnational capitalist class in which 80 families own half of the wealth of the world. Not only do worker-owners feel better about their work, themselves and their enterprises, and while mainstream critics may scoff, many of these cooperatives, communes and worker owned enterprises are alive and doing quite well and rapidly growing. The model here is Mondragon, the Spanish collective that is the seventh largest company in Spain which is entirely employee owned. As some advocates of worker owned and managed enterprises note, a truly just society may be dependent on the abolition of private property, but such a transition may take generations. Consequently, worker-owned businesses represent a first step. On the one hand, we are quite sympathetic and supportive about toward the various movements toward worker managers, worker owners, co-ops communes etc. The humanization of work, creative productive work that provides agency, allows self-fulfillment and grants recognition rather than the alienated forms of wage labor, is an absolutely necessary first step toward a "sane society," but alas, not sufficient. Given our social psychological frame, the focus on the economic suffers from a productivist bias. Even as workers take ownership of businesses, they still face the same competitive market forces that require increasing productivity and lowering costs, which often means elimination of jobs. Advanced technologies of capitalism render more and more workers redundant, even those at many higher levels of skill. For example, computers conduct a vast amount of global trading using highly sophisticated algorithms that have nothing to do with the skill and cunning of old-time brokers haggling on the trading floor. The staff at the Henn-Na Hotel in Japan consists entirely of robots which are designed to look like attractive humans (one receptionist is a talking velociraptor who wears a cute little round hat) and can engage in intelligent conversations. At present, the Henn-Na is more of a theme park for high-end tourists (although it received a five-star hospitality rating), it is also a prototype for removing the human elements (wages, unions) from hotel services (Wong,

2015). Medical diagnoses over the internet or robo-pilots do not form unions, do not demand overtime and will work 24/7 without complaint. Basically, capitalism forces people to work for employers that are at the same time always trying to reduce their work force. The result is involuntary servitude, and then involuntary layoff.

To the Barricades

At the moment, dynamic and humanistic character changes have only just begun and it will take a while before we reach the point of a large critical mass to support truly progressive mass movements. Only long term, organized and sustained social movements perhaps lasting a generation or two, seem likely to achieve substantive change and demonstrate that system change is possible. As the characterological and normative changes proceed, this will not change economic relations, but given the underlying fragility of the system another crisis, far more cataclysmic than 2007–2008 could precipitate massive mobilizations in short order. Perhaps much less than a crisis will expose the inherent injustice of the US economy. Recall how the immolation of one person precipitated a series of events that overthrew the longtime dictator of Tunisia in less than a year. Hedges (2015a) has put it quite distinctly:

> Radical change always comes from below. As long as our gaze is turned upward to the powerful, as long as we invest hope in reforming the system of corporate power, we will remain enslaved ... We must build mass movements that are allied with independent political parties—a tactic used in Greece by Syriza and in Spain by Podemos. Political action without the support of radical mass movements inevitably becomes hollow ... Only by building militant mass movements that are unrelentingly hostile to the system of corporate capitalism, imperialism, militarism and globalization can we wrest back our democracy ... And until you see the rich fleeing in panic from the halls of Congress, the temples of finance, the universities, the media conglomerates, the war industry and their exclusive gated communities and private clubs, all politics in America will be farce.[5]

Such a revolution is not simply about the redistribution of wealth or power but the transformations of consciousness and values.

---

5 http://www.truthdig.com/report/print/make_the_rich_panic_20150503 Accessed 11/26.2015.

Considerations of subjectivity, namely, social character, enables us to see how and why certain ideological frames depend upon particular constellations of social character. These very same constellations of character selectively operate to reproduce the dominant ideology that sustains class relationships. But sometimes the nature of social character, never fully socialized, can resist, critique and challenge those ideological frameworks, especially at times when capitalism faces various crises of legitimacy. This is especially clear to us in so far as we have suggested that American exceptionalism is a central element of American civil religion and as such, has provided the fundamental moral foundations of the society in terms of its beliefs and practices. The most important of these beliefs, as we claimed in Chapter 2 are the ways that Americans have seen themselves were a people chosen by God that like a lost tribe of Israel, come to the Promised Land, to rebuild a new Jerusalem that would be home to the third Temple. Thus Americans were exceptional meaning that anything they might do from slavery to genocide to imperialism was permissible since God had blessed America. Many found comfort, refuge and security in the apparent miracles of mass production, wealth, famous celebrities, thrills and consumption to alleviate the fragmentations of community, the emptiness of materialism, the ersatz gratification of shopping and the shallowness of the possession of goods. A sane society must provide spiritual and humanist frameworks of meaning that provide more fulfillment than alienated labor, more gratification than consumerism, and more meaning than the accumulation of wealth. In the American case, exceptionalism remains when all else fails—we are the best country on earth, no matter what the problems of the present. As an integral aspect of American civil religion, it hold the door open for fanatic patriotism, provides mass support for military adventurism abroad and police domination here at home.

Summary

America today is a highly polarized society riven by crises, conflicts and powerful emotions, fear, anger, aggression, hostility and contempt. Sadly, and a bit fearfully, we are reminded of Weimar Germany and endless economic crises that the impotent government could do little to stop let alone reverse the plunge into chaos. The failure of capitalism circa 1929 added credibility to various extremist factions, all of whom called for the death of democracy. Fierce street battles erupted as the various socialists and communists battled and brawled with the reactionary brown shirts of Nazi Party. No, we haven't gotten there yet nor do we believe we will soon, but the memories of those days yet haunt the present. Government in the US is firmly in power, but for the most part simply has little concerns for anyone with less than a seven-figure income, except at the periodic moments when they would harvest votes to simulate a "democracy" that instead cloaks power. But we must ask how and why a charismatic dictator enthralled the people of one of the most sophisticated civilizations in the history of the world, gained a mass following, and plunged the world into the most horrendous and destructive war in all human history. To be sure there is a small cottage industry devoted to understanding the rise and fall of the Third Reich, which includes one of the better books on the topic by that title. But that is not our concern; we seek to understand what's happening in the United States, why it's happening and what can be done. One of the earliest and for us quite admittedly most important set of explanations came from the works of the scholars of the Frankfurt School of Critical Theory and for our purposes, the most relevant of those scholars was Erich Fromm's profound analysis that interwove the Marxist critique of capitalist domination, alienation and exploitation with Weber's analysis of domination, religion and the nature of modern rationality as the basis of dehumanization and the entrapment of people within the iron cages of rationality. But Fromm, a sociologist trained as a psychoanalyst brought Freud's analysis of the unconscious into the emancipatory critique of the Frankfurt school and his initial book, *Escape from Freedom*, has remained a major inspiration and model for the analysis of the crisis of the present time. Moreover, his subsequent books expanded the ideas and further explained the nature of social character, nihilism, narcissism and destructiveness. While many critics of the Frankfurt school see it as an excursion leading to gloom, doom, hopelessness and despair culminating in cynicism and withdrawal, Fromm drew quite different conclusions. Along with Frankfurt school scholars such as Bloch and Benjamin, he never gave up hope and the articulation of that hope could be found in his *Sane Society, The Art of Loving*, and *To Have or to Be?* Inspired by his work, we have attempted to understand the nature of the contemporary American crisis, and offer analysis that concludes with the possibilities of hope.

As we've repeatedly noted the problems of our times can be analytically separated into three areas, (1), capitalist political economy, (2), a plutocracy in which a small number of the Uber rich largely control the government that serves their interests in capital accumulation, and which has otherwise become completely dysfunctional and ill serves the majority of people including the vast numbers of people that fervently support political parties and agendas that ultimately work against their own self interests. (3) Finally, American culture, or what is sometimes called American character that privileges religion, phallic aggressive violence, unbridled pursuits of wealth and the collective narcissistic grandiosity of America as a not only being special, but inherently exceptional and chosen by God. The main point of our analysis has been to show that the current capitalist economy, the government it owns, and culture it produces is undergirded by a historically specific form of American social character which is largely not only unconscious, but as such largely invisible indeed repressed. On the one hand that social character enabled the ascent of America to the very pinnacle of world power, in some ways creating the most powerful Empire in the history of the world. At the same time, dialectically understood, the same character now serves to undermine the nation and slowly but surely contributes to a period of descent, marked by the growing chaos, conflicts and discontents that negate hope for a better future. As we began our journey, we noted that the fault dear reader, was not in our stars but in ourselves. And from within ourselves, a transformed social character is emergent that we believe will spearhead progressive change.

In the previous chapter we pointed out how the process of dynamic change led to the transformation of social character as the market society spread throughout Europe and one indication of that transformation was the emergence of Protestantism. The only essential goal of capitalism is to increase its profits, and using scientific discoveries and technological innovations, capitalism fostered industrialization and mass production which made mass consumption possible. Accordingly, a new social character type emerged that regarded consumerism as a desirable lifestyle. Commodities can satisfy all necessities and desires whether physical, emotional, spiritual, or aspiring social status. Given the dysfunctions of contemporary capitalism that led to stagnation for the majority and decline for many, the process of dynamic change is forging a new social character even as economic inequality forces an end to consumerism. People can't consume what they can't afford.

The unconscious psychodynamics of American social character have not only enabled the current state of affairs, but within that social character, essential to its overt manifestations, a variety of human desires have been repressed, primarily the needs for attachments and community, compassion and caring and an inclusive framework of meaning. Thus, borrowing an important concept from psychoanalytic theory, we call for a "return of the repressed" in which those positive qualities of social character that have been repressed may come forth and regenerate. We've suggested that that return of the repressed enables a "regression in the service of humanity" a takeoff on psychoanalytic ego psychology in which recovering the repressed memories images and desires of childhood has been essential for the creative process. In our case however what we are seeking is a recovery of what we call the Commune, referring of course to the Paris Commune which for a period of several months in 1871, the city residents established an alternative society of equality, mutual aid, and perhaps most importantly—dignity for all. Indeed, the success of that Commune threatened to inspire other French communities and perhaps spread to other countries as well. As an ideological exemplar and working model that directly threatened the capitalist class, the former enemies France and Prussia joined forces, attacked the Commune, slaughtered the residents and destroyed the Commune. Still, we believe that its spirit of moral regeneration, reproduced in the progressive era and the civil rights movement and anti-war movements, women's rights, animal rights, Occupy, The Arab Spring, and countless other moments all over the world has lived on, repressed at both the level of the individual and forgotten by a "cultural amnesia," such that as Margaret Thatcher once said about capitalism, TINA, "there is no alternative" to capitalism. Yes Maggie, there is an alternative, and we call it humanistic socialism.

The well-known images of America, a society of hard-working individuals seeking to maximize their self-interest and acquire their own pot of gold through their own hard work in a land of free and hardworking people, has been the dominant economic mythos common to the early Puritans, and then the more affluent later colonialists, and then again for the citizens of the new nation for whom the new nation, the "land of plenty." Industrialization ultimately led to an extremely well-paid working-class and managerial cadres, but now financialization and digitalization has shredded that industrial employer-worker contract so that the economy no longer functions for the majority of people. A small class of social dominators not only garners most of the income and hordes the wealth, but they control the political power as well.

The received wisdom of our government, taught in schools, celebrated in the mass media and an inherent part of every politician's speech is that America threw off the yoke of English oppression and "we the people" formed a democratic government that would guarantee life, liberty and the pursuit of happiness for all. But the "we" of the founders were largely the "we" of rich, white, businessmen and merchants of the northern and middle colonies while most of the southern representatives of that "we" were slave owners which meant that slaves, as dehumanized instruments of production, were not included in the "we." Indigenous peoples were never part of the "we;" they were almost always the despised Other. Given economic and cultural differences among the ruling elite, the dominant model of American government was generally pluralism, which also accommodated the interests of farmers and organized labor at various times. As time has gone by we've seen that an unelected power elite largely dominates government by moving or threatening to move capital around the country or out of the country, and large campaign contributions further help to ensure political cooptation. For the most part, elections have become entertaining diversions which mask the real nature of power in the United States.

The final part of our analysis rested upon the valorization of religion and celebrations of God. Yes, we know that the Puritans came to America in order to freely practice their religion. Yes, we know that the Constitution of the United States was very clear about the separation of church and state and the founding fathers, in their wisdom, proclaimed freedom of religion for all and that included Christians whether Protestant or Catholic, Jews and Mohammedans (or Musselmen), the 18th Century term for Muslims. Although the country has experienced extensive violence, religious persecution has not been a primary motivation. We mentioned the Salem witch trials and the murder of innocent, marginal people, but gender more than religion shaped these moments. The public humiliation, torture, and execution was an attack on marginal women (and occasionally men), not marginal religious beliefs. Founded partly but significantly on slavery, violence was a typical means of domination, and the nation still experiences frequent racially motivated violence, by police and others. Although the genocide of Native Americans was initially justified by the fact that they were heathens, we also showed that the later and more common justification were transgressions that violated conventional gender roles of Euro-American society generally and certain male privileges specifically, especially wife-beating and rape. Let us not forget the long history of "good" Christians in the KKK who not only burned crosses but tortured, mutilated and lynched or burned "uppity" African Americans. Here again, we see the primacy of race. Throughout the 20th Century, right-wing religion has always included a code language for race and/or gender oppression. Today, Donald Trump rode a wave of ethnocentrism and racism to the Republican nomination. As he clarified, it's not just Mexican immigrants who are rapists and murderers, but all immigrants. His call to ban Muslims from entering the country plays on the popular stereotype that all Muslims are swarthy and deceitful bandits, probably terrorists from the deserts of the middle-east.

Given everything that we said, how might we move toward a sane society for the 21st Century? Let us first note that the capitalist system of production has largely produced vast inequality and in so far as corporate America has automated, exported jobs, and decimated corporate careers in favor of short-term contracts, consultancies and even unpaid internships, the majority of Americans have found their standards of living stagnate or decline—especially the working classes and the youth. The extremely powerful capitalists have done almost everything possible to keep wages low, benefits even lower and job security a remembrance of things past. But we are reminded that within the forgotten history of America is another history, a history of communes and co-ops. From the beginning, however, the earliest colonies depended on the compacts of mutual aid. Secondly, perhaps most clearly in the traditions of Howard Zinn, there is another history of resistance to domination, a history of workers strikes, antiwar movements and various forms of resistance. In view of the actual successes of a number of communal, cooperative economic ventures, we see that the foundations of a sane society need rest upon the abolition of private income-producing property and the restoration of the spirit of the Commune, or later anarcho-syndicalist organizations or even more recently the Mondragon Cooperative of Spain that now includes over 200 separate companies, it represents about 1/7 of the economy and is entirely owned and managed by the workers.

Classical fascism and Soviet Communism were both overtly hostile to democracy in any form. For both, one party and a totalitarian cultural system, typically led by a military or quasi-military hero (notice how every Soviet leader prior to Gorbachev were covered in military honors) has no use for the deliberations of political parties that may negotiate and compromise political principles and ideological purity. Unfortunately, the governance of today, aptly described by Wolin as an "inverted totalitarianism" uses the façade of deliberative democracy to cloak the fact that the political process from nomination to political campaign and fundraising is largely a diversion from the actual nature of power which is largely controlled by the elite. No, we are not conspiracy theorists. This has nothing to do with conspiracies. Rather, we have described a system in which a small groups of extremely wealthy elites and major corporations use their wealth to dominate the political process in order to gain more wealth. There is no need for conspiracies; the process is legal and straightforward. As we noted several times however, this does not mean they manage their affairs efficiently or practically. Recently for example, after a wild period of gambling, selling clearly volatile "subprime" loans, the economy went ahead and imploded, as many economists warned it would. Not only did the Bush government begin the bailouts that the Obama government enthusiastically continued, but they furthermore provided the upper echelon of bankers with multimillion dollar bonuses. The supposedly liberal Obama packed his administration with longtime Wall Street insiders such as Timothy Geithner, Larry Summers, and Harry Wilson, just as the Bush administration did with Henry Paulson. In short, representative democracy is a façade, a diversion from the realities of power in America today. But again if we look into the repressed history of America we do find a history of participatory democracy in which most people acted democratically to run their own local governments. This is a course noted by de Tocqueville and seen as one of the great virtues of

America, but surely as we know small communities cannot perform the functions required by government today from food and product safety to building and maintaining airports, superhighways, transportation networks, ports, utility networks, and education.

That said, there are number of ways democracy can be made more democratic. The first thing would be undoing The Citizens United decision that allows unlimited campaign contributions. Secondly, as is being done in many communities throughout the world, the notions of participatory budgeting give people a more direct say in their governance. Third, while religion sometimes serves to maintain race, class, and gender hierarchies, and to justify interventionist foreign policies, unlike our Marxist brethren, or the intransigent, authoritarian "new atheists" who tolerate no religion of any kind (except their own zealous atheism), we see that religion is more complex and indeed contradictory. Just as American Protestantism justified slavery, the anti-slavery movement began when Quakers and others sought to stop the slave trade. Much of the impetus for emancipation came from what were then progressive churches, in the same way the Civil Rights movement was organized through Black churches and church networks. As with Durkheim and especially Erich Fromm, and others like Peter Berger or Mircea Eliade, we see that religion, at least humanistic forms remain a major means of sustaining communities of caring and sharing. We have also shown how they actively challenge injustice. Although religion in America often takes an authoritarian form, which is part of the reason that the millennial generation youth are leaving institutional religion, the growing popularity of alternative sources of spirituality from Zen to Wicca and various progressive humanistic movements in evangelical Christianity demonstrate the desire for community and living faith to temper otherwise insatiable appetites—not the least of which has been the unbridled quest for wealth and endless economic growth although almost all of that growth goes to the very upper echelons of society and very little has gone to either the struggling people or the rebuilding of the deteriorating infrastructure.

Our final concern suggests that many of the problems that we've discussed, from inequality to consumerism and ostentatious consumption is part of the dominant orientation of what Erich Fromm called "having," the accumulation of things as more important than relationships, meaning, or surely social justice. But as every religious leader has taught (except for the recent prosperity gospel), the accumulation of material goods tends to be shallow, superficial and never brings the happiness people expect. As Lao Tzu said, never honor the rich man, for he always brings strife, or as Jesus instructed the disciples with the parable of the Good Samaritan who helped a man just because the man needed help: "go and do likewise." Thus we argue that a crucial part of the recovery of the repressed to enable the moral regeneration of American society requires the simple joys of being, of finding awe in nature and pleasure in each other's company. Yes, this would mean more modest standards of living but in turn, people would enjoy a more secure and gratifying life. Yes, this would greatly reduce our carbon footprint, and perhaps slow down if not stop or even reverse the trends toward ecological disasters that we now face.

Epilogue

When authors write a book, at the end, they usually try to bring all the threads of each chapter together and come to certain conclusions. But we cannot do that do that since we are looking at an ongoing process, witnessing the changing social character of America, and the directions in which it changes, which much like a switchman on the track of world history, may be quite crucial in determining an eventual outcome. But given the nature of current situation, the outcome is uncertain. Our discipline has for the most part, concerned itself with what is enduring, regular and typical of an institution, an organization, or even the habitus that serves to reproduce social structure. But quite often, a unique event, perhaps little noticed at the time can have important ramifications down the line. Consider only for a moment, if the 2000 election had not been stolen in Florida, it is unlikely that a president Al Gore would've attacked Iraq, there would be no Islamic State, and Syria would have remained more stable. We do/did not support the governments of Saddam Hussein nor Muammar Gaddafi nor of Bashar al-Assad, but their regimes were preferable to years of war that have left three countries in ruins, killed hundreds of thousands, and created millions of refugees and many eager fighters for the Islamic State. Middle East turmoil will likely endure for generations. As we write in an election year, we do worry that a major terrorist attack on United States soil could impact the election.

Resurrecting the Frankfurt School

Perhaps our most important contributions have been threefold (1) Our dialectal approach to history, suggested by dialectical materialism, has argued that the values, motives and frameworks of understanding, the factors that enabled America's assent from a remote backwater colony of England to the apex of world power, are now such that those very same qualities serve to undermine the nation and systematically thwart the possibilities of making the changes necessary to adapt to the contemporary world. As we have seen, its rampant individualism frustrates any and all social or political efforts that benefit the collective good; as a gunslinger nation of "tough guys" that exalt the gun, at least 30,000 people die every year.

Its intense ambition for worldly success, rooted in its early Puritanism, transformed in every era and stage of capital, yet motivates ambitions for unbridled wealth but given the nature of the current system and the nature of its social dominators, most of its wealth goes primarily to its an elite few, devoid of any concerns besides power and profit. Their success, based upon how they made their profits, how they control the government and how they game the system, has meant hardships for the majority. Finally, the persistence of authoritarian religion, as a cloak to preserve patriarchy, racism, sexism, and homophobia and to protect the purity of young women has led to a deterioration of critical thought and indeed education in general.

Secondly, our work was inspired by the groundbreaking efforts of the early Frankfurt School of Critical Theory whose interests were shaped in part by attempting to understand the rise of fascism in Germany. Old ideas are not necessarily irrelevant, especially when they speak to an essential reality that still dominates social life. We believe that the insights, tools and emancipatory values of the early Frankfurt school of Critical Theory, and the work of Erich Fromm in particular remain highly relevant so long as capitalism and emotions are relevant to the human experience. Thus a major thrust of our work is part of an effort update the tradition and make it relevant for the world of the 21st Century. Our interests are primarily in using the legacy of the Frankfurt school to understand the crucial issues of our age within global capitalism rather than offer history or critique of that effort or a new biography, neither by dint of temperament nor interest, and given that many other scholars have done so and there is indeed little we can really add to those biographies and critiques. Capitalism is not just highly relevant; it has taken over the entire world and while it is created vast wealth, and has moved hundreds of millions of people from grinding poverty and hunger to the lower rungs of the middle classes, it has also impacted the economies of the advanced countries. We are not however giving capitalism the status of an actor, rather it is a system of actions and choices employed by various capitalists in such ways to maximize their profits. Corporations do not exploit workers. The various executives and managers do. Banks do not force people from their homes in foreclosures, account auditors and law enforcement officers do. What is essential however, is that part and part of its elite leaders in America, the social dominators, much of their ruthless, the predatory capitalism stems in part from the nature of traditional American character. Further, as our own work has attempted to understand other aspects of contemporary society, from the carnivalization of its popular culture, to various right-wing mobilizations to the critique of American culture and social character, concerns no longer relevant ever since the linguistic turn of Habermas led away from the critique of capitalist domination, how it's culture industries have colonized consciousness and has been internalized as an enduring moment of the psyche.

Lastly, (3), we feel that the concept of national character has not been given sufficient attention in recent academic discourses, and where it has, the focus has been more limited to specific topics like individualism, anti-intellectualism, and attitudes. Moreover, most such work avoids taking a stance that is in any way controversial, and consequently it doesn't really explain anything of importance.

The Resurrection of Critical Theory

Thus a major theme of our work is the resurrection and renewal of the critical tradition of the early iteration of critical theory which is being either lost, ignored or sanitized for the sake of what Michael Thompson has called the domestication of critical theory, that is to say, rendering it as just another bland philosophical tradition that ignores the real world. Critical Theory is not among the dominant explanatory frameworks of our discipline, sociology, nor does it have much purchase in other social sciences such as political science, economics, or even what might seem its natural home, philosophy. Why is that? First and foremost, for us Critical Theory, as an emancipatory critique of domination is not simply value laden, a no-no in the supposedly "objective," value free world of the Academy. Insofar as we remain beholden to Marx, our approach is generally regarded as somewhere between philosophical obscurantism and unrealistic political radicalism which have no place in sociology—maybe because it doesn't bring in the corporate-government grant money. Moreover, we duly note, that even among our Marxist comrades who also offer critiques of domination, inequality, globalization, and predatory speculative capitalism, most of these analyses are primarily structural and typically not only disdain looking at the social psychological moments that underpin capitalist domination, but insofar as our critical social psychology is clearly rooted in Freudian psychoanalysis, emotions, and the unconscious—aspects of human life that don't even exist for self-professed "structuralists." For the structuralists, capitalism is the actor and people are merely parts of the system, either as abstract predator or prey. Even though classical Freudian theory has undergone a number of metamorphoses and permutations, we still find value in concepts like the unconscious, desire and defense, ambivalence and character structure that many do not take. Thus for example we've more than freely embraced other, more recent developments in psychoanalytic theory such as ego psychology object relations, interpersonal, that helped us to understand denial, splitting, and what is been central to our analysis, the return of the repressed and regression in the service of humanity to capture the emancipatory thrust that lies within ourselves that can empower and resist.

Even in the highly rarefied realm of Frankfurt school critical theory, when Habermas elaborated his communication theory of society, the Freudian theories of subjectivity, desire and defense were replaced by symbolic interactionist approaches, especially the work of George Herbert Mead, a behaviorist who acknowledged no internal life at all and considered the self to be completely shaped by social forces external to the individual. Moreover, the repressive superego, sustaining conformity through guilt was sanitized by cognitive developmental approaches to morality pioneered by Piaget and refined by Kohlberg. While we do not simply dismiss these approaches, they offer us little in terms of understanding the nature of domination, how that domination fosters the reproduction of social arrangements that in turn lead to immiseration and ambivalence, nor can these more cognitive linguistic approaches speak to the intense emotions and irrationality that may be aroused by economic hardships, or manipulated by political leaders.

Notwithstanding the many critiques of the Frankfurt School approach, of which we are well aware, we nevertheless remain convinced that just as the original Frankfurt school provided us with a number of insights on the role of character, desire and mass media that helped us to understand the rise of Nazism, and the subsequent flourishing of consumerism, we believe that the analytic tools provided by Horkheimer and Adorno, Marcuse, and especially Erich Fromm remain highly useful in illuminating what is hidden by powerful forces at the level of both culture and character to keep certain aspects of society and the individual hidden.

But that said, the conditions of the 20th Century, beginning perhaps with World War I and the end of empires, the economic crisis that led to the rise of fascism, World War II, has demanded rethinking and redevelopment of Marx's insights. Toward this effort, the Frankfurt school incorporated a critique of capitalist culture both in terms of hegemonic ideology in which Instrumental Reason rendered the impersonal nature of modern domination somewhere between "normal" and invisible. Further, and again indebted to that work, is the importance of even considering popular culture, much as we noted the westward movement of the frontier fostered the "tough guy monomyth" rendering cowboys, sheriffs, soldiers and bounty hunters, heroic celebrities a tradition that was long continued with the rise of motion pictures and the stars of the silver screen. And as we have seen, two of the tough guys became governors of California, one of whom became president and as we finish our writing, another media celebrity, a tough guy of reality TV won the Republican presidential nomination. (Our analysis of character change suggests that his angry, authoritarian, older white male constituency will not provide the demographics for a victory.)

For our purposes however, the most important contribution of the Frankfurt school has been its critical social psychology rooted in Freudian psychodynamics that through the work of Wilhelm Reich, Erich Fromm and Herbert Marcuse has enabled us to understand the psychodynamics of domination that began primarily with the studies of authoritarianism. For Fromm, the concern with authoritarianism, moved psychodynamic theory away from its biologism to the psychodynamics of social interaction. More specifically Erich Fromm pointed out how given the social changes and crises that arose with the rise of capitalism, again seen in its transformations, there were widespread fears and anxieties over abandonment, powerlessness, and meaninglessness. To escape those fears that Fromm subsumed as freedom, people might submit themselves to seemingly powerful leaders, father figures, or causes, that demands subservience from those below. Some people might become aggressive and seek to destroy their enemies, finally they might find blind conformity comforting. We still find Fromm's analyses insightful for understanding many of the conservative if not reactionary social movements of today from the John Birch society, to the Moral Majority, the Tea Party and even the mass support of the economically distressed blue-collar workers supporting Donald Trump. But as useful and is central as authoritarianism may be for studying social character, there are indeed other aspects of social character that are salient. True to a psychoanalytic perspective, certain aspects of character and ambivalence, contradictory aspects exist side-by-side as a polarity, and given certain social conditions, an internal balance may change and impact the person's thoughts and behaviors. As one joke goes what's a conservative? A liberal who's just been mugged. What's a liberal? A conservative who has just been indicted. Besides the note of humor, what we wish to illustrate is the flexibility of the person, his or her ability to shift and change that is the prelude for character change, and when that becomes more general, and the population begins to change, other social changes take place. Fromm's perspective then helped us explain how and why social character changed and as it did, as different cohorts move through the lifecycle they bring with them the values shaped by the context of their youth. The changing values of generations as we've seen has been a major factor enabling social change social change. Fromm's perspective on dynamic change is one of the core arguments that we made for understanding how and why the younger generations of today are moving away from more traditional, authoritarian organizations and values.

One of our primary points, informed by the critical social psychology of the Frankfurt school (Langman, 2016) is the absolute naïveté of progressives, especially their chattering classes of journalists and pundits that may write columns in elite newspapers and/or appear as "infotainment" on television networks, and often, both that little appreciate the role of social psychological factors beginning with authoritarianism, and perhaps ending with various aspects of motivated reasoning and denial. They fail to appreciate how certain people can so strongly reject facts, evidence and logic. No, such people are neither stupid nor crazy, but certain beliefs resonate with their underlying social character, especially under the conditions of social stress and strain. Indeed, we have now reached the point where membership in the Republican Party requires a complete and total rejection of facts of any kind. Even before Obama's election there were endless claims that he's Kenyan, Muslim, atheist, communist, socialist and worst of all, he is the Antichrist. He hates America, has created death panels to exterminate Americans over 65, he has had FEMA build detention camps to house American patriots, and as we go to press we found out that Obama just had justice Scalia killed so that he might appoint a gay minority lesbian, a dedicated communist to the Supreme Court. But rather than laugh at them, much as Marx had noted that prayer was the wail of the oppressed, psychologically we need to understand how these bizarre, hostile rantings, and projections are indeed the wails of those hurting from the consequences of America's predatory capitalism, and much as Fromm explained, they assuage their pains through both their delusions, projections and succumbing to the lure of the tough, but benevolent, charismatic father figure. We saw that movie before, when the star had a little black mustache. This time he has a mane of orange comb-over hair. First as tragedy, then as a reality TV farce. To paraphrase Benjamin, we must have empathy for those whom have lost the capacity for empathy.

Following the insights of the Frankfurt school tradition, we can have been able to show how American character enabled the United States to become the most powerful hegemon in the history the world. At the same time, the consequences of its underlying social character have included the ascent of various social dominators which has led to unprecedented levels of inequality and extreme hardships for many. In contrast, FDR was born rich into an old-money family, but he also realized that general prosperity is a pre-requisite for social stability and continued prosperity. Works programs, economic regulation and other intervention, and active efforts to correct the ecological catastrophe of the Dust Bowl demonstrated a different attitude than the wealthy of today. For leaders like FDR or JFK (both born rich), the country is only as strong as its weakest link. Today, the richest seek only more wealth and power, will claim anything of value, and let the rest of the world burn.

Our interests are a bit broader than simply following the insights of the early Frankfurt school and Erich Fromm, but rekindling an interest in national character has been marginalized by the various approaches to globalization and its various processes and consequences. We would argue that in recent years, there have been too few studies and critiques of national character which one might lead one to assume that it is no longer a relevant concern. *Au contraire*, we dissent and might simply ask why so many other countries have seen such different trajectories, for example the Scandinavian countries, whose people are among the happiest in the world, are not only highly taxed but with little complaint because vulnerable people receive the support they need and the country can maintain itself. Yes, progressive political parties have been important but that still leaves us with the question as to why one country might have progressive political parties, while another is so completely controlled by the rich that political parties are irrelevant.

But our concern was not to offer a scholarly critique and analysis of the history of national character studies as such, but rather to understand the role of national character at least at the level of collective values and how it has impacted contemporary American society and was sustained by an underlying social character. Moreover, for various reasons, not least of which was the explosion of studies of globalization and transnational studies, concerns with nations, nation states, and nationalism have tended to wane, regrettably since the concern with the global economy serves to obscure so many of the conflicts and rivalries today that feed upon nationalism and national interests, often cloaked as ethnic conflicts, religious conflicts etc. but as Craig Calhoun put it so succinctly, nations do matter, and as the dominant superpower of the world since 1945 what America has done matters a great deal.

Recent empires, such as Germany, Japan, Russia, France and Great Britain offer some direction to understand the conflicting passions of nationalism and humanitarianism. They are not identical to the US in the present, however. Today, we see a much more gradual self-destruction of the United States as it pursues various national and international policies and agendas consistent with its traditional social character that have so weakened the foundations of the Colossus, that it too is in a process of gradual self-destruction.

Toward a Better Future

Inspired by the emancipatory spirit of the Frankfurt School, especially the analyses and visions of Erich Fromm, we are hopeful. As he showed, the characterological changes from feudalism to the early market society, to late capital then its bureaucratic/consumerist moments were such that each constellation of social character was well adapted to a particular form of work and domination, whether by the Church-State elite, the early market, the later factory based industrialization, and finally, 20th Century consumerism that simultaneously "erased" class consciousness and critical thought at the same time. But we contend, each epic has fostered a form or selfhood that may have been "well adapted" variant of what Fromm called "pathological normality" in which adaptation at the level of social character that impelled different forms work and social domination, but necessarily led to the thwarting, distorting and truncating of selfhood in each epoch, serving the interests of the elites of each period albeit at the cost of personal immiseration. But today, we are witnessing something different. Firstly, the system is not working very well for most folks and many want a change. On the one hand, we now have the technologies and models of work organization that can minimize work, and make it a more fulfilling activity that can empower and enable self-creation-realizing one's unique talents.[1] But such an economic change must also depend on overcoming cultural barriers and a new expression of social character that will resist the old and usher in the new. Given the processes of dynamic change, the emergent social character of our times is more flexible, more open, more pluralistic, multi-dimensional, and perhaps protean. Such a social character is not only more open economically, politically and culturally, but psychologically as well. S/he is more amenable to, and perhaps actively seeks to recapture long lost, suppressed elements of American society that provide a framework that is democratic, inclusive, dedicated to equality, genuine freedom, justice and dignity. Such a social character portends the coming of a truly democratic society, a sane society that unlike the pathological normality of the society in which we now live, may not only be desirable, and fulfilling, but necessary for the very survival of human civilization.

We are optimistic, our analysis suggests that a new phoenix of social character is a rising from the ashes of the present. We have argued that the tectonic plates of American culture and subjectivity are shifting. Spearheaded by youth as the bearers of a changing social character, one more disposed to caring, sharing and empathy, embracing active democracy, inclusion and toleration. Thus we offer not a conclusion, but an informed hope for a new beginning, for what we will call a sane society for the 21st Century. Will it happen? We believe it must. The world can live without the United States, but the United States can no longer live without the rest of the world. Collapsed empires crowd the annals of history and not one has ever been reconstituted in a more progressive and sustainable form—that would surely be an *exceptional* accomplishment.

---

1   Paul Mason has shown how we now have new forms of owners, work, the technologies, social conditions and emerging subjectivities that can enable a fulfilling post capitalist world, and while many may see a declining standard of living, many more will move upward, but all would have a more gratifying life. http://www.theguardian.com/books/2015/jul/17/postcapitalism-end-of-capitalism-begun Accessed 08/23/2015.

Bibliography

ACWS—Alberta Council of Women's Shelters. 2012. "Men's Attitudes and Behaviours Toward Violence Against Women." https://acws.ca/sites/default/files/documents/PresentationACWSMensAttitudesBehaviorsTowardViolenceAgainstWomenreleasedCalgaryBWTG.pdf.

Abramsky, Sasha. 2013. *The American Way of Poverty: How the Other Half Still Lives.* New York, NY: Nation Books.

Acemoglu, Daron and James Robinson. 2013. *Why Nations Fail: The Origins of Power, Prosperity, and Poverty.* New York, NY: Crown Publishing.

Adamczyk, Ed. 2015. "Birmingham, England, Laughs at Fox News Comments." *UPI News*: http://www.upi.com/Top_News/World-News/2015/01/12/Birmingham-England-laughs-at-Fox-News-comments/7191421078689/.

Adorno, Theodor, Else Frenkel-Brunswik, Daniel J. Levinson, and R. Nevitt Sanford. 1950. *The Authoritarian Personality.* New York, NY: Harper and Brothers.

Agnew, Jeremy. 2011. *Entertainment in the Old West: Theater, Music, Circuses, Medicine Shows, Prizefighting and Other Popular Amusements.* Jefferson, NC: McFarland Press.

Allen, Theodore. 1994. *The Invention of the White Race, Vol. I.* New York, NY: Verso Press.

Alperovitz, Gar. 2013. *What Then Must We Do? Straight Talk about the Next American Revolution.* White River Junction, VT: Chelsea Green Publishing.

Altemeyer, Bob. 1988. *Enemies of Freedom: Understanding Right-Wing Authoritarianism.* San Francisco, CA: Jossey-Bass.

Altemeyer, Bob. 1996. *The Authoritarian Specter.* Cambridge, MA: Harvard University Press.

Altemeyer, Bob. 2004. "Highly Dominating, Highly Authoritarian Personalities." *The Journal of Social Psychology* 144, 4: 421–447.

Altemeyer, Bob. 2006. *The Authoritarians.* Winnipeg, Manitoba: University of Manitoba Press.

Amarasingam, Amarnath. 2010. "What is the New Atheism?" *Religion and the New Atheism: A Critical Appraisal.* Leiden, The Netherlands: Brill.

Anderson, Elijah. 2014. "City of Detroit hosts water affordability fair for past-due accounts today." *Detroit Free Press*: http://www.freep.com/story/news/local/michigan/detroit/2014/08/23/city-of-detroit-hosts-water-affordability-fair-for-past-due-accounts-today/14488441/.

Anderson, Terry L. and Peter J. Hill. 2004. *The Not so Wild, Wild West: Property Rights on the Frontier.* Stanford, CA: Stanford University Press.

Apple, Michael W. 2001. "Bringing the World to God: education and the politics of authoritarian religious populism." *Discourse: Studies in the Cultural Politics of Education*, Vol.22, 2: 149–172.

Appy, Christian G. 2015. *American Reckoning: The Vietnam War and Our National Identity*. New York, NY: Viking Press.

AP/NBC News. 2006. "Haggard Admits Sexual Immorality, Apologizes. Evangelical Leader Contrite After Dismissal From Colorado Church." http://www.nbcnews.com/id/15536263/ns/us_news-life/t/haggard-admits-sexual-immorality-apologizes/#.VmDo8-Jep8E.

Armstrong, James. 2014. *If Only: George McGovern and the America That Might Have Been*. North Berwick, ME: PSA Communications.

Aronowitz, Stanley. 1990. *Crisis In Historical Materialism: Class, Politics, and Culture in Marxist Theory*. Minneapolis, MN: University of Minnesota Press.

Babiak, Paul and Robert D. Hare. 2006. *Snakes in Suits: When Psychopaths go to Work*. New York, NY: HarperCollins.

Baden-Meyer, Alexis. 2015. "Monsanto's Roundup: Enough to Make You Sick." *Nation of Change*, January 25: http://www.nationofchange.org/2015/01/24/monsantos-roundup-enough-make-sick/.

Bader, Michael. 2015. *More than Bread and Butter: A Psychologist Speaks to Progressives About What People Really Need in Order to Win and Change the World*. San Francisco, CA: Amazon Kindle/Michael Bader.

Bageant, Joe. 2008. *Deer Hunting with Jesus: Dispatches from America's Class War*. New York, NY: Crown Books.

Bailey, Richard A. 2011. *Race and Redemption in Puritan New England (Religion in America)*. New York, NY: Oxford University Press.

Bakhtin, Mikhail. 1968. *Rabelais and His World*. Bloomington, IN: Indiana University Press.

Barnett, Cynthia. 2013. "The Measurement of White-Collar Crime Using Uniform Crime Reporting (UCR) Data." Washington, DC: U.S. Department of Justice, Federal Bureau of Investigation, Criminal Justice Information Services (CJIS) Division.

Barrett, David M. 1993. *Uncertain Warriors: Lyndon Johnson and His Vietnam Advisors*. Lawrence, KS: University of Kansas Press.

Barry, John M. 2012. *Roger Williams and the Creation of the American Soul: Church, State, and the Birth of Liberty*. New York, NY: Viking Penguin.

Barstow, Anne L. 1994. *Witchcraze: A New History of the European Witch Hunts*. San Francisco, CA: HarperCollins.

Bartkowski, John P. 2004. *The Promise Keepers: Servants, Soldiers, and Godly Men*. New Brunswick, NJ: Rutgers University Press.

Battalora, Jacqueline. 2013. *Birth of a White Nation: The Invention of White People and Its Relevance Today*. Houston, TX: Strategic Book Publishing.

BBC News. 2015. "Paris Mayor to sue Fox News over Muslim Claims." *BBC News*: http://www.bbc.com/news/entertainment-arts-30915395.

Becker, Ernst. 1997 [1973]. *The Denial of Death*. New York, NY: Basic Books.

Bell, Rob. 2011. *Love Wins: A Book About Heaven, Hell, and the Fate of Every Person Who Ever Lived.* New York, NY: HarperCollins.

Bellah, Robert N. 1992. *The Broken Covenant: American Civil Religion on Trial, Second Edition.* Chicago, IL: University of Chicago Press.

Bellah, Robert N., Richard Madsen, Steve Tipton, William Sullivan, and Ann Swidler. 1992 [1976]. *The Good Society.* New York, NY: Vintage Books.

Benski, Tova and Lauren Langman. 2013. "The Effects Of Affects: The Place Of Emotions In The Mobilizations Of 2011." *Current Sociology* 61, 4: 525–540.

Berger, Peter. 1990 [1967]. *The Sacred Canopy: Elements of a Sociological Theory of Religion.* New York, NY: Random House.

Berlet, Chip and Matthew N. Lyons. 2000. *Right-Wing Populism in America: Too Close for Comfort.* New York, NY: Guilford Press.

Berman, Ari. 2014. "North Carolina's Moral Monday Movement Kicks Off 2014 With a Massive Rally in Raleigh." *The Nation Online,* http://www.thenation.com/article/north-carolinas-moral-monday-movement-kicks-2014-massive-rally-raleigh/.

Bershidsky, Leonid. 2016. "Germany's Middle Class Is Endangered, Too." *Bloomberg Business Online:* https://www.bloomberg.com/view/articles/2016-05-10/germany-s-middle-class-is-endangered-too.

Bivens, Josh and Laurence Mishel. 2015. "Understanding the Historic Divergence Between Productivity and a Typical Worker's Pay: Why It Matters and Why It's Real." Washington, DC: Economic Policy Institute.

Block, Sharon. 2006. *Rape and Sexual Power in Early America.* Chapel Hill, NC: University of North Carolina Press.

Blogowska, Joanna, Catherine Lambert, and Vassilis Saroglou. 2013. "Religious Prosociality and Aggression: It's Real." *Journal for the Scientific Study of Religion* 52, 3:524–536.

Bolloten, Burnett. 1991. *The Spanish Civil War: Revolution and Counterrevolution.* Chapel Hill, NC: University of North Carolina Press.

Bonilla-Silva, Eduardo. 2013. *Racism without Racists: Color-Blind Racism and the Persistence of Racial Inequality in America.* Lanham, MD: Rowman and Littlefield.

Borchers, Callum. 2016. "Hillary Clinton's Goldman Sachs speech transcripts are now a campaign issue. Why weren't they before?" *Washington Post* Online: https://www.washingtonpost.com/news/the-fix/wp/2016/02/05/hillary-clintons-goldman-sachs-speech-transcripts-are-now-a-campaign-issue-why-werent-they-before/.

Borger, Julian. 2014. "US report on 'enhanced interrogation' concludes: torture doesn't work." The Guardian: http://www.theguardian.com/us-news/2014/dec/09/senate-committee-cia-torture-does-not-work.

Bourne, Russell. 2002. *Gods of War, Gods of Peace: How the Meeting of Native and Colonial Religions Shaped Early America.* Orlando, FL: Harcourt Books.

Bradbury, Ray. [1951] 2013. *Fahrenheit 451: A Novel.* New York, NY: Simon and Schuster.

Brands, H.W. 2005. *Andrew Jackson: His Life and Times.* New York, NY: Random House.

Bray, Robert. 2005. *Peter Cartwright, Legendary Frontier Preacher.* Champaign, IL: University of Illinois Press.

Bronner, Stephen. 2004. *Reclaiming the Enlightenment: Toward a Politics of Radical Engagement.* New York, NY: Columbia University Press.

Bronner, Stephen. 2010. "Democracy, Foreign Policy, and War." In *Where Do We Go from Here?: American Democracy and the Renewal of the Radical Imagination*, Mark Majors, ed. Lanham, MD: Lexington Books.

Brown, Dee. 1995. *The American West.* New York, NY: Touchstone Press.

Brown, Kathleen M. 1996. *Good Wives, Nasty Wenches, and Anxious Patriarchs: Gender, Race, and Power in Colonial Virginia.* Chapel Hill, NC: University of North Carolina Press.

Brown, Sterling A. 1996. *The Collected Poems of Sterling A. Brown.* Evanston, IL: Triquarterly/Northwestern University Press.

Bruggemann, Walter. 2014. *Sabbath as Resistance: Saying NO to the Culture of NOW.* Louisville, KY: Westminster John Knox Press.

Bureau of Labor Statistics. 2015. "Economic News Release USDL-15-0072." January 23: http://www.bls.gov/news.release/union2.nro.htm.

Burrough, Bryan and John Helyar. 1990. *Barbarians at the Gates: The Fall of RJR-Nabisco.* New York, NY:

Carney, John. 2009. "Lloyd Blankfein Says He Is Doing 'God's Work.'" *Business Insider*, November 9: http://www.businessinsider.com/lloyd-blankfein-says-he-is-doing-gods-work-2009-11.

Carney, John. 2010. "Bonus Watch 2010: Goldman Sachs Pays Huge Bonuses And Gives Junior Bankers A 50% Salary Raise." *Business Insider*, Jan 28: http://www.businessinsider.com/bonus-watch-2009-goldman-sachs-pays-huge-bonuses-and-gives-junior-bankers-a-50-salary-raise-2010-1?op=1.

Casselman, Ben. 2016. "Americans Don't Miss Manufacturing—They Miss Unions." FiveThirtyEight.com: http://fivethirtyeight.com/features/americans-dont-miss-manufacturing-they-miss-unions/.

Cassidy, John. 2014. "The Winner of the Spending Bill Vote: Jamie Dimon." *New Yorker Magazine*: http://www.newyorker.com/news/john-cassidy/spending-bill-vote-winner-jamie-dimon.

Cattani, Daiane, Vera Lúcia de Liz Oliveira Cavalli, Carla Elise Heinz Rieg, Juliana Tonietto Domingues, Tharine Dal-Cim, Carla Inês Tasca, Fátima Regina Mena Barreto Silva, and Ariane Zamoner. 2014. "Mechanisms Underlying The Neurotoxicity Induced By Glyphosate-Based Herbicide In Immature Rat Hippocampus: Involvement Of Glutamate Excitotoxicity." *Toxicology* 320, 5: 34–45.

Cavanaugh, Jack. 2010. *The Gipper: George Gipp, Knute Rockne, and the Dramatic Rise of Notre Dame Football.* New York, NY: Skyhorse Press.

CBS News. 2015. "Koch Brothers' network will drop almost $1 billion on 2016 election." http://www.cbsnews.com/news/koch-brothers-network-will-spend-almost-1-billion-on-2016-election/.

Chang, Ha-Joon. 2010. *23 Things They Don't Tell You about Capitalism.* New York, NY: Bloomsbury Press.

Chomsky, Noam and Robert W. McChesney. 2011. *Profit Over People: Neoliberalism and Global Order.* New York, NY: Seven Stories Press.

Chen, Tim. 2015. "American Household Debt Statistics, 2015." http://www.nerdwallet .com/blog/credit-card-data/average-credit-card-debt-household/.

Chengu, Garikai. 2014. "America Created Al-Qaeda and the ISIS Terror Group." Montreal, Canada: Centre for Research on Globalization.

Choksi, Niraj. 2016. "The Oregon standoff is far bigger than a group of armed men in a refuge." *WashingtonPost* online, January 4: https://www.washingtonpost.com/news/post-nation/wp/2016/01/04/the-oregon-standoff-is-far-bigger-than-a-group-of-armed-men-in-a-forest/.

Cicero, Marcus Tullius. 1960 [c. 40 BCE]. *Cicero: Selected Works.* New York, NY: Penguin Classics.

Clinch, Matt. 2014. "Rich hoard cash as their wealth reaches record high." *CNBC News*: http://www.cnbc.com/id/102198213#.

CNN Money 2014. "Income is on the Rise...Finally!" CNN.com, http://money.cnn .com/2014/08/20/news/economy/median-income/index.html.

Cohen, William. 1991. *At Freedom's Edge: Black Mobility and the Southern White Quest for Racial Control, 1861–1915.* Baton Rouge, LA: Louisiana State University Press.

Cohrs, Christopher J., and Frank Asbrock. 2009. "Right-wing authoritarianism, social dominance orientation and prejudice against threatening and competitive ethnic groups." *European Journal of Social Psychology* 39, 2: 270–289.

Coleman, Michael C. 1993. *American Indian Children at School, 1850–1930.* Oxford, MS: University of Mississippi Press.

Conroy, David W. 1995. *In Public Houses: Drink and the Revolution of Authority in Colonial Massachusetts.* Chapel Hill, NC: University of North Carolina Press.

Crane, Elaine Forman. 2012. *Witches, Wife Beaters, and Whores: Common Law and Common Folk in Early America.* Ithaca, NY: Cornell University Press.

Crawford, Jarret T. and Jane M. Pilanski. 2014. "The Differential Effects of Right-Wing Authoritarianism and Social Dominance Orientation on Political Intolerance." *Political Psychology* 35, 4: 557–576.

Crawford, Jarret T., Lee Jussim, Thomas R. Cain, and Florette Cohen. 2013. "Right-wing authoritarianism and social dominance orientation differentially predict biased evaluations of media reports." *Journal of Applied Social Psychology* 43: 163–174.

Cribbs, Sarah E. and D. Mark Austin. 2011. "Enduring Pictures in Our Heads: The Continuance of Authoritarianism and Racial Stereotyping." *Journal of Black Studies* 42, 3:334–359.

Crouse, James and Douglas Stalker. 2007. "Do Right-Wing Authoritarian Beliefs Originate From Psychological Conflict?" *Psychoanalytic Psychology* 24, 1: 25–44.

Crouse, James and Douglas Stalker. 2007. "Do Right-Wing Authoritarian Beliefs Originate From Psychological Conflict?" *Psychoanalytic Psychology* 24, 1: 25–44.

Crowson, H. Michael and Teresa K. Debacker. 2008. "Belief, Motivational, and Ideological Correlates of Human Rights Attitudes." *The Journal of Social Psychology* 148, 3: 293–310.

Curl, John. 2007. *Memories of Drop City: The First Hippie Commune of the 1960s and the Summer of Love.* Lincoln, NE: iUniverse.

Curl, John. 2012. *For All the People: Uncovering the Hidden History of Cooperation, Cooperative Movements, and Communalism in America.* Oakland, CA: PM Press.

Cusick, Daniel. 2015. "Solar Power Sees Unprecedented Boom in U.S." *Scientific American Online*: http://www.scientificamerican.com/article/solar-power-sees-unprecedented-boom-in-u-s/.

Dean, John. 2006. *Conservatives Without Conscience.* New York, NY: Penguin Group.

De Crevecoeur, J. Hector St. John. 1981 [1782]. *Letters from an American Farmer and Sketches of Eighteenth-Century America.* New York, NY: Penguin Books.

Demos, John. 1995. *The Unredeemed Captive: A Family Story from Early America.* New York, NY: Vintage Books.

Densley, James A., Tianji Cai, and Susan Hilal. 2014. "Social dominance orientation and trust propensity in street gangs." *Group Processes Intergroup Relations* 17, 6: 763–779.

De Tocqueville, Alexis. 1945 [1840]. *Democracy in America.* New York, NY: Alfred A. Knopf.

Detroit Free Press. 2016. "Indictments don't absolve Snyder in Flint water crisis." Detroit Free Press online: http://www.freep.com/story/opinion/editorials/2016/04/21/flint-criminal-charges/83293934/.

Diamond, Larry. 2008. *The Spirit of Democracy: The Struggle to Build Free Societies Throughout the World.* New York, NY: Henry Holt.

Di Mento, Maria. 2014. "Philanthropy 50: No. 23 Stephen Schwarzman." *The Chronicle of Philanthropy*, http://philanthropy.com/article/No-23-Stephen-Schwarzman/144485/.

Dio, Cassius Cocceianus. 1987 [c. 229] *The Roman History: The Reign of Augustus.* New York, NY: Penguin Classics.

Donald, David Herbert. 1996. *Lincoln.* New York: Touchstone Books.

Duckitt, John and Boris Bizumic. 2013. "Multidimensionality of Right-Wing Authoritarian Attitudes: Authoritarianism-Conservatism-Traditionalism." *Political Psychology* 34, 6: 841–862.

Dunbar-Ortiz, Roxanne. 2014. *An Indigenous Peoples' History of the United States.* Boston, MA: Beacon Press.

Durieza, Bart and Alain Van Hiel. 2002. "The march of modern fascism. A comparison of social dominance orientation and authoritarianism." *Personality and Individual Differences* 32: 1199–1213.

Duriez, Bart and Bart Soenens. 2009. "The intergenerational transmission of racism: The role of Right-Wing Authoritarianism and Social Dominance Orientation." *Journal of Research in Personality* 43: 906–909.

Durkheim, Emile. 1951 [1897]. *Suicide: A Study in Sociology*. New York, NY: MacMillan and Company.

Dworkin, Shari and Faye Linda Wachs. 2009. *Body Panic: Gender, Health, and the Selling of Fitness*. New York, NY: New York University Press.

Dwyer, Devin. 2014. "Former Vice President Dick Cheney Says CIA Torture Report Is 'Full of Crap'." ABC News, December 10: http://abcnews.go.com/Politics/vice-president-dick-cheney-cia-torture-report-full/story?id=27513355.

Economic Policy Institute. 2014. "Raising America's Pay: A summary of the initiative." Washington, DC: Economic Policy Institute.

Edwards, Sarah R., Kathryn A. Bradshaw, and Verlin B. Hinsz. 2014. "Denying Rape but Endorsing Forceful Intercourse: Exploring Differences Among Responders." *Violence And Gender* 1, 4: 188–193.

Einolf, Christopher J. 2011. "The Link Between Religion and Helping Others: The Role of Values, Ideas, and Language." *Sociology of Religion* 72, 4: 435–455.

Ekehammar, Bo, Nazar Akrami, Magnus Gylje, and Ingrid Zakrisson. 2004. "What matters most to prejudice: Big Five personality, Social Dominance Orientation, or Right-Wing Authoritarianism?" *European Journal of Personality* 18, 6: 463–482.

Elias, Norbert. 1969. *The Civilizing Process, The History of Manners, Vol. I*. Oxford: Blackwell.

Engel, Jeffery A. 2014. "When George Bush Believed the Cold War Ended and Why that Mattered." In *Inside the Presidency of George H.W. Bush*. Michael Nelson and Barbara A. Perry, eds. Ithaca, NY: Cornell University Press.

Epstein, Catherine A. 2015. *Nazi Germany: Confronting the Myths*. Malden, MA: John A. Wiley and Sons.

Everett, Burgess. 2015. "Chuck Schumer Bucks White House on Iran." *Politico*: http://www.politico.com/story/2015/04/chuck-schumer-bucks-white-house-on-iran-116713.html.

Falk, Gerhard. 2011. *Football and American Culture*. New York, NY: Routledge.

Fanon, Franz. 2004 [1961]. *The Wretched of the Earth*. New York, NY: Grove Press.

Fanon, Franz. 2008 [1952]. *Black Skins: White Masks*. New York, NY: Grove Press.

Ferguson, Charles H. 2012. *Predator Nation: Corporate Criminals, Political Corruption, and the Hijacking of America*. New York, NY: Crown Business.

Fieldhouse, Andrew. 2013. *Rising income inequality and the role of shifting market-income distribution, tax burdens, and tax rates*. Washington, DC: Economic Policy Institute.

Fischer, D.H. 1989. *Albion's seed: Four British folkways in America*. New York, NY: Oxford University Press.

Fischer, Kirsten. 2002. *Suspect Relations: Sex, Race, and Resistance in Colonial North Carolina*. Ithaca, NY: Cornell University Press.

Frank, Thomas. 2004. *What's the Matter with Kansas?: How Conservatives Won the Heart of America*. New York, NY: Henry Holt.

Frankl, Victor. 1992 [1959]. *Man's Search for Meaning*. Cutchogue, NY: Buccaneer Books.

Fromm, Erich. 1990 [1955]. *The Sane Society*. New York, NY: Henry Holt.

Fromm, Erich. [1972] 1992. *You Shall Be as Gods*. New York, NY: Henry Holt.

Fromm, Erich. 1992 [1973]. *The Anatomy of Human Destructiveness*. New York, NY: Henry Holt.

Fromm, Erich. 1994 [1941]. *Escape from Freedom*. New York, NY: Henry Holt.

Fromm, Erich. 2013 [1976]. *To Have or to Be?* New York, NY: Bloomsbury Academic.

Fromm, Erich and Michael Maccoby. 1996 [1972]. *Social Character in a Mexican Village*. Piscataway, NJ: Transaction Publishers.

Frosh, Stephen. 2013. "Psychoanalysis, colonialism, racism." Journal of Theoretical and Philosophical Psychology 33, 3: 141–154.

Fry, Richard, and Rakesh Kochhar. 2014. "America's wealth gap between middle-income and upper-income families is widest on record." *Pew Research Center*: http://www.pewresearch.org/fact-tank/2014/12/17/wealth-gap-upper-middle-income/.

Gallagher, John. 2015. "Insider emails: Wall Street Pushed Bad Detroit Mortgage Loans." *Detroit Free Press*, January 25. http://www.freep.com/story/money/business/michigan/2015/01/24/subprime-detroit-morgan-stanley/22286935/.

Garry, Vincent F., Mary E. Harkins, Leanna L. Erickson, Leslie K. Long-Simpson, Seth E. Holland, and Barbara L. Burroughs. 2002. "Birth defects, season of conception, and sex of children born to pesticide applicators living in the Red River Valley of Minnesota, USA." *Environmental Health Perspectives* 110, Suppl. 3: 441–449.

Gilens, Martin and Benjamin I. Page, "Testing Theories of American Politics: Elites, Interest Groups, and Average Citizens," Perspectives on Politics, Volume 12, 03, September, 2014, pp. 564–581.

Gilens, Martin and Benjamin I. Page. 2014. "Testing Theories of American Politics: Elites, Interest Groups, and Average Citizens." *Perspectives on Politics* 12, 3: 564–581.

Gilpatric, Katy. 2010. "Violent Female Action Characters in Contemporary American Cinema." *Sex Roles* 62: 734–746.

Giroux, Henry A. 2014. *Neoliberalism's War on Higher Education*. Chicago, IL: Haymarket Books.

Giving USA Foundation. 2013. *Giving USA 2013: The Annual Report on Philanthropy for the Year 2012*. Chicago, IL: Giving USA Foundation.

Glover, Scott and Maeve Reston. 2015. "A Tale of Two Carsons." *CNN Online*, http://www.cnn.com/2015/11/05/politics/ben-carson-2016-childhood-violence/index.html.

Gormley, Barbara and Frederick G. Lopez. 2010. "Authoritarian and Homophobic Attitudes: Gender and Adult Attachment Style Differences." *Journal of Homosexuality*, 57: 525–538.

Gorn, Elliott J. 1986. *The Manly Art: Bare-Knuckle Prize Fighting in America.* Ithaca, NY: Cornell University Press.

Gray, Kathleen. 2015. "Courser, Gamrat Return To Capitol In Wake Of Scandal." *Detroit Press Online,* http://www.freep.com/story/news/politics/2015/08/19/house-resumes-session-amidst-ongoing-scandal-roads-debate/31907759/.

Greven, Philip J. 1991. *Spare the Child: The Religious Roots of Punishment and the Psychological Impact of Physical Abuse.* New York, NY: Knopf Doubleday Publishing.

Habermas, Jürgen. 1975. *Legitimation Crisis.* Boston: Beacon Press.

Haidt, Jonathan. 2012. *The Righteous Mind: Why Good people are Divided by Politics and Religion.* New York, NY: Random House.

Hale, Grace Elizabeth. 1999. Making Whiteness: The Culture of Segregation in the South, 1890–1940. New York, NY: Random House.

Hammer, Richard and Martin A. Gosch. [1975] 2013. *The Last Testament of Lucky Luciano.* New York: Enigma Books.

Harding, Kate. 2015. *Asking for It: The Alarming Rise of Rape Culture—and What We Can Do about It.* Boston, MA: Da Capo Press.

Harris, Sam. 2004. *The End of Faith: Religion, Terror, and the Future of Reason.* New York, NY: W.W. Norton.

Harris, Sam. 2010. *The Moral Landscape: How Science Can Determine Human Values.* New York, NY: The Free Press.

Hartz, Louis. 1991 [1955]. *The Liberal Tradition in America.* Orlando, FL: Harcourt Brace and Company.

Heaven, Patrick C.L., Joseph Ciarrochi, and Peter Leeson. 2011. "Cognitive ability, right-wing authoritarianism, and social dominance orientation: A five-year longitudinal study amongst adolescents." *Intelligence* 39, 1:15–21.

Hedges, Chris. 2015. *The Wages of Revolt.* New York, NY: Nation Books.

Hedges, Chris. 2015a. "Make the Rich Panic." *Truthdig.org,* http://www.truthdig.com/report/item/make_the_rich_panic_20150503.

Heitmann, John. 2009. *The Automobile and American Life.* Chapel Hill, NC: University of North Carolina Press.

Helms, Matt, Nancy Kaffer, and Stephen Henderson. 2012. "Detroit files for bankruptcy, setting off battles with creditors, pensions, unions." *Detroit Free Press:* http://www.freep.com/article/20130718/NEWS01/307180107/Detroit-bankruptcy-filing-Kevyn-Orr-emergency-manager.

Hetherington, Marc and Jonathan D. Weiler. 2009. *Authoritarianism and Polarization in American Politics.* New York, NY: Cambridge University Press.

Hewitt, Glenn A. 1988. *Regeneration and Morality: A Study of Charles Finney, Charles Hodge, John W. Nevin, and Horace Bushnell.* Chicago, IL: University of Chicago Press.

Hodge, Charles D. 1866. *Systematic Theology.* New York, NY: Scribner, Armstrong, and Company.

Hofstadter, Richard. 1963. *Anti-Intellectualism in American Life*. New York, NY: Vintage Books/Random House.

Hofstadter, Richard. 1964. *The Paranoid Style in American Politics, and Other Essays*. New York, NY: Vintage Books.

Hogg, Michael A. and Janice Adelman. 2013. "Uncertainty–Identity Theory: Extreme Groups, Radical Behavior, and Authoritarian Leadership." *Journal of Social Issues* 69, 3: 436–454.

Holtzman, Elizabeth and Cynthia Cooper. 2012. *Cheating Justice: How Bush and Cheney Attacked the Rule of Law and Plotted to Avoid Prosecution? and What We Can Do about It*. Boston, MA: Beacon Press.

Horkheimer, Max and Theodor Adorno. 1969 [1947]. *The Dialectic of Enlightenment*. New York, NY: Continuum Publishers.

Huckabee, Mike. 2014. *God, Guns, Grits, and Gravy*. New York, NY: St. Martin's Press.

Ignatiev, Noel. 1995. How the Irish Became White. New York, NY: Routledge.

Inkeles, Alex. 1997. *National Character: A Psycho-Social Perspective*. New Brunswick, NJ: Transaction Publishers.

Inskeep, Steve. 2014. "YMCA Campers Mistaken For Migrant Kids Headed For Detention." http://www.npr.org/2014/07/16/331899913/ymca-campers-mistaken-for-migrant -kids-headed-for-detention.

Irigaray, Luce. 1985. *The Sex which is not One*. Ithaca, NY: Cornell University Press.

Jacoby, Susan. 2009. *The Age of American Unreason*. New York, NY: Vintage Books/ Random House.

Jaffe, Greg. 2015. "Obama budget's boost for military spending points to brewing national security debate." *Washington Post* Online: http://www.washingtonpost.com/ politics/obama-budgets-boost-for-military-spending-points-to-brewing-national -security-debate/2015/02/01/914c5030-a967-11e4-a2b2-776095f393b2_story.html.

James, William. 2000 [1907]. *Pragmatism and Other Essays*. New York, NY: The Penguin Group.

Jehl, Douglas, 2005. "Report Urged Action Against General for Speeches." *The New York Times*, March 4: http://www.nytimes.com/2005/03/04/politics/report-urged-action -against-general-for-speeches.html.

Jerschow, Elina, Aileen P. McGinn, Gabriele de Vos, Natalia Vernon, Sunit Jariwala, Golda Hudes, David Rosenstreich. 2012. "Dichlorophenol-containing pesticides and allergies: results from the US National Health and Nutrition Examination Survey 2005–2006." *Annals of Allergy, Asthma & Immunology* 109, 6: 420–430.

Jewett, Robert and John Shelton Lawrence. 2003. *Captain America and the Crusade Against Evil: The Dilemma of Zealous Nationalism*. Grand Rapids, MI: William B. Eerdmans Press.

Johnson, Chalmers. 2004. *The Sorrows of Empire: Militarism, Secrecy, and the End of the Republic.* New York, NY: Metropolitan.

Johnson, Jamie. 2004. *Born Rich.* Los Angeles, CA: Shout Factory Studios.

Johnson, Chalmers. 2010. *Dismantling the Empire: America's Last Best Hope.* New York, NY: Metropolitan/Henry Holt Books.

Juergensmeyer, Mark. 2003. *Terror in the Mind of God: The Global Rise of Religious Violence.* Berkeley, CA: University of California Press.

Kimmel, Michael. 2008. *Guyland: The Perilous World Where Boys Become Men.* New York, NY: HarperCollins.

Klein, Naomi. 2000. *No Logo.* New York, NY: St. Martin's Press.

Klein, Naomi. 2007. *The Shock Doctrine.* New York, NY, Picador.

Krantz, Matt. 2015. "$194B! Apple's Cash Pile Hits Record." *USA Today Online*, http://americasmarkets.usatoday.com/2015/04/27/194b-apple-cash-pile-hits-record/.

Krattenmaker, Tom. 2013. *The Evangelicals You Don't Know: Introducing the Next Generation of Christians.* Lanham, MD: Rowman and Littlefield.

Krauthammer, Charles. 2015. "Krauthammer on Iran Nuclear Deal: 'This Is Quite Insane.'" Fox News Online: http://insider.foxnews.com/2015/07/14/charles-krauthammer-iran-nuclear-deal-quite-insane.

Krier, Daniel and William J. Swart. 2014. "The Commodification of Spectacle: Spectators, Sponsors and the Outlaw Biker Diegesis at Sturgis." *Critical Sociology* Online, May 2. Print version forthcoming.

Kris, Ernst. 1952. *Psychoanalytic Explorations in Art.* New York, NY: Alfred A. Knopf.

Kroh, Kiley. 2014. "Germany Sets New Record, Generating 74% of Power from Renewable Sources." ClimateProgress.org: http://thinkprogress.org/climate/2014/05/13/3436923/germany-energy-records/Germany/.

Kteily, Nour S., Jim Sidanius, and Shana Levin. 2011. "Social dominance orientation: Cause or 'mere effect'?: Evidence for SDO as a causal predictor of prejudice and discrimination against ethnic and racial outgroups." *Journal of Experimental Social Psychology* 47, 1: 208–214.

Lackoff, George. 2009. *The Political Mind: A Cognitive Scientist's Guide to Your Brain and Its Politics.* New York, NY: The Penguin Group.

La Monica, Paul R. 2015. "Apple has 203B in Cash. Why?" *CNNMoney Online*: http://money.cnn.com/2015/07/22/investing/apple-stock-cash-earnings/index.html.

Langman, Lauren. 2012. "Cycles of Contention: The Rise and Fall of the Tea Party." *Critical Sociology* 38, 4: 449–469.

Langman, Lauren. 2013. "Occupy: A New Social Movement." *Current Sociology* 61, 4: 510–524.

Langman, Lauren. 2015. "An Overview: Hegemony, Ideology and the Reproduction of Domination." *Critical Sociology* 41, 3: 425–432.

Langman, Lauren. 2015a. "Why Is Assent Willing? Culture, Character and Consciousness." *Critical Sociology* 41, 3: 463–481.

Langman, Lauren, 2016, "The Critical Social Psychology of Critical Theory." *Handbook of Critical Theory*, Michael Thompson, ed. New York, NY: Palgrave McMillan.

Langman, Lauren and Meghan A. Burke. 2006. "From Exceptionalism to Imperialism: Culture, Character, and American Foreign Policy." In *Globalization between the Cold War and Neo-Imperialism*, Jennifer M. Lehmann and Harry F. Dahms, eds.: 189–228.

Langman, Lauren, and George Lundskow. 2012. "Down the Rabid Hole to a Tea Party." *Critical Sociology* 38, 4: 589–597.

La Roche, Julia. 2013. "Here's How Much 10 Of The Richest People In The World Made Per Minute In 2013." *Business Insider Online*, Retrieved 9-15-2014 from http://www .businessinsider.com/what-warren-buffett-makes-per-hour-2013-12.

Lasch, Christopher. 1979. *The Culture of Narcissism: American Life in an Age of Diminishing Expectations*. New York, NY: W.W. Norton and Company.

Lawrence, D.H. 2003 [1910]. *Studies in Classic American Literature*. New York, NY: Cambridge University Press.

Leeson, Peter, Patrick C.L. Heaven, and Joseph Ciarrochi. 2012. "Revisiting the link between low verbal intelligence and ideology." *Intelligence* 40, 2: 213–216.

Legomsky, Joanne. 1999. "How Nabisco's New Cookie Crumbles." *The New York Times*, http://www.nytimes.com/1999/08/15/business/investing-how-nabisco-s-new -cookie-crumbles.html.

Leopold, Todd. 2012. "We're #1...We're #1...We're not?" CNN, July 2: http://www.cnn .com/2012/07/02/us/american-exceptionalism-other-countries-lessons/index.html.

Lerner, Michael. 2007. *The Left Hand of God*. New York, NY: Harper Colllins.

Lerner, Jennifer S., Julie H. Goldberg, and Philip E. Tetlock. 1998. "Sober Second Thought: The Effects of Accountability, Anger, and Authoritarianism on Attributions of Responsibility." *Personality and Social Psychology Bulletin* 24, 6: 563–574.

Levin, Shana, Christopher M. Federico, Jim Sidanius, and Joshua L. Rabinowitz. 2002. "Social Dominance Orientation and Intergroup Bias: The Legitimation of Favoritism for High-Status Groups." *Personality and Social Psychology Bulletin* 28, 2: 144–157.

Lewis, Tanya. 2014. "New Rankings Reveal Teen Pregnancy Rates In Each State." *HuffingtonPost*: http://www.huffingtonpost.com/2014/05/05/teen-pregnancy-rate_n _5269203.html.

Liberman, Peter. 2014. "War and Torture as 'Just Deserts.'" *Public Opinion Quarterly* 78, 1: 47–70.

Lifton, Robert. 1993. *The Protean Self: Human Resilience in an Age of Fragmentation* Chicago, IL: University of Chicago Press.

Lipset, Seymour Martin. 1979. *The First New Nation: The United States in Historical and Comparative Perspective*. New York, NY: W.W. Norton and Company.

Lipset, Seymour Martin. 1990. *Continental Divide: The Values and Institutions of the United States and Canada*. New York, NY: Routledge.

Livengood, Chad and Melissa Nann Burke. 2015. "Carson's Westmoreland Story Doesn't Match Records." *The Detroit News Online*, http://www.detroitnews.com/story/news/politics/2015/11/06/carsons-westmoreland-story-match-records/75328960/.

Loewen, James. 2009. *Teaching What Really Happened: How to Avoid the Tyranny of Textbooks and Get Students Excited About Doing History.* New York, NY: Teachers College Press.

Lofgren, Mike. 2012. "Revolt of the Rich." *The American Conservative*, retrieved 9-15-2014 from http://www.theamericanconservative.com/articles/revolt-of-the-rich/.

Lundskow, George. 2002. *Awakening to an Uncertain Future: A Case Study of the Promise Keepers.* New York, NY: Peter Lang.

Lundskow, George. 2012. "Authoritarianism and Destructiveness in the Tea Party Movement." *Critical Sociology* 38, 4: 529–547.

Lupsha. Peter A. "American Values: Suckers and Wiseguys." pp. 294–309 in *American Social Character: Modern Interpretations.* Rupert Wilkinson, ed. New York: HarperCollins.

Lutz, Bob. 2011. *Car Guys versus Bean Counters: The Battle for the Soul of American Business.* New York, NY: Penguin Books.

Lynch, Conor. 2015. "Welcome to 'Libertarian Island': Inside the Frightening Economic Dreams of Silicon Valley's Super Rich." Alternet.org: http://www.alternet.org/news-amp-politics/welcome-libertarian-island-inside-frightening-economic-dreams-silicon-valleys.

Macias, Amanda. 2015. "The Rest of the World Doesn't Even Come Close to US Military Spending." Business Insider, http://www.businessinsider.com/map-of-us-military-spending-2015-2?op=1.

MacWilliams, Matthew. 2016. "The One Weird Trait That Predicts Whether You're a Trump Supporter: And it's not gender, age, income, race or religion." *Politico*: http://www.politico.com/magazine/story/2016/01/donald-trump-2016-authoritarian-213533.

Manders, Dean. 2006. *The Hegemony of Common Sense: Wisdom and Mystification in Everyday Life.* New York, NY: Peter Lang Publishing.

Mangan, J.A. 2012. *'Manufactured' Masculinity: Making Imperial Manliness, Morality and Militarism.* New York, NY: Routledge.

Mann, Thomas A. and Norman J. Ornstein. 2012. *It's Even Worse Than It Looks: How the American Constitutional System Collided With the New Politics of Extremism.* New York, NY: Basic Books.

Marcuse, Herbert. 1991 [1964]. *One-Dimensional Man.* Boston, MA: Beacon Press.

Markon, Jerry. 2015. "Huckabee: Iran nuclear deal will march Israelis 'to the door of the oven'" Washington Post, July 26: http://www.washingtonpost.com/politics/huckabee-iran-nuclear-deal-will-march-israelis-to-the-door-of-the-oven/2015/07/26/bc963910-33bc-11e5-94ce-834ad8f5c50e_story.html.

Martelle, Scott. 2007. *Blood Passion: The Ludlow Massacre and Class War in the American West.* New Brunswick, NJ: Rutgers University Press.

Mataconis, Doug. 2012. "House And Senate Incumbent Re-Election Rates Top 90%." *OutsidetheBeltway* Online: http://www.outsidethebeltway.com/house-and-senate -incumbent-re-election-rates-top-90/.

Matthews, Chris. 2014. *Tip and the Gipper: When Politics Worked.* New York, NY: Simon and Schuster.

Mayer, Jane. 2009. *The Dark Side: The Inside Story of How The War on Terror Turned into a War on American Ideals.* New York, NY: Doubleday.

McBride, James. 1995. *War, Battering, and Other Sports.* Amherst, NY: Humanity/ Prometheus Books.

McCormick, John. 2015. "Cruz, Gaining on Trump in Iowa, Intensifies War Rheto- ric." Bloomberg News, December 5: http://www.bloomberg.com/politics/articles/ 2015-12-06/cruz-gaining-on-trump-in-iowa-intensifies-war-rhetoric.

McLaren, Brian. 2012. *Why Did Jesus, Moses, the Buddha, and Mohammed Cross the Road?: Christian Identity in a Multi-Faith World.* New York, NY: Jericho Books.

McLean, Bethany and Peter Elkind. 2003. *The Smartest Guys in the Room: The Amazing Rise and Scandalous Fall of Enron.* New York, NY: Fortune Publishing, a Division of Time, Inc.

McLean, Bethany, and Joe Nocera. 2010. *All the Devils are Here: The Hidden History of the Financial Crisis.* New York, NY: Portfolio/Penguin Books.

McWhiney, G. 1988. *Cracker culture: Celtic ways in the old South.* Tuscaloosa, AL: University of Alabama Press.

Mee, Bob. 2001. *Bare Fists: The History of Bare Knuckle Prize Fighting.* New York, NY: HarperCollins.

Merchant, Carolyn. 1989. *The Death of Nature: Women, Ecology, and the Scientific Revo- lution.* New York, NY: HarperCollins.

Merton, Robert K. 1967 [1949]. *Social Theory and Social Structure.* New York, NY: The Free Press.

Mills, C. Wright. 1956 [2000]. *The Power Elite.* New York, NY: Oxford University Press.

Mirisola, Alberto, Michele Roccato, Silvia Russo, Giulia Spagna, and Alessio Vieno. 2013. "Societal Threat to Safety, Compensatory Control, and Right-Wing Authori- tarianism." *Political Psychology* 35, 6: 795–812.

Molina, Natalia. 2014. *How Race Is Made in America: Immigration, Citizenship, and the Historical Power of Racial Scripts.* Berkeley and Los Angeles, CA: University of Cali- fornia Press.

Mooney, Chris. 2006. *The Republican War on Science.* New York, NY: Basic Books.

Mooney, Chris. 2012. *The Republican Brain: The Science of Why They Deny Science—and Reality.* Hoboken, NJ: John Wiley and Sons.

Morrison, Kimberly Rios and Oscar Ybarra. 2008. "The effects of realistic threat and group identification on social dominance orientation." *Journal of Experimental So- cial Psychology* 44, 1: 156–163.

Mossad Report. 2012. "Iran/Nuclear/Program Status." Report No. 9342. 22 October.

Murphy, Kevin. 2014. "Kansas looks to sex toy sale as payback for overdue taxes." *Reuters News Service*, http://www.reuters.com/article/2014/09/25/us-usa-kansas-auction-id USKCN0HK2BB20140925#Jfdz3R4yHp2FdTTt.99.

Neiwert, David. 2009. *Eliminationists: How Hate Talk Radicalized the American Right.* Sausalito, CA: PoliPointPress.

Nelson, Mariah Burton. 1995. *The Stronger Women Get, the More Men Love Football: Sexism and the American Culture of Sports.* New York, NY: Avon Books.

Nietzsche, Friedrich. 1989 [1886]. *Beyond Good and Evil: Prelude to a Philosophy of the Future.* New York, NY: Vintage Books.

Nietzsche, Friedrich. 1990 [1889]. *Twilight of the Idols/The Anti-Christ.* New York: Penguin Group.

Nisbett, Richard E. 1993. "Violence and US Regional Culture." *American Psychologist* 48, 4: 441–449.

Norris, Gareth and Heather Reeves. 2013. "Fear of Crime and Authoritarianism: A comparison of rural and urban attitudes." *Crime Prevention and Community Safety* 15, 2: 134–150.

OECD. 2011. *Divided We Stand: Why Inequality Keeps Rising.* OECD Publishing. http://dx.doi.org/10.1787/9789264119536-en.

OECD. 2013. "Crisis Squeezes Income and Puts Pressure on Inequality and Poverty." www.oecd.org/inequality.

Ogilvy, James. 1979. *Many Dimensional Man,* New York, NY: Harper Collins Publishers.

Oppliger. Patrice A. 2004. *Wrestling and Hypermasculinity.* Jefferson, NC: McFarland and Company.

Oriard, Michael. 1991. *Sporting with the Gods: The Rhetoric of Play and Game in American Literature.* New York, NY: Cambridge University Press.

Packer, George. 2013. *The Unwinding: An Inner History of the New America.* New York, NY: Farrar, Straus, Giroux.

Pachterbecke, Matthieu Van, Christopher Freyer and Vassilis Saroglou. 2011. "When authoritarianism meets religion: Sacrificing others in the name of abstract deontology." *European Journal of Social Psychology* 41, 7: 898–903.

Paganelli, Alejandra, Victoria Gnazzo, Helena Acosta, Silvia L. López, and Andrés E. Carrasco. 2010. "Glyphosate-Based Herbicides Produce Teratogenic Effects on Vertebrates by Impairing Retinoic Acid Signaling." *Chemical Research in Toxicology* 23, 10: 1586–1595.

Paine, Thomas. 2010 [1796]. *Agrarian Justice.* Rockville, MD: Wildside Press.

Patel, Eboo. 2012. *Sacred Ground: Pluralism, Prejudice, and the Promise of America.* Boston, MA: Beacon Press.

Pear, Robert. 2014. "From Contribution Limits to the Sage Grouse." *New York Times,* Dec. 13, p. A10.

Perry, Ryan and Chris G. Sibley. 2012. "Big-Five personality prospectively predicts Social Dominance Orientation and Right-Wing Authoritarianism." *Personality and Individual Differences* 52, 1: 3–8.

Pettis, Jeffrey S., Elinor M. Lichtenberg, Michael Andree, Jennie Stitzinger, Robyn Rose, and Dennis vanEngelsdorp. 2013. "Crop Pollination Exposes Honey Bees to Pesticides Which Alters Their Susceptibility to the Gut Pathogen Nosema ceranae." *PLoS ONE* 8(7): e70182. doi: 10.1371/journal.pone.0070182.

PEW Charitable Trusts. 2015. *The Precarious State of Family Balance Sheets.* Philadelphia, PA, and Washington, DC: PEW Charitable Trusts.

Pew Research. 2012. *Religion and Public Life Project.* Retrieved 8-20-2014 from http://www.pewforum.org/2012/10/09/nones-on-the-rise/.

Pew Research Center. 2012. *Fewer, Poorer, Gloomier: The Lost Decade of the Middle Class.* Pew Social and Demographic Trends: Washington, DC.

Pew Research Center. 2014. "Beyond Red vs. Blue: The Political Typology." Pew Social and Demographic Trends: Washington, DC.

Pew Research Center. 2014a. "Stark Racial Divisions in Reactions to Ferguson Police Shooting." Pew Social and Demographic Trends: Washington, DC.

Pew Research Center. 2015. "Public's Policy Priorities Reflect Changing Conditions At Home and Abroad." Pew Social and Demographic Trends: Washington, DC.

Phares, Ross. 1971. *Bible in Pocket, Gun in Hand: The Story of Frontier Religion.* Lincoln, NE: University of Nebraska Press.

Phillips, Brian, Phyllis Curtiss, and George Lundskow. 2010. "Workers' Relationships To Their Union: The Effects Of Transfer Status And Race At A U.S. Automobile Plant." *The Social Science Journal* 47, 2: 392–417.

Pierce Charles P. 2009. *Idiot America: How Stupidity Became a Virtue in the Land of the Free* New York, NY: Random House.

Pierce, Charles P. 2012. *Am I a Democrat or a Republican? An Effort to Save America.* Otego, NY: Harmonic Creations.

Piketty, Charles. 2014. *Capital in the Twenty-First Century.* Cambridge, MA: Harvard University Press.

Pinder, Sherrow O. 2013. Whiteness and Racialized Ethnic Groups in the United States: The Politics of Remembering. Lanham, MD: Lexington Books.

Pinsky, Drew and S. Mark Young. 2009. *The Mirror Effect: How Celebrity Narcissism Is Seducing America.* New York, NY: HarperCollins.

Potter, David. 1954. *People of Plenty*, Chicago, IL: University of Chicago Press.

Pratto, Felicia, Jim Sidanius, Lisa M. Stallworth, and Bertram Malle. 1994. "Social dominance orientation: A personality variable predicting social and political attitudes." *Journal of Personality and Social Psychology* 67, 4: 741–763.

Preston, Darrell, and Chris Christoff. 2013. "Only Wall Street Wins in Detroit Reaping 473 Million Fee." *Bloomberg News*: http://www.bloomberg.com/news/2013-03-14/only-wall-street-wins-in-detroit-crisis-reaping-474-million-fee.html.

Pronger, Brian. 1990. *The Arena of Masculinity: Sports, Homosexuality, and the Meaning of Sex.* New York, NY: St. Martin's Press.

Prothero, Stephen. 2003. *American Jesus: How the Son of God Became a National Icon.* New York, NY: Farrar, Straus, Giroux.

Putnam, Robert D. 2000. *Bowling Alone: The Collapse and Revival of American Community.* New York, NY: Simon and Schuster.

Putnam, Robert D., Lewis Feldstein and Donald J. Cohen. 2004. *Better Together: Restoring the American Community.* New York, NY: Simon and Shuster.

Rajan, Sangeetha and Venkat R. Krishnan. 2002. "Impact of gender on influence, power and authoritarianism." *Women in Management Review* 17, 5/6: 197–206.

Ramadan, Tariq. 2009. *Radical Reform: Islamic Ethics and Liberation.* New York, NY: Oxford University Press.

Rattner, Steven. 2010. *Overhaul: An Insider's Account of the Obama Administration's Emergency Rescue of the Auto Industry.* Boston, MA and New York, NY: Houghton Mifflin Harcourt.

Rauh, Virginia A., Frederica P. Pererab, Megan K. Horton, Robin M. Whyatt, Ravi Bansale, Xuejun Haoe, Jun Liue, Dana Boyd Barrf, Theodore A. Slotking, and Bradley S. Peterson. 2012. "Brain Anomalies In Children Exposed Prenatally To A Common Organophosphate Pesticide." *PNAS* 109, 20: 7871–7876.

Ravitch, Diane. 2010. *The Death and Life of the Great American School System: How Testing and Choice Are Undermining Education.* New York, NY: Perseus/Basic Books.

Ravitch, Diane. 2014. *Reign of Error: The Hoax of the Privatization Movement and the Danger to America's Public Schools.* New York, NY: Random House.

Reich, Wilhem. 1990 [1946]. *The Mass Psychology of Fascism.* New York, NY: Farrar, Straus, Giroux.

Reis, Elizabeth. 1999. *Damned Women: Sinners and Witches in Puritan New England.* Ithaca, NY: Cornell University Press.

Reis, Elizabeth. 2014. *American Sexual History.* New York, NY: Wiley-Blackwell.

Reitman, Janet. 2013. "Jahar's World: He was a charming kid with a bright future. But no one saw the pain he was hiding or the monster he would become." *Rolling Stone* 1188, August: 46–57.

Remini, Robert V. 2001. *Andrew Jackson and His Indian Wars.* New York, NY: Viking Press.

Rice, Doyle. 2015. "Fla. gov. bans the terms climate change, global warming." USA Today: http://www.usatoday.com/story/weather/2015/03/09/florida-governor-climate-change-global-warming/24660287/.

Richard, Wilkinson and Kate, Pickett. 2010. *The Spirit Level: Why Greater Equality Makes Societies Stronger.* Penguin books Limited.

Rieder, Joerg. 2009. *No Rising Tide: Theology, Economics, and the Future.* Minneapolis, MN: Augsburg Fortress Press.

Riesman, David. 2001 [1961]. *The Lonely Crowd.* New Haven, CT: Yale University Press.

Robinson, William I. 2004. *A Theory of Global Capitalism: Production, Class, and State in a Transnational World.* Baltimore, MD: John Hopkins University Press.

Rodriguez, Dylan. 2011. "White Supremacy as Substructure: Towards a Geneology of a Racial Animus, for Reconstruction to Pacification." *State of White Supremacy: Racism, Governance, and the United States.* Jung, Moon-Kie, João Costa Vargas, and Eduardo Bonilla-Silva, eds. Stanford, CA: Stanford University Press.

Roediger, David R. 2005. *Working Toward Whiteness: How America's Immigrants Became White: The Strange Journey from Ellis Island to the Suburbs.* New York, NY: Basic Books.

Rojek, Chris. 2001. *Celebrity.* London, England: Reaktion Press.

Rojek, Chris. 2013. *Event Power: How Global Events Manage and Manipulate.* Thousand Oaks, CA: Sage Publications.

Rojek, Chris. 2016. "F.J. Turner's Frontier Thesis: The Ruse of American Character." *European Journal of Social Theory.* Forthcoming.

Rosen, Hannah. 2009. *Terror in the Heart of Freedom: Citizenship, Sexual Violence, and the Meaning of Race in the Post-Emancipation South.* Chapel Hill, NC: University of North Carolina Press.

Rosenberg, Paul. 2015. "Paul Krugman Has Taught Them Nothing: Republicans Would Tank the Economy Again, Given Another Chance." *Alternet.org,* Nov. 1: http://www.alternet.org/economy/paul-krugman-has-taught-them-nothing-republicans-would-tank-economy-again-given-another.

Roston, Eric. 2015. "For Some Wisconsin State Workers, 'Climate Change' Isn't Something You Can Talk About." *Bloomberg Business*: http://www.bloomberg.com/news/articles/2015-04-08/for-some-wisconsin-state-workers-climate-change-isn-t-something-you-can-talk-about.

Roubini, Nouriel. 2004. *Bailouts or Bail-Ins: Responding to Financial Crises in Emerging Markets.* Washington, DC: Institute for International Economics.

Rountree, Helen C. 1990. *Pocahontas's People: The Powhatan Indians of Virginia through Four Centuries.* Norman, OK: University of Oklahoma Press.

Roustan, A., M. Aye, M. De Meo, and C. Di Giorgio. 2014. "Genotoxicity of mixtures of glyphosate and atrazine and their environmental transformation products before and after photoactivation." *Chemosphere* 108: 93–100.

Rowling, J.K. 1997. *Harry Potter and the Sorcerer's Stone.* New York, NY: Scholastic.

RT News. 2015. "Monsanto gets approval for new GMO corn, soybeans designed for potent new biocide." January 25: http://rt.com/usa/223451-monsanto-gmo-pesticide-approved/.

Saccaro, Matt. 2014. "Professors on food stamps: The shocking true story of academia in 2014." *Salon.com*: http://www.salon.com/2014/09/21/professors_on_food_stamps_the_shocking_true_story_of_academia_in_2014/.

Salerno, Roger A. 2003. *Landscapes of Abandonment: Capitalism, Modernity, and Estrangement.* Albany, NY: State University of New York Press.

Samsel, Anthony and Stephaine Seneff. 2013. "Enzymes and Amino Acid Biosynthesis by the Gut Microbiome: Pathways to Modern Diseases." *Entropy* 15: 1416–1463.

Samsel, Anthony and Stephaine Seneff. 2013. "Glyphosate's Suppression of P450 Enzymes and Amino Acid Biosynthesis by the GUt Microbe: Pathways to Modern Diseases." *Entropy* 15, 4: 1416–1463.

Samsel, Anthony and Stephanie Seneff. 2013a. "Glyphosate, pathways to modern diseases II: Celiac sprue and gluten intolerance." *Interdisciplinary Toxicology* 6, 4: 159–184.

Sanday, Peggy Reeves. 2007. *Fraternity Gang Rape: Sex, Brotherhood, and Privilege on Campus, Second Edition.* New York, NY: New York University Press.

Sandburg, Carl. 1939. *Abraham Lincoln: The Prairie Years.* New York: Harcourt Brace.

Sassen, Saskia. 2014. *Expulsions: Brutality and Complexity in the Global Economy.* Cambridge, MA: Harvard University Press.

Scahill, Jeremy. 2013. *Dirty Wars: The World Is a Battlefield.* New York, NY: Nation Books.

Schinasi, Leah and Maria E. Leon. 2014. "Non-Hodgkin Lymphoma and Occupational Exposure to Agricultural Pesticide Chemical Groups and Active Ingredients: A Systematic Review and Meta-Analysis." *International Journal of Environmental Research and Public Health*: 11, 4: 4449–4527.

Schlesinger, Arthur. 2004. *War and the American Presidency.* New York, NY: W.W. Norton.

Schwartz, David. 2011. "Arizona House Votes to Make Colt Revolver Official State Gun." Reuters, Wed. April 20: http://www.reuters.com/article/2011/04/20/us-colt-arizona-idUSTRE73J4E820110420.

Seelye, Katharine Q. 2004. "Cheney's Five Draft Deferments During the Vietnam Era Emerge as a Campaign Issue." The New York Times, May 1st: http://www.nytimes.com/2004/05/01/politics/campaign/01CHEN.html?ex=1398830400&en=1c0259e620183dd6&ei=5007&partner=USERLAND.

Sennett, Richard. 1998. *The Corrosion of Character: The Personal Consequences of Work in the New Capitalism.* New York, NY: W.W. Norton.

Sennett, Richard. 2006. *The Culture of the New Capitalism.* New Haven, CT: Yale University Press.

Séralini, Gilles-Eric, Robin Mesnage, Emilie Clair, Steeve Gress, Joël Spiroux de Vendômois, and Dominique Cellier. 2011. "Genetically modified crops safety assessments: present limits and possible improvements." *Environmental Sciences Europe* 23, 10: doi:10.1186/2190-4715-23-10.

Serna, Joseph, Kate Linthicum, and Matt Hansen. 2014. "Protesters of undocumented immigrants vow to block new arrivals." Los Angeles Times, July 3, http://www.latimes.com/local/lanow/la-me-ln-murrieta-protesters-undocumented-immigrants-20140703-story.html.

Serrano, Richard A. 1998. *One of Ours: Timothy McVeigh and the Oklahoma City Bombing.* New York, NY: W.W. Norton.

Shaffer, Barbara A., and Brad M. Hastings. 2007. "Authoritarianism and religious identification: Response to threats on religious beliefs." *Mental Health, Religion & Culture* 10, 2: 151–158.

Shapiro, Emily. 2016. "The History Behind the Donald Trump 'Small Hands' Insult." ABC-News Online: http://abcnews.go.com/Politics/history-donald-trump-small-hands -insult/story?id=37395515.

Shim, Youn K., Steven P. Mlynarek, and Edwin van Wijngaarden. 2009. "Parental Exposure to Pesticides and Childhood Brain Cancer: U.S. Atlantic Coast Childhood Brain Cancer Study." *Environmental Health Perspectives* 117, 6: 1002–1006.

Shorrocks, Anthony, Jim Davies, and Rodrigo Lluberas. 2015. *Global Wealth Data Book, 2015*. Zurich, Switzlerland: Credit Suisse Research Institute.

Sidanius, Jim, Felicia Pratto, and Joshua L. Rabinowitz. 1994. "Gender, Ethnic Status, and Ideological Asymmetry A Social Dominance Interpretation." *Journal of Cross-Cultural Psychology* 25, 2: 194–216.

Sklair, Leslie. 2001. *The Transnational Capitalist Class*. Malden, MA: Blackwell.

Slater, Phillip. 1971. *The Pursuit of Loneliness: American Culture at the Breaking Point*. New York, NY: Houghton-Mifflin.

Slotkin, Richard. 1998 [1985]. *The Fatal Environment: The Myth of the Frontier in the Age of Industrialization*. Norman, OK: University of Oklahoma Press.

Slotkin, Richard. 1998 [1992]. *Gunfighter Nation: The Myth of the Frontier in Twentieth-Century America*. Norman, OK: University of Oklahoma Press.

Slotkin, Richard. 2000 [1973]. *Regeneration Through Violence: The Mythology of the American Frontier, 1600–1860*. Norman, OK: University of Oklahoma Press.

Smedley, Audrey, and Brian D. Smedley. 2012. *Race in North America: Origin and Evolution of a Worldview*. Boulder, CO: Westview Press.

Sowell, Thomas. 2001. *The Quest for Cosmic Justice*. New York, NY: Simon and Schuster.

Sparrow, Bartholomew. 2014. "Organizing Security: How the Bush Presidency Made Decisions on war and Peace." *Inside the Presidency of George H.W. Bush*. Michael Nelson and Barbara A. Perry, eds. Ithaca, NY: Cornell University Press.

Stahl, William A. "One-Dimensional Rage: The Social Epistemology of the New Atheism and Fundamentalism." *Religion and the New Atheism: A Critical Appraisal*. Leiden, The Netherlands: Brill.

Stenner, Karen. 2005. *The Authoritarian Dynamic*. New York, NY: Cambridge University Press.

Stevenson, Alexandra. 2016. "Hedge Funds Faced Choppy Waters in 2015, but Chiefs Cashed In." *NyTimes.com*: http://www.nytimes.com/2016/05/10/business/dealbook/ hedge-fund-manager-compensation.html?_r=0.

Stieglitz, Joseph E. 2015. *The Great Divide: Unequal Societies and What We Can Do About Them*. New York, NY: W.W. Norton.

Stout, Mary A. 2012. *Native American Boarding Schools*. Santa Barbara, CA: ABC-CLIO Press.

Strange, Susan. 1997. *Casino Capitalism*. Manchester, England: Manchester University Press.

Straus, Murray A. and Denise A. Donnelly. 2001. *Beating the Devil Out of Them: Corporal Punishment in American Families and Its Effects on Children*. Piscataway, NJ: Transaction Publishers.

Sue, Derald Wing. 2004. "Whiteness and Ethnocentric Monoculturalism: Making the 'Invisible' Visible." *American Psychologist* 59, 8: 761–769.

Sunday, Billy. [1919] 2005. *The Sawdust Trail: Billy Sunday in His Own Words*. Iowa City, IA: University of Iowa Press.

Sweeney, Kathleen. 2006. "Supernatural Girls." *Afterimage* 33, 5: 13–16.

Swift, Lindsay 2008 [1911]. *William Lloyd Garrison*. Whitefish, MT: Kessinger Publishing.

Tagar, Michal Reifen, Christopher M. Federico, Kristen E. Lyons, Steven Ludeke, and Melissa A. Koenig. 2014. "Heralding the Authoritarian? Orientation Toward Authority in Early Childhood." *Psychological Science* 25, 4: 883–892.

Taibbi, Matt. 2010. *Griftopia: Bubble Machines, Vampire Squids, and the Long Con that is Breaking America*. New York, NY: Spiegel and Grau.

Taibbi, Matt. 2014. *The Divide: American Injustice in the Age of the Wealth Gap*. New York, NY: Spiegel and Grau.

Tasini. 2011. "A Country is not a Company: CEOs Should Sit Down And Shut Up." Daily Kos, http://www.dailykos.com/story/2011/09/12/1016095/-A-COUNTRY-is-not-a-COMPANY-CEOs-Should-Sit-Down-And-Shut-Up.

Tawney, R.H. 1926. *Religion and the Rise of Capitalism*. New York, NY: Harcourt Brace Jovanovich.

Taylor, Adam. 2015. "Why do Italian soccer fans and other foreigners fly the Confederate flag?" *The Washington Post* Online, https://www.washingtonpost.com/news/worldviews/wp/2015/06/22/why-do-italian-soccer-fans-and-other-foreigners-fly-the-confederate-flag/.

Taylor, Paul. 2016. *The Next America: Boomers, Millennials, and the Looming Generational Showdown*. New York, NY: Perseus Group.

Tesfaye, Sophia. 2015. "A Staggering Number of Republicans believe President Obama is a Muslim." *Salon.com*, http://www.salon.com/2015/09/14/a_staggering_number_of_republicans_believe_president_obama_is_a_muslim/.

Teymoori, Ali, Arash Heydari, and Hedayat Nasiri. 2014. "Relationship between dimensions of religiosity, authoritarianism, and moral authority." *Social Compass* 6, 1: 92–107.

Thompson, Peter. 1999. *Rum Punch & Revolution: Taverngoing & Public Life in Eighteenth Century Philadelphia*. Philadelphia, PA: University of Pennsylvania Press.

Thompson, Michael J. 2012. *The Politics of Inequality: A Political History of the Idea of Economic Inequality in America.* New York, NY: Columbia University Press.

Thongprakaisanga, Siriporn, Apinya Thiantanawatb, Nuchanart Rangkadiloka, Tawit Suriyoc, and Jutamaad Satayavivad. 2013. "Glyphosate induces human breast cancer cells growth via estrogen receptors." *Food and Chemical Toxicology* 59: 129–136.

Truman, Jennifer L. and Lynn Langton. 2014. "Criminal Victimization, 2013." Washington, DC: U.S. Department of Justice, Office of Justice Programs, Bureau of Justice Statistics.

Turner, Frederick Jackson. 1921. *The Frontier in American History.* New York, NY: Henry Holt.

Turner, Victor. 1995. *The Ritual Process: Structure and Anti-Structure.* Piscataway, NJ: Transaction Publishers.

Turse, Nick. 2013. *Kill Anything that Moves.* New York, NY: Picador Press.

Ulrich, Laurel. 1991. *Good Wives: Image and Reality in the Lives of Women in Northern New England, 1650–1750.* New York, NY: Vintage Books.

Valenti, Jessica. 2010. *The Purity Myth: How America's Obsession with Virginity is Hurting Women.* Berkeley, CA: Perseus Group.

Vande Bunte, Matt. 2015. "Counterintuitive redesign of I-96/Cascade junction right tool to ease congestion, MDOT director says." MLive.com: http://www.mlive.com/news/grand-rapids/index.ssf/2015/02/mdot_cascade_i-96.html.

Vaughan, Alden T. 1995. *New England Frontier: Puritans and Indians, 1620–1675, 3rd Edition.* Norman, OK: University of Oklahoma Press.

VPC Report. 2015. *Gun Deaths Outpace Motor Vehicle Deaths in 17 States and the District of Columbia in 2013.* Washington, DC: Violence Policy Center.

Wakeley, J.B. 2014. *The Bold Frontier Preacher: A Portraiture of Rev. William Cravens of Virginia.* Staunton, VA: Clarion Press.

Warner, Loyd, J O Low, Paul S Lunt, and Leo Srole. 1963. *Yankee City.* New Haven, CT: Yale University Press.

Washington Post-ABC News Poll. 2014. "Majority Say CIA Harsh Interrogations Justified." December 14, http://www.washingtonpost.com/page/2010-2019/Washington-Post/2014/12/16/National-Politics/Polling/release_376.xml.

Weber, Max. 2002 [1920]. *The Protestant Ethic and the Spirit of Capitalism.* Los Angeles, CA: Roxbury Publishing.

Weinstein, Michael and Davin Seay. 2006. *With God On Our Side: One Man's War Against an Evangelical Coup in the Military.* New York, NY: St. Martin's Press.

Weiss, Mitchell D. 2015. "Student Loan Debt: America's Next big Crisis." USA Today, August 23: http://www.usatoday.com/story/money/personalfinance/2015/08/23/credit-dotcom-student-loan-crisis/32015421/.

Wessinger, Cathy. 2000. *How the Millennium Comes Violently.* New York, NY: Seven Bridges Press.

Whyte, William H. 1956. *The Organization Man*. New York, NY: Simon and Schuster.

Wilkinson, Rupert. 1972. *The Broken Rebel: A Study In Culture, Politics, And Authoritarian Character*. New York, NY: Harper and Row.

Wilkinson, Rupert. 1986. *American Tough: The Tough-Guy Tradition and American Character*. New York, NY: HarperCollins.

Wilkinson, Tracy. 2010. "Latin America, Caribbean Creating a Bloc without the US and Canada." La Times, February 22: http://latimesblogs.latimes.com/laplaza/2010/02/latin-america-caribbean-creating-a-new-organization-minus-the-us.html.

Wilkinson, Melinda. 2011. "Alabama county files biggest municipal bankruptcy." *Reuters*, http://www.reuters.com/article/2011/11/10/us-usa-alabama-jeffersoncounty-idUSTRE7A87WW20111110.

Will, George. 2013. "Break up the big banks." *The Washington Post*, February 8: http://www.washingtonpost.com/opinions/george-will-break-up-the-big-banks/2013/02/08/2379498a-714e-11e2-8b8d-e0b59a1b8e2a_story.html.

Winthrop, John. 1838 [1630]. "A Model of Christian Charity." *Collections of the Massachusetts Historical Society, Vol. 7* (3rd series): 31–48.

Wolff, Richard D. 2012. *Democracy at Work: A Cure for Capitalism*. Chicago, IL: Haymarket Books.

Wolff, Richard D. 2013. *Capitalism Hits the Fan: The Global Economic Meltdown and What to Do About It*. Northampton, MA: Interlink Publishing.

Wolin, Sheldon S. 2008. *Democracy Incorporated: Managed Democracy and the Specter of Inverted Totalitarianism*. Princeton, NJ: Princeton University Press.

Woodard, Colin. 2011. *American Nations: A History of the Eleven Rival Regional Cultures of North America*. New York, NY: Viking Press.

WRAL News. 2013. "Civil rights rally draws thousands in downtown Raleigh." http://www.wral.com/nc-advocates-to-rally-with-urgency-in-raleigh/12086224/.

Yee Hee Lee, Michelle. 2015. "Does the United States really have 5 percent of the world's population and one quarter of the world's prisoners?" Washington Post online: https://www.washingtonpost.com/news/fact-checker/wp/2015/04/30/does-the-united-states-really-have-five-percent-of-worlds-population-and-one-quarter-of-the-worlds-prisoners/.

Young, Ralph. 2015. *Dissent: The History of an American Idea*. New York, NY: New York University Press.

Zeese, Kevin and Margaret Flowers. 2013. "Cooperatives and Community Work Are Part of American DNA." *Truthout.org*, http://www.truth-out.org/opinion/item/14076-cooperatives-and-community-work-are-part-of-american-dna.

Zinn, Howard. 2005 [1908]. *A People's History of the United States*. New York, NY: HarperPerennial.

Zizek, Slavoj. 1994. *Mapping Ideology*. Brooklyn, NY: Verso.

Index

CPSIA information can be obtained
at www.ICGtesting.com
Printed in the USA
LVHW051039290623
751112LV00004B/336